THE
CAMBRIDGE EDITION OF
THE LETTERS AND WORKS OF
D. H. LAWRENCE

THE WORKS OF D. H. LAWRENCE

EDITORIAL BOARD

AARON'S ROD

D. H. LAWRENCE

EDITED BY
MARA KALNINS

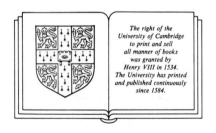

The right of the
University of Cambridge
to print and sell
all manner of books
was granted by
Henry VIII in 1534.
The University has printed
and published continuously
since 1584.

CAMBRIDGE UNIVERSITY PRESS

CAMBRIDGE

NEW YORK   NEW ROCHELLE

MELBOURNE   SYDNEY

Published by the Press Syndicate of the University of Cambridge
The Pitt Building, Trumpington Street, Cambridge CB2 1RP
32 East 57th Street, New York, NY 10022, USA
10 Stamford Road, Oakleigh, Melbourne 3166, Australia

Printed in Great Britain at the University Press, Cambridge

British Library cataloguing in publication data
Lawrence, D. H.
Aaron's rod. – (The Cambridge edition of the letters and works
of D. H. Lawrence)
I. Title   II. Kalnins, Mara   III. Series
823'.912 [F]   PR6023.A93

Library of Congress cataloguing in publication data
Lawrence, D. H. (David Herbert), 1885–1930.
Aaron's rod.
(The Cambridge edition of the letters and works of
D. H. Lawrence)
Bibliography.
E Kalnins, Mara.   II. Title.   III. Series:
Lawrence, D. H. (David Herbert), 1885–1930. Works. 1979.
PR6023.A93A65   1988   823'.912   87–23907

ISBN 0 521 25250 4 hard covers
ISBN 0 521 27246 7 paperback

CE

CONTENTS

GENERAL EDITORS' PREFACE

D. H. Lawrence is one of the great writers of the twentieth century – yet the texts of his writings, whether published during his lifetime or since, are, for the most part, textually corrupt. The extent of the corruption is remarkable; it can derive from every stage of composition and publication. We know from study of his MSS that Lawrence was a careful writer, though not rigidly consistent in matters of minor convention. We know also that he revised at every possible stage. Yet he rarely if ever compared one stage with the previous one, and overlooked the errors of typists or copyists. He was forced to accept, as most authors are, the often stringent house-styling of his printers, which overrode his punctuation and even his sentence-structure and paragraphing. He sometimes overlooked plausible printing errors. More important, as a professional author living by his pen, he had to accept, with more or less good will, stringent editing by a publisher's reader in his early days, and at all times the results of his publishers' timidity. So the fear of Grundyish disapproval, or actual legal action, led to bowdlerisation or censorship from the very beginning of his career. Threats of libel suits produced other changes. Sometimes a publisher made more changes than he admitted to Lawrence. On a number of occasions in dealing with American and British publishers Lawrence produced texts for both which were not identical. Then there were extraordinary lapses like the occasion when a compositor turned over two pages of MS at once, and the result happened to make sense. This whole story can be reconstructed from the introductions to the volumes in this edition; cumulatively they will form a history of Lawrence's writing career.

The Cambridge edition aims to provide texts which are as close as can now be determined to those he would have wished to see printed. They have been established by a rigorous collation of extant manuscripts and typescripts, proofs and early printed versions; they restore the words, sentences, even whole pages omitted or falsified by editors or compositors; they are freed from printing-house conventions which are imposed on Lawrence's style; and interference on the part of frightened publishers has been eliminated. Far from doing violence to the texts Lawrence would have wished to see published, editorial intervention is essential to recover them. Though we have to accept that some cannot now be recovered in their entirety because early states have not survived, we must be glad that so much evidence remains. Paradoxical as it may seem, the outcome of this recension will be texts which differ, often radically and certainly frequently, from those seen by the author himself.

Editors have adopted the principle that the most authoritative form of the text is to be followed, even if this leads sometimes to a 'spoken' or a 'manuscript' rather than a 'printed' style. We have not wanted to strip off one house-styling in order to impose another. Editorial discretion has been allowed in order to regularise Lawrence's sometimes wayward spelling and punctuation in accordance with his most frequent practice in a particular text. A detailed record of these and other decisions on textual matters, together with the evidence on which they are based, will be found in the textual apparatus or an occasional explanatory note. These give significant deleted readings in manuscripts, typescripts and proofs; and printed variants in forms of the text published in Lawrence's lifetime. We do not record posthumous corruptions, except where first publication was posthumous.

In each volume, the editor's introduction relates the contents to Lawrence's life and to his other writings; it gives the history of composition of the text in some detail, for its intrinsic interest, and because this history is essential to the statement of editorial principles followed. It provides an account of publication and reception which will be found to contain a good deal of hitherto unknown information. Where appropriate, appendixes make available extended draft manuscript readings of significance, or important material, sometimes unpublished, associated with a particular work.

Though Lawrence is a twentieth-century writer and in many respects remains our contemporary, the idiom of his day is not invariably intelligible now, especially to the many readers who are not native speakers of British English. His use of dialect is another difficulty, and further barriers to full understanding are created by now obscure literary, historical, political or other references and allusions. On these occasions explanatory notes are supplied by the editor; it is assumed that the reader has access to a good general dictionary and that the editor need not gloss words or expressions that may be found in it. Where Lawrence's letters are quoted in editorial matter, the reader should assume that his manuscript is alone the source of eccentricities of phrase or spelling. An edition of the letters is still in course of publication: for this reason only the date and recipient of a letter will be given if it has not so far been printed in the Cambridge edition.

ACKNOWLEDGEMENTS

I would like to thank James T. Boulton, general editor of the edition, for his generous encouragement and advice in the preparation of this volume, Lindeth Vasey for her meticulous help on editorial matters, Michael Black and the staff of Cambridge University Press for their unfailing patience and assistance and George Donaldson and John Worthen for their valuable criticism.

I also wish to thank the following for their particular contributions: Carl and Helen Baron, Fiona Bune, Tom Creighton, Marianne Creedy, Mary Donaldson, Katherine Jarvis, Howard Mills, Iona Opie, Melissa Partridge, Jacques and Margaret Prieu, Terry Rogers, Keith Sagar, Eric Stocker and Pamela Wordley.

Finally I must thank the Harry Ransom Humanities Research Center, University of Texas at Austin, for making available the materials in its collection, and Van Mildert College, Durham University, for awarding me a fellowship to complete the work.

May 1987   M.K.

CHRONOLOGY

11 September 1885	Born in Eastwood, Nottinghamshire
September 1898–July 1901	Pupil at Nottingham High School
1902–1908	Pupil teacher; student at University College, Nottingham
7 December 1907	First publication: 'A Prelude', in *Nottinghamshire Guardian*
October 1908	Appointed as teacher at Davidson Road School, Croydon
November 1909	Publishes five poems in *English Review*
3 December 1910	Engagement to Louie Burrows; broken off on 4 February 1912
9 December 1910	Death of his mother, Lydia Lawrence
19 January 1911	*The White Peacock* published in New York (20 January in London)
19 November 1911	Ill with pneumonia; resigns his teaching post on 28 February 1912
March 1912	Meets Frieda Weekley; they elope to Germany on 3 May
23 May 1912	*The Trespasser*
September 1912–March 1913	At Gargnano, Lago di Garda, Italy
February 1913	*Love Poems and Others*
29 May 1913	*Sons and Lovers*
June–August 1913	In England
August 1913–June 1914	In Germany, Switzerland and Italy
July 1914–December 1915	In London, Buckinghamshire and Sussex
13 July 1914	Marries Frieda Weekley in London
26 November 1914	*The Prussian Officer*
30 September 1915	*The Rainbow*; suppressed by court order on 13 November
June 1916	*Twilight in Italy*
July 1916	*Amores*
15 October 1917	After twenty-one months' residence in Cornwall, ordered to leave by military authorities
20 October–30 November 1917	At 44 Mecklenburgh Square, London. Begins *Aaron's Rod*: 'I began it in the Mecklenburg Square days'
26 November 1917	*Look! We Have Come Through!*

February 1918	Works on *Aaron's Rod*: 'another daft novel. It goes ... very slowly and fitfully'
17 March 1918	*Aaron's Rod*: 'done 150 pages ... as blameless as *Cranford*'
mid–September 1918	Continues 'slowly working' on *Aaron's Rod*
October 1918	*New Poems*
December 1918	Spends Christmas with his sister Ada Clarke at Ripley, Derbyshire
June 1919	Still hoping to complete his 'quite "proper" novel' but probably ceases work on *Aaron's Rod* shortly afterwards
14 November 1919	Travels to Italy
15–17 November 1919	Stays at Sir Walter Becker's villa near Turin
19 November–10 December 1919	At the Pensione Balestra, Florence; probably writes essay 'Looking Down'
20 November 1919	*Bay*
March 1920	Moves to Taormina, Sicily
5 May 1920	Finishes *The Lost Girl*
by 18 July 1920	Resumes work on *Aaron's Rod*: '⅓ done ... But it stands still just now'
12 September 1920	*Aaron's Rod* 'half done'
November 1920	Private publication of *Women in Love* (New York), *The Lost Girl*
End November 1920	Abandons *Aaron's Rod*: 'can't end it'; begins *Mr Noon*
December 1920	Works on *Mr Noon*
5–13 January 1921	Visits Sardinia
by 21 January–February 1921	Writes *Sea and Sardinia*
4 April 1921	At Taormina 'I shall try and finish *Aarons Rod*'
6 May 1921	At Baden-Baden 'I am working on *Aaron's Rod*'
c. 9 May 1921	Sends first third of *Aaron's Rod* to Violet Monk for typing.
10 May 1921	*Psychoanalysis and the Unconscious* (New York)
12 May 1921	*Aaron's Rod* '⅔ done'
27 May 1921	'*Aaron* is finished, save for the last chapter'
1 June 1921	'*Aaron* is complete'
21 July 1921	Sends second part of *Aaron's Rod* to Curtis Brown for typing
Late July–early August 1921	Revises first third of *Aaron's Rod* TS
7 August 1921	Receives rest of *Aaron's Rod* TS and begins revising
14 August 1921	'Foreword' (unlocated) to *Aaron's Rod* sent to Thomas Seltzer

8 October 1921   Sends revised TS to Robert Mountsier for
                                Seltzer
by 22 October 1921   Writes an 'explanatory foreword' (unlocated)
                                to the novel
23 November 1921   Sends second revised typescript to Curtis
                                Brown for Martin Secker
12 December 1921   *Sea and Sardinia* (New York)
December 1921–January 1922   Refuses Seltzer's request to alter *Aaron's Rod*
by 18 January 1922   Returns a clean typescript copy (unlocated)
                                sent him by Seltzer earlier in January
                                without any corrections 'or only a few'

February 1922   Part of chapter XIV published in the *Dial* as
                                'An Episode'
26 February 1922   Leaves for Ceylon
March–August 1922   In Ceylon and Australia
14 April 1922   *Aaron's Rod* published by Seltzer in USA
June 1922   *Aaron's Rod* published by Secker in England
September 1922–March 1923   In New Mexico
23 October 1922   *Fantasia of the Unconscious* (New York)
24 October 1922   *England, My England* (New York)
March 1923   *The Ladybird, The Fox, The Captain's Doll*
March–November 1923   In Mexico and USA
27 August 1923   *Studies in Classic American Literature* (New
                                York)
September 1923   *Kangaroo*
9 October 1923   *Birds, Beasts and Flowers* (New York)
December 1923–March 1924   In England, France and Germany
March 1924–September 1925   In New Mexico and Mexico
August 1924   *The Boy in the Bush* (with Mollie Skinner)
10 September 1924   Death of his father, John Arthur Lawrence
14 May 1925   *St. Mawr Together with the Princess*
September 1925–June 1928   In England and, mainly, in Italy
7 December 1925   *Reflections on the Death of a Porcupine*
                                (Philadelphia)
January 1926   *The Plumed Serpent*
June 1927   *Mornings in Mexico*
24 May 1928   *The Woman Who Rode Away and Other Stories*
June 1928–March 1930   In Switzerland and, principally, in France
July 1928   *Lady Chatterley's Lover* privately published
                                (Florence)
September 1928   *Collected Poems*
July 1929   Exhibition of paintings in London raided by
                                police. *Pansies* (manuscript earlier seized in
                                the mail)
September 1929   *The Escaped Cock* (Paris)
2 March 1930   Dies at Vence, Alpes Maritimes, France

CUE-TITLES

(The place of publication is London unless otherwise stated.)

Asquith
: Lady Cynthia Asquith. *Diaries 1915–1918*. Hutchinson, 1968.

Carswell
: Catherine Carswell. *The Savage Pilgrimage*. Chatto and Windus, 1932; reprinted by Cambridge University Press, 1981.

Letters, i.
: James T. Boulton, ed. *The Letters of D. H. Lawrence.* Volume I. Cambridge: Cambridge University Press, 1979.

Letters, ii.
: George J. Zytaruk and James T. Boulton, eds. *The Letters of D. H. Lawrence.* Volume II. Cambridge: Cambridge University Press, 1981.

Letters, iii.
: James T. Boulton and Andrew Robertson, eds. *The Letters of D. H. Lawrence.* Volume III. Cambridge: Cambridge University Press, 1984.

Letters, iv.
: Warren Roberts, James T. Boulton and Elizabeth Mansfield, eds. *The Letters of D. H. Lawrence.* Volume IV. Cambridge: Cambridge University Press, 1987.

Movements
: D. H. Lawrence. *Movements in European History.* Introd. James T. Boulton. Oxford: Oxford University Press, 1971.

Nehls
: Edward Nehls, ed. *D. H. Lawrence: A Composite Biography.* 3 Volumes. Madison: University of Wisconsin Press, 1957–9.

Phoenix
: Edward D. McDonald, ed. *Phoenix: The Posthumous Papers of D. H. Lawrence.* New York: Viking, 1936.

Weintraub
: Stanley Weintraub. *Reggie: A Portrait of Reginald Turner.* New York: Braziller, 1965.

INTRODUCTION

INTRODUCTION

When D. H. Lawrence began writing *Aaron's Rod* in the autumn of 1917 he was living in London following his expulsion from Cornwall in October – 'I began it in the Mecklenburg Square days.'[1] It was a dreary, hopeless period in his life when, depressed by the recent banning for obscenity of *The Rainbow* – the novel in which he had expressed his deepest belief in marriage as the way to earthly fulfilment – and by the poverty and police persecution of the war years, he was writing little: 'ones self seems to contract more and more away from everything, and especially from people. It is a kind of wintering. The only thing to do is to let it *be* winter' (iii. 197). Nevertheless by the end of January 1918 he had resumed work on the critical essays which were to become *Studies in Classic American Literature* (hereafter *Studies*) and in February he began to work on *Aaron's Rod* again: 'I am doing some philosophic essays, also, very spasmodically, another daft novel. It goes slowly – very slowly and fitfully. But I don't care' (iii. 216). The novel continued to develop 'slowly and fitfully' and indeed was not completed in its final – and radically different – form until the end of May 1921 (iii. 729, 730). However, by mid-March 1918 Lawrence had written something like a third of the book: 'I have begun a novel now – done 150 pages – which is as blameless as *Cranford*. It shall not have one garment disarranged, but shall be buttoned up like a member of Parliament. Still, I wouldn't vouch that it is like *Sons and Lovers*: it is funny. It amuses me terribly' (iii. 227).

But although he continued to work on the novel at intervals – 'I am slowly working at another novel: though I feel it's not much use. No publisher will risk my last, and none will risk this, I expect'[2] – and as late as 8 June 1919 still spoke of wanting to finish his 'quite "proper" novel' (iii. 364), his interest in novel writing was flagging: 'I can't do anything in the world today – am just choked' (iii. 280). He probably abandoned *Aaron*

---

[1] *Letters*, iii. 728. DHL and Frieda were lent a bed-sitting room at 44 Mecklenburgh Square, London, by a friend Hilda Doolittle (see Explanatory note on 26:31 and *Letters*, ii. 203 n. 3) after their expulsion from Cornwall. (Subsequent references to *Letters*, i.–iv. are given in the text with volume and page number.)

[2] *Letters*, iii. 280. 'My last' refers to *Women in Love*, still unpublished though first completed in November 1916.

shortly after June since there is no further reference to it in correspondence that year. It was not until July 1920 that he began writing the novel again (iii. 567, 572). One can only guess what the early 'blameless' *Aaron* could have been like, lacking as it did the important Italian material of the later version (which was based on Lawrence's experience of Florence in November 1919 and later). He may have drawn on his life in London in the autumn of 1917 for some of the early *Aaron's Rod* as indeed he did for the novel as we have it now. Certainly many of the characters as finally created are thinly disguised, often satirical, portraits of the circle he moved in during the autumn of 1917. The young musician Cecil Gray, whom Lawrence met in Cornwall in the summer of 1917 (iii. 154) became Cyril Scott (the name of an actual person and also a musician);[3] the Lawrences' friend Hilda Doolittle (who had lent them a bed-sitting room at Mecklenburgh Square) became Julia Cunningham, and her husband Richard Aldington became Robert Cunningham; while 'Dorothy Yorke – Arabella, the American girl at Mecklenburgh Sq' (iii. 259) was the prototype for Josephine Ford. Various incidents such as the episode of 'The Lighted Tree' in chapter III of *Aaron's Rod* had their origins in actual events,[4] but of course Lawrence drew very widely on his past for material and it would be dangerous to infer too much about the content, dating and composition of *Aaron's Rod* from such evidence. Lawrence often reworked old material. Indeed, Aaron's surname 'Sisson' appears in an early story 'The Shades of Spring' in the character John Adderley 'Syson',[5] while the Bricknells of *Aaron's Rod* (like the Crich family of *Women in Love* and the Barlows of *Touch and Go* who were in some measure modelled on the real-life Barbers of Lamb Close) were partly based on a local Eastwood family, the Brentnalls. How much of the material in the early *Aaron's Rod* was transmuted into the novel as it emerged in the summer of 1921 must therefore remain conjectural since no manuscript survives, but it is reasonable to suppose that when Lawrence began the novel again he incorporated the memories of his past in the Midlands and those of the war years, in particular the autumn of 1917 when he was in London, in the first part of the novel, much as he used the flight to Italy in 1919 and the time in Florence for the second half.

The early *Aaron* appears to have had only a transient interest for Lawrence. His commitment to fiction temporarily declined after the

---

[3] See Asquith 338 where Lady Cynthia Asquith mentions Cyril Scott as one of a party at Glynde in September 1917. DHL also wrote to another Cyril Scott on 23 March 1921 (*Letters*, iii. 691–2).

[4] See Asquith 341–5.

[5] 'Sisson' was a common name in the Eastwood area; see Explanatory note on 5:8.

banning of *The Rainbow* and the difficulty of finding a publisher for its sequel, *Women in Love* which he nevertheless went on revising. However, he wrote in May 1917: 'Philosophy interests me most now – not novels or stories. I find people ultimately boring: and you can't have fiction without people. So fiction does not, at the bottom, interest me any more. I am weary of humanity and human things' (iii. 127). Much of his best writing at this time and in the immediate post-war period, therefore, is to be found not in fiction but in the essays and in the poems which were to be collected in *Birds, Beasts and Flowers*. As he later wrote, 'Once be disillusioned with the man-made world, and you can still see the magic, the beauty, the delicate realness of all other life.'[6] However by July 1918 he was becoming absorbed again by just those 'human things', and he wrote the first chapters of *Movements in European History*, a textbook for school children, commissioned by Oxford University Press (iii. 261, 268–9). During the summer and autumn of that year he continued to revise the essays for *Studies*. These were to become much more than literary essays on American fiction: they contain a searching analysis, and a telling condemnation, of the civilisation that produced the first world war, but it is characteristic of Lawrence that they are equally statements of his belief in man's ability to emerge from that destruction, to create 'a new era of living':[7]

At present there is a vast myriad-branched human engine, the very thought of which is death. But in the winter even a tree looks like iron. Seeing the great trunk of dark iron and the swaying steel flails of boughs, we cannot help being afraid. What we see of buds looks like sharp bronze stud-points. The whole thing hums elastic and sinister and fatally metallic, like some confused scourge of swinging steel throngs. Yet the lovely cloud of green and summer lustre is within it ... It only wants the miracle, the new, soft, creative wind: which does not blow yet. Meanwhile we can only stand and wait, knowing that what is, is not.[8]

Gradually Lawrence's enthusiasm for writing kindled again, and the second half of 1918 saw the completion of several essays on education as well as some short stories[9] and the play *Touch and Go* which 'fired up my last sparks of hope in the world, as it were, and cried out like a Balaams ass. I believe the world yet might get a turn for the better, if it but had a little

---

[6] 'Review of *Gifts of Fortune*, by H. M. Tomlinson', *Phoenix* 345. Although this review dates from November 1926 the quotation aptly expresses DHL's feelings at this time.

[7] 'The Spirit of Place', *The Symbolic Meaning*, ed. Armin Arnold (Arundel, 1962), pp. 30–1.

[8] Ibid., pp. 30–1.

[9] See *Letters*, iii. 285–6, 302–3, 298, 299–300. The stories were 'The Blind Man', 'The Fox' and 'Tickets Please'. By December DHL had written '4 little essays for the *Times* – "Education of the People" '; see *Letters*, iii. 306.

shove that way' (iii. 293). In December 1918 and January 1919 he continued his efforts to give the world that 'shove', and he worked on *Movements in European History* which he completed early in February 1919.[10] But his health, never robust, had been undermined by the strain and poverty of the war years and the frustration of being trapped in England – 'I do so want to *get out* – out of England – really, out of Europe. And I *will* get out' (iii. 312). And the early months of 1919 found Lawrence ill again with little interest in writing anything, although he continued to revise his history book (iii. 347): 'I have not written anything these last few months – not since I have been ill. I feel I don't want to write – still less do I want to publish anything' (iii. 348).

During the summer months of 1919, however, Lawrence rallied and wrote some stories and essays, further revised *Studies* and, with his friend Koteliansky, embarked on a translation of the Russian philosopher Shestov's *All Things Are Possible*.[11] At last in October the long awaited passports and visas (applied for in August) arrived. Lawrence's wife Frieda left for Germany in the middle of the month and on the 14th of November Lawrence himself left England for Italy. He first stayed near Turin as the guest of Sir Walter Becker (whom he portrayed in *Aaron's Rod* as Sir William Franks)[12] and then continued to Florence where he stayed at the Pensione Balestra, Piazza Mentana (described in *Aaron's Rod* as the Pension Nardini):

On a dark, wet, wintry evening in November, 1919, I arrived in Florence, having just got back to Italy for the first time since 1914. My wife was in Germany, gone to see her mother, also for the first time since that fatal year 1914. We were poor; who was going to bother to publish me and to pay for my writings, in 1918 and 1919? I landed in Italy with nine pounds in my pocket and about twelve pounds lying in the bank in London. Nothing more.[13]

Nevertheless, after the bleakness of the war years in Cornwall and London, the flight to Italy seemed like an entry into another world: 'Italy is still gay – does all her weeping in her press – takes her politics with her wine, and enjoys them' (iii. 417). And in December Lawrence travelled to Rome, to Picinisco (which he described in the last chapters of *The Lost*

10 See *Letters*, iii. 304, 322, 326 and 323.
11 DHL wrote 'Fanny and Annie' and 'Monkey Nuts' in May (see *Letters*, iii. 360). He was editing Koteliansky's translation of Shestov in August (iii. 380–3) and probably finished the work on Shestov around the end of the month (iii. 387). He also revised *Studies* during September (iii. 400).
12 See *Letters*, iii. 417. See also Sir Walter's account of DHL's visit in Nehls, ii. 12–13, and Explanatory note on 130:39.
13 'Introduction' to *Memoirs of the Foreign Legion* by Maurice Magnus (Secker, 1924), p. 11.

Girl) and Capri, although he wrote little.[14] When he did resume work in January 1920 he was to channel his energy first into *Psychoanalysis and the Unconscious* (iii. 466) and, in February, into the novel which had originally started as 'The Insurrection of Miss Houghton' in 1913, had lain fallow and was now to be completely rewritten and entitled *The Lost Girl*. Lawrence worked on *The Lost Girl* over the next few months while living at the Fontana Vecchia, Taormina, Sicily, where he had moved early in March (iii. 497) and where much of *Aaron's Rod* was also to be written. *The Lost Girl* was finished early in May (iii. 515) – 'quite amusing: and quite moral' (iii. 525) – and although Lawrence mentions that he intended to begin work on a new novel, *Mr Noon* (iii. 537), by June he had set this aside to write poems for his *Birds, Beasts and Flowers* volume and to revise *Studies* and *The Lost Girl*.

When Lawrence finally returned to *Aaron's Rod* in July 1920, he seems to have followed a pattern similar to that which governed the writing of *The Lost Girl*: that is, he scrapped his early work and began the novel afresh, as the subsequent references to his 'new' novel (and indeed his general habit of entirely rewriting his novels) suggest. His correspondence in this month does not specifically mention the novel by title – 'I have begun another novel – amusing it is' (iii. 565) and 'I'm working with ever-diminishing spasms of fitfulness at a novel which I know won't go forward many more steps' (iii. 567). It is just possible that some of the references to the 'new' novel may be to *Mr Noon*, whose composition history is intertwined with that of *Aaron's Rod*, but Lawrence's letter to his English publisher Martin Secker on 18 July clearly establishes that the text he is working on is *Aaron's Rod*: 'Yes, I have another novel in hand. I began it two years ago. I have got it ⅓ done, and it is very amusing. But it stands still just now, awaiting events. Once it starts again it will steam ahead' (iii. 572). However, the novel progressed very slowly. Already in September when he was again in Florence, Lawrence was complaining: 'My novel jerks one chapter forward now and then. It is half done. But where the other ½ is coming from, ask the Divine Providence' (iii. 594), and by the end of the month: 'My novel – the new one – has stuck half way, but I don't care. I may get a go on him at Taormina. If not, I think I can sort of jump him picaresque' (iii. 602). Early in October Lawrence seemed determined to finish the novel: 'I am still stuck in the middle of *Aaron's Rod*, my novel. But at Taormina I'll spit on my hands and lay fresh hold' (iii. 608) and, a little

---

[14] DHL mentions that he is 'going to do various small things – on Italy and on Psycoanalysis – for the periodicals' and that he has sent 'Murry an essay from here', which may be 'David' (*Letters*, iii. 426–7, 428).

later, 'I am half way through a novel called *Aaron's Rod*, – hope to finish before Christmas' (iii. 613). There is no evidence in the correspondence to indicate precisely where Lawrence was 'stuck' but it seems reasonable to assume from the meticulous account of the November days spent as Sir Walter Becker's guest and the arrival in Florence which became chapters XII and XIII, the half-way point of the novel, that Lawrence had written at least this much. The thinly disguised portraits of leading figures in the Anglo-Italian community in Florence at this time – Norman Douglas as Argyle, Reggie Turner as Algy Constable, and Maurice Magnus (for whose *Memoirs of the Foreign Legion* Lawrence was later to write an introduction) as Louis Mee[15] – could possibly have been written by then. But since these characters and the events surrounding them do not occur until three-quarters of the way through the finished novel (chapters XVI and XVII) it seems more likely that they were written rather later.

Meanwhile Lawrence was finishing poems for *Birds, Beasts and Flowers* and was correcting *The Lost Girl* proofs, although he appears to have been working only sporadically (iii. 609). In November 1920 any work he may have been doing on *Aaron* was further disrupted by a request from Oxford University Press to write a new penultimate chapter on Italian history for *Movements in European History* (iii. 622). The new chapter, like some of the Italian scenes in *Aaron's Rod* and the correspondence of 1920 and 1921, reflects both his growing disenchantment with post-war Italy and Italian politics[16] and his instinct for sensing the mood of a country and its people, as well as his shrewd understanding of that era of political unrest which saw the rise of fascism and communism.

And so Italy was made—modern Italy. Fretfulness, irritation, and nothing in life except money: this is what the religious fervour of Garibaldians and Mazzinians works out to—in united, free Italy as in other united, free countries. No wonder liberty so often turns to ashes in the mouth, after being so fair a fruit to contemplate. Man needs more than liberty.[17]

In the meantime work on *Aaron's Rod* had simply ceased: 'Am doing no serious work' (iii. 624) and 'I did more than half of *Aaron's Rod*, but can't end it: the flowering end missing, I suppose – so I began a comedy, which I hope will end' (iii. 626). Presumably the 'comedy' was *Mr Noon* which Lawrence specifically mentions to Secker a fortnight later: 'Probably between *Women in Love* and *The Rainbow* best insert another incensorable

---

15 See Weintraub 189–99 and Nehls, ii. 61–6.
16 See letter to Mackenzie, 7 October 1920: 'Italy feels awfully shaky and nasty, and for the first time my unconscious is uneasy of the Italians' (*Letters*, iii. 609).
17 *Movements* 291.

novel – either *Aaron's Rod*, which I have left again, or *Mr Noon*, which I am doing.'[18] For the rest of December 1920 and part of January 1921 – except for a quick jaunt to Sardinia – he continued work on *Mr Noon*[19] but he seemed unable to recommence work on *Aaron's Rod*: '*Mr Noon* will be, I think, *most* dangerous: but humorously so. It will take me about a month still to finish – this month was lost moving about. *Aaron* will not be dangerous – if only his rod would start budding, poor dear' (iii. 653).

However, Lawrence set aside both *Mr Noon* and *Aaron's Rod* in February to write *Sea and Sardinia* – 'I have nearly done a little travel-book: "Diary of a Trip to Sardinia": which will have photographs, and which I hope, through the magazines, will make me something' (iii. 664) – which he finished in February and revised during March (iii. 667, 681, 686). Although at the time he still intended to 'try to finish *Aaron's Rod*. But am not in a good work-mood' (iii. 688), his enthusiasm for writing anything at all had waned, and the familiar urge to travel seized him. In the early months of the year he proposed various schemes, which varied from the romantic one of sailing the South Seas with a few congenial souls, to working a farm in New England, or touring the Mediterranean by boat:[20] 'This is a sort of crisis for me. I've got to come unstuck from the old life and Europe, and I can't know beforehand. So have patience' (iii. 693).

In April Lawrence did travel: he visited Palermo, Capri, Rome and Florence and, by the end of the month, Baden-Baden in Germany, where he was finally to complete *Aaron's Rod*. 'I shall try and finish *Aarons Rod* this summer, before finishing *Mr Noon II* – which is funny, but a hair-raiser. First part innocent – *Aarons Rod* innocent' (iii. 702). At last, early in May 1921, residing in Baden-Baden with Frieda, Lawrence resumed work on *Aaron's Rod*: 'have some hope of finishing it here' (iii. 714), he told his friend and agent in America, Robert Mountsier. To his Buddhist friends Earl and Achsah Brewster he wrote: 'I am finishing Aaron. And you won't like it *at all*. Instead of bringing him nearer to heaven, in leaps and bounds, he's misbehaving and putting ten fingers to his nose at everything. Damn heaven. Damn holiness. Damn Nirvana. Damn it all' (iii. 720). On 12 May he informed Curtis Brown, now his official agent in England, that he was 'having a shot at finishing another novel *Aaron's Rod* – which is ⅔ done' (iii. 717), and to Secker on 16 May he wrote: 'Here I have got *Aaron's Rod* well under weigh again, and have the end in sight. Nothing impossible in it, at

---

[18] *Letters*, iii. 638; see also iii. 439, 459.
[19] See *Letters*, iii. 639, 645; and especially 'I left off *Aaron's Rod* and began "Lucky Noon" ' (*Letters*, iii. 646).
[20] See *Letters*, iii. 655, 664–5, 667–8, 689, 702.

all.'[21] Indeed he had sent the first part of the novel to be typed by Violet Monk in England early in May with instructions to Mountsier to bring both typed copies (ribbon and carbon) with him when he came on his proposed visit to the Lawrences.[22] By 27 May Lawrence was confident of completing the novel and he wrote both to Secker and to Koteliansky:

I have *nearly* finished my novel *Aarons Rod*, which I began long ago and could never bring to an end. I began it in the Mecklenburg Square days. Now suddenly I had a fit of work – sitting away in the woods. And save for the last chapter, it is done. But it won't be popular. (iii. 728)

You will be glad to hear I have as good as finished *Aaron's Rod*: that is, it is all done except the last chapter – two days work. It all came quite suddenly here. But it is a queer book: I've no idea what you or anybody will think of it. When it is typed I will let you see it. (iii. 729)

The book was completed by the end of the month: on 1 June Lawrence wrote to both Mountsier and Curtis Brown that he had just finished the novel (iii. 730, 731).

Lawrence called *Aaron's Rod* 'the last of my serious English novels – the end of *The Rainbow*, *Women in Love* line. It had to be written – and had to come to such an end' (iv. 92–3). *The Rainbow* and *Women in Love* – 'an organic artistic whole' as he termed them (iii. 459) – move chronologically from the rural England of the mid-nineteenth century to the very brink of the first world war, while *Aaron's Rod*, opening with the Christmas of 1918 after the armistice, follows the travels of a character who leaves England altogether. All these novels chronicle the individual's search in each generation for fulfilment, and all question the quality of existence possible in an increasingly materialistic and technological England where the value of the individual seems to be diminished and his needs reduced to insignificance. The novels in this 'line' dramatise the question which Lawrence thought faced every generation: *how* to live, how to bring the needs of the intellectual and emotional selves into harmony and into equilibrium with the outside world, how to find a rule of conduct that both

---

[21] *Letters*, iii. 722. It seems likely that DHL had written at least as far as chaps. XVI and XVII by this time and may have been working on the scenes between Aaron and the Marchesa, which makes his assurance to Secker that there was 'nothing impossible', in the novel ironic, in view of later censoring by his publisher.

[22] '... the first part of *Aaron's Rod* was being typed by *Miss V. Monk, Grimsbury Farm, Long Lane, near Newbury, Berks*. I wrote a week ago and asked her please to post me the carbon copy only. You might ask her if she has done so: and if she hasn't, bring the whole, both type copies, *if you like*. I really think I may finish *Aaron's Rod* while I am here' (*Letters*, iii. 724). The Lawrences knew Violet Monk during their time at nearby Chapel Farm Cottage in 1918 and 1919; see Nehls, i. 463–7, 486–7 and 501–6. (The reference on p. 505 to Violet Monk typing *The Lost Girl* is an error for her work on *Aaron's Rod*.)

interprets man's role in the world and sustains his inner being. Like Nietzsche (whom he quotes in *Aaron's Rod*), Lawrence saw human existence as a dialectic, a continual process of conflict between elements within the self as well as outside it, a conflict however which was a necessary condition for the creation of oneself into new being. In *The Rainbow* and *Women in Love* this quest for integration is achieved to a greater or lesser degree through the coming together of opposites, male and female, in the sacrament of marriage. *Aaron's Rod*, however, completed in the desolation of post-war Germany ('Germany helped me to the finish of *Aaron*' iv. 259), not only rejects the civilisation that had rushed into that cataclysm – 'I am feeling absolutely at an end with the civilised world' (iii. 689) – but questions marriage itself as the goal of human fulfilment: 'How we hang on to the marriage clue! Doubt if its really a way out' (iii. 521). Indeed it suggests that marriage is only a prelude:

The best thing I have known is the stillness of accomplished marriage, when one possesses one's own soul in silence ... And I must confess that I feel this selfsame 'accomplishment' of the fulfilled being is only a preparation for new responsibilities ahead, new unison in effort and conflict, the effort to make, with other men, a little new way into the future, and to break through the hedge of the many.[23]

The writings of the post-war period reveal two important developments in the direction of Lawrence's thinking: first a desire to explore the nature of human relationship outside the marriage bond, in particular that of political man; and second a growing fascination with the unknown forces within the psyche itself, 'the source and well-head of creative activity'[24] as he called it. It is no accident that the major essays Lawrence wrote while engaged on *Aaron's Rod* (and which, with *Studies*, may be said to stand in the same relation to that novel as 'Study of Thomas Hardy' does to *The Rainbow* and 'The Crown' to *Women in Love*) should have been studies in psychology: *Psychoanalysis and the Unconscious* and *Fantasia of the Unconscious*. *Aaron's Rod*, then, set at first in the industrial Midlands, belongs in one sense to the old world of Lawrence's 'English novels', but in the Italian chapters it also looks forward to the exploration of man's deepest impulses as they manifest themselves in his political, social and religious activity. These are the issues that were to inform the novels Lawrence wrote next, *Kangaroo* and *The Plumed Serpent*.

Writing to Katherine Mansfield in December 1918, Lawrence had already recognised a decisive change in his conception of the novel and in

---

[23] *Fantasia of the Unconscious* (Seltzer, 1922), chap. XI. Cf. 'Whitman' in *The Symbolic Meaning*, ed. Arnold, p. 263; cf. also below pp. 104 and 266.

[24] 'Introduction' to *All Things Are Possible* by Leo Shestov, *Phoenix* 216.

the purpose of his writing: 'It seems to me, if one is to do fiction now, one must cross the threshold of the human psyche' (iii. 302). The letter is revealing, and may suggest one reason why Lawrence had such difficulty in completing *Aaron's Rod*: he was in a period of transition, reluctant merely to continue the 'picaresque' adventures, as he rather dismissively called them, of his hero and concerned to move away from the vividly realised physical settings and events of post-war England and Italy to a deeper exploration of the spiritual process of his age, for which Aaron's experiences were to provide a vehicle. Of course the novel also renders particular places and characters, but the story of Aaron's search, as the last chapters of the novel reveal, also becomes the presentation of Lawrence's – and everyman's – quest: 'Allons, there is no road yet, but we are all Aarons with rods of our own', as he wrote in *Fantasia of the Unconscious*,[25] and again: 'Men live and see according to some gradually developing and gradually withering vision. This vision exists also as a dynamic idea or metaphysic—exists first as such. Then it is unfolded into life and art.'[26]

The Rainbow, Women in Love and *Aaron's Rod* chronicle that 'gradually developing and gradually withering vision': *Aaron's Rod*, with its discussion of the obscure but powerful forces which move men and civilisations, offers a glimpse of the vision to come. In the concluding chapters Lilly (who often articulates Lawrence's beliefs) discusses the two primary impulses in man, love and power, and questions the nature of the political and religious ideologies which have shaped western civilisation, suggesting that the love mode is outworn and that the new era will be one of power. But what becomes clear in the novel, as elsewhere in Lawrence's writings, is that Lilly's idea of power transcends any notion of mere authoritarianism. Lawrence's vision of man is not political but spiritual, not a denial of man's freedom and individuality but a confirmation of it because it is based on a recognition of the innate and inexplicable differences between each unique human being. 'Power—the power-urge. The will-to-power—but not in Nietzsche's sense', says Lilly and he goes on to explain the doctrine of power as a creative force, that which causes individuals and cultures to rise into being, to create themselves: 'you develop the one and only phoenix of your own self' and 'your soul inside you is your only Godhead'.[27]

[25] Chap. I.
[26] 'Foreword' to *Fantasia of the Unconscious*.
[27] See below 297:28–9, 295:38–9 and 296:26.

An account of a conversation between Lawrence and Earl and Achsah Brewster in May 1921, shortly before he completed the novel, reveals a fascinating glimpse of an alternative ending to *Aaron's Rod*:

We were alone, and he told us that he was writing *Aaron's Rod*, and began outlining the story. It seemed more beautiful as he narrated it in his low sonorous voice with the quiet gesture of his hands, than it ever could written in a book. Suddenly he stopped, after Aaron had left his wife and home and broken with his past, gravely asking what he should do with him now.

We ventured that only two possible courses were left to a man in his straits – either to go to Monte Cassino and repent, or else to go through the whole cycle of experience.

He gave a quiet chuckle of surprise and added that those were the very possibilities he had seen, that first he had intended sending him to Monte Cassino, but found instead that Aaron had to go to destruction to find his way through from the lowest depths.[28]

Neither for Aaron nor for the England of his time was a retreat into the peace of a monastery possible, as Lawrence recognised. On finishing the novel he wrote: 'the old order has gone ... And the era of love and peace and democracy with it. There will be an era of war ahead' (iii. 732). Lawrence's words have proved all too prophetic: the novel ends with an anarchist's bomb which destroys Aaron's flute – his rod, the emblem of his quest and the means by which he has followed it. Yet, characteristically, the final message of the novel is one of hope: 'It'll grow again. It's a reed, a water-plant—you can't kill it'.[29]

Like Aaron, fleeing the devastation of post-war England, Lawrence struggled with his writings which were, as he wrote on finishing *The Lost Girl*, 'the crumpled wings of my soul. They get me free before I get myself free ... I get some sort of wings loose' (iii. 522). His post-war works, particularly *Aaron's Rod*, *Fantasia of the Unconscious* and the essays in *Studies*, are a record of that struggle to find a new vision of regeneration for modern man. In the travels that were to come – Ceylon and the Far East, Australia, and the Americas and finally his eventual return to Europe – and in the literature that arose out of them, Lawrence sought to understand the creative and vital forces in man which alone can reshape his world.

---

[28] Nehls, ii. 58–9. DHL visited Monte Cassino in February 1920 and later recorded his impression of the monastery in his 'Introduction' to Maurice Magnus's *Memoirs of the Foreign Legion*. Also cf. Nietzsche: 'Whoever, at any time, has undertaken to build a new heaven has found the strength for it in his own hell', *The Genealogy of Morals*, trans. F. Golffing (New York, 1956), p. 251.

[29] See below 285:12.

Publication

Although Lawrence had sent the first part of *Aaron's Rod* to England to be
typed by Violet Monk *c.* 9 May 1921, he did not actually get the 143 pages
of typescript back (iv. 54) until 27 June 1921, when he wrote to Mountsier:
'Have received *Aaron* MS.'[30] There was a delay of three weeks before
Lawrence sent the second part of the novel to be typed, but there is no
indication in the correspondence of the reason for the delay. Presumably
Lawrence was revising the manuscript. Although on 12 June he had
written to Mountsier, 'Hear from Miss Monk she has sent you *Aaron*'s first
part. I must see it: and then I must sent this Conclusion to be typed' (iv.
36), he did not post the second portion of *Aaron's Rod* until 21 July, and
then it was to his agent Curtis Brown.

> This is the remainder of *Aarons Rod*. I had planned to type it myself, but find no
> type-writing machine available. Have it done as quick as possible, then send it back
> to me for revision – true copy and carbon copy both. I have the first 143 pages here
> ready typed. But I want to do a lot of revision on the typescript. (iv. 54)

The revisions in the first 143 pages, however, are relatively minor; only
chapter II contains any substantially rewritten passages, while chapter III
has a few altered phrases and sentences and chapter VII some rewritten
dialogue. Presumably Lawrence was making these revisions to both ribbon
and carbon copy (only the latter has survived) during the last part of July
and early in August.

Curtis Brown duly sent the two copies of the remainder of the novel
which Lawrence had requested and these arrived on 7 August 1921:

> I was very glad to get the two copies of *Aaron's Rod* this morning – beautifully typed
> and bound. Very many thanks. I was just beginning to be uneasy, having had no
> word from you.
>   Tell me please what the cost is, so that I can compare with what I pay in Italy.
>   (iv. 65)

Although Lawrence went on to promise to 'return the whole MS. directly',
he actually revised the second part extensively, and on 14 August warned
Curtis Brown (and through him his American publisher Thomas Seltzer)

---

[30] *Letters*, iv. 44. As the June correspondence reveals, DHL sometimes meant the typescript
rather than the autograph manuscript by 'MS'. His letter to Mountsier of 7 June 1921
differentiates between the two states of the text but in letters to Secker, Mountsier and
Curtis Brown, all dated 12 June 1921, DHL confirms that he is waiting for the *typed* copy
of *Aaron's Rod* to arrive from Mountsier, but speaks of this to Curtis Brown as the 'MS'
(ibid., 28, 34–6). On 20 June 1921 he was still waiting for Mountsier to bring the
typescript with him 'which lies at American Express' (ibid. 39). In the end Mountsier
actually posted the copy.

that there would be some delay in despatching the novel: 'I may be some time sending the *Aaron* MSS: must go through it carefully. Surely it is just as well also if Secker publishes it next Spring: is there really any hurry? Please answer' (iv. 69). Seltzer, impatient to have the novel, had hoped to receive it earlier and wrote to Mountsier on 20 August: 'I am definitely determined to bring it out this fall.'[31] But the only thing Seltzer did receive from Lawrence in August was a brief foreword to *Aaron's Rod*, dated 14 August 1921, of which no trace has survived beyond a description in a public sale catalogue of 1936.[32]

There were, then, *two* complete corrected typescripts of *Aaron's Rod*, ribbon and carbon, (pp. 1–143 typed by Violet Monk, pp. 144–490 typed by Curtis Brown's agency). The one destined for Seltzer through Mount-sier has survived, the other for Secker through Curtis Brown has been lost. Lawrence sent Mountsier the typescript (mixed ribbon and carbon copy) he had revised for Seltzer (hereafter TS) on 8 October and confirmed this in his letter of the same date to Seltzer himself:

I hope Mountsier has sent you the MS of *Aarons Rod*. He emphatically dislikes the book, but then he is not responsible for it. I want you to write and tell me simply what you feel about it. It is the last of my serious English novels – the end of *The Rainbow*, *Women in Love* line. It had to be written – and had to come to such an end. If you wish, I will write a proper little explanatory foreword to it – not the one I sent from Zell am See. I want you to tell me if you consider it 'dangerous' – and what bit of it you think so – and if you'd like any small alteration made. If you would, please name the specific lines. (iv. 92–3)

This second 'little explanatory foreword' was written as 'a small intro-duction to *Aaron's Rod*' (iv. 104) and posted to Seltzer on 22 October but as with the first (written in August) no copy has been located. In the same letter to Seltzer Lawrence confirmed that he had sent the TS to Mountsier who would be responsible for forwarding it to Seltzer: 'I hear from Mountsier that he is posting you *Aaron's Rod*. I hope you won't dislike it as much as he does. – But I want you to publish it about as it stands. I will

[31] *Letters to Thomas and Adele Seltzer*, ed. Gerald M. Lacy (Los Angeles, 1976), p. 214. See also *Letters*, iv. 57.

[32] The catalogue of the American Art Association (Anderson Galleries Inc., New York) advertised the following items in their public sale of 29 and 30 January 1936: an autograph manuscript of about 285 words, 'Foreword to Aaron's Rod', signed and dated 14 August 1921; a letter of about 145 words written from Thumersbach, Zell-am-See, and dated 15 August 1921, to Thomas Seltzer. The catalogue quotes part of the letter which relates to *Aaron's Rod* and the 'Foreword': 'Probably you won't like it; probably it won't sell. Yet it is what I want it to be. I am satisfied with it. It is the end of the *Rainbow–Women in Love* novels: and my last word. I enclosed a little Foreword to it, which you print or not, as you like' (*Letters*, iv. 71). See also ibid. 93.

make any small modification you wish. So write at once.' Presumably Seltzer received the TS around 22 October or shortly thereafter. It was not until 10 November, however, that Lawrence wrote to Secker promising to send the second corrected typescript of *Aaron's Rod* to Curtis Brown,[33] and in the end this second copy was not posted until 23 November. However, although Lawrence sent this second copy to Secker a month later there is no reason to suppose that he made any additional corrections to it. His letter to Secker on that date also states: 'I am sending Curtis Brown the MS. of *Aarons Rod*. I want it to be published simultaneously with Seltzer's' (iv. 129).

The direction for simultaneous publication, however, is misleading and at variance with Lawrence's determination that Seltzer not be at a publishing disadvantage. His letter to Curtis Brown of the same date clearly states: 'I am sending you today the MS. of *Aaron's Rod*, for Secker. I don't want him by *any means* to publish it before Seltzer is ready at the American end: if Secker wants to publish it' (iv. 129). This is further confirmed by other references to publication policy: for example, in an earlier letter to Curtis Brown (where he acknowledged receipt of the two typescripts, ribbon and carbon, of *Aaron's Rod*) Lawrence specifically states: 'But *please* see that Seckers date of publication does not precede Seltzers' (iv. 65). And in an earlier letter still of 30 July 1921 Lawrence had actually announced his intention to give Seltzer the edge in publishing *Aaron's Rod*.

Your letter of 15 July today. I had your cable in Baden. – I had to send 2nd half of *Aaron's Rod* to England to be typed after all. Expect it back next week. Then shall post it to you. I shall post your copy two weeks sooner than Secker's. He hasn't seen the book yet. Mountsier read the first half and didn't like it: takes upon himself to lecture me about it. Says it will be unpopular. Can't help it. It is what I mean, for the moment. It isn't 'improper' at all: only it never turns the other cheek, and spits on ecstasy. I like it, because it kicks against the pricks. I'll send it the first possible moment. (iv. 57)

As we have seen, however, Lawrence did not post the TS to Seltzer 'next week' and, during August, on the advice of Curtis Brown and Mountsier he suggested a spring publication date. On 12 September he wrote: '*I* think better withold *Aaron* till spring'.[34]

---

[33] 'I am going to send *Aaron's Rod* to Curtis Brown. He and Mountsier hate it. Probably you will too. But I want you to publish it none the less. That is to say, I don't in the least want you to if you don't wish to. But I will have the book published. It is my last word in one certain direction' (*Letters*, iv. 116).

[34] *Letters*, iv. 85. Curtis Brown had written to DHL on 26 August 1921, while he was revising the novel, that he thought 'Next spring will be all right for "AARON'S ROD". In fact I

Certainly relations between Lawrence and Secker were strained at this time, partly because Lawrence was irritated by Secker's capitulation over the threatened libel suits regarding *Women in Love* and partly because of their disagreement over the five-book contract he had signed on 14 April 1920 giving Secker first refusal on the five books following *Women in Love*. Secker insisted that the contract implied five *novels*, whereas Lawrence and Mountsier rightly pointed out that the contract specified *books*. The various negotiations and compromises that this and other misunderstandings led to are not the concern here[35] but undoubtedly Lawrence was annoyed with Secker.[36] He negotiated a separate contract with Seltzer for *Aaron's Rod*[37] and clearly felt little concern about his English publisher: 'Whether Secker turns it down or not is all one to me. English publication no longer interests me much' (iv. 96); and as late as 9 January 1922 he wrote: 'If Secker doesn't want to do *Aaron's Rod*, I don't mind a bit' (iv. 159). Seltzer himself readily fell in with Lawrence's wishes that the novel should wait until the following spring for publication, although originally he had wavered between publishing *Mr Noon* or *Aaron's Rod* in the autumn of 1921.[38] But in any case he was anxious to bring out *Aaron* in America

believe it would be better, unless the book can be put in hand instantly, for it isn't a Christmas book' to which DHL agreed (Harry Ransom Humanities Research Center, University of Texas at Austin – hereafter UT).

[35] See 'Introduction' to *Women in Love*, ed. David Farmer, Lindeth Vasey and John Worthen (Cambridge, 1987), pp. xliv–xlvii for an account of the strained relations between DHL and Secker. See also 'Introduction' to *The Lost Girl*, ed. John Worthen (Cambridge, 1981), pp. li–lii.

[36] This was not least because of his dilatoriness in paying DHL, and his suggestion that *Mr Noon* not be counted as one of the five books he was entitled to: 'Secker has paid £50. in to my bank, after a sharp letter from me. Now I hear from CB. that he, Secker, wants to count this little *Mr Noon* novel as not a novel, but a bit thrown in with his legal five' (*Letters*, iii. 730).

[37] The contract for *Aaron's Rod* between Seltzer and DHL was signed on 1 September 1921, giving DHL an advance of $500 on a royalty of 10% on the first 2500 copies, 12½% on 5000 and 15% on copies over 5000. The selling price of the volume was $2. Clause 8 in the contract is ironic in view of later events: 'The Publisher shall not abridge, expand or otherwise alter the said work without the written consent of the Author or his representative.' Seltzer had sole publishing rights in the United States. Secker's terms were: a royalty of 1 shilling per copy on the first 2000 copies, one shilling and sixpence per copy on the next 3000 and two shillings per copy thereafter 'in calculating which thirteen copies shall be reckoned as twelve' (a clause which understandably infuriated DHL); and finally a royalty of threepence per copy on the sale of sheets for the Colonial market.

[38] Letter from Seltzer to Mountsier, 17 June 1921, *Letters to Thomas and Adele Seltzer*, ed. Lacy, pp. 207–8. 'I have done some thinking about the wisdom of publishing *Mr. Noon* in the fall. The more I think of it the more I am convinced that if *Aaron's Rod* has the possibility of a popular success, that is, if we believe it has a chance of selling at least as well as *The Lost Girl*, and if it is really unobjectionable, then *Aaron's Rod* ought to be the next novel for us. To have another novel against which there is no definite objection follow *The*

well before the English edition: 'By all means I want to publish it before Secker does' he wrote to Mountsier.[39]

At the same time Lawrence was also considering the idea of serialising part of *Aaron's Rod*, and as early as mid-August had written: 'I don't know whether it is any good thinking of trying any bit of *Aaron* for *The Dial*: the Florence part, if any: or the Sir William Franks part' (iv. 74), although earlier he had expressed his doubts about such a scheme: '*Aaron* won't serialise' (iv. 28). But on 12 September he repeated the idea to Mountsier:

I think the 'Novara' chapters – leaving out that long Aaron-introspect bit about his wife: i.e., just the chapters about the Sir Wm Franks place – would do for magazines: also the Florence chapters: also the Milan incident: all separate. But I am not very keen on English magazines' doing the book, really. I *don't want it hawked around.* – Curtis has a duplicate of the latter half – all that is any way fit for serial. He could correct this from your copy, if he wanted. *But don't let him go raggedly around with bits of the novel in England.*[40]

Part of chapter XIV of *Aaron's Rod* duly appeared with Seltzer's permission (before his edition came out in April 1922) as 'An Episode' in the February 1922 volume of the American periodical, the *Dial*.[41] To Lawrence's annoyance however it was only a four-page extract: 'I'm sorry the *Dial*

Lost Girl would give Lawrence a very strong position here. After that we need fear no antagonism. *Mr. Noon* may arouse a storm of protest which we could stand very well after a second success like *The Lost Girl* but not so well before. So I would very much like to see the MS of *Aaron's Rod* before we decide.'

[39] *Letters to Thomas and Adele Seltzer*, ed. Lacy, p. 210.

[40] *Letters*, iv. 85. DHL also states in his letter of 18? August 'I shall send you today the MS. of *Aaron's Rod*' (ibid. 74) – presumably the autograph manuscript – which Mountsier must have returned at some point since DHL makes it clear in November of the same year that the original handwritten manuscript was in his own possession: 'I have only my hand-written MS – which luckily I haven't yet burned' (ibid. 131). It seems probable that Curtis Brown had more than one carbon copy of the second half of the novel made in August from the original manuscript. But if other copies of *Aaron's Rod* or part of it were made, they have not survived; in any case they would not have had DHL's final corrections and hence would possess no textual authority.

[41] Negotiations with the *Dial* had begun in August 1921 with correspondence between Curtis Brown, Mountsier and Thayer, the editor of the periodical at that time. The decision to print the self-contained descriptions of the fascist march in Milan which forms part of chapter XIV was taken by the *Dial* staff (although as DHL's letter to Mountsier of 12 September quoted above indicates, it was one of the portions he thought might serialise) to avoid any of the controversial issues in the book (see *D. H. Lawrence and "The Dial"*, ed. Nicholas Joost and Alvin Sullivan (Carbondale, Illinois, 1970), p. 117 and pp. 60–1). DHL had been doubtful about publishing *Aaron's Rod* in the *Dial*. His 26 November 1921 letter to Mountsier reveals his annoyance at the way they had recently published mutilated extracts from *Sea and Sardinia* in the October and November 1921 issues: 'I dont think I want *The Dial* to mess about with *Aarons Rod*. I hated their snipping up such bits of *Sardinia*' (*Letters*, iv. 130).

takes that scrap of *Aaron* – What good are 35 dollars anyway? – one cheapens oneself' (iv. 187).

Early private reactions to *Aaron's Rod*, despite Lawrence's belief that there was 'nothing impossible in it, at all', were predictably negative. Curtis Brown had written to Mountsier as early as 17 September 1921:

In view of the enclosed in "John Bull", and the likelihood of police suppression, of "Women in Love" I think there can be no question about the advisability and the necessity of eliminating the portions of "AARON'S ROD" that deal in such anatomical detail with sex. We can't get the book published normally here if these are included, and I doubt if its private printing would really help Lawrence's reputation. It seems to me that his future now hangs delicately in the balance. If only he would turn out the great story which everyone expects of him, without any appearance or shadow of sex-obsession, he could have the world at his feet. Otherwise, those who maintain that his readers buy his books not for art, as they pretend, but for pornography, are going to get the upper hand, and a really big man's chance will be lost.[42]

Lawrence himself noted 'Everybody hated *Aaron's Rod* – even Frieda' (iv. 124) and although Seltzer was enthusiastic and cabled Lawrence that he thought the book 'wonderful, overwhelming'[43] both he and Secker voiced reservations as profound as those of Curtis Brown and Mountsier.[44] Lawrence was faced with the familiar and uncongenial task of trying to modify and censor his own work. On 26 November, after he had posted the second typescript to Secker, he replied to Seltzer's objections:

About *Aaron*: I haven't got any type-written corrected MS. so don't quite know how it stands. I have only my hand-written MS – which luckily I haven't yet burned. If you really must modify Argyle – I think he is so funny, though Mountsier calls him a foul-mouthed Englishman – you can do so at your discretion, by just lifting a word or two. I'll go through the Marchesa MS. tonight.

Seltzer was to 'lift' considerably more than just 'a word or two'. Lawrence's postscript to the letter shows his frustration at the limitations imposed on him by his publishers:

I have looked through the original MS. It is no good, I can't alter it. But if you like to follow the type-script, which I have often written over, in the scenes you mention, and if you like to leave out what is written over, I don't think you need fear

[42] UT. *John Bull*, a weekly journal established and edited by Horatio Bottomley, had that day published a particularly hostile review of *Women in Love* (see Nehls, ii. 89–91).

[43] Quoted by DHL in his letter to Secker, 23 November 1921 (iv. 129).

[44] See *Letters*, iv. 127. Secker wrote to Curtis Brown on 16 January 1922 that he feared the novel would 'do little to assist his reputation' (UT).

the public much. And if you like to leave out a sentence or two, or alter a phrase or two, do so. But I can't write anything different. Follow the original typescript.[45]

Seltzer's letter has not survived but from the cuts he made (recorded in the Textual apparatus), principally in modifying the rather racy speech of Argyle and the love-making scenes between Aaron and the Marchesa, one can gather the tenor of his objections.[46] Secker received proof sheets of the novel from Seltzer eventually (although he had set up his own edition from Lawrence's typescript – see below), and adopted some of the American publisher's cuts but also made some of his own. In a revealing letter to Curtis Brown he records his initial reaction to the typescript sent him: 'There are certain paragraphs and passages which are quite unpublishable and as Mr. Lawrence has given Seltzer a free hand to make certain amendments, I gather that this permission applies to me also.'[47]

Lawrence himself can have altered very little, if any, of the text. On 1 December he repeated, 'Seltzer must make himself any small modifications of *Aarons Rod*' (iv. 134) and although he seems to have relented a little when he wrote to Secker (for his information) later that month, 'I am making some modifications in *Aaron's Rod*, for Seltzer. You can see them when they're done' (iv. 152), subsequent correspondence indicates that he never in fact made these alterations. In mid-January 1922 Lawrence received a clean typescript of the novel (which has not survived) from Seltzer, presumably based on the definitive and corrected TS he had sent him, but confessed:

The typed MS. of *Aaron's Rod* came today. I again tried altering it. I can modify the bits of Argyle's speech. But the essential scenes of Aaron and the Marchesa it is impossible to me to alter. With all the good-will towards you and the general public that I am capable of, I can no more alter those chapters than if they were cast-iron. You can lift out whole chunks if you like. You can smash them if you like. But you can no more alter them than you can alter cast iron.

There you are. It's your dilemma. You can now do what you like with the book. Print only a limited edition – leave out anything you like for a popular edition – even if you like substitute something of your own for the offensive passages. But it is useless asking me to do any more. I shall return you the MS. on Monday. Then say no more to me. I am tired of this miserable, paltry, haffling and caffling world – dead sick of it. (iv. 167)

---

[45] *Letters*, iv. 131, 132. The 'Marchesa MS.' must refer to chap. XVIII 'The Marchesa', parts of which are extensively rewritten in TS.
[46] See Textual apparatus for examples of this censorship, especially 235:11–36, 261:25–262:11 and 272:7–273:35.
[47] 28 February 1922 (Secker Letter-Book, University of Illinois at Urbana–Champaign).

But it is doubtful whether Lawrence even altered any of Argyle's speech, since on 18 January he wrote to Mountsier: 'I sent back the type MS. of *Aaron* to Seltzer because it was just physically impossible to me to alter it. He may do as he likes now. I just won't alter it: can't, the alterations won't come: and the general public can go to hell in any way it likes' (iv. 168). And a few days later he wrote in reply to Curtis Brown, who had asked about Seltzer's demand for changes ('Did you alter the original manuscript very much?'):[48]

I didn't alter the original MS. at all, of *Aarons Rod*. Or only a few words. I couldn't. Seltzer sent me a clean typed copy of the book, begging for the alterations for the sake of the 'general public' (he didn't say *jeune fille*). I sat in front of the MS and tried: but it was like Balaams Ass, and wouldn't budge. I couldn't do it: So I sent it back to Seltzer to let him do as he pleases. I would rather Secker followed the true MS, if he will – and vogue la galère.[49]

Seltzer, then, must have made his own cuts and alterations either on the fresh typescript or at proof stage (neither of these states of the text is extant) since the published text certainly does not follow the sole surviving corrected typescript (TS) which was the basis for his retyped setting copy. Lawrence's original autograph MS has not survived either, nor have the foreword and introduction to *Aaron's Rod* that he mentioned to Seltzer; and of the two complete corrected typescripts (i.e. the ribbon and carbon copy of 143 pages typed by Violet Monk and the two bound copies of pp. 144–490 sent by Curtis Brown which were duly forwarded to Secker and Seltzer), only one complete typescript remains. This is Seltzer's TS, the copy Lawrence sent on 8 October to Mountsier to be forwarded to Seltzer later that month. A comparison of first England and American impressions with the surviving TS reveals that on those occasions (which cannot be attributed to censoring or house-styling) where the editions differ in substantives it is Seltzer's edition which follows the TS most closely.[50]

Originally of course the two typescripts were identical, being ribbon and carbon copies. Both were revised by Lawrence but it is probable that given his habit of continual revision he made some further alterations when transcribing corrections from the first (Seltzer's) to the second (Secker's) typescript, as indeed some of the substantive differences between A1 and

---

[48] Letter from Curtis Brown to DHL, 20 January 1922 (UT).
[49] *Letters*, iv. 177. The 'true MS' refers to Secker's copy of the corrected typescript.
[50] For example, chap. XVII is entitled 'High Up over the Cathedral Square' in both TS and A1 whereas E1 titles the chapter 'Nel Paradiso'. Both TS and A1 read: ' "In November?" laughed Lilly' but E1 has ' "So late in the year?" laughed Lilly' (see Textual apparatus for 233:11).

E1 suggest. However, since the second typescript has not survived, precisely which alterations were Lawrence's and which Secker's must remain conjectural.[51] It is also possible that Lawrence may have made a few, very minor alterations to the clean copy that Seltzer sent him in January 1922 but he expressly disclaims having corrected this copy – 'or only a few words' – so that in the absence of this lost typescript there is no way of ascertaining which differences, if any, were made by Lawrence and which by Seltzer. The original TS sent to Seltzer is therefore authoritative. Secker, however, seemed under the impression that Lawrence *was* going to alter the novel extensively, for he was at first anxious to obtain Seltzer's proof sheets and to set up his own edition from them. On 16 January 1922 Secker wrote to Curtis Brown: 'Will you please ask Seltzer to let me have the proofs of *Aaron's Rod* with the author's latest alterations. I will then put the book in hand at once.'[52] And on 20 January Curtis Brown wrote to Lawrence: 'Seltzer is bringing out "AARON'S ROD" in May or June' and 'Mr. Secker wants to do "AARON'S ROD" here and I am asking Mr. Mountsier to let us have a complete set of Seltzer's revised proofs so that Secker may set from them.'[53] But as we have seen, in response to Curtis Brown's query 'Did you alter the original manuscript very much?' Lawrence replied that he had not, although Secker would not have known that.

It is therefore unlikely that Lawrence had anything to do with the alterations made to *Aaron's Rod* after he had returned the fresh copy (typed from the definitive TS) to Seltzer on 18 January. There is no indication of his being involved in proof correction and some evidence against it. On 26 February 1922 he left for Ceylon and was in no position to correct and return further copy (it is significant that he never saw the proofs of *Sea and Sardinia* either, published just before *Aaron's Rod*, in December 1921). Furthermore, his letter to Seltzer of 11 June 1922, acknowledging receipt of the published copy of *Aaron's Rod*, suggests that he didn't know what cuts had been made: ' – today come the copies of *Aaron* – Many thanks – book looks so nice – haven't plucked up courage to look out the cut parts yet' (iv. 260).

Secker was anxious to see Seltzer's proofs but by 17 March 1922, less than a month before the publication of the novel in America, he still had not obtained them. He had decided in any case by the end of February to

51 This kind of continual, slightly modified revision can be seen in works such as *Women in Love* where both the typescripts for Seltzer and Secker survive. See 'Introduction' to *Women in Love*, ed. Farmer, Vasey and Worthen, p. xxxii.
52 UT.   53 UT.

set up his edition from the typescript Lawrence had sent him, imposing his own cuts and alterations, although he also wanted to discover what cuts Seltzer had seen fit to make, as the correspondence below reveals. Curtis Brown wrote to Mountsier: 'Secker will be glad to have Seltzer's revised proofs of "AARON'S ROD" as soon as possible although he is setting up from the MS. Mr. Lawrence sent him, as there are apparently only very slight corrections.'[54] On 27 March Curtis Brown confirmed that Secker was hoping to publish *Aaron's Rod* in June[55] and on 21 April 1922 he wrote to Mountsier: 'We have sent on to Messrs Secker the proofs of "AARON'S ROD" which came to us from Seltzer, and hope to be able to let you know soon about the eliminations.'[56] No further correspondence on the subject of the cut passages exists but it is clear from his letters that substantial cuts were made by Seltzer which Secker was anxious to see.[57] At whatever stage the cuts were made, however, they were done without Lawrence's sanction, although, as the letters cited above and the terms of his contract required, he had given Seltzer permission to censor. Seltzer published the first American edition of *Aaron's Rod* on 14 April 1922 and Secker followed with the first English edition in June.

The two first editions are textually quite similar; most of the significant alterations and cuts in both occur in the chapters dealing with Aaron's affair with the Marchesa and his dialogue with Argyle. Occasionally the cuts themselves differ when Seltzer and Secker disagreed in their estimation of what would offend public opinion. Two striking examples of this occur in chapter X and in chapter XVII. In chapter X Secker, fearful of his British readers, censored a conversation that was critical of the 'Battenbergs' (i.e. 'Mount Battens') whereas Seltzer, either unaware of the implied criticism of the Royal family or guessing that the American public would not grasp the significance of the name, left the passage in. Chapter XVII contains an innocent conversation about friendship and love which passed Seltzer's scrutiny, but was considered dangerous and was cut by Secker: four pages of dialogue which appear in the American edition are

---

[54] 17 March 1922 (UT). See also letter from Secker to Curtis Brown, 28 February 1922: 'In accordance with your letter of the 22nd, I have now sent the typescript of this book to the printer' (Secker Letter-Book, University of Illinois at Urbana–Champaign). See also 'Introduction' to *Women in Love*, ed. Farmer, Vasey and Worthen, pp. xlv–xlvii where the editors discuss similar negotiations between Seltzer and Secker over *Women in Love*.

[55] See letter from Curtis Brown to Mountsier, 27 March 1922 where he states: 'We have just heard from Mr Martin Secker that he is hoping to publish "AARON'S ROD" in June' (UT).

[56] UT.

[57] See 'Introduction' to *Women in Love*, ed. Farmer, Vasey and Worthen, p. xlv where a similar story is told.

entirely omitted from the English text. There is also a puzzling anomaly in the Secker first edition at 272:9 where an alteration has been made, presumably by someone in the publisher's office, to one of the censored passages. The English first edition at this point reads: 'a long, live thread of electric fire' but there is a variant of this: 'a long, live thread excruciating, but also an intensely gratifying sensation'. Of the seven copies of E1 at the Harry Ransom Humanities Research Center, four have the former reading, three the latter; there is no evidence to indicate how many copies of Secker's original edition of 3000 were printed with each reading. The surviving correspondence offers no explanation of why or when this alteration was made nor are there any other discrepancies of this kind in the Secker edition.[58]

All subsequent printings of the novel have derived from these two first editions. Seltzer brought out three impressions of *Aaron's Rod* in 1922 alone, and sales of the novel in America were substantial. Writing to Mountsier on the verso of Seltzer's letter of 6 September 1922 (which read 'AARON'S ROD is now in the third edition and is selling fairly ...') Lawrence commented that Seltzer had said in a letter to Australia that *Aaron* had already sold 6000 copies' (iv. 315, 316). English sales, however, lagged behind as Curtis Brown explained in a letter in December of that year to Mountsier about Secker's publication and sales.

I do not think he advertises well, although apparently he pushes his books pretty hard in other directions. He certainly gets some considerable successes. Personally, I do not doubt the correctness of his royalty statements. This question arises so often in the case of authors like Lawrence, who do the sort of distinguished work that attracts great critical attention, leading to the general supposition that the sales are large. I hope and believe these large sales will come over here, as they already have, apparently, in America, if only we can persevere in patience.[59]

In the following month Curtis Brown told Lawrence that Secker's sales of *Aaron's Rod* to the end of November had been 2559 copies.[60]

There is little other evidence available about the sales of *Aaron's Rod* during Lawrence's lifetime, but the important feature about the publication of the novel is that all subsequent editions in America (with the exception of Viking below) were based on Seltzer's text, perpetuating his

---

[58] Subsequent reprints preserved 'a long, live thread of electric fire' so it is probable that this was the original reading which Secker chose to adopt rather than the more explicit revision, given his anxiety about sexual connotations.

[59] 29 December 1922 (UT).

[60] 2 January 1923 (UT). Sales of *The Lost Girl* and *Women in Love* by comparison, for a similar period, were rather better: 2949 and 3173 copies, respectively.

cuts and alterations. These included Albert & Charles Boni (1922, 1930), Avon Book Division (1922, 1960), Grosset & Dunlap (1930). Viking Press re-issued the text of Secker's original edition in 1959 with several subsequent reprintings. In England Secker (who also had the rights to *Aaron's Rod* in the British Empire, Colonies and Dependencies)[61] reprinted his first edition in 1924, 1927, 1929 and 1930. Heinemann (who subsequently acquired the rights to all Lawrence's books in 1935) issued *Aaron's Rod* in 1933, following Secker's text, with many later reprintings; Penguin issued their paperback edition in 1950, also using the Secker text. There were three other editions also derived from Secker: Albatross (Leipzig, 1937, 1952), Harborough (1960), and Heron Books (1968). None of these texts, however, was amended from Lawrence's corrected and authoritative typescript – none therefore has any textual authority.

Reception

Although after completing his novel Lawrence had written 'Everybody hated *Aaron's Rod*', few English reviews were entirely hostile. If most were equivocal in their assessment of the novel, reviewers nevertheless paid tribute to Lawrence's genius and acknowledged his importance in modern literature. Responses to *Aaron's Rod* were generally of two kinds: those reviewers who uneasily saw the novel as a continuation of *The Rainbow* and *Women in Love* and who thus criticised Lawrence's obsession, as they saw it, with sex even while admitting the power of his writing and the beauty of the Italian scenes; and those few critics who recognised *Aaron's Rod* as a new kind of novel, concerned not so much with the colour of events, places and characters as with the manifold workings of the human psyche. The first review in England appeared on 7 June 1922 in the *Nation*. The reviewer, Joseph Wood Krutch, rather unwillingly confessed to a fascination for Lawrence's work, seeing his novels 'less as a means of describing the variety of life than as a means of projecting his personality upon the world'. He sensed that the story of Aaron's journey also chronicles the processes of Lawrence's own thought, commenting that 'in "Aaron's Rod" he has created a group of people who for all their superficial differences are really the same person'. Krutch went on to reveal a narrow conception of the novel's theme, however, seeing it as 'exclusively a world of love – of passionate attraction and repulsion', and concluded therefore that *Aaron's Rod* was 'an epic of love's exasperations' (p. 696). By contrast *The Times Literary Supplement* for 22 June 1922 acknowledged Lawrence's power 'to

---

[61] Letter from Curtis Brown to Mountsier, 5 October 1922 (UT).

test our faith and our reason' and saw *Aaron's Rod* as 'the story, picaresque in form, of a man – a miner by occupation, a musician in soul – who wandered away from all ties except that of his friendship for another man, in search of himself'. Echoing Lawrence's own dissatisfaction with the development of his novel ('I can sort of jump him picaresque') the review criticised its form as 'a little too picaresque. It has no end', and concluded with the guarded admission: 'There is very great power in this angry genius' (p. 411).

The *Spectator* reviewer, remembering the negative reception of *Women in Love* and wary of Lawrence's new novel, summed up its place in his *œuvre*:

Most of his readers regarded *Sons and Lovers* as a work of genius, but in the later *Women in Love* most of them saw a book crazy and pathological ... it was the generally-held opinion that in *Women in Love* Mr. Lawrence had written under the influence of a tiresome sex obsession. In *Aaron's Rod* we have the reaction.

The review criticised 'the heavy opening' and 'the incoherence of construction', pronouncing *Aaron's Rod* 'a faulty book' but nonetheless a great one because of Lawrence's ability to render the states which not only the mind but also the body pass through:

He performs what many of us still believe to be the prime function of the novelist, that of letting a little window into the heads of the kind of people a reader may be expected to meet. What is remarkable about Mr. Lawrence's windows, however, is that they 'give' not only into the heads and hearts of his characters, but into their deep, instinctive, emotional processes. The very core of a personality is, in the case of one or two of the characters, slowly laid bare to us.

The review concluded, however, with the familiar warning to readers that *Aaron's Rod* 'is not an agreeable book for young adolescents of either sex' (p. 23).

Perhaps the most disappointing English review was Rebecca West's for the *New Statesman* on 8 July 1922. She recognised the 'unique poetic talent' of the descriptive sections of the novel, particularly the Italian chapters, but noted that 'there is also, unfortunately, an as unique idiocy in the metaphysical theories which to its detriment, shape its development'. The review concluded with a sadly mistaken prophecy of Lawrence's future career: 'The consolation is that the literary life of a writer of Mr. Lawrence's vitality is bound to be very long, and he is a man hardly halfway up the thirties' (p. 388). Less than eight years later, of course, Lawrence was dead. Rebecca West had visited Lawrence in 1919 when he was in Florence working on an essay which was probably 'Looking Down' and which contains an early working out of some of the ideas he was later to develop in the Florence chapters of *Aaron's Rod*. She later came to see her rejection of these 'metaphysical' aspects of his writing as misguided, and although her retrospective account of that recognition, written in 1930, does not technically constitute a review of *Aaron's Rod*, it is worth quoting for its perceptive assessment of his achievement in that novel and its insight into the process and direction of his creative work at that time.

He was tapping out an article on the state of Florence at that moment without knowing enough about it to make his views of real value. Is that the way I looked at it? Then I was naïve. I know now that he was writing about the state of his own soul at that moment, which, since our self-consciousness is incomplete, and since in consequence our vocabulary also is incomplete, he could only render in symbolic terms; and the city of Florence was as good a symbol as any other. If he was foolish in taking the material universe and making allegations about it that were true only of the universe within his own soul, then Rimbaud was a great fool also. Or to go further back, so too was Dante who made a new Heaven and Hell and Purgatory as a symbol for the geography within his own breast, and so too was St. Augustine, when in *The City of God* he writes an attack on the pagan world, which is unjust so long as it is regarded as an account of events on the material plane, but which is beyond price as an account of the conflict in his soul between that which tended to death and that which tended to life. Lawrence was in fact no different from any other great artist who has felt the urgency to describe the unseen so keenly that he has rifled the seen of its vocabulary and diverted it to that purpose; and it took courage to do that in a land swamped with naturalism as England was when Lawrence began to write.[62]

Other reviewers in 1922 were less discerning and some actually hostile. Gerald Gould, writing for the *Saturday Review* (15 July 1922), condemned 'Mr. Lawrence's demented miners, tearful cavalry officers and sinister and brooding ladies' and dismissed the novel's 'distortion of values', denouncing the characters whom he saw 'tainted with a specific mental disease ... Their sweetest songs are those that tell of Sadist thought' (p. 109). Happily other reviews were less damning. A brief, if rather puzzled, paragraph appeared in the *English Review* for August 1922 which tentatively suggested that *Aaron's Rod* was 'a prelude to something more definite', and concluded 'In Aaron we can detect a rod, but it is not yet magic' (p. 184). Of all the English reviews only those by Edward Shanks in the *London Mercury* and John Middleton Murry in *Nation and Athenæum* recognised the striking originality of *Aaron's Rod*. The former criticised the novel's plot as weak but spoke with admiration of Lawrence's novels as 'slices of the real life which lies under the surface of action and expression'

[62] *D. H. Lawrence* (Secker, 1930), pp. 34–6.

– and praised Lawrence for 'stripping off the physical superfluities and revealing the spiritual essentials. And it is an extraordinary performance, one which is full of promise for the future of the novel.'[63]

Murry, who had written a scathing attack on *Women in Love* which he felt showed Lawrence 'far gone in the maelstrom of his sexual obsession' and had seen his last novel, *The Lost Girl*, as 'full of noxious exasperation', now praised his new work: 'The exasperation, the storm and stress are gone. He has dragged us with him through the valley of the shadow; now we sail with him in the sunlight. Mr. Lawrence's new book ripples with the consciousness of victory; he is gay, he is careless, he is persuasive. To read "Aaron's Rod" is to drink of a fountain of life.' His review pays tribute to *Aaron's Rod* as 'the most important thing that has happened to English literature since the war', recognising that it marked Lawrence's emergence from the crisis of the war and a change in the nature of his writing:

'Aaron's Rod' shows that he has gained the one thing he lacked: serenity. Those who do not know his work may read it and wonder where the serenity is to be found. They must read all Mr. Lawrence's work to discover it fully. They must allow themselves to be manhandled and shattered by 'The Rainbow' and by 'Women in Love' before they can appreciate all the significance of his latest book. For the calm is but partly on the surface of 'Aaron's Rod', it lies chiefly in the depths. As before, Mr. Lawrence offers a violent challenge to conventional morality; as before, he covers us with the spume of his ungoverned eloquence. But the serenity is there. Mr. Lawrence can now laugh at himself without surrendering a jot of his belief in the truth he proclaims. It is as though he looked back whimsically at his own struggling figure in the past, saw all his violence and extravagance, and recognised that he could not have become what he is if he had not been what he was.[64]

Murry does indeed criticise aspects of the novel, its careless construction, 'the host of minor characters who refuse to become properly substantial', but he sees these features as minor blemishes in a work of profound morality and commitment, the story 'of the effort of a man to lose the whole world and gain his own soul'. Alone of English reviewers, Murry both recognised the theme of the novel as 'the self-sufficiency of the human soul' and noted its importance for the future of the English novel. 'There is beauty everywhere in "Aaron's Rod", beauty of the thing seen, beauty of the seeing spirit; and everywhere the careless riches of true creative

[63] *London Mercury* (October 1922), p. 656. Quoted in R. P. Draper, ed. *D. H. Lawrence: The Critical Heritage* (1970), p. 183.

[64] *Nation and Athenæum* (12 August 1922), p. 655. Quoted in Draper, p. 178.

power. "Aaron's Rod" – truly symbolic name – satisfies Arnold's test of magic of style. It is life-imparting.'[65]

Notwithstanding the good sales of *Aaron's Rod* in America, reviews of the novel were few and largely negative. Most English reviewers had recognised the power of Lawrence's writing, however grudgingly, and had acknowledged his place in contemporary fiction; only two American reviews did either. L. M. Field, writing for the *New York Times Book Review* for 30 April 1922, began with a shrewd assessment of the novel's early chapters, rightly recognising their accuracy as portraits of a 'nerve exhausted generation shattered by the first world war', but soon turned to the hackneyed and trite criticism of Lawrence's work as rooted 'consciously or unconsciously, in the well-known complex of sex-fear – ' (p. 14). D. S. Ogburn, writing for the *Literary Review* (3 June 1922), liked the descriptive writing but similarly saw the novel as an expression of sexual neurosis and Lawrence himself as 'a wilfully perverse young man' (p. 699). Other American reviews were even less favourable. They ranged from the *Independent* (27 May 1922) which dismissed *Aaron's Rod* 'as a piece of elaborate piffle' (p. 489) and its writer as 'a sentimental pervert' (p. 492), to a short paragraph in the *Freeman* (26 July 1922) which acknowledged that 'Mr. Lawrence's writing is still full of glamour, still conveys the sense of his own wonder at the strangeness of life's adventure', but rejected the novel as 'not one of Mr. Lawrence's notable achievements' (p. 478). Similarly, H. L. Mencken, writing an article for the *Smart Set* in July 1922, attacked both *The Lost Girl* and *Aaron's Rod* as 'infinitely profound in tone, and infinitely hollow in content' (p. 143), while a short notice in the *Chapbook* for January 1923 merely remarked that the book was worth reading. Of all the reviews on either side of the Atlantic, only that by Murry astutely recognised the importance of *Aaron's Rod* as a creative work in its own right and a significant advance in Lawrence's development as a writer. In answer to the uncomprehending and negative reviews in both England and America it is worth quoting Murry's final assessment of *Aaron's Rod*: 'We could riddle this book with criticism, but not one of the shafts would touch its soul. It is real; it is alive.'[66]

Base-text

The surviving corrected typescript of *Aaron's Rod* (TS) is now at the Harry Ransom Humanities Research Center, University of Texas at Austin. TS is revised throughout in Lawrence's handwriting in black ink. There are

[65] Ibid., p. 656 (Draper, p. 179).   [66] Ibid., p. 655 (Draper, p. 179).

also a number of corrections and instructions in pencil. Nearly all the latter however are not by Lawrence; they concern accidentals, paragraphing instructions and alterations to the spelling and have no textual authority. They are probably house-styling alterations made after Lawrence had finished his own revision, that is, when TS was with Seltzer. It is probable that these pencilled corrections were incorporated into the later clean copy sent to Lawrence, and were thus tacitly accepted by him, but no evidence exists to prove this. There are no type-setting or compositor's marks on TS; presumably when Seltzer set up his edition he used the clean typescript that he had sent to Lawrence for last-minute changes and which has not survived.

The base-text for the present edition is TS – 'the true MS' as Lawrence called it (iv. 177) – which he sent to Seltzer in October 1921. The Textual apparatus records variants between this TS and the first American and English editions. The variants in A1 may derive from Seltzer's cuts, errors, house-styling and substantive and accidental changes by either Seltzer or his printer. The variants in E1 come from differences between TS and the missing copy which formed the basis for Secker's edition, or from Secker's own cuts, substantive and accidental changes. It is now impossible to determine in all cases which of the variants in E1 resulted from Lawrence correcting Secker's typescript differently from Seltzer's, and which from Secker's own cuts and changes, but for the first time an edition of *Aaron's Rod* is printed which restores the cuts and emendations imposed by both Seltzer and Secker in their respective first editions, and perpetuated by all later publishers of the novel, and which eliminates the house-styling of previous editions.

Appendix I

Lawrence extensively revised TS before sending it to Seltzer. Two passages in particular, which were entirely rewritten, are the account of the riot in chapter XIV and the love-making episode between Aaron and the Marchesa in chapter XIX. Although Lawrence cancelled these versions in TS, they are included here as given in the unrevised TS for their intrinsic interest and for their importance in revealing the kinds of conceptual and stylistic changes that occurred in Lawrence's revisions.

AARON'S ROD

Note on the text

The base-text for this edition is the surviving corrected typescript (TS) of *Aaron's Rod* which DHL sent to his American publisher Thomas Seltzer in October 1921 and from which a copy was made for setting the first American edition (A1). The TS is owned by the Harry Ransom Humanities Research Center, University of Texas at Austin.

The apparatus records all textual variants including editorial interventions on the few occasions when it has been necessary to emend the text.

The following emendations have been made silently:

1 Clearly accidental spelling errors by DHL or the typist and obvious typesetters' mistakes have been corrected.

2 Accidental omissions have been supplied in the case of incomplete quotation marks, final stops, apostrophes in colloquial contractions and the stop following a title, e.g. 'Mrs.'.

3 The English edition (E1) consistently printed 'to-day', 'to-morrow', 'to-night', 'good-night' and 'good-bye' whereas these appear as one unhyphenated word (with only a few exceptions which have been recorded) in TS and A1. The spelling of the base-text has been preserved here.

4 The English edition consistently capitalised 'Socialist' and 'Socialism' which appear in the lower case in both the base-text and A1; the base-text usage has been retained. Similarly A1 consistently spells 'ffrench' as 'French'; the base-text (and E1) reading has been used throughout.

5 DHL often followed a full stop, quotation or exclamation mark with a dash before beginning the next sentence with a capital letter. E1 nearly always – and A1 sometimes – omitted the dash, which has been restored here.

6 DHL's typist was not always consistent in placing punctuation inside or outside quotation marks indicating speech. The most usual practice in TS of placing punctuation within quotation marks has been adopted. Similarly the typist occasionally typed a full stop within quotation marks in error for a comma at the end. The normal convention of the comma has been used here.

7 The convention for indicating ellipses varies in the base-text and is four full stops in A1 and either three or six full stops in E1. The convention adopted here is three full stops.

8 Italic chapter and number (TS, chapters x to xxi) appear in roman type and numerals and chapter titles (unlike those in A1 and E1 which were given in capital letters) follow DHL's upper and lower case letters in TS. Full stops, omitted after some chapter numbers in TS, have been supplied.

9 A1 did not always follow DHL's habit in TS of beginning a new paragraph after a line or two of direct speech, particularly when there were only a few narrative lines to follow, i.e. one or two or three sentences. The paragraphing of the base-text (which E1 also followed) has been retained throughout; any other departures from this paragraphing have been recorded.

10 Italic punctuation in A1 is recorded only when it is part of another variant.

Contents

Chapter I.

The Blue Ball*

There was a large, brilliant evening star in the early twilight, and underfoot the earth was half frozen. It was Christmas Eve. Also the War was over, and there was a sense of relief that was almost a new menace. A man felt the violence of the nightmare released now into the general air. Also there had been another wrangle among the men on the pit-bank that evening.*

Aaron Sisson* was the last man on the little black railway-line climbing the hill home from work. He was late because he had attended a meeting of the men on the bank. He was secretary to the Miners Union* for his colliery, and had heard a good deal of silly wrangling that left him nettled.

He strode over a stile, crossed two fields, strode another stile, and was in the long road of colliers' dwellings. Just across was his own house: he had built it himself. He went through the little gate, up past the side of the house to the back. There he hung a moment, glancing down the dark, wintry garden.

"My father—my father's come!" cried a child's excited voice, and two little girls in white pinafores ran out in front of his legs.

"Father, shall you set the Christmas tree—?" they cried. "We've got one!"

"Afore I have my dinner?" he answered amiably.

"Set it now. Set it now.—We got it through Fred Alton."

"Wheer is it?"

The little girls were dragging a rough, dark object out of a corner of the passage into the light of the kitchen door.

"It's a beauty!" exclaimed Millicent.

"Yes, it is," said Marjory.

"I should think so," he replied, striding over the dark bough. He went to the back kitchen to take off his coat.

"Set it now, Father. Set it now," clamoured the girls.

"You might as well. You've left your dinner so long, you might as well do it now before you have it," came a woman's plangent voice, out of the brilliant light of the middle room.

5

Aaron Sisson had taken off his coat and waistcoat and his cap. He stood bare-headed in his shirt and braces, contemplating the tree.

"What am I to put it in?" he queried. He picked up the tree, and held it erect by the top-most twig. He felt the cold as he stood in the yard coat-less, and he twitched his shoulders.

"Isn't it a beauty!" repeated Millicent.

"Ay!—lop-sided though."

"Put something on, you two!" came the woman's high imperative voice, from the kitchen.

"We aren't cold," protested the girls from the yard.

"Come and put something on," insisted the voice.

The man started off down the path, the little girls ran grumbling indoors. The sky was clear, there was still a crystalline, non-luminous light in the under air.

Aaron rummaged in his shed at the bottom of the garden, and found a spade and a box that was suitable. Then he came out to his neat, bare, wintry garden. The girls flew towards him, putting the elastic of their hats under their chins as they ran. The tree and the box lay on the frozen earth. The air breathed dark, frosty, electric.

"Hold it up straight," he said to Millicent, as he arranged the tree in the box. She stood silent and held the top bough, he filled in round the roots.

When it was done, and pressed in, he went for the wheel-barrow. The girls were hovering excited round the tree. He dropped the barrow and stooped to the box. The girls watched him hold back his face—the boughs pricked him.

"Is it very heavy?" asked Millicent.

"Ay!" he replied, with a little grunt.

Then the procession set off—the trundling wheel-barrow, the swinging hissing tree, the two excited little girls. They arrived at the door. Down went the legs of the wheel-barrow on the yard. The man looked at the box.

"Where are you going to have it?" he called.

"Put it in the back kitchen," cried his wife.

"You'd better have it where it's going to stop. I don't want to hawk it about."

"Put it on the floor against the dresser, Father. Put it there," urged Millicent.

"You come and put some paper down, then," called the mother hastily.

The two children ran indoors, the man stood contemplative in the cold, shrugging his uncovered shoulders slightly. The open inner door showed a bright linoleum on the floor, and the end of a brown side-board on which stood an aspidistra.

Again with a wrench Aaron Sisson lifted the box. The tree pricked   5
and stung. His wife watched him as he entered staggering, with his face averted.

"Mind where you make a lot of dirt," she said.

He lowered the box with a little jerk on to the spread-out newspaper on the floor. Soil scattered.   10

"Sweep it up," he said to Millicent.

His ear was lingering over the sudden, clutching hiss of the tree-boughs.

A stark white incandescent light filled the room and made everything sharp and hard. In the open fire-place a hot fire burned   15
red. All was scrupulously clean and perfect. A baby was cooing in a rocker-less wicker cradle by the hearth. The mother, a slim, neat woman with dark hair, was sewing a child's frock. She put this aside, rose, and began to take her husband's dinner from the oven.

"You stopped confabbing long enough tonight," she said.   20

"Yes," he answered, going to the back kitchen to wash his hands.

In a few minutes he came and sat down to his dinner. The doors were shut close, but there was a draught, because the settling of the mines under the house made the doors not fit. Aaron moved his chair, to get out of the draught. But he still sat in his shirt and   25
trousers.

He was a good-looking man, fair, and pleasant, about thirty-two years old. He did not talk much, but seemed to think about something. His wife resumed her sewing. She was acutely aware of her husband, but he seemed not very much aware of her.   30

"What were they on about today, then?" she said.

"About the throw-in."

"And did they settle anything?"

"They're going to try it—and they'll come out if it isn't satis-factory."   35

"The butties* won't have it, I know," she said.

He gave a short laugh, and went on with his meal.

The two children were squatted on the floor by the tree. They had a wooden box, from which they had taken many little newspaper packets, which they were spreading out like wares.   40

"Don't open any. We won't open any of them till we've taken them all out—and then we'll undo one in our turns. Then we s'll both undo equal," Millicent was saying.

"Yes, we'll take them *all* out first," re-echoed Marjory.

5 "And what are they going to do about Job Arthur Freer? Do they want him?"

A faint smile came on her husband's face.

"Nay, I don't know what they want.—Some of 'em want him—whether they're a majority, I don't know."

10 She watched him closely.

"Majority! I'd give 'em majority. They want to get rid of you, and make a fool of you, and you want to break your heart over it. Strikes me you need something to break your heart over."

He laughed silently.

15 "Nay," he said. "I s'll never break my heart."

"You'll go nearer to it over that, than over anything else: just because a lot of ignorant monkeys want a monkey of their own sort to do the Union work, and jabber to them, they want to get rid of you, and you eat your heart out about it. More fool you, that's all I 20 say—more fool you. If you cared for your wife and children half what you care about your Union, you'd be a lot better pleased in the end. But you care about nothing but a lot of ignorant colliers, who don't know what they want except it's more money just for themselves. Self, self, self—that's all it is with them—and ignorance."

25 "You'd rather have self without ignorance?" he said, smiling finely.

"I would, if I've got to have it. But what I should like to see is a man that has thought for others, and isn't all self and politics."

Her colour had risen, her hand trembled with anger as she sewed. 30 A blank look had come over the man's face, as if he did not hear or heed any more. He drank his tea in a long draught, wiped his moustache with two fingers, and sat looking abstractedly at the children.

They had laid all the little packets on the floor, and Millicent was 35 saying:

"Now I'll undo the first, and you can have the second. I'll take this—"

She unwrapped the bit of newspaper and disclosed a silvery ornament for a Christmas tree: a frail thing like a silver plum, with 40 deep rosy indentations on each side.

"Oh!" she exclaimed. "Isn't it *lovely!*"

Her fingers cautiously held the long bubble of silver and glowing rose, cleaving to it with a curious, irritating possession. The man's eyes moved away from her. The lesser child was fumbling with one of the little packets.

"Oh!"—a wail went up from Millicent—. "You've taken one!—You didn't wait." Then her voice changed to a motherly admonition, and she began to interfere. "This is the way to do it, look! Let me help you."

But Marjory drew back with resentment.

"Don't Millicent!—Don't!" came the childish cry. But Millicent's fingers itched.

At length Marjory had got out her treasure—a little silvery bell, with a glass drop hanging inside. The bell was made of frail glassy substance, light as air.

"Oh, the bell!" rang out Millicent's clanging voice. "The bell! It's my bell. My bell! It's mine! Don't break it, Marjory. Don't break it, will you?"

Marjory was shaking the bell against her ear. But it was dumb, it made no sound.

"You'll break it, I know you will—. You'll break it. Give it *me*—" cried Millicent, and she began to take away the bell. Marjory set up an expostulation.

"*Let her alone,*" said the father.

Millicent let go as if she had been stung, but still her brassy, impudent voice persisted:

"She'll break it. She'll break it. It's *mine*—"

"You undo another," said the mother, politic.

Millicent began with hasty, itching fingers to unclose another package.

"Aw—aw Mother, my peacock—aw, my peacock, my green peacock!" Lavishly she hovered over a sinuous greenish bird, with wings and tail of spun glass, pearly, and body of deep electric green.

"It's *mine*—my green peacock! It's mine, because Marjory's had one wing off, and mine hadn't.—My green peacock that I love! I love it!" She swung it softly from the little ring on its back. Then she went to her mother.

"Look Mother, isn't it a beauty?"

"Mind the ring doesn't come out," said her mother.—"Yes, it's lovely!" The girl passed on to her father.

"Look Father, don't you love it!"

"Love it?" he re-echoed, ironical over the word love.

She stood for some moments, trying to force his attention. Then she went back to her place.

5 Marjory had brought forth a golden apple, red on one cheek, rather garish.

"Oh!" exclaimed Millicent feverishly, instantly seized with desire for what she had not got, indifferent to what she had. Her eye ran quickly over the packages. She took one.

10 "Now!" she exclaimed loudly, to attract attention. "Now! What's this?—What's this? What will this beauty be?"

With finicky fingers she removed the newspaper. Marjory watched her wide-eyed. Millicent was self-important.

"The blue ball!" she cried in a climax of rapture. "I've got *the blue*
15 *ball.*"

She held it gloating in the cup of her hands. It was a little globe of hardened glass, of a magnificent full dark-blue colour. She rose and went to her father.

"It was *your* blue ball, wasn't it father?"

20 "Yes."

"And you had it when you were a little boy, and now I have it when I'm a little girl."

"Ay," he replied drily.

"And it's never been broken all those years."

25 "No, not yet."

"And perhaps it never will be broken."

To this she received no answer.

"Won't it break?" she persisted. "Can't you break it?"

"Yes, if you hit it with a hammer," he said.

30 "Aw!" she cried. "I don't mean that. I mean if you just drop it. It won't break if you drop it, will it?"

"I daresay it won't."

"But *will* it?"

"I sh'd think not."

35 "Should I try?"

She proceeded gingerly to let the blue ball drop. It bounced dully on the floor-covering.

"Oh-h-h!" she cried, catching it up. "I love it."

"Let *me* drop it," cried Marjory, and there was a performance of
40 admonition and demonstration from the elder sister.

But Millicent must go further. She became excited.

"It won't break," she said, "even if you toss it up in the air."

She flung it up, it fell safely. But her father's brow knitted slightly. She tossed it wildly: it fell with a little splashing explosion: it had smashed. It had fallen on the sharp edge of the tiles that protruded 5 under the fender.

"*Now* what have you done!" cried the mother.

The child stood with her lip between her teeth, a look, half of pure misery and dismay, half of satisfaction, on her pretty sharp face.

"She wanted to break it," said the father. 10

"No she didn't! What do you say that for!" said the mother. And Millicent burst into a flood of tears.

He rose to look at the fragments that lay splashed on the floor.

"You must mind the bits," he said, "and pick 'em all up."

He took one of the pieces to examine it. It was fine and thin and 15 hard, lined with pure silver, brilliant. He looked at it closely. So— this was what it was. And this was the end of it. He felt the curious soft explosion of its breaking still in his ears. He threw his piece in the fire.

"Pick all the bits up," he said. "Give over! give over! Don't cry any 20 more."

The good-natured tone of his voice quieted the child, as he intended it should.

He went away into the back kitchen to wash himself. As he was bending his head over the sink before the little mirror, lathering to 25 shave, there came from outside the dissonant voices of boys, pouring out the dregs of carol-singing.

"While Shep-ep-ep-ep-herds watched—"*

He held his soapy brush suspended for a minute. They called this singing! His mind flitted back to early carol music. Then again he 30 heard the vocal violence outside.

"Aren't you off there!" he called out, in masculine menace. The noise stopped, there was a scuffle. But the feet returned and the voices resumed. Almost immediately the door opened, boys were heard muttering among themselves. Millicent had given them a 35 penny. Feet scraped on the yard, then went thudding along the side of the house, to the street.

To Aaron Sisson this was home, this was Christmas: the unspeakably familiar. The war over, nothing was changed. Yet everything changed. The scullery in which he stood was painted green, quite 40

fresh, very clean, the floor was red tiles. The wash-copper of red bricks was very red, the mangle with its put-up board was white-scrubbed, the American oil-cloth* on the table had a gay pattern, there was a warm fire, the water in the boiler hissed faintly. And in
5 front of him, beneath him as he leaned forward shaving, a drop of water fell with strange, incalculable rhythm from the bright brass tap into the white enamelled bowl, which was now half full of pure, quivering water. The war was over, and everything just the same. The acute familiarity of this house, which he had built for his
10 marriage twelve years ago, the changeless pleasantness of it all seemed unthinkable. It prevented his thinking.

When he went into the middle room to comb his hair he found the Christmas tree sparkling, his wife was making pastry at the table, the baby was sitting up propped in cushions.

15 "Father," said Millicent, approaching him with a flat blue-and-white angel of cotton-wool, and two ends of cotton..."tie the angel at the top."

"Tie it at the top?" he said, looking down.

"Yes. At the very top—because it's just come down from the sky."
20 "Ay my word!" he laughed. And he tied the angel.

Coming downstairs after changing he went into the icy cold parlour, and took his music and a small handbag. With this he retreated again to the back kitchen. He was still in trousers and shirt and slippers: but now it was a clean white shirt, and his best black
25 trousers, and new pink and white braces. He sat under the gas-jet of the back kitchen, looking through his music. Then he opened the bag, in which were sections of a flute and a piccolo. He took out the flute, and adjusted it. As he sat he was physically aware of the sounds of the night: the bubbling of water in the boiler, the faint sound of the
30 gas, the sudden crying of the baby in the next room, then noises outside, distant boys shouting, distant rags of carols, fragments of voices of men. The whole country was roused and excited.

The little room was hot. Aaron rose and opened a square ventilator over the copper, letting in a stream of cold air, which was
35 grateful to him. Then he cocked his eye over the sheet of music spread out on the table before him. He tried his flute. And then at last, with the odd gesture of a diver taking a plunge, he swung his head and began to play. A stream of music, soft and rich and fluid, came out of the flute. He played beautifully. He moved his head and
40 his raised bare arms with slight, intense movements, as the delicate

music poured out. It was sixteenth-century Christmas melody, very limpid and delicate.

The pure, mindless, exquisite motion and fluidity of the music delighted him with a strange exasperation. There was something tense, exasperated to the point of intolerable anger, in his good-humoured breast, as he played the finely-spun peace-music. The more exquisite the music, the more perfectly he produced it, in sheer bliss; and at the same time, the more intense was the maddened exasperation within him.

Millicent appeared in the room. She fidgetted at the sink. The music was a bugbear to her, because it prevented her from saying what was on her own mind. At length it ended, her father was turning over the various books and sheets. She looked at him quickly, seizing her opportunity.

"Are you going out, Father?" she said.

"Eh?"

"Are you going out?" She twisted nervously.

"What do you want to know for?"

He made no other answer, and turned again to the music. His eye went down a sheet—then over it again—then more closely over it again.

"Are you?" persisted the child, balancing on one foot.

He looked at her, and his eyes were angry under knitted brows.

"What are you bothering about?" he said.

"I'm not bothering—I only wanted to know if you were going out," she pouted, quivering to cry.

"I expect I am," he said quietly.

She recovered at once, but still with timidity asked:

"We haven't got any candles for the Christmas tree—shall *you* buy some, because mother isn't going out?"

"Candles!" he repeated, settling his music and taking up the piccolo.

"Yes—shall you buy us some, Father? Shall you?"

"Candles!" he repeated, putting the piccolo to his mouth and blowing a few piercing, preparatory notes.

"Yes, little Christmas-tree candles—blue ones and red ones, in boxes—Shall you, Father?"

"We'll see—if I see any—"

"But *shall* you?" she insisted desperately. She wisely mistrusted his vagueness.

But he was looking unheeding at the music. Then suddenly the piccolo broke forth, wild, shrill, brilliant. He was playing Mozart. The child's face went pale with anger at the sound. She turned, and went out, closing both doors behind her to shut out the noise.

5 The shrill, rapid movement of the piccolo music seemed to possess the air, it was useless to try to shut it out. The man went on playing to himself, measured and insistent. In the frosty evening the sound carried. People passing down the street hesitated, listening. The neighbours knew it was Aaron practicing his piccolo. He was 10 esteemed a good player: was in request at concerts and dances, also at swell balls. So the vivid piping sound tickled the darkness.

He played on till about seven o'clock: he did not want to go out too soon, in spite of the early closing of the public houses. He never went with the stream, but made a side current of his own. His wife said he 15 was contrary.—When he went into the middle room to put on his collar and tie, the two little girls were having their hair brushed, the baby was in bed, there was a hot smell of mince-pies baking in the oven.

"You won't forget our candles, will you Father?" asked Millicent, 20 with assurance now.

"I'll see," he answered.

His wife watched him as he put on his overcoat and hat. He was well-dressed, handsome-looking. She felt there was a curious glamour about him. It made her feel bitter. He had an unfair 25 advantage—he was free to go off, while she must stay at home with the children.

"There's no knowing what time you'll be home," she said.

"I shan't be late," he answered.

"It's easy to say so," she retorted, with some contempt. He took 30 his stick, and turned towards the door.

"Bring the children some candles for their tree, and don't be so selfish," she said.

"All right," he said, going out.

"Don't say *All right* if you never mean to do it," she cried, with 35 sudden anger, following him to the door.

His figure stood large and shadowy in the darkness.

"How many do you want?" he said.

"A dozen," she said. "And holders too, if you can get them," she added, with barren bitterness.

40 "Yes—all right," he turned and melted into the darkness. She went indoors, worn with a strange and bitter flame.

He crossed the fields towards the little town, which once more fumed its lights under the night. The country ran away, rising on his right hand. It was no longer a great bank of darkness. Lights twinkled freely here and there, though forlornly, now that the war-time restrictions were removed. It was no glitter of pre-war nights, pit-heads glittering far-off with electricity. Neither was it the black gulf of the war darkness: instead, this forlorn sporadic twinkling.

Everybody seemed to be out of doors. The hollow dark country-side re-echoed like a shell with shouts and calls and excited voices. Restlessness and nervous excitement, nervous hilarity were in the air. There was a sense of electric surcharge everywhere, frictional, a neurasthenic haste for excitement.

Every moment Aaron Sisson was greeted with Goodnight— Goodnight Aaron—Goodnight Mr. Sisson. People carrying parcels, children, women, thronged home on the dark paths. They were all talking loudly, declaiming loudly about what they could and could not get, and what this or the other had lost.

When he got into the main street, the only street of shops, it was crowded. There seemed to have been some violent but quiet contest, a subdued fight, going on all the afternoon and evening: people struggling to buy things, to get things. Money was spent like water, there was a frenzy of money-spending. Though the necessities of life were in abundance, still the people struggled in frenzy for cheese, sweets, raisins, pork-stuff, even for flowers and holly, all of which were scarce, and for toys and knick-knacks, which were sold out. There was a wild grumbling, but a deep satisfaction in the fight, the struggle. The same fight and the same satisfaction in the fight was witnessed whenever a tram-car stopped, or when it heaved its way into sight. Then the struggle to mount on board became desperate and savage, but stimulating. Souls surcharged with hostility found now some outlet for their feelings.

As he came near the little market-place he bethought himself of the Christmas-tree candles. He did not intend to trouble himself. And yet, when he glanced in passing into the sweet-shop window, and saw it bare as a board, the very fact that he probably *could not* buy the things made him hesitate, and try.

"Have you got any Christmas-tree candles?" he asked as he entered the shop.

"How many do you want?"

"A dozen."

"Can't let you have a dozen. You can have two boxes—four in a box—eight. Sixpence a box."

"Got any holders?"

"Holders? Don't ask. Haven't seen one this year."

5   "Got any toffee—?"

"Cough-drops—twopence an ounce—nothing else left."

"Give me four ounces."

He watched her weighing them in the little brass scales.

"You've not got much of a Christmas show," he said.

10   "Don't talk about Christmas, as far as sweets is concerned. They ought to have allowed us six times the quantity—there's plenty of sugar, why didn't they? We s'll have to enjoy ourselves with what we've got. We mean to, anyhow."

"Ay," he said.

15   "Time we had a bit of enjoyment, *this* Christmas. They ought to have made things more plentiful."

"Yes," he said, stuffing his package in his pocket.

Chapter II.

Royal Oak*

The war had killed the little market of the town. As he passed the market-place on the brow, Aaron noticed that there were only two miserable stalls. But people crowded just the same. There was a loud 5 sound of voices, men's voices. Men pressed round the doorways of the public houses.

But he was going to a pub out of town. He descended the dark hill. A street-lamp here and there shed parsimonious light. In the bottoms, under the trees, it was very dark. But a lamp glimmered in 10 front of the "Royal Oak." This was a low white house sunk three steps below the highway. It was darkened, but sounded crowded.

Opening the door, Sisson found himself in the stone passage. Old Bob, carrying three cans, stopped to see who had entered—then went on into the public bar on the left. The bar itself was a sort of 15 little window-sill on the right: the pub was a small one. In this window-opening stood the landlady, drawing and serving to her husband. Behind the bar was a tiny parlour or den, the landlady's preserve.

"Oh, it's you," she said, bobbing down to look at the new-comer. 20 None entered her bar-parlour unless invited.

"Come in," said the landlady.

There was a peculiar intonation in her complacent voice, which showed she had been expecting him, a little irritably.

He went across into her bar-parlour. It would not hold more than 25 eight or ten people, all told—just the benches along the walls, the fire between—and two little round tables.

"I began to think you weren't coming," said the landlady, bringing him a whiskey.

She was a large, stout, high-coloured woman, with a fine profile, 30 probably Jewish. She had chestnut-coloured eyes, quick, intelligent. Her movements were large and slow, her voice laconic.

"I'm not so late, am I?" asked Aaron.

"Yes, you *are* late, I should think." She looked up at the little clock. "Close on nine."

35

"I did some shopping," said Aaron, with a quick smile.

"Did you indeed. That's news, I'm sure. May we ask what you bought?"

This he did not like. But he had to answer.

5 "Christmas-tree candles, and toffee."

"For the little children? Well you've done well for once! I must say I recommend you. I didn't think you had so much in you."

She sat herself down in her seat at the end of the bench, and took up her knitting. Aaron sat next to her. He poured water into his glass,

10 and drank.

"It's warm in here," he said, when he had swallowed the liquor.

"Yes, it is. You won't want to keep that thick good overcoat on," replied the landlady.

"No," he said, "I think I'll take it off."

15 She watched him as he hung up his overcoat. He wore black clothes, as usual. As he reached up to the pegs, she could see the muscles of his shoulders, and the form of his legs. Her reddish-brown eyes seemed to burn, and her nose, that had a subtle, beautiful Hebraic curve, seemed to arch itself. She made a little place for him

20 by herself, as he returned. She carried her head thrown back, with dauntless self-sufficiency.

There were several colliers in the room, talking quietly. They were the superior type all, favoured by the landlady, who loved intellectual discussion. Opposite, by the fire, sat a little, greenish

25 man—evidently an oriental.

"You're very quiet all at once, Doctor," said the landlady in her slow, laconic voice.

"Yes.—May I have another whiskey, please!"

She rose at once, powerfully energetic.

30 "Oh, I'm sorry," she said. And she went to the bar.

"Well," said the little Hindu doctor, "and how are things going now, with the men?"

"The same as ever," said Aaron.

"Yes," said the stately voice of the landlady. "And I'm afraid

35 they will always be the same as ever. When will they learn wisdom?"

"But what do you call wisdom?" asked Sherardy, the Hindu.* He spoke with a little, childish lisp.

"What do I call wisdom?" repeated the landlady. "Why all acting

40 together for the common good. That is wisdom in my idea."

"Yes, very well, that is so. But what do you call the common good?" replied the little doctor, with childish pertinence.

"Ay," said Aaron, with a laugh, "that's it."

The miners were all stirring now, to take part in the discussion.

"What do I call the common good?" repeated the landlady. "That all people should study the welfare of other people, and not only their own."

"They are not to study their own welfare?" said the doctor.

"Ah, that I did not say," replied the landlady. "Let them study their own welfare, and that of others also."

"Well then," said the doctor, "what is the welfare of a collier?"

"The welfare of a collier," said the landlady, "is that he shall earn sufficient wages to keep himself and his family comfortable, to educate his children, and to educate himself; for that is what he wants, education."

"Ay, happen so," put in Brewitt, a big, fine, good-humoured collier. "Happen so, Mrs. Houseley.* But what if you haven't got much education, to speak of?"

"You can *always* get it," she said patronising.

"Nay—I'm blest if you can. It's no use tryin' to educate a man over forty—not by book-learning. That isn't saying he's a fool, neither."

"And what better is them that's got education?" put in another man. "What better is the manager, or th' under-manager, than we are?—Pender's yaller enough i' th' face."

"He is that," assented the men in chorus.

"But because he's yellow in the face, as you say, Mr. Kirk," said the landlady largely, "that doesn't mean he has no advantages higher than what you have got."

"Ay," said Kirk. "He can ma'e more money than I can—that's about a' as it comes to."

"He can make more money," said the landlady. "And when he's made it, he knows better how to use it."

"'Appen so, an' a' !—What does he do, more than eat and drink and work?—an' take it out of hisself a sight harder than I do, by th' looks of him.—What's it matter, if he eats a bit more or drinks a bit more—"

"No," reiterated the landlady. "He not only eats and drinks. He can read, and he can converse."

"Me an' a',"* said Tom Kirk, and the men burst into a laugh. "I can read—an' I've had many a talk an' conversation with you in this house, Mrs. Houseley—am havin' one at this minute, seemingly."

"*Seemingly*, you are," said the landlady ironically. "But do you think there would be no difference between your conversation, and
5   Mr. Pender's, if he were here so that I could *enjoy* his conversation?"

"An' what difference would there be?" asked Tom Kirk. "He'd go home to his bed just the same."

"*There*, you are mistaken. He would be the better, and so should I, a great deal better, for a little genuine conversation."

10   "If it's conversation as ma'es his behind drop—" said Tom Kirk.

"An' puts th' bile in his face—" said Brewitt.

There was a general laugh.

"I can see it's no use talking about it any further," said the landlady, lifting her head dangerously.

15   "But look here, Mrs. Houseley, do you really think it makes much difference to a man, whether he can hold a serious conversation or not?" asked the doctor.

"I do indeed, all the difference in the world—To me, there is no greater difference, than between an educated man and an unedu-
20   cated man."

"And where does it come in?" asked Kirk.

"But wait a bit, now," said Aaron Sisson. "You take an educated man—take Pender. What's his education for? What does he scheme for?—What does he contrive for? What does he talk for?—"

25   "For all the purposes of his life," replied the landlady.

"Ay, an' what's the purpose of his life?" insisted Aaron Sisson.

"The purpose of his life," repeated the landlady, at a loss. "I should think he knows that best himself."

"No better than I know it—and you know it," said Aaron.

30   "Well," said the landlady, "if you know, then speak out. What is it?"

"To make more money for the firm—and so make his own chance of a rise better."

The landlady was baffled for some moments. Then she said:

35   "Yes, and suppose that he does. Is there any harm in it? Isn't it his duty to do what he can for himself? Don't you try to earn all you can?"

"Ay," said Aaron. "But there's soon a limit to what I can earn.—It's like this. When you work it out, everything comes to
40   money. Reckon it as you like, it's money on both sides. It's money we

live for, and money is what our lives is worth—nothing else. Money we live for, and money we are when we're dead: that or nothing. An' it's money as is between the masters and us. There's a few educated ones got hold of one end of the rope, and all the lot of us hanging on to th' other end, an' we s'll go on pulling our guts out, time in, time out—" 5

"But they've got th' long end o' th' rope, th' masters has," said Brewitt.

"For as long as one holds, the other will pull," concluded Aaron Sisson philosophically. 10

"An' I'm almighty sure o' that," said Kirk.

There was a little pause.

"Yes, that's all there is in the minds of *you men*," said the landlady. "But what can be done with the money, that you never think of—— the education of the children, the improvement of conditions—" 15

"Educate the children, so that they can lay hold of the long end of the rope, instead of the short end," said the doctor, with a little giggle.

"Ay, that's it," said Brewitt. "I've pulled at th' short end, an' my lads may do th' same." 20

"A selfish policy," put in the landlady.

"Selfish or not, they may do it."

"Till the crack o' doom," said Aaron, with a glistening smile.

"Or the crack o' th' rope," said Brewitt.

"Yes, and *then what?*" cried the landlady. 25

"Then we s'll all drop on our backsides," said Kirk.

There was a general laugh, and an uneasy silence.

"All I can say of you men," said the landlady, "is that you have a narrow, selfish policy.—Instead of thinking of the children, instead of thinking of improving the world you live in—" 30

"We hang on, British bulldog breed," said Brewitt.

There was a general laugh.

"Yes, and little wiser than dogs, wrangling for a bone," said the landlady.

"Are we to let t'other side run off wi' th' bone, then, while we sit 35 on our stunts* an' yowl for it?" asked Brewitt.

"No indeed. There can be wisdom in everything.—It's what you *do* with the money, when you've got it," said the landlady, "that's where the importance lies."

"It's Missis as gets it," said Kirk. "It doesn't stop wi' us." 40

"Ay, it's the wife as gets it, ninety per cent," they all concurred.

"And who *should* have the money, indeed, if not your wives? They have everything to *do* with the money. What idea have you, but to waste it!"

5   "Women waste nothing—they couldn't if they tried," said Aaron Sisson.

There was a lull for some minutes. The men were all stimulated by drink. The landlady kept them going. She herself sipped a glass of brandy—but slowly. She sat near to Sisson—and the great fierce
10 warmth of her presence enveloped him particularly. He loved so to luxuriate, like a cat, in the presence of a violent woman. He knew that tonight she was feeling very nice to him—a female glow that came out of her to him. Sometimes when she put down her knitting, or took it up again from the bench beside him, her fingers just touched
15 his thigh, and the fine electricity ran over his body, as if he were a cat tingling at a caress.

And yet he was not happy—nor comfortable. There was a hard, opposing core in him, that neither the whiskey nor the woman could dissolve or soothe, tonight. It remained hard, nay, became harder
20 and more deeply antagonistic to his surroundings, every moment. He recognised it as a secret malady he suffered from: this strained, unacknowledged opposition to his surroundings, a hard core of irrational, exhausting withholding of himself. Irritating, because he still *wanted* to give himself. A woman and whiskey, these were usually
25 a remedy—and music. But lately these had begun to fail him. No, there was something in him that would not give in—neither to the whiskey, nor the woman, nor even the music. Even in the midst of his best music, it sat in the middle of him, this invisible black dog, and growled and waited, never to be cajoled. He knew of its presence—
30 and was a little uneasy. For of course he *wanted* to let himself go, to feel rosy and loving and all that. But at the very thought, the black dog showed its teeth.

Still he kept the beast at bay—with all his will he kept himself as it were genial. He wanted to melt and be rosy, happy.

35 He sipped his whiskey with gratification, he luxuriated in the presence of the landlady, very confident of the strength of her liking for him. He glanced at her profile—that fine throwback of her hostile head, wicked in the midst of her benevolence; that subtle, really very beautiful delicate curve of her nose, that moved him exactly like a
40 piece of pure sound. But tonight it did not overcome him. There was

a devilish little cold eye in his brain that was not taken in by what he saw.

A terrible obstinacy located itself in him. He saw the fine, rich-coloured, secretive face of the Hebrew woman, so loudly self-righteous, and so dangerous, so destructive, so lustful—and he waited for his blood to melt with passion for her. But not tonight. Tonight his innermost heart was hard and cold as ice. The very danger and lustfulness of her, which had so pricked his senses, now made him colder. He disliked her at her tricks. He saw her once too often. Her and all women. Bah, the love game! And the whiskey that was to help in the game! He had drowned himself once too often in whiskey and in love. Now he floated like a corpse in both, with a cold, hostile eye.

And at least half of his inward fume was anger because he could no longer drown. Nothing would have pleased him better than to feel his senses melting and swimming into oneness with the dark. But impossible! Cold, with a white fury inside him, he floated wide-eyed and apart as a corpse. He thought of the gentle love of his first married years, and became only whiter and colder, set in more intense obstinacy. A wave of revulsion lifted him.

He became aware that he was deadly antagonistic to the landlady, that he disliked his whole circumstances. A cold, diabolical consciousness detached itself from his state of semi-intoxication.

"Is it pretty much the same out there in India?" he asked of the doctor suddenly.

The doctor started, and attended to him on his own level.

"Probably," he answered, "it is worse."

"Worse!" exclaimed Aaron Sisson. "How's that?"

"Why, because, in a way the people of India have an easier time even than the people of England. Because they have no responsibility. The British Government takes the responsibility. And the people have nothing to do, except their bit of work—and talk perhaps about national rule,* just for a pastime."

"They have to earn their living?" said Sisson.

"Yes," said the little doctor, who had lived for some years among the colliers, and become quite familiar with them. "Yes, they have to earn their living—and then no more. That's why the British Government is the worst thing possible for them. It is the worst thing possible. And not because it is a bad government. Really, it is not a bad government. It is a good one—and they know it—much better than they would make for themselves, probably. But for that reason it is so very bad."

The little oriental laughed a queer, sniggering laugh. His eyes were very bright, dilated, completely black. He was looking into the ice-blue, pointed eyes of Aaron Sisson. They were both intoxicated—but grimly so. They looked at each other in elemental difference.

The whole room was now attending to this new conversation: which they all accepted as serious. For Aaron was considered a special man, a man of peculiar understanding, even though as a rule he said little.

"If it is a good government, doctor, how can it be so bad for the people?" said the landlady.

The doctor's eyes quivered for the fraction of a second, as he watched over the other man. He did not look at the landlady.

"It would not matter what kind of mess they made—and they would make a mess, if they governed themselves, the people of India. They would probably make the greatest muddle possible—and start killing one another. But it wouldn't matter if they exterminated half the population, so long as they did it themselves, and were responsible for it."

Again his eyes dilated, utterly black, to the eyes of the other man, and an arch little smile flickered on his face.

"I think it would matter very much indeed," said the landlady. "They had far better *not* govern themselves."

She was, for some reason, becoming angry. The little greenish doctor emptied his glass, and smiled again.

"But what difference does it make," said Aaron Sisson, "whether they govern themselves or not?—They only live till they die, either way." And he smiled faintly. He had not really listened to the doctor. The terms "British Government," and "bad for the people—good for the people," made him malevolently angry.

The doctor was nonplussed for a moment. Then he gathered himself together.

"It matters," he said, "it matters.—People should always be responsible for themselves. How can any people be responsible for another race of people, and for a race much older than they are, and not at all children."

Aaron Sisson watched the other dark face, with its utterly exposed eyes. He was in a state of semi-intoxicated anger and clairvoyance. He saw in the black, void, glistening eyes of the oriental only the same danger, the same menace that he saw in the landlady. Fair, wise, even benevolent words: always the human good speaking, and always underneath, something hateful, something detestable and murderous. Wise speech and good intentions—they were invariably maggoty with these secret inclinations to destroy the man in a man. 5 Whenever he heard anyone holding forth: the landlady, this doctor, the spokesman on the pit-bank: or when he read the all-righteous newspaper; his soul curdled with revulsion, as from something foul. Even the infernal love and good-will of his wife. To hell with good-will! It was more hateful than ill-will. Self-righteous bullying, 10 like poison gas!

The landlady looked at the clock.

"Ten minutes to, gentlemen," she said coldly. For she too knew that Aaron was spoiled for her for that night.

The men began to take their leave, shakily. The little doctor 15 seemed to evaporate. The landlady helped Aaron on with his coat. She saw the curious whiteness round his nostrils and his eyes, the fixed hellish look on his face.

"You'll eat a mince-pie in the kitchen with us, for luck?" she said to him, detaining him till last. 20

But he turned laughing to her.

"Nay," he said, "I must be getting home."

He turned and went straight out of the house. Watching him, the landlady's face became yellow with passion and rage.

"That little poisonous Indian viper," she said aloud, attributing 25 Aaron's mood to the doctor. Her husband was noisily bolting the door.

Outside it was dark and frosty. A gang of men lingered in the road near the closed door. Aaron found himself among them, his heart bitterer than steel. 30

The men were dispersing. He should take the road home. But the devil was in it, if he could take a stride in the homeward direction. There seemed a wall in front of him. He veered. But neither could he take a stride in the opposite direction. So he was destined to veer round, like some sort of weather-cock, there in the middle of the 35 dark road outside the "Royal Oak."

But as he turned, he caught sight of a third exit. Almost opposite was the mouth of Shottle Lane, which led off under trees, at right angles to the high-road, up to New Brunswick Colliery.* He veered towards the off-chance of this opening, in a delirium of icy fury, 40 and plunged away into the dark lane, walking slowly, on firm legs.

Chapter III.

The Lighted Tree*

It is remarkable how many odd or extraordinary people there are in England. We hear continual complaints of the stodgy dullness of the English. It would be quite as just to complain of their freakish, unusual characters. Only *en masse* the metal is all Britannia.

In an ugly little mining town we find the odd ones just as distinct as anywhere else. Only it happens that dull people invariably meet dull people, and odd individuals always come across odd individuals, no matter where they may be. So that to each kind society seems all of a piece.

At one end of the dark, tree-covered Shottle Lane stood the "Royal Oak" public house; and Mrs. Houseley was certainly an odd woman. At the other end of the lane was Shottle House, where the Bricknells lived;* the Bricknells were odd, also. Alfred Bricknell, the old man, was one of the partners in the Colliery firm. His English was incorrect, his accent, broad Derbyshire, and he was not a gentleman in the snobbish sense of the word. Yet he was well-to-do, and very stuck-up. His wife was dead.

Shottle House stood two hundred yards beyond New Brunswick Colliery. The colliery was imbedded in a plantation, whence its burning pit-hill glowed, fumed, and stank sulphur in the nostrils of the Bricknells. Even war-time efforts had not put out this refuse fire. Apart from this, Shottle House was a pleasant square house, rather old, with shrubberies and lawns. It ended the lane in a dead end. Only a field-path trekked away to the left.

On this particular Christmas Eve Alfred Bricknell had only two of his children at home. Of the others, one daughter was unhappily married, and away in India weeping herself thinner; another was nursing her babies in Streatham. Jim,* the hope of the house, and Julia, now married to Robert Cunningham,* had come home for Christmas.

The party was seated in the drawing-room, that the grown-up daughters had made very fine during their periods of courtship. Its walls were hung with fine grey canvas, it had a large, silvery grey,

26

silky carpet, and the furniture was covered with dark green silky material. Into this reticence pieces of futurism, Omega cushions* and Van-Gogh-like pictures exploded their colours. Such *chic* would certainly not have been looked for up Shottle Lane.

The old man sat in his high grey arm-chair very near an enormous 5 coal fire. In this house there was no coal-rationing. The finest coal was arranged to obtain a gigantic glow such as a coal-owner may well enjoy, a great, intense mass of pure red fire. At this fire Alfred Bricknell toasted his tan, lambs-wool-lined slippers.

He was a large man, wearing a loose grey suit, and sprawling in the 10 large grey arm-chair. The soft lamp-light fell on his clean, bald, Michelangelo head, across which a few pure hairs glittered. His chin was sunk on his breast, so that his sparse but strong-haired white beard, in which every strand stood distinct, like spun glass lithe and elastic, curved now upwards and inwards, in a curious curve 15 returning upon him. He seemed to be sunk in stern, prophet-like meditation. As a matter of fact, he was asleep after a heavy meal.

Across, seated on a pouffe on the other side of the fire, was a cameo-like girl with neat black hair done tight and bright in the French mode. She had strangely-drawn eyebrows, and her colour 20 was brilliant. She was hot, leaning back behind the shaft of old marble of the mantel-piece, to escape the fire. She wore a simple dress of apple-green satin, with full sleeves and ample skirt and a tiny bodice of green cloth. This was Josephine Ford,* the girl Jim was engaged to. 25

Jim Bricknell himself was a tall big fellow of thirty-eight. He sat in a chair in front of the fire, some distance back, and stretched his long legs far in front of him. His chin too was sunk on his breast, his young forehead was bald, and raised in odd wrinkles, he had a silent half-grin on his face, a little tipsy, a little satyr-like. His small 30 moustache was reddish.

Behind him a round table was covered with cigarettes, sweets, and bottles. It was evident Jim Bricknell drank beer for choice. He wanted to get fat—that was his idea. But he couldn't bring it off: he was thin, though not too thin, except to his own thinking. 35

His sister Julia was bunched up in a low chair between him and his father. She too was a tall stag of a thing, but she sat hunched up like a witch. She wore a wine-purple dress, her arms seemed to poke out of the sleeves, and she had dragged her brown hair into straight, untidy strands. Yet she had real beauty. She was talking to the young man 40

who was not her husband: a fair, pale, fattish young fellow in
pince-nez and dark clothes. This was Cyril Scott,* a friend.

The only other person stood at the round table pouring out red
wine. He was a fresh, stoutish young Englishman in khaki, Julia's
husband, Robert Cunningham, a lieutenant about to be demobilised,
when he would become a sculptor once more. He drank red wine in
large throatfuls, and his eyes grew a little moist. The room was hot
and subdued, everyone was silent.

"I say," said Robert suddenly, from the rear—"anybody have a
drink? Don't you find it rather hot?"

"Is there another bottle of beer there?" said Jim, without moving,
too settled even to stir an eyelid.

"Yes—I think there is," said Robert.

"Thanks—don't open it yet," murmured Jim.

"Have a drink, Josephine?" said Robert.

"No thank you," said Josephine, bowing slightly.

Finding the drinks did not go, Robert went round with the
cigarettes. Josephine Ford looked at the white rolls.

"Thank you," she said, and taking one, suddenly licked her rather
full, dry red lips with the rapid tip of her tongue. It was an odd
movement, suggesting a snake's flicker. She put her cigarette
between her lips, and waited. Her movements were very quiet and
well-bred; but perhaps too quiet, they had the dangerous impassivity
of the Bohemian, Parisian or American rather than English.

"Cigarette, Julia?" said Robert to his wife.

She seemed to start or twitch, as if dazed. Then she looked up at
her husband with a queer smile, puckering the corners of her eyes.
He looked at the cigarettes, not at her. His face had the blunt,
voluptuous gravity of a young lion, a great cat. She kept him standing
for some moments impassively. Then suddenly she hung her long,
delicate fingers over the box, in doubt, and spasmodically jabbed at
the cigarettes, clumsily raking one out at last.

"Thank you, dear—thank you," she cried, rather high, looking up
and smiling once more. He turned calmly aside, offering the
cigarettes to Scott, who refused.

"Oh!" said Julia, sucking the end of her cigarette. "Robert is so
happy with all the good things—aren't you dear?" she sang, breaking
into a hurried laugh. "We aren't used to such luxurious living, we
aren't—*are we dear?*—No, we're not such swells as this, we're not.
Oh *Robbie*, isn't it all right, isn't it just all right!" She tailed off into

her hurried, wild, repeated laugh. "We're so happy in a land of plenty, *aren't we dear?*"

"Do you mean I'm greedy, Julia?" said Robert.

"Greedy!—Oh, greedy!—he asks if he's greedy?—No you're not greedy, Robbie, you're not greedy. I want you to be happy."

"I'm quite happy," he returned.

"Oh, he's happy!—Really!—he's happy! Oh, what an accomplishment! Oh, my word!" Julia puckered her eyes and laughed herself into a nervous, twitching silence.

Robert went round with the matches. Julia sucked her cigarette.

"Give us a light, Robbie, if you *are* happy!" she cried.

"It's coming," he answered.

Josephine smoked with short, sharp puffs. Julia sucked wildly at her light. Robert returned to his red wine. Jim Bricknell suddenly roused up, looked round on the company, smiling a little vacuously and showing his odd, pointed teeth.

"Where's the beer?" he asked, in deep tones, smiling full into Josephine's face, as if she were going to produce it by some sleight of hand. Then he wheeled round to the table, and was soon pouring beer down his throat as down a pipe. Then he dropped supine again. Cyril Scott was silently absorbing gin and water.

"I say," said Jim, from the remote depths of his sprawling. "Isn't there something we could do to while the time away?"

Everybody suddenly laughed—it sounded so remote and absurd.

"What, play bridge or poker or something conventional of that sort?" said Josephine in her distinct voice, speaking to him as if he were a child.

"Oh damn bridge," said Jim in his sleep-voice. Then he began pulling his powerful length together. He sat on the edge of his chair-seat, leaning forward, peering into all the faces and grinning.

"Don't look at me like that—so long—" said Josephine, in her self-contained voice. "You make me uncomfortable." She gave an odd little grunt of a laugh, and the tip of her tongue went over her lips as she glanced sharply, half furtively round the room.

"I like looking at you," said Jim, his smile becoming more malicious.

"But you shouldn't, when I tell you not," she returned.

Jim twisted round to look at the state of the bottles. The father also came awake. He sat up.

"Isn't it time," he said, "that you all put away your glasses and cigarettes, and thought of bed?"

Jim rolled slowly round towards his father, sprawling in the long chair.

5 "Ah Dad," he said, "tonight's the night! Tonight's some night, Dad.—You can sleep any time—" his grin widened—"but there aren't many nights to sit here—like this—Eh?"

He was looking up all the time into the face of his father, full and nakedly lifting his face to the face of his father, and smiling fixedly.
10 The father, who was perfectly sober, except for the contagion from the young people, felt a wild tremor go through his heart as he gazed on the face of his boy. He rose stiffly.

"You want to stay?" he said. "You want to stay!—Well then—well then, I'll leave you. But don't be long." The old man rose to his full
15 height, rather majestic. The four younger people also rose respectfully—only Jim lay still prostrate in his chair, twisting up his face towards his father.

"You won't stay long," said the old man, looking round a little bewildered. He was seeking a responsible eye. Josephine was the
20 only one who had any feeling for him.

"No, we won't stay long, Mr. Bricknell," she said gravely.

"Goodnight Dad," said Jim, as his father left the room.

Josephine went to the window. She had rather a stiff, *poupée** walk.
25 "How is the night?" she said, as if to change the whole feeling in the room. She pushed back the thick grey-silk curtains. "Why?" she exclaimed. "What is that light burning? A red light?"

"Oh, that's only the pit-bank on fire," said Robert, who had followed her.
30 "How strange!—Why is it burning now?"

"It always burns, unfortunately—it is most consistent at it. It is the refuse from the mines. It has been burning for years, in spite of all efforts to the contrary."

"How very curious! May we look at it?" Josephine now turned the
35 handle of the French windows, and stepped out.

"Beautiful!" they heard her voice exclaim from outside.

In the room, Julia laid her hand gently, protectively over the hand of Cyril Scott.

"Josephine and Robert are admiring the night together!" she said,
40 smiling with subtle tenderness to him.

"Naturally! Young people always do these romantic things," replied Cyril Scott. He was twenty-two years old, so he could afford to be cynical.

"Do they?—Don't you think it's nice of them?" she said, gently removing her hand from his. His eyes were shining with pleasure. 5

"I do. I envy them enormously. One only needs to be sufficiently naïve," he said.

"One does, doesn't one!" cooed Julia.

"I say, do you hear the bells?" said Robert, poking his head into the room. 10

"No, dear! Do you?" replied Julia.

"Bells! Hear the bells! Bells!" exclaimed the half-tipsy and self-conscious Jim. And he rolled in his chair in an explosion of sudden, silent laughter, showing his mouthful of pointed teeth, like a dog. Then he gradually gathered himself together, found his feet, 15 smiling fixedly.

"Pretty cool night!" he said aloud, when he felt the air on his almost bald head. The darkness smelt of sulphur.

Josephine and Robert had moved out of sight. Julia was abstracted, following them with her eyes. With almost supernatural keen- 20 ness she seemed to catch their voices from the distance.

"Yes Josephine, *wouldn't* that be *awfully* romantic!"—she suddenly called shrilly.

The pair in the distance started.

"What—!" they heard Josephine's sharp exclamation. 25

"What's that?—What would be romantic?" said Jim as he lurched up and caught hold of Cyril Scott's arm.

"Josephine wants to make a great illumination of the grounds of the estate," said Julia, magniloquent.

"No—no—I didn't say it," remonstrated Josephine. 30

"What Josephine said," explained Robert, "was simply that it would be pretty to put candles on one of the growing trees, instead of having a Christmas tree indoors."

"Oh Josephine, how sweet of you!" cried Julia.

Cyril Scott giggled. 35

"Good egg! Champion idea, Josey, my lass. Eh? What—!" cried Jim. "Why not carry it out—eh? Why not? Most attractive." He leaned forward over Josephine, and grinned.

"Oh no!" expostulated Josephine. "It all sounds so silly now. No. Let us go indoors and go to bed." 40

"*No* Josephine dear—*No*! It's a *lovely* idea!" cried Julia. "Let's get candles and lanterns and things—"

"Let's!" grinned Jim. "Let's, everybody—let's."

"Shall we really?" asked Robert. "Shall we illuminate one of the
5 fir-trees by the lawn."

"Yes! How lovely!" cried Julia. "I'll fetch the candles."

"The women must put on warm cloaks," said Robert.

They trooped indoors for coats and wraps and candles and lanterns. Then, lighted by a bicycle lamp, they trooped off to the
10 shed to twist wire round the candles for holders. They clustered round the bench.

"I say," said Julia, "doesn't Cyril look like a pilot on a stormy night! Oh I say—!" and she went into one of her hurried laughs.

They all looked at Cyril Scott, who was standing sheepishly in the
15 background, in a very large overcoat, smoking a large pipe. The young man was uncomfortable, but assumed a stoic air of philosophic indifference.

Soon they were busy round a prickly fir-tree at the end of the lawn. Jim stood in the background vaguely staring. The bicycle lamp sent
20 a beam of strong white light deep into the uncanny foliage, heads clustered and hands worked. The night above was silent, dim. There was no wind. In the near distance they could hear the panting of some engine at the colliery.

"Shall we light them as we fix them," asked Robert, "or save them
25 for one grand rocket at the end?"

"Oh, as we do them," said Cyril Scott, who had lacerated his fingers and wanted to see some reward.

A match spluttered. One naked little flame sprang alight among the dark foliage. The candle burned tremulously, naked. They all
30 were silent.

"We ought to do a ritual dance! We ought to worship the tree," sang Julia, in her high voice.

"Hold on a minute. We'll have a little more illumination," said Robert.

35 "Why yes. We want more than one candle," said Josephine.

But Julia had dropped the cloak in which she was huddled, and with arms slung asunder was sliding, waving, crouching in a *pas seul*⁕ before the tree, looking like an animated bough herself.

Jim, who was hugging his pipe in the background, broke into a
40 short, harsh, cackling laugh.

"Aren't we fools!" he cried. "What? Oh God's love, aren't we fools!"

"No—why?" cried Josephine, amused but resentful.

But Jim vouchsafed nothing further, only stood like a Red Indian gripping his pipe.

The beam of the bicycle lamp moved and fell upon the hands and faces of the young people, and penetrated the recesses of the secret trees. Several little tongues of flame clipped sensitive and ruddy on the naked air, sending a faint glow over the needle foliage. They gave a strange, perpendicular aspiration in the night. Julia waved slowly in her tree dance. Jim stood apart, with his legs straddled, a motionless figure.

The party round the tree became absorbed and excited as more ruddy tongues of flame pricked upward from the dark tree. Pale candles became evident, the air was luminous. The illumination was becoming complete, harmonious.

Josephine suddenly looked round.

"Why—y—y!" came her long note of alarm.

A man in a bowler hat and a black overcoat stood on the edge of the twilight.

"What is it?" cried Julia.

"*Homo sapiens!*" said Robert, the lieutenant. "Hand the light, Cyril."

He played the beam of light full on the intruder: a man in a bowler hat, with a black overcoat buttoned to his throat, a pale, dazed, blinking face. The hat was tilted at a slightly jaunty angle over the left eye, the man was well-featured. He did not speak.

"Did you want anything?" asked Robert, from behind the light.

Aaron Sisson blinked, trying to see who addressed him. To him, they were all illusory. He did not answer.

"Anything you wanted?" repeated Robert, military, rather peremptory.

Jim suddenly doubled himself up and burst into a loud harsh cackle of laughter. Whoop! he went, and doubled himself up with laughter. Whoop! Whoop! he went, and fell on the floor,* and writhed with laughter. He was in that state of intoxication when he could find no release from maddening self-consciousness. He knew what he was doing, he did it deliberately. And yet he was also beside himself, in a sort of hysterics. He could not help himself, in exasperated self-consciousness.

The others all began to laugh, unavoidably. It was a contagion. They laughed helplessly and foolishly. Only Robert was anxious.

"I'm afraid he'll wake the house," he said, looking at the doubled-up figure of Jim writhing on the grass and whooping loudly.

5   "No—no!" cried Josephine, weak with laughing in spite of herself. "No—it's too long—I'm like to die laughing—"

Jim embraced the earth in his convulsions. Even Robert shook quite weakly with laughter. His face was red, his eyes full of dancing water. Yet he managed to articulate.

10   "I say, you know, you'll bring the old man down." Then he went off again into spasms.

"Hu! Hu!" whooped Jim, subsiding. "Hu!"

He rolled over on to his back, and lay silent. The others also became weakly silent.

15   "What's amiss?" said Aaron Sisson, breaking this spell.

They all began to laugh again, except Jim, who lay on his back looking up at the strange sky.

"What're you laughing at?" repeated Aaron.

"We're laughing at the man on the floor," replied Josephine. "I
20   think he's drunk a little too much."

"Or not enough," put in Cyril Scott. He twigged Jim's condition.

"Ay," said Aaron, standing mute and obstinate.

"Did you want anything?" Robert enquired once more.

"Eh?" Aaron looked up. "Me? No, not me." A sort of inertia kept
25   him rooted. The young people looked at one another and began to laugh, rather embarrassed.

"Another!" said Cyril Scott cynically.

They wished he would go away. There was a pause.

"What do you reckon stars are?" asked the sepulchral voice of Jim.
30   He still lay flat on his back on the grass.

Josephine went to him and pulled at his coat.

"Get up," she said. "You'll take cold. Get up now, we're going indoors."

"What do you reckon stars are?" he persisted.

35   Aaron Sisson stood on the edge of the light, smilingly staring at the scene, like a boy out of his place, but stubbornly keeping his ground.

"Get up now," said Josephine. "We've had enough." But Jim would not move.

40   Robert went with the bicycle lamp and stood at Aaron's side.

"Shall I show you a light to the road—you're off your track," he said. "You're in the grounds of Shottle House."

"I can find my road," said Aaron. "Thank you."

Jim suddenly got up and went to peer at the stranger, poking his face close to Aaron's face.

"Right-o," he remarked. "You're not half a bad sort of chap— Cheery-o! What's your drink?"

"Mine—whiskey," said Aaron.

"Come in and have one. We're the only sober couple in the bunch—what?" cried Jim.

Aaron stood unmoving, static in everything. Jim took him by the arm affectionately. The stranger looked at the flickering tree, with its tiers of lights.

"A Christmas tree," he said, jerking his head and smiling.

"That's right old man," said Jim, seeming thoroughly sober now. "Come indoors and have a drink."

Aaron Sisson negatively allowed himself to be led off. The others followed in silence, leaving the tree to flicker the night through. The stranger stumbled at the open window-door.

"Mind the step," said Jim affectionately.

They crowded to the fire, which was still hot. The new-comer looked round vaguely. Jim took his bowler hat and gave him a chair. He sat without looking round, a remote, abstract look on his face. He was very pale, and seemed inwardly absorbed.

The party threw off their wraps and sat around. Josephine turned to Aaron Sisson, who sat with a glass of whiskey in his hand, rather slack in his chair, in his thickish overcoat. He did not want to drink. His hair was blond, quite tidy, his mouth and chin handsome but a little obstinate, his eyes inscrutable. His pallor was not natural to him. Though he kept the appearance of a smile, underneath he was hard and opposed. He did not wish to be with these people, and yet, mechanically, he stayed.

"Do you feel quite well?" Josephine asked him.

He looked at her quickly.

"Me?" he said. He smiled faintly. "Yes, I'm all right." Then he dropped his head again and seemed oblivious.

"Tell us your name," said Jim affectionately.

The stranger looked up.

"My name's Aaron Sisson, if it's anything to you," he said.

Jim began to grin.

"It's a name I don't know," he said. Then he named all the party present. But the stranger hardly heeded, though his eyes looked curiously from one to the other, slow, shrewd, clairvoyant.

"Were you on your way home?" asked Robert, huffy.

5 The stranger lifted his head and looked at him.

"Home!" he repeated. "No. The other road—." He indicated the direction with his head, and smiled faintly.

"Beldover?"* enquired Robert.

"Yes."

10 He had dropped his head again, as if he did not want to look at them.

To Josephine, the pale, impassive, blank-seeming face, the blue eyes with the smile which wasn't a smile, and the continual dropping of the well-shaped head was curiously affecting. She wanted to cry.

15 "Are you a miner?" Robert asked, *de haut en bas.**

"No," cried Josephine. She had looked at his hands.

"Men's checkweighman,"* replied Aaron. He had emptied his glass. He put it on the table.

"Have another?" said Jim, who was attending fixedly, with curious 20 absorption, to the stranger.

"No," cried Josephine, "no more."

Aaron looked at Jim, then at her, and smiled slowly, with remote bitterness. Then he lowered his head again. His hands were loosely clasped between his knees.

25 "What about the wife?" said Robert—the young lieutenant.

"What about the wife and kiddies? You're a married man, aren't you?"

The sardonic look of the stranger rested on the subaltern.

"Yes," he said.

30 "Won't they be expecting you?" said Robert, trying to keep his temper and his tone of authority.

"I expect they will—"

"Then you'd better be getting along, hadn't you?"

The eyes of the intruder rested all the time on the flushed 35 subaltern. The look on Aaron's face became slowly satirical.

"Oh dry up the army touch," said Jim contemptuously, to Robert. "We're all civvies here.—We're all right, aren't we?" he said loudly, turning to the stranger with a grin that showed his pointed teeth.

40 Aaron gave a brief laugh of acknowledgement.

"How many children have you?" sang Julia from her distance.

"Three."

"Girls or boys?"

"Girls."

"All girls? Dear little things! How old?"

"Oldest eight—youngest nine months—"

"So small!" sang Julia, with real tenderness now—Aaron dropped his head.

"But you're going home to them, aren't you?" said Josephine, in whose eyes the tears had already risen. He looked up at her, at her tears. His face had the same pale perverse smile.

"Not tonight," he said.

"But why? You're wrong!" cried Josephine.

He dropped his head and became oblivious.

"Well!" said Cyril Scott, rising at last with a bored exclamation. "I think I'll retire."

"Will you?" said Julia, also rising. "You'll find your candle outside."

She went out. Scott bade goodnight, and followed her. The four people remained in the room, quite silent. Then Robert rose and began to walk about, agitated.

"Don't you go back to 'em. Have a night out. You stop here tonight," Jim said suddenly, in a quiet, intimate tone.

The stranger turned his head and looked at him, considering.

"Yes?" he said. He seemed to be smiling coldly.

"Oh but!" cried Josephine. "Your wife and your children! Won't they be awfully bothered? Isn't it awfully unkind to them?"

She rose in her eagerness. He sat turning up his face to her. She could not understand his expression.

"Won't you go home to them?" she said, hysterical.

"Not tonight," he replied quietly, again smiling.

"You're wrong!" she cried. "You're wrong!"

And so she hurried out of the room in tears.

"Er—what bed do you propose to put him in?" asked Robert rather officer-like.

"Don't propose at all my lad," replied Jim ironically—he did not like Robert. Then to the stranger he said:

"You'll be all right on the couch in my room?—it's a good couch, big enough, plenty of rugs—" His voice was easy and intimate.

Aaron looked at him, and nodded.

They had another drink each, and at last the two set off, rather stumbling, upstairs. Aaron carried his bowler hat with him.

Robert remained pacing in the drawing-room for some time. Then he went out, to return in a little while. He extinguished the lamps and saw that the fire was safe. Then he went to fasten the window-doors securely. Outside he saw the uncanny glimmer of candles across the lawn. He had half a mind to go out and extinguish them—but he did not. So he went upstairs and the house was quiet. Faint crumbs of snow were falling outside.

When Jim woke in the morning Aaron had gone. Only on the floor were two packets of Christmas-tree candles, fallen from the stranger's pockets. He had gone through the drawing-room door, as he had come. The housemaid said that while she was cleaning the grate in the dining-room she heard someone go into the drawing-room: a parlour-maid had even seen someone come out of Jim's bedroom. But they had both thought it was Jim himself, for he was an unsettled house mate.

There was a thin film of snow, a lovely Christmas morning.

Chapter IV.

The Pillar of Salt*

Our story will not yet see daylight. A few days after Christmas, Aaron
sat in the open shed at the bottom of his own garden, looking out on
the rainy darkness. No one knew he was there. It was some time after   5
six in the evening.

From where he sat, he looked straight up the garden to the house.
The blind was not drawn in the middle kitchen, he could see the
figures of his wife and one child. There was a light also in the
upstairs window. His wife was gone upstairs again. He wondered if   10
she had the baby ill. He could see her figure vaguely behind the lace
curtains of the bedroom. It was like looking at his home through the
wrong end of a telescope. Now the little girls had gone from the
middle room: only to return in a moment.

His attention strayed. He watched the light falling from the   15
window of the next-door house. Uneasily, he looked along the whole
range of houses. The street sloped downhill, and the backs were
open to the fields. So he saw a curious succession of lighted
windows, between which jutted the intermediary back premises,
scullery and outhouse, in dark little blocks. It was something like the   20
keyboard of a piano: more still, like a succession of musical notes.
For the rectangular planes of light were of different intensities, some
bright and keen, some soft, warm, like candle-light, and there was
one surface of pure red light, one or two were almost invisible, dark
green. So the long scale of lights seemed to trill across the dark-   25
ness, now bright, now dim, swelling and sinking. The effect was
strange.

And thus the whole private life of the street was threaded in lights.
There was a sense of indecent exposure, from so many backs. He felt
himself almost in physical contact with this contiguous stretch of   30
back premises. He heard the familiar sound of water gushing from
the sink into the grate, the dropping of a pail outside the door, the
clink of a coal shovel, the banging of a door, the sound of voices. So
many houses cheek by jowl, so many squirming lives, so many back
yards, back doors giving on to the night. It was revolting.   35

Away in the street itself, a boy was calling the newspaper: "—'*ning Post!*—'*ning Po-o-st!*" It was a long, melancholy howl, and seemed to epitomise the whole of the dark, wet, secretive, thickly-inhabited night. A figure passed the window of Aaron's own house, entered,
5 and stood inside the room talking to Mrs. Sisson. It was a young woman in a brown mackintosh and a black hat. She stood under the incandescent light, and her hat nearly knocked the globe. Next door a man had run out in his shirt sleeves: this time a young, dark-headed collier running to the gate for a newspaper, running bare-headed,
10 coat-less, slippered in the rain. He had got his news-sheet, and was returning. And just at that moment the young man's wife came out, shading her candle with a lading tin. She was going to the coal-house for some coal. Her husband passed her on the threshold. She could be heard breaking the bits of coal and placing them on the dustpan.
15 The light from her candle fell faintly behind her. Then she went back, blown by a swirl of wind. But again she was at the door, hastily standing her iron shovel against the wall. Then she shut the back door with a bang. These noises seemed to scrape and strike the night.
20 In Aaron's own house, the young person was still talking to Mrs. Sisson. Millicent came out, sheltering a candle with her hand. The candle blew out. She ran indoors, and emerged again, her white pinafore fluttering. This time she performed her little journey safely. He could see the faint glimmer of her candle emerging secretly from
25 the closet.

The young person was taking her leave. He could hear her sympathetic—"Well—goodnight! I hope she'll be no worse. Goodnight Mrs. Sisson!" She was gone—he heard the windy bang of the street-gate. Presently Millicent emerged again, flitting indoors.
30 So he rose to his feet, balancing, swaying a little before he started into motion, as so many colliers do. Then he moved along the path towards the house, in the rain and darkness, very slowly edging forwards.

Suddenly the door opened. His wife emerged with a pail. He
35 stepped quietly aside, on to his side garden, among the sweet herbs. He could smell rosemary and sage and hyssop. A low wall divided his garden from his neighbour's. He put his hand on it, on its wetness, ready to drop over should his wife come forward. But she only threw the contents of her pail on the garden and retired again. She might
40 have seen him had she looked. He remained standing where he was,

listening to the trickle of rain in the water-butt. The hollow countryside lay beyond him. Sometimes in the windy darkness he could see the red burn of New Brunswick bank, or the brilliant jewels of light clustered at Bestwood Colliery. Away in the dark hollow, nearer, the glare of the electric power-station disturbed the night. So again the wind swirled the rain across all these hieroglyphs of the countryside, familiar to him as his own breast.

A motor-car was labouring up the hill. His trained ear attended to it unconsciously. It stopped with a jar. There was a bang of the yard-gate. A shortish dark figure in a bowler hat passed the window. Millicent was drawing down the blind. It was the doctor. The blind was drawn, he could see no more.

Stealthily he began to approach the house. He stood by the climbing rose of the porch, listening. He heard voices upstairs. Perhaps the children would be downstairs. He listened intently. Voices were upstairs only. He quietly opened the door. The room was empty, save for the baby, who was cooing in her cradle. He crossed to the hall. At the foot of the stairs he could hear the voice of the Indian doctor: "Now little girl, you must just keep still and warm in bed, and not cry for the moon." He said "*de* moon," just as ever.—Marjory must be ill.

So Aaron quietly entered the parlour. It was a cold, clammy room, dark. He could hear footsteps passing outside on the asphalt pavement below the window, and the wind howling with familiar cadence. He began feeling for something in the darkness of the music-rack beside the piano. He touched and felt—he could not find what he wanted. Perplexed, he turned and looked out of the window. Through the iron railing of the front wall he could see the little motor-car sending its straight beams of light in front of it, up the street.

He sat down on the sofa by the window. The energy had suddenly left all his limbs. He sat with his head sunk, listening. The familiar room, the familiar voice of his wife and his children—he felt weak as if he were dying. He felt weak like a drowning man who acquiesces in the waters. His strength was gone, he was sinking back. He would sink back to it all, float henceforth like a drowned man.

So he heard voices coming nearer from upstairs, feet moving. They were coming down.

"No Mrs. Sisson, you needn't worry," he heard the voice of the doctor on the stairs. "If she goes on as she is, she'll be all right. Only she must be kept warm and quiet—warm and quiet—that's the chief thing."

"Oh, when she has those bouts I can't bear it," Aaron heard his wife's voice.

5 They were downstairs. Their feet click-clicked on the tiled passage. They had gone into the middle room. Aaron sat and listened.

"She won't have any more bouts. If she does, give her a few drops from the little bottle, and raise her up. But she won't have any 10 more," the doctor said.

"If she does, I s'll go off my head, I know I shall."

"No you won't. No you won't do anything of the sort. You won't go off your head. You'll keep your head on your shoulders, where it ought to be," protested the doctor.

15 "But it nearly drives me mad."

"Then don't let it. The child won't die, I tell you. She will be all right, with care. Who have you got sitting up with her? You're not to sit up with her tonight, I tell you. Do you hear me?"

"Miss Smitham's coming in. But it's no good—I shall have to sit 20 up. I shall *have* to."

"I tell you you won't. You obey *me*. I know what's good for you as well as for her. I am thinking of you as much as of her."

"But I can't bear it—all alone." This was with the beginning of tears. There was a dead silence—then a sound of Millicent weeping 25 with her mother. As a matter of fact, the doctor was weeping too, for he was an emotional sympathetic soul, over forty.

"Never mind—never mind—you aren't alone," came the doctor's matter-of-fact voice, after a loud nose-blowing. "I am here to help you. I will do whatever I can—whatever I can."

30 "I can't bear it. I can't bear it," wept the woman.

Another silence, another nose-blowing, and again the doctor:

"You'll *have* to bear it—I tell you there's nothing else for it. You'll have to bear it—but we'll do our best for you. I will do my best for you—always—*always*—in sickness or out of sickness—There!"

35 He pronounced *there* oddly, not quite *dhere*.

"You haven't heard from your husband?" he added.

"I had a letter—"—sobs—"from the bank this morning."

"*From de bank?*"

"Telling me they were sending me so much per month, from him, 40 as an allowance, and that he was quite well, but he was travelling."

"Well then, why not let him travel? You can live."

"But to leave me *alone*," there was burning indignation in her voice. "To go off and leave me with every responsibility, to leave me with all the burden."

"Well I wouldn't trouble about him. Aren't you better off without him?" 5

"I am. I am," she cried fiercely. "When I got that letter this morning, I said *May evil befall you, you selfish demon*. And I hope it may."

"Well-well, well-well, don't fret. Don't be angry, it won't make it any better, I tell you." 10

"Angry! I *am* angry. I'm worse than angry. A week ago I hadn't a grey hair in my head. Now look here—" There was a pause.

"Well-well, well-well, never mind. You will be all right, don't you bother. Your hair is beautiful anyhow." 15

"What makes me so mad is that he should go off like that—never a word—coolly takes his hook.* I could kill him for it."

"Were you ever happy together?"

"We were all right at first. I know I was fond of *him*. But he'd kill anything.—He kept himself back, always kept himself back, couldn't 20 give himself—"

There was a pause.

"Ah well," sighed the doctor. "Marriage is a mystery. I'm glad I'm not entangled in it."

"Yes, to make some woman's life a misery.—I'm sure it was death 25 to live with him, he seemed to kill everything off inside you. He was a man you couldn't quarrel with, and get it over. Quiet—quiet in his tempers, and selfish through and through. I've lived with him twelve years—I know what it is. Killing! You don't know what he was—"

"I think I knew him. A fair man? Yes?" said the doctor. 30

"Fair to look at.—There's a photograph of him in the parlour—taken when he was married—and one of me.—Yes, he's fair-haired."

Aaron guessed that she was getting a candle to come into the parlour. He was tempted to wait and meet them—and accept it all 35 again. Devilishly tempted, he was. Then he thought of her voice, and his heart went cold. Quick as thought he obeyed his first impulse. He felt behind the couch, on the floor where the curtains fell. Yes—the bag was there. He took it at once. In the next breath he stepped out of the room and tip-toed into the passage. He retreated to the far end, 40

near the street door, and stood behind the coats that hung on the
hall-stand.

At that moment his wife came into the passage, holding a candle.
She was red-eyed with weeping, and looked frail.

5   "Did *you* leave the parlour door open?" she asked of Millicent,
suspiciously.

"No," said Millicent from the kitchen.

The doctor, with his soft, oriental tread followed Mrs. Sisson into
the parlour. Aaron saw his wife hold up the candle before his

10 portrait, and begin to weep. But he knew her. The doctor laid his
hand softly on her arm, and left it there, sympathetically. Nor did he
remove it when Millicent stole into the room, looking very woe-
begone and important. The wife wept silently, and the child joined
in.

15 "Yes, I know him," said the doctor. "If he thinks he will be
happier when he's gone away, you must be happier too, Mrs. Sisson.
That's all. Don't let him triumph over you by making you miserable.
You enjoy yourself as well. You're only a girl—."

But a tear came from his eye, and he blew his nose vigorously on a

20 large white silk handkerchief, and began to polish his *pince-nez*.
Then he turned, and they all bundled out of the room.

The doctor took his departure. Mrs. Sisson went almost immediately upstairs, and Millicent shortly crept after her. Then Aaron,
who had stood motionless as if turned to a pillar of salt, went quietly

25 down the passage and into the living room. His face was very pale,
ghastly-looking. He caught a glimpse of himself in the mirror over
the mantel, as he passed, and felt weak, as if he were really a
criminal. But his heart did not relax, nevertheless. So he hurried into
the night, down the garden, climbed the fence into the field, and

30 went away across the field in the rain, towards the high-road.

He felt sick in every fibre. He almost hated the little handbag he
carried, which held his flute and piccolo. It seemed a burden just
then—a millstone round his neck. He hated the scene he had
left—and he hated the hard, inviolable heart that stuck unchanging

35 in his own breast.

Coming to the high-road, he saw a tall, luminous tram-car roving
along through the rain. The trams ran across country from town to
town. He dared not board, because people knew him. So he took a
side road, and walked in a detour for two miles. Then he came out on

40 the high-road again, and waited for a tram-car. The rain blew on his
face. He waited a long time for the last car.

Chapter V.

At the Opera

A friend had given Josephine Ford a box at the opera* for one evening: our story continues by night. The box was large and important, near the stage. Josephine and Julia were there, with Robert and Jim—also two more men. The women sat in front of the box, conspicuously. They were both poor, they were rather excited. But they belonged to a set which looked on social triumphs as a downfall that one allows oneself. The two men, Lilly and Struthers, were artists, the former literary, the latter a painter.* Lilly sat by Josephine in front of the box: he was her little lion of the evening.

Few women can sit in front of a big box, on a crowded and full-swing opera night, without thrilling and dilating. There is an intoxication in being thus thrust forward, conspicuous and enhanced, right in the eye of the vast crowd that lines the hollow shell of the auditorium. Thus even Josephine and Julia leaned their elbows and poised their heads regally, looking condescendingly down upon the watchful world. They were two poor women, having nothing to do with society. Half Bohemians.

Josephine was an artist. In Paris she was a friend of a very fashionable dressmaker and decorator, master of modern elegance. Sometimes she designed dresses for him, and sometimes she accepted from him a commission to decorate a room. Usually at her last sou, it gave her pleasure to dispose of costly and exquisite things for other people, and then be rid of them.

This evening her dress was a simple, but a marvellously poised thing of black and silver: in the words of the correct journal. With her tight black, bright hair, her arched brows, her dusky-ruddy face and her bare shoulders; her strange equanimity, her long, slow, slanting looks; she looked foreign and frightening, clear as a cameo, but dark, far-off. Julia was the English beauty, in a lovely blue dress. Her hair was becomingly untidy on her low brow, her dark blue eyes wandered and got excited, her nervous mouth twitched. Her high-pitched, sing-song voice and her hurried laugh could be heard in the theatre. She twisted a beautiful little fan that a dead artist had given her.

45

Not being fashionable, they were in the box when the overture
began. The opera was Verdi—*Aida*.* If it is impossible to be in an
important box at the opera without experiencing the strange intoxication of social pre-eminence, it is just as impossible to be there
5   without some feeling of horror at the sight the stage presents.

Josephine leaned her elbow and looked down: she knew how
arresting that proud, rather stiff bend of her head was. She had some
aboriginal American in her blood. But as she looked, she pursed her
mouth. The artist in her forgot everything, she was filled with
10 disgust. The sham Egypt of *Aida* hid from her nothing of its shame.
The singers were all colour-washed, deliberately colour-washed to a
bright orange tint. The men had oblong dabs of black wool under
their lower lip; the beard of the mighty Pharaohs. This oblong dab
shook and wagged to the singing.

15 The vulgar bodies of the fleshy women were unendurable. They
all looked such good meat. Why were their haunches so prominent?
It was a question Josephine could not solve. She scanned their really
expensive, brilliant clothing. It was *nearly* right—nearly splendid. It
only lacked that last subtlety which the world always lacks, the last
20 final clinching which puts calm into a sea of fabric, and yet is the
opposite pole to machine fixity.

But the leading tenor was the chief pain. He was large, stout,
swathed in a cummerbund, and looked like a eunuch. This fattish,
emasculated look seems common in stage heroes—even the
25 extremely popular. The tenor sang bravely, his mouth made a large
coffin-shaped, yawning gap in his orange face, his little beard
fluttered oddly, like a tail. He turned up his eyes to Josephine's box
as he sang—that being the regulation direction. Meanwhile his
abdomen shook as he caught his breath, the flesh of his fat naked
30 arms swayed.

Josephine looked down with the fixed gravity of a Red Indian,
immovable, inscrutable. It was not till the scene was ended that she
lifted her head as if breaking a spell, sent the point of her tongue
rapidly over her dried lips, and looked round into the box. Her
35 brown eyes expressed shame, fear, and disgust. A curious grimace
went over her face—a grimace only to be expressed by the exclamation *Merde!** But she was mortally afraid of society, and its fixed
institutions. Rapidly she scanned the eyes of her friends in the box.
She rested on the eyes of Lilly, a dark, ugly man.

40 "Isn't it nasty?" she said.

"You shouldn't look so closely," he said. But he took it calmly, easily, whilst she felt floods of burning disgust, a longing to destroy it all.

"Oh-ho-ho!" laughed Julia. "It's so fu-nny—so funny!"

"Of course we are too near," said Robert. 5

"Say you admire that pink fondant over there," said Struthers, indicating with his eyebrows a blonde large woman in white satin with pink edging, who sat in a box opposite, on the upper tier.

"Oh the fondant—exactly—the fondant! Yes, I admire her immensely! Isn't she exactly *it*!" sang Julia. 10

Josephine was scanning the auditorium. So many myriads of faces—like beads on a bead-work pattern—all bead-work, in different layers. She bowed to various acquaintances—mostly Americans in uniform, whom she had known in Paris. She smiled to Lady Cochrane, two boxes off—Lady Cochrane had given her the box. 15
But she felt rather coldly towards her.

The curtain rose, the opera wound its slow length along. The audience loved it. They cheered with mad enthusiasm. Josephine looked down on the choppy sea of applause, white gloves clapping, heads shaking. The noise was strange and rattling. What a curious 20
multiple object a theatre-audience was! It seemed to have a million heads, a million hands, and one monstrous, unnatural consciousness. The singers appeared before the curtain—the applause rose up like clouds of dust.

"Oh, isn't it *too wonderful*!" cried Julia. "I am wild with excite- 25
ment. Are you all of you?"

"Absolutely wild," said Lilly laconically.

"Where is Scott tonight?" asked Struthers.

Julia turned to him and gave him a long, queer look from her dark blue eyes. 30

"He's in the country," she said, rather enigmatic.

"Don't you know, he's got a house down in Dorset," said Robert, verbally rushing in. "He wants Julia to go down and stay."

"Is she going?" said Lilly.

"She hasn't decided," replied Robert. 35

"Oh! What's the objection?" asked Struthers.

"Well, none whatsoever, as far as can be seen, except that she can't make up her mind," replied Robert.

"Julia's got no mind," said Jim rudely.

"Oh! Hear the brotherly verdict!" laughed Julia hurriedly. 40

"You mean go down to Dorset alone?" said Struthers.

"Why not?" replied Robert, answering for her.

"And stay how long?"

"Oh—as long as it lasts," said Robert again.

5   "Starting with eternity," said Lilly, "and working back to a fortnight."

"And what's the matter?—looks bad in the eyes of the world?"

"Yes—about that. Afraid of compromising herself—"

Lilly looked at them.

10   "Depends what you take the world to mean. Do you mean us in this box, or the crew outside there?" he jerked his head towards the auditorium.

"Do you think, Lilly, that we're the world?" said Robert ironically.

15   "Oh yes, I guess we're shipwrecked in this box, like Robinson Crusoes. And what we do on our own little island matters to us alone. As for the infinite crowds of howling savages outside there in the unspeakable, all you've got to do is mind they don't scalp* you."

20   "But *won't* they?" said Struthers.

"Not unless you put your head in their hands," said Lilly.

"I don't know—" said Jim.

But the curtain had risen, they hushed him into silence.

All through the next scene Julia puzzled herself, as to whether she 25 should go down to the country and live with Scott. She had carried on a nervous kind of *amour** with him, based on soul sympathy and emotional excitement. But whether to go and live with him? She didn't know if she wanted to or not: and she couldn't for her life find out. She was in that nervous state when desire seems to evaporate the 30 moment fulfilment is offered.

When the curtain dropped she turned.

"You see," she said, screwing up her eyes, "I have to think of Robert." She cut the word in two, with an odd little hitch in her voice—"*Rob*-ert."

35   "My dear Julia, can't you believe that I'm *tired* of being thought of," cried Robert, flushing.

Julia screwed up her eyes in a slow smile, oddly cogitating.

"Well, who *am* I to think of?" she asked.

"Yourself," said Lilly.

40   "Oh yes! Why yes! I never thought of that!" She gave a hurried

little laugh. "But then it's no *fun* to think about oneself," she cried flatly. "I think about *Rob*-ert and *Scott*." She screwed up her eyes and peered oddly at the company.

"Which of them will find you the greatest treat," said Lilly sarcastically.

"Anyhow," interjected Robert nervously, "it will be something new for Scott."

"Stale buns for you, old boy," said Jim drily.

"I don't say so. But—" exclaimed the flushed, full-blooded Robert, who was nothing if not courteous to women.

"How long ha' you been married? Eh?" asked Jim.

"Six years!" sang Julia sweetly.

"Good God!"

"You see," said Robert, "Julia can't decide anything for herself. She waits for someone else to decide, then she puts her spoke in."

"Put it plainly—" began Struthers.

"But don't you know, it's no *use* putting it plainly," cried Julia.

"But *do* you want to be with Scott, out and out, or *don't* you?" said Lilly.

"Exactly!" chimed Robert.—"That's the question for you to answer Julia."

"I *won't* answer it," she cried. "Why should I?"

And she looked away into the restless hive of the theatre. She spoke so wildly that she attracted attention. But it half pleased her. She stared abstractedly down at the pit.

The men looked at one another in some comic consternation.

"Oh damn it all!" said the long Jim, rising and stretching himself. "She's dead nuts on Scott. She's all over him. She'd have eloped with him weeks ago if it hadn't been so easy. She can't stand it that Robert offers to hand her into the taxi."

He gave his malevolent grin round the company, then went out. He did not re-appear for the next scene.

"Of course, if she loves Scott—" began Struthers.

Julia suddenly turned with wild desperation, and cried:

"I like him tremendously—tre-men-dous-ly! He *does* understand."

"Which we don't," said Robert.

Julia smiled her long, odd smile in their faces: one might almost say she smiled in their teeth.

"What do *you* think, Josephine?" asked Lilly.

Josephine was leaning forward. She started. Her tongue went rapidly over her lips. "Who—? I—?" she exclaimed.

"Yes."

"I think Julia should go with Scott," said Josephine. "She'll
5 bother with the idea till she's done it. She loves him, really."

"Of course she does," cried Robert.

Julia, with her chin resting on her arms, in a position which irritated the neighbouring Lady Cochrane sincerely, was gazing with unseeing eyes down upon the stalls.

10 "Well then—" began Struthers. But the music struck up softly. They were all rather bored. Struthers kept on making small, half audible remarks—which was bad form, and displeased Josephine, the hostess of the evening.

When the curtain came down for the end of the act, the men got
15 up. Lilly's wife Tanny suddenly appeared. She had come on after a dinner engagement.

"Would you like tea or anything?" Lilly asked.

The women refused. The men filtered out on to the crimson and white, curving corridor. Julia, Josephine and Tanny remained in the
20 box. Tanny was soon hitched on to the conversation in hand.

"Of course," she replied, "one can't decide such a thing like drinking a cup of tea."

"Of course one can't, dear Tanny," said Julia.

"After all, one doesn't leave one's husband every day, to go and
25 live with another man. Even if one looks on it as an experiment—"

"It's difficult!" cried Julia. "It's difficult! I feel they all want to *force* me to decide. It's cruel."

"Oh, men with their beastly logic, their either-this-or-that stunt, they are an awful bore.—But of course, Robert can't love you *really*,
30 or he'd want to keep you. I can see Lilly discussing such a thing for *me*. But then you don't love Robert either," said Tanny.

"I do! Oh I do, Tanny! I *do* love him, I love him dearly. I think he's beautiful. Robert's beautiful. And he *needs* me. And I need him too. I need his support. Yes, I do love him."

35 "But you like Scott better," said Tanny.

"Only because he—he's different," sang Julia, in long tones. "You see Scott has his art. His art matters. And *Rob*-ert—Robert is a dilettante, don't you think—he's dilettante—" She screwed up her eyes at Tanny. Tanny cogitated.

40 "Of course I don't think that matters," she replied.

"But it does, it matters tremendously, dear Tanny, tremendously."

"Of course," Tanny sheered off, "I can see Scott has great attractions—a great warmth somewhere—"

"Exactly!" cried Julia. "He *understands*—"

"And I believe he's a real artist. You might even work together. You might write his librettos."

"Yes!—Yes!—" Julia spoke with a long, pondering hiss.

"It might be *awfully* nice," said Tanny rapturously.

"Yes!— It might!—It might—!" pondered Julia. Suddenly she gave herself a shake. Then she laughed hurriedly, as if breaking from her line of thought.

"And wouldn't Robert be an *awfully* nice lover for Josephine! Oh, wouldn't that be splendid!" she cried with her high laugh.

Josephine, who had been gazing down into the orchestra, turned now, flushing darkly.

"But I don't want a lover, Julia," she said, hurt.

"Josephine dear! Dear old Josephine! Don't you really! Oh yes you do.—I want one so *badly*," cried Julia, with her shaking laugh. "Robert's awfully *good* to me. But we've been married six years. And it does make a difference, doesn't it, Tanny dear?"

"A great difference," said Tanny.

"Yes, it makes a difference, it makes a difference," mused Julia. "Dear old Rob-ert—I wouldn't hurt him for worlds. I wouldn't. Do you think it would hurt Robert?"

She screwed up her eyes, looking at Tanny.

"Perhaps it would do Robert good to be hurt a little," said Tanny. "He's so well-nourished."

"Yes!—Yes!—I see what you mean, Tanny!—Poor old *Rob*-ert! Oh, poor old Rob-ert, he's so young!"

"He *does* seem young," said Tanny. "One doesn't forgive it."

"He is young," said Julia. "I'm five years older than he. He's only twenty-seven. Poor old Robert."

"Robert is young, and inexperienced," said Josephine, suddenly turning with anger. "But I don't know why you talk about him."

"Is he inexperienced, Josephine dear? *Is* he?" sang Julia. Josephine flushed darkly, and turned away.

"Ah, he's not so innocent as all that," said Tanny roughly. "Those young young men, who seem so fresh, they're deep enough, really. They're far less innocent really than men who *are* experienced."

"They are, aren't they Tanny," repeated Julia softly. "They're old—older than the Old Man of the Seas, sometimes, aren't they? Incredibly old, like little boys who know too much—aren't they? Yes!" She spoke quietly, seriously, as if it had struck her.

Below, the orchestra was coming in. Josephine was watching closely. Julia became aware of this.

"Do you see anybody we know, Josephine?" she asked.

Josephine started.

"No," she said, looking at her friends quickly and furtively.

"Dear old Josephine, she knows all sorts of people," sang Julia.

At that moment the men returned.

"Have you actually come back!" exclaimed Tanny to them.

They sat down without answering. Jim spread himself as far as he could, in the narrow space. He stared upwards, wrinkling his ugly, queer face. It was evident he was in one of his moods.

"If only somebody loved me!" he complained. "If only somebody loved me I should be all right. I'm going to pieces." He sat up and peered into the faces of the women.

"But we *all* love you," said Josephine, laughing uneasily, "Why aren't you satisfied?"

"I'm not satisfied. I'm not satisfied," murmured Jim.

"Would you like to be wrapped in swaddling bands and laid at the breast?" asked Lilly, disagreeably.

Jim opened his mouth in a grin, and gazed long and malevolently at his questioner.

"Yes," he said. Then he sprawled his long six foot of limb and body across the box again.

"You should try loving somebody, for a change," said Tanny. "You've been loved too often. Why not try and love somebody?"

Jim eyed her narrowly.

"I couldn't love *you*," he said, in vicious tones.

"*À la bonne heure!*"* said Tanny.

But Jim sank his chin on his chest, and repeated obstinately:

"I want to be loved."

"How many times *have* you been loved?" Robert asked him. "It would be rather interesting to know."

Jim looked at Robert long and slow, but did not answer.

"Did you ever keep count?" Tanny persisted.

Jim looked up at her, malevolent.

"I believe I did," he replied.

"Forty is the age when a man should begin to reckon up," said Lilly.

Jim suddenly sprang to his feet, and brandished his fists.

"I'll pitch the lot of you over the bloody rail," he said.

He glared at them, from under his bald, wrinkled forehead. Josephine glanced round. She had become a dusky white colour. She was afraid of him, and she disliked him intensely nowadays.

"Do you recognise anyone in the orchestra?" she asked.

The party in the box had become dead silent. They looked down. The conductor was at his stand. The music began. They all remained silent and motionless during the next scene, each thinking his own thoughts. Jim was uncomfortable. He wanted to make good. He sat with his elbows on his knees, grinning slightly, looking down. At the next interval he stood up suddenly.

"It *is* the chap—What?" he exclaimed excitedly, looking round at his friends.

"Who?" said Tanny.

"It *is* he?" said Josephine quietly, meeting Jim's eye.

"Sure!" he barked.

He was leaning forward over the ledge, rattling a programme in his hand, as if trying to attract attention. Then he made signals.

"There you are!" he exclaimed triumphantly. "That's the chap."

"Who? Who?" they cried.

But neither Jim nor Josephine would vouchsafe an answer.

The next was the long interval. Jim and Josephine gazed down at the orchestra. The musicians were laying aside their instruments and rising. The ugly fire-curtain began slowly to descend. Jim suddenly bolted out.

"Is it that man Aaron Sisson?" asked Robert.

"Where? Where?" cried Julia. "It can't be."

But Josephine's face was closed and silent. She did not answer.

The whole party moved out on to the crimson-carpeted gangways. Groups of people stood about chatting, men and women were passing along, to pay visits or to find drinks. Josephine's party stared around, talking desultorily. And at length they perceived Jim stalking along, leading Aaron Sisson by the arm. Jim was grinning, the flautist looked unwilling. He had a comely appearance, in his white shirt—a certain comely blondness and repose. And as much a gentleman as anybody.

"Well!" cried Josephine to him. "How do you come here?"

"I play the flute," he answered, as he shook hands.

The little crowd stood in the gangway and talked.

"How wonderful of you to be here!" cried Julia.

He laughed.

"Do you think so?" he answered.

"Yes, I do.—It seems so *far* from Shottle House and Christmas Eve.—Oh, wasn't it exciting!" cried Julia.

Aaron looked at her, but did not answer.

"We've heard all about you," said Tanny playfully.

"Oh yes," he replied.

"Come!" said Josephine, rather irritated. "We crowd up the gangway." And she led the way inside the box.

Aaron stood and looked down at the dishevelled theatre.

"You get all the view," he said.

"We do, don't we!" cried Julia.

"More than's good for us," said Lilly.

"Tell us what you are doing. You've got a permanent job?" asked Josephine.

"Yes—at present."

"Ah! It's more interesting for you than at Beldover."

She had taken her seat. He looked down at her dusky young face. Her voice was always clear and measured.

"It's a change," he said, smiling.

"Oh, it must be more than that," she said. "Why, you must feel a whole difference. It's a whole new life."

He smiled, as if he were laughing at her silently. She flushed.

"But isn't it?" she persisted.

"Yes. It can be," he replied.

He looked as if he were quietly amused, but dissociated. None of the people in the box were quite real to him. He was not really amused. Julia found him dull, stupid. Tanny also was offended that he could not *perceive* her. The men remained practically silent.

"You're a chap I always hoped would turn up again," said Jim.

"Oh yes!" replied Aaron, smiling as if amused.

"But perhaps he doesn't like us! Perhaps he's not glad that *we've* turned up," said Julia, leaving her sting.

The flautist turned and looked at her.

"You can't *remember* us, can you?" she asked.

"Yes," he said. "I can remember you."

"Oh," she laughed. "You *are* unflattering."

He was annoyed. He did not know what she was getting at.

"How are your wife and children?" she asked spitefully.

"All right, I think."

"But you've been back to them?" cried Josephine in dismay.

He looked at her, a slow, half-smiling look, but did not speak. 5

"Come an' have a drink. Damn the women," said Jim uncouthly, seizing Aaron by the arm and dragging him off.

Chapter VI.

Talk*

The party stayed to the end of the interminable opera. They had agreed to wait for Aaron. He was to come around to the vestibule for them, after the show. They trooped slowly downstairs into the crush of the entrance hall. Chattering, swirling people, red carpet, palms green against cream-and-gilt walls, small whirlpools of life at the open, dark doorways, men in opera hats steering decisively about—it was the old scene. But there were no taxis—absolutely no taxis. And it was raining. Fortunately the women had brought shoes. They slipped these on. Jim rocked through the crowd, in his tall hat, looking for the flautist.

At last Aaron was found—wearing a bowler hat. Julia groaned in spirit. Josephine's brow knitted. Not that anybody cared, really. But as one must frown at something, why not at the bowler hat?* Acquaintances and elegant young men in uniforms insisted on rushing up and bowing and exchanging a few words, either with Josephine, or Jim, or Julia, or Lilly. They were coldly received. The party veered out into the night.

The women hugged their wraps about them, and set off sharply, feeling some repugnance for the wet pavements and the crowd. They had not far to go—only to Jim's rooms in Adelphi. Jim was leading Aaron, holding him by the arm and slightly pinching his muscles. It gave him great satisfaction to have between his fingers the arm-muscles of a working-man, one of the common people, the *fons et origo** of modern life. Jim was talking rather vaguely about Labour and Robert Smillie, and Bolshevism.* He was all for revolution and the triumph of Labour.

So they arrived, mounted a dark stair, and entered a large, handsome room, one of the Adams rooms. Jim had furnished it from Heal's* with striped hangings, green and white and yellow and dark purple, and with a green-and-black checked carpet, and great stripe-covered chairs and chesterfield. A big gas-fire was soon glowing in the handsome old fire-place, the panelled room seemed cosy.

56

While Jim was handing round drinks and sandwiches, and Josephine was making tea, Robert played Bach on the piano—the pianola, rather. The chairs and lounge were in a half-circle round the fire. The party threw off their wraps and sank deep into this expensive comfort of modern Bohemia. They needed the Bach to take away the bad taste that *Aida* had left in their mouths. They needed the whiskey and curaçao to rouse their spirits. They needed the profound comfort in which to sink away from the world. All the men, except Aaron, had been through the war in some way or other. But here they were, in the old setting exactly, the old bohemian routine.

The bell rang, Jim went downstairs. He returned shortly with a frail, elegant woman—fashionable rather than bohemian. She was cream and auburn, Irish, with a slightly-lifted upper lip that gave her a pathetic look. She dropped her wrap and sat down by Julia, taking her hand delicately.

"How are you, darling?" she asked.

"Yes—I'm happy," said Julia, giving her odd, screwed-up smile.

The pianola stopped, they all chatted indiscriminately. Jim was watching the new-comer—Mrs. Browning*—with a concentrated wolfish grin.

"I like her," he said at last. "I've seen her before, haven't I?—I like her awfully."

"Yes," said Josephine, with a slight grunt of a laugh. "He wants to be loved."

"Oh," cried Clariss. "So do I!"

"Then there you are!" cried Tanny.

"Alas no, there we aren't," cried Clariss. She was beautiful too, with her lifted upper lip. "We both want to be loved, and so we miss each other entirely. We run on in two parallel lines, that can never meet." She laughed low and half sad.

"Doesn't *she* love you?" said Aaron to Jim amused, indicating Josephine. "I thought you were engaged."

"*Her!*" leered Jim vindictively, glancing at Josephine. "*She* doesn't love me."

"Is that true?" asked Robert hastily, of Josephine.

"Why," she said, "yes. Why should he make me say out here that I don't love him!"

"Got you my girl," said Jim.

"Then it's no engagement?" said Robert.

"Listen to the row fools make, rushing in,"* said Jim maliciously.

"No, the engagement is broken," said Josephine.

"World coming to pieces bit by bit," said Lilly. Jim was twisting in his chair, and looking like a Chinese dragon, diabolical. The room
5 was uneasy.

"What gives you such a belly-ache for love, Jim?" said Lilly, "or for being loved? Why do you want so badly to be loved?"

"Because I like it, damn you," barked Jim. "Because I'm in need of it."

10 None of them quite knew whether they ought to take it as a joke. It was just a bit too real to be quite pleasant.

"Why are you such a baby?" said Lilly. "There you are, six foot in length, have been a cavalry officer and fought in two wars, and you spend your time crying for somebody to love you. You're a
15 comic."

"Am I though," said Jim. "I'm losing life. I'm getting thin."

"You don't look as if you were losing life," said Lilly.

"Don't I? I am though. I'm dying."

"What of? Lack of life?"

20 "That's about it, my young cock. Life's leaving me."

"Better sing Tosti's 'Farewell'* to it."

Jim who had been sprawling full length in his arm-chair, the centre of interest of all the company, suddenly sprang forward and pushed his face, grinning, in the face of Lilly.

25 "You're a funny customer, you are," he said.

Then he turned round in his chair, and saw Clariss sitting at the feet of Julia, with one white arm over her friend's knee. Jim immediately stuck forward his muzzle and gazed at her. Clariss had loosened her masses of thick, auburn hair, so that it hung half free.
30 Her face was creamy pale, her upper lip lifted with odd pathos! She had rose-rubies in her ears.

"I like *her*," said Jim. "What's her name?"

"Mrs. Browning. Don't be so rude," said Josephine.

"Browning for gravies. Any relation of Robert?"

35 "Oh yes! You ask my husband," come the slow, plangent voice of Clariss.

"You've got a husband, have you?"

"Rather! Haven't I, Juley?"

"Yes," said Julia, vaguely and wispily. "Yes dear, you have."

40 "And two fine children," put in Robert.

"No! You don't mean it!" said Jim. "Who's your husband? Anybody?"

"Rather!" came the deep voice of Clariss. "He sees to that."

Jim stared, grinning, showing his pointed teeth, reaching nearer and nearer to Clariss who, in her frail scrap of an evening dress, 5 amethyst and silver, was sitting still in the deep black hearth-rug, her arm over Julia's knee, taking very little notice of Jim, although he amused her.

"I like you awfully, I say," he repeated.

"Thanks, I'm sure," she said. 10

The others were laughing, sprawling in their chairs, and sipping curaçao and taking a sandwich or a cigarette. Aaron Sisson alone sat upright smiling flickeringly. Josephine watched him, and her pointed tongue went from time to time over her lips.

"But I'm sure," she broke in, "this isn't very interesting for the 15 others. Awfully boring! Don't be silly all the time, Jim, or we must go home."

Jim looked at her with narrowed eyes. He hated her voice. She let her eye rest on his for a moment. Then she put her cigarette to her lips. Robert was watching them both. 20

Josephine took her cigarette from her lips again.

"Tell us about yourself, Mr. Sisson," she said. "How do you like being in London?"

"I like London," said Aaron.

Where did he live? Bloomsbury.* Did he know many people? 25 No—nobody except a man in the orchestra. How had he got his job? Through an agent. Etc. Etc.

"What do you make of the miners?" said Jim, suddenly taking a new line.

"Me?" said Sisson. "I don't make anything of them." 30

"Do you think they'll make a stand against the government?"

"What for?"

"Nationalisation."

"They might, one day."

"Think they'd fight?" 35

"Fight?"

"Yes."

Aaron sat laughing.

"What have they to fight for?"

"Why everything! What haven't they to fight for?" cried Josephine 40 fiercely. "Freedom, liberty, an escape from this vile system. Won't they fight for that?"

Aaron sat smiling, slowly shaking his head.

"Nay," he said, "you mustn't ask me what they'll do—I've only just left them, for good. They'll do a lot of cavilling."

"But won't they *act?*" cried Josephine.

"Act?" said Aaron. "How, act?"

"Why, defy the government, and take things in their own hands," said Josephine.

"They might, some time," said Aaron, rather indifferent.

"I wish they would!" cried Josephine. "My, wouldn't I love it if they'd make a bloody revolution!"

They were all looking now at her. Her black brows were twitching, in her black and silver dress she looked like a symbol of young disaster.

"Must it be bloody, Josephine?" said Robert.

"Why yes. I don't believe in revolutions that aren't bloody," said Josephine. "Wouldn't I love it! I'd go in front with a red flag."

"It would be rather fun," said Tanny.

"Wouldn't it!" cried Josephine.

"Oh Josey, dear!" cried Julia hysterically. "Isn't she a red-hot Bolsher! *I* should be frightened."

"No!" cried Josephine. "I should love it."

"So should I," said Jim, in a luscious sort of voice. "What price* machine guns at the end of the Strand! That's a day to live for, what?"

"Ha! Ha!" laughed Clariss, with her deep laugh. "We'd all Bolsh together. I'd give the cheers."

"I wouldn't mind getting killed. I'd love it, in a real fight," said Josephine.

"But Josephine," said Robert, "don't you think we've had enough of that sort of thing in the war? Don't you think it all works out rather stupid and unsatisfying?"

"Ah but a civil war would be different. I've no interest in fighting Germans. But a civil war would be different."

"That's a fact, it would," said Jim.

"Only rather worse," said Robert.

"No, I don't agree," cried Josephine. "You'd feel you were doing something, in a civil war."

"Pulling the house down," said Lilly.

"Yes," she cried. "Don't you hate it, the house we live in—London—England—America! Don't you hate them?"

"I don't like them. But I can't get much fire in my hatred. They pall on me rather," said Lilly.

"Ay!" said Aaron, suddenly stirring in his chair.

Lilly and he glanced at one another with a look of recognition.

"Still," said Tanny, "there's got to be a clearance some day or other."

"Oh," drawled Clariss. "I'm all for a clearance. I'm all for pulling the house down. Only while it stands I do want central heating and a good cook."

"May I come to dinner?" said Jim.

"Oh yes. You'd find it rather domestic."

"Where do you live?"

"Rather far out now—Amersham."*

"Amersham? Where's that—?"

"Oh it's on the map."

There was a little lull. Jim gulped down a drink, standing at the side-board. He was a tall, fine, soldierly figure, and his face, with its little sandy moustache and bald forehead, was odd. Aaron Sisson sat watching him, unconsciously.

"Hello you!" said Jim. "Have one?"

Aaron shook his head, and Jim did not press him. It saved the drinks.

"You believe in love, don't you?" said Jim sitting down near Aaron, and grinning at him.

"Love!" said Aaron.

"*Love!* he says," mocked Jim, grinning at the company.

"What about it, then?" asked Aaron.

"It's life! Love is life," said Jim fiercely.

"It's a vice, like drink," said Lilly.

"Eh? A vice!" said Jim. "May be for you, old bird."

"More so still for you," said Lilly.

"It's life. It's life!" reiterated Jim. "Don't you agree?" He turned wolfishly to Clariss.

"Oh yes—every time—" she drawled nonchalant.

"Here, let's write it down," said Lilly. He found a blue pencil and printed in large letters on the old creamy marble of the mantel-piece panel:—LOVE IS LIFE.

Julia suddenly rose and flung her arms asunder wildly.

"Oh, I hate love. I hate it," she protested.

Jim watched her sardonically.

"Look at her!" he said. "Look at Lesbia who hates love."

"No, but perhaps it is a disease. Perhaps we are all wrong, and we
5 can't love properly," put in Josephine.

"Have another try," said Jim.—"I know what love is. I've thought
about it. Love is the soul's respiration."

"Let's have that down," said Lilly.

LOVE IS THE SOUL'S RESPIRATION. He printed it on the
10 old mantel-piece.

Jim eyed the letters.

"It's right," he said. "Quite right. When you love, your soul
breathes in. If you don't breath in, you suffocate."

"What about breathing out?" said Robert. "If you don't breathe
15 out, you asphyxiate."

"Right you are, Mock Turtle—"* said Jim maliciously.

"Breathing out is a bloody revolution," said Lilly.

"You've hit the nail on the head," said Jim solemnly.

"Let's record it then," said Lilly. And with the blue pencil he
20 printed:—

WHEN YOU LOVE, YOUR SOUL BREATHES IN

And then on the next line.

WHEN YOUR SOUL BREATHES OUT, IT'S A BLOODY
REVOLUTION.

25 "I say Jim," he said. "You must be busting yourself, trying to
breathe in."

"Don't you be too clever. I've thought about it," said Jim. "When
I'm in love, I get a great inrush of energy. I actually feel it rush
in—here!" He poked his finger on the pit of his stomach. "It's the
30 soul's expansion. And if I can't get these rushes of energy, I'M
DYING, AND I KNOW I AM."

He spoke the last words with sudden ferocity and desperation.

"All *I* know is," said Tanny, "you don't look it."

"I *am*. I *am*," Jim protested. "I'm dying. Life's leaving me."

35 "Maybe you're choking with love," said Robert. "Perhaps you
have breathed in so much, you don't know how to let it go again.
Perhaps your soul's got a crick in it, with expanding so much."

"You're a bloody young sucking pig, you are," said Jim.

"Even at that age, I've learned my manners," replied Robert.

40 Jim looked round the party. Then he turned to Aaron Sisson.

"What do you make of 'em, eh?" he said.

Aaron shook his head, and laughed.

"Me?" he said.

But Jim did not wait for an answer.

"I've had enough," said Tanny, suddenly rising. "I think you're all silly. Besides, it's getting late."

"She!" said Jim, rising and pointing luridly to Clariss. "She's Love. And *he's* the working people. The hope is in these two—" He jerked a thumb at Aaron Sisson, after having indicated Mrs. Browning.

"Oh how awfully interesting. It's quite a long time since I've been a personification.—I suppose you've never been one before?" said Clariss, turning to Aaron in conclusion.

"No, I don't think I have," he answered.

"I hope personification is right—Ought it to be *allegory* or something else?" This from Clariss to Robert.

"Or a parable, Clariss," laughed the young lieutenant.

"Goodbye," said Tanny. "I've been awfully bored."

"Have you?" grinned Jim. "Goodbye! Better luck next time."

"We'd better look sharp," said Robert, "if we want to get the tube."

The party hurried through the rainy narrow streets down to the Embankment station. Robert and Julia and Clariss were going west, Lilly and his wife Tanny were going to Hampstead, Josephine and Aaron Sisson were going both to Bloomsbury.

"I suppose," said Robert, on the stairs—"Mr. Sisson will see you to your door, Josephine. He lives your way."

"There's no need at all," said Josephine.

The four who were going north went down to the low tube level. It was nearly the last train. The station was half deserted, half rowdy, several fellows were drunk, shouting and crowing. Down there in the bowels of London, after midnight, everything seemed horrible and unnatural.

"How I hate this London," said Tanny. She was half Norwegian, and had spent a large part of her life in Norway, before she married Lilly.

"Yes, so do I," said Josephine. "But if one must earn one's living one must stay here. I wish I could get back to Paris. But there's nothing doing for me in France.—When do you go back into the country, both of you?"

"Friday," said Lilly.

"How lovely for you!—And when will you go to Norway, Tanny?"

"In about a month," said Tanny.

"You must be awfully pleased."

"Oh—thankful—*thankful* to get out of England—"

"I know. That's how I feel. Everything is so awful—so dismal and dreary, I find it—"

They crowded into the train. Men were still yelling like wild beasts—others were asleep—soldiers were singing.

"Have you really broken your engagement with Jim?" shrilled Tanny in a high voice, as the train roared.

"Yes, he's impossible," said Josephine. "Perfectly hysterical and impossible."

"And *selfish*—" cried Tanny.

"Oh terribly—" cried Josephine.

"Come up to Hampstead to lunch with us," said Lilly to Aaron.

"Ay—thank you," said Aaron.

Lilly scribbled directions on a card. The hot, jaded, midnight underground rattled on. Aaron and Josephine got down to change trains.

Chapter VII.

The Dark Square Garden

Josephine had invited Aaron Sisson to dinner at a restaurant in Soho,* one Sunday evening. They had a corner to themselves, and with a bottle of burgundy she was getting his history from him.

His father had been a shaft-sinker, earning good money, but had been killed by a fall down the shaft when Aaron was only four years old. The widow had opened a shop: Aaron was her only child. She had done well in her shop. She had wanted Aaron to be a schoolteacher. He had served three years apprenticeship, then suddenly thrown it up and gone to the pit.

"But why?" said Josephine.

"I couldn't tell you. I felt more like it."

He had a curious quality of an intelligent, almost sophisticated mind, which had repudiated education. On purpose he kept the midland accent in his speech. He understood perfectly what a personification was—and an allegory. But he preferred to be illiterate.

Josephine found out what a miner's checkweighman was. She tried to find out what sort of wife Aaron had—but, except that she was the daughter of a publican and was delicate in health, she could learn nothing.

"And do you send her money!" she asked.

"Ay," said Aaron. "The house is mine. And I allow her so much a week out of the money in the bank. My mother left me a bit over a thousand when she died."

"You don't mind what I say, do you?" said Josephine.

"No, I don't mind," he laughed.

He had this pleasant-seeming courteous manner. But he really kept her at a distance. In some things he reminded her of Robert: blond, erect, nicely built, fresh and English-seeming. But there was a curious cold distance to him, which she could not get across. An inward indifference to her—perhaps to everything. Yet his laugh was so handsome.

"Will you tell me why you left your wife and children?—Didn't you love them?"

65

Aaron looked at the odd, round, dark muzzle of the girl. She had had her hair bobbed, and it hung in odd dark folds, very black, over her ears.

"Why I left her?" he said. "For no particular reason. They're all right without me."

Josephine watched his face. She saw a pallor of suffering under its freshness, and a strange tension in his eyes.

"But you couldn't leave your little girls for no reason at all—"

"Yes, I did. For no reason—except I wanted to have some free room round me—to loose myself—"

"You mean you wanted love?" flashed Josephine, thinking he said *lose*.

"No, I wanted fresh air. I don't know what I wanted. Why should I know?"

"But we must know: especially when other people will be hurt," said she.

"Ah well! A breath of fresh air, by myself. I felt forced to feel—I feel if I go back home now, I shall be *forced*—forced to love—or care—or something."

"Perhaps you wanted more than your wife could give you," she said.

"Perhaps less. She's made up her mind she loves me, and she's not going to let me off."

"Did you never love her?" said Josephine.

"Oh yes. I shall never love anybody else. But I'm damned if I want to be a lover any more. To her or to anybody. That's the top and bottom of it. I don't want to *care*, when care isn't in me. And I'm not going to be forced to it."

The fat, aproned French waiter was hovering near. Josephine let him remove the plates and the empty bottle.

"Have more wine," she said to Aaron. "Do?"

But he refused. She liked him because of his dead-level indifference to his surroundings. French waiters and foreign food—he noticed them in his quick, amiable-looking fashion—but he was indifferent. Josephine was piqued. She wanted to pierce this amiable aloofness of his.

She ordered coffee and brandies.

"But you don't want to get away from *everything*, do you? I myself feel so *lost* sometimes—so dreadfully alone: not in a silly sentimental fashion, because men keep telling me they love me, don't you know. But my *life* seems alone, for some reason—"

"Haven't you got relations?" he said.

"No one, now mother is dead. Nothing nearer than aunts and cousins in America. I suppose I shall see them all again one day. But they hardly count over here."

"Why don't you get married?" he said. "How old are you?"

"I'm twenty-five. How old are you?"

"Thirty-three."

"You might almost be any age.—I don't know why I don't get married. In a way, I hate earning my own living—yet I go on—and I like my work—"

"What are you doing now?"

"I'm painting scenery for a new play—rather fun—I enjoy it. But I often wonder what will become of me."

"In what way?"

She was almost affronted.

"What becomes of me? Oh, I don't know. And it doesn't matter, not to anybody but myself."

"What becomes of anybody, anyhow? We live till we die. What do you want?"

"Why, I keep saying I want to get married and feel sure of something. But I don't know—I feel dreadful sometimes—as if every minute would be the last. I keep going on and on—I don't know what for—and *it* keeps going on and on—goodness knows what it's all for."

"You shouldn't bother yourself," he said. "You should just let it go on and on—"

"But I *must* bother," she said. "I must think and feel—"

"You've no occasion," he said.

"How—?" she said, with a sudden grunting, unhappy laugh. Then she lit a cigarette.

"No," she said. "What I should really like more than anything would be an end of the world. I wish the world would come to an end."

He laughed, and poured his drops of brandy down his throat.

"It won't, for wishing," he said.

"No, that's the awful part of it. It'll just go on and on.—Doesn't it make you feel you'd go mad?"

He looked at her, and shook his head.

"You see it doesn't concern me," he said. "So long as I can float by myself."

"But *are* you *satisfied*!" she cried.

"I like being by myself—I hate feeling and caring, and being forced into it. I want to be left alone—"

"You aren't very polite to your hostess of the evening," she said, laughing a bit miserably.

5   "Oh, we're all right," he said. "You know what I mean—"

"You like your own company? Do you?—Sometimes I think I'm nothing when I'm alone. Sometimes I think I surely must be nothing—nothingness."

He shook his head.

10   "No," he said. "No. I only want to be left alone."

"Not to have anything to do with anybody?" she queried ironically.

"Not to any extent."

She watched him—and then she bubbled with a laugh.

"I think you're funny," she said. "You don't mind?"

15   "No—why—It's just as you see it.—Jim Bricknell's a rare comic, to my eye."

"Oh him!—no, not actually. He's self-conscious and selfish and hysterical. It isn't a bit funny after a while."

"I only know what I've seen," said Aaron. "You'd both of you like

20 a bloody revolution, though."

"Yes. Only when it came he wouldn't be there."

"Would you?"

"Yes, indeed I would. I would give everything to be in it. I'd give heaven and earth for a great big upheaval—and then darkness."

25   "Perhaps you'll get it, when you die," said Aaron.

"Oh, but I don't want to die and leave all this standing. I hate it so."

"Why do you?"

"But don't you?"

30   "No, it doesn't really bother me."

"It makes me feel I can't live."

"I can't see that."

"But you always disagree with one!" said Josephine. "How do you like Lilly? What do you think of him?—"

35   "He seems sharp," said Aaron.

"But he's more than sharp."

"Oh yes! He's got his finger in most pies."

"And doesn't like the plums in any of them," said Josephine tartly.

"What does he do?"

40   "Writes—stories and plays."

"And makes it pay?"

"Hardly at all.—They want us to go. Shall we?"

She rose from the table. The waiter handed her her cloak, and they went out into the blowy dark night. She folded her wrap round her, and hurried forward, with short, sharp steps. There was a certain Parisian *chic* and mincingness about her, even in her walk: but underneath, a striding, savage suggestion, as if she could leg it in great strides, like some savage squaw.

Aaron pressed his bowler hat down on his brow.

"Would you rather take a bus?" she said in a high voice, because of the wind.

"I'd rather walk."

"So would I."

They hurried across the Charing Cross Road, where great buses rolled and rocked, crammed with people. Her heels clicked sharply on the pavement, as they walked east. They crossed Holborn, and passed the Museum. And neither of them said anything.

When they came to the corner, she held out her hand.

"Look!" she said. "Don't come any further: don't trouble."

"I'll walk round with you: unless you'd rather not."

"No—But do you want to bother?"

"It's no bother."

So they pursued their way through the high wind, and turned at last into the old, beautiful square. It seemed dark and deserted, dark like a savage wilderness in the heart of London. The wind was roaring in the great bare trees of the centre, as if it were some wild dark grove deep in a forgotten land.

Josephine opened the gate of the Square garden with her key, and let it slam to behind him.

"How wonderful the wind is!" she shrilled. "Shall we listen to it for a minute?"

She led him across the grass past the shrubs to the big tree in the centre. There she climbed up to a seat. He sat beside her. They sat in silence, looking at the darkness. Rain was blowing in the wind. They huddled against the big tree-trunk, for shelter, and watched the scene.

Beyond the tall shrubs and the high, heavy railings the wet street gleamed silently. The houses of the Square rose like a cliff on this inner dark sea, dimly lighted at occasional windows. Boughs swayed and sang. A taxi-cab swirled round a corner like a cat, and purred to a standstill. There was a light of an open hall door. But all far away, it seemed, unthinkably far away. Aaron sat still and watched. He was frightened, it all seemed so sinister, this dark, bristling heart of London. Wind boomed and tore like waves ripping a shingle beach. The two white lights of the taxi stared round and departed, leaving the coast at the foot of the cliffs deserted, faintly spilled with light from the high lamp. Beyond there, on the outer rim, a policeman passed solidly.

Josephine was weeping steadily all the time, but inaudibly. Occasionally she blew her nose and wiped her face. But he had not realised. She hardly realised herself. She sat near the strange man. He seemed so still and remote—so fascinating.

"Give me your hand," she said to him, subduedly.

He took her cold hand in his warm, living grasp. She wept more bitterly. He noticed at last.

"Why are you crying?" he said.

"I don't know," she replied, rather matter-of-fact, through her tears.

So he let her cry, and said no more, but sat with her cold hand in his warm, easy clasp.

"You'll think me a fool," she said. "I don't know why I cry."

"You can cry for nothing, can't you?" he said.

"Why yes, but it's not very sensible."

He laughed shortly.

"Sensible!" he said.

"You are a strange man," she said.

But he took no notice.

"Did you ever intend to marry Jim Bricknell?" he asked.

"Yes, of course."

"I can't imagine it," he said.

"Why not?"

Both were watching blankly the roaring night of mid-London, the phantasmagoric old Bloomsbury Square. They were still hand in hand.

"Such as you shouldn't marry," he said.

"But why not? I want to."

"You think you do."

"Yes indeed I do."

He did not say any more.

"Why shouldn't I?" she persisted.

"I don't know—"

And again he was silent.

"You've known some life, haven't you?" he asked.

"Me? Why?"

"You seem to."

"Do I? I'm sorry. Do I seem vicious?—No, I'm not vicious.—I've seen some life, perhaps—in Paris mostly. But not much. Why do you ask?"

"I wasn't thinking."

"But what do you mean? What *are* you thinking?"

"Nothing. Nothing."

"Don't be so irritating," said she.

But he did not answer, and she became silent also. They sat hand in hand.

"Won't you kiss me?" came her voice out of the darkness.

He waited some moments, then his voice sounded gently, half mocking, half reproachful.

"Nay!" he said.

"Why not?"

"I don't want to."

"Why not?" she asked.

He laughed, but did not reply.

She sat perfectly still for some time. She had ceased to cry. In the darkness her face was set and sullen. Sometimes a spray of rain blew across it. She drew her hand from his, and rose to her feet.

"I'll go in now," she said.

"You're not offended, are you?" he asked.

"No. Why?"

They stepped down in the darkness from their perch.

"I wondered."

She strode off for some little way. Then she turned and said:

"Yes, I think it is rather insulting."

"Nay," he said. "Not it! Not it!"

And he followed her to the gate.

She opened with her key, and they crossed the road to her door.

"Goodnight," she said, turning and giving him her hand.

"You'll come and have dinner with me—or lunch—will you? When shall we make it?" he asked.

"Well, I can't say for certain. I'm very busy just now. I'll let you know."

A policeman shed his light on the pair of them as they stood on the step.

"All right," said Aaron, dropping back, and she hastily opened the big door, and entered.

Chapter VIII.

A Punch in the Wind*

The Lillys had a labourer's cottage in Hampshire*—pleasant enough. They were poor. Lilly was a little, dark, thin, quick fellow, his wife a fine blonde.* They had known Robert and Julia for some years, but Josephine and Jim were new acquaintances,—fairly new.

One day in early spring Lilly had a telegram, "Coming to see you arrive 4.30—Bricknell." He was surprised, but he and his wife got the spare room ready. And at four o'clock Lilly went off to the station. He was a few minutes late, and saw Jim's tall, rather elegant figure stalking down the station path. Jim had been an officer in the regular army, and still spent hours with his tailor. But instead of being a soldier he was a sort of socialist, and a red-hot revolutionary of a very ineffectual sort.

"Good lad!" he exclaimed, as Lilly came up. "Thought you wouldn't mind."

"Not at all. Let me carry your bag."

Jim had a bag and a knapsack.

"I had an inspiration this morning," said Jim. "I suddenly saw that if there was a man in England who could save me, it was you."

"Save you from what?" asked Lilly, rather abashed.

"Eh—?" and Jim stooped grinning at the smaller man.

Lilly was somewhat puzzled, but he had a certain belief in himself as a saviour. The two men tramped rather incongruously through the lanes to the cottage.

Tanny was in the doorway as they came up the garden path.

"So nice to see you! Are you all right?" she said.

"A.1." said Jim, grinning. "Nice of you to have me."

"Oh we're awfully pleased."

Jim dropped his knapsack on the broad sofa.

"I've brought some food," he said.

"Have you! That's sensible of you. We can't get a great deal here, except just at week-ends," said Tanny.

Jim fished out a pound of sausages and a pot of fish paste.

"How lovely the sausages," said Tanny. "We'll have them for

dinner tonight—and we'll have the other for tea now. You'd like a wash?"

But Jim had already opened his bag, taken off his coat, and put on an old one.

5   "Thanks," he said.

Lilly made the tea, and at length all sat down.

"Well how unexpected this is—and how nice," said Tanny.

"Jolly—eh?" said Jim.

He ate rapidly, stuffing his mouth too full.

10   "How is everybody?" asked Tanny.

"All right. Julia's gone with Cyril Scott. Can't stand that fellow, can you? What?"

"Yes, I think he's rather nice," said Tanny. "What will Robert do?"

15   "Have a shot at Josephine, apparently."

"Really? Is he in love with her? I thought so. And she likes him too, doesn't she?" said Tanny.

"Very likely," said Jim.

"I suppose you're jealous," laughed Tanny.

20   "Me!" Jim shook his head. "Not a bit. Like to see the ball kept rolling."

"What have you been doing lately?"

"Been staying a few days with my wife."

"No really! I can't believe it."

25   Jim had a French wife, who had divorced him, and two children. Now he was paying visits to this wife again: purely friendly. Tanny did most of the talking. Jim excited her, with his way of looking in her face and grinning wolfishly, and at the same time asking to be saved.

After tea he wanted to send telegrams, so Lilly took him round to
30   the village postoffice. Telegrams were a necessary part of his life. He had to be suddenly starting off to keep sudden appointments, or he felt he was a void in the atmosphere. He talked to Lilly about social reform, and so on. Jim's work in town was merely nominal. He spent his time wavering about and going to various meetings, philandering
35   and weeping.

Lilly kept in the back of his mind the Saving which James had come to look for. He intended to do his best. After dinner the three sat cosily round the kitchen fire.

"But what do you really think will happen to the world?" Lilly
40   asked Jim, amid much talk.

"What? There's something big coming," said Jim.

"Where from?"

"Watch Ireland, and watch Japan—they're the two poles of the world," said Jim.

"I thought Russia and America," said Lilly.

"Eh? What? Russia and America! They'll depend on Ireland and Japan. I know it. I've had a vision of it. Ireland on this side and Japan on the other—they'll settle it."

"I don't see how," said Lilly.

"*I* don't see *how*—But I had a vision of it."

"What sort of vision?"

"Couldn't describe it."

"But you don't think much of the Japanese, do you?" asked Lilly.

"Don't I! Don't I!" said Jim. "What, don't you think they're wonderful?"

"No. I think they're rather unpleasant."

"I think the salvation of the world lies with them."

"Funny salvation," said Lilly. "I think they're anything but angels."

"Do you though? Now that's funny. Why?"

"Looking at them even. I knew a Russian doctor who'd been through the Russo-Japanese war,* and who had gone a bit cracked. He said he saw the Japs rush a trench. They threw everything away and flung themselves through the Russian fire, and simply dropped in masses. But those that reached the trenches jumped in with bare hands on the Russians and tore their faces apart and bit their throats out—fairly ripped the faces off the bone.—It had sent the doctor a bit cracked. He said the wounded were awful,—their faces torn off and their throats mangled—and dead Japs with flesh between the teeth—God knows if it's true. But that's the impression the Japanese had made on this man—It had affected his mind really."

Jim watched Lilly, and smiled as if he were pleased.

"No—really—!" he said.

"Anyhow they're more demon than angel, I believe," said Lilly.

"Oh, no, Rawdon, but you always exaggerate," said Tanny.

"Maybe," said Lilly.

"I think Japanese are fascinating—fascinating—so quick, and such *force* in them—"

"Rather!—eh?" said Jim, looking with a quick smile at Tanny.

"I think a Japanese lover* would be marvellous," she laughed riskily.

"I s'd think he would," said Jim, screwing up his eyes.

"Do you hate the normal British as much as I do?" she asked him.

5   "Hate them! Hate them!" he said, with an intimate grin.

"Their beastly virtue," said she. "And I believe there's nobody more vicious underneath."

"Nobody!" said Jim.

"But you're British yourself," said Lilly to Jim.

10   "No, I'm Irish. Family's Irish—my mother was a Fitzpatrick."

"Anyhow you live in England."

"Because they won't let me go to Ireland."

The talk drifted. Jim finished up all the beer, and they prepared to go to bed. Jim was a bit tipsy, grinning. He asked for bread and
15 cheese to take upstairs.

"Will you have supper?" said Lilly. He was surprised, because Jim had eaten strangely much at dinner.

"No—where's the loaf?" And he cut himself about half of it. There was no cheese.

20   "Bread'll do," said Jim.

"Sit down and eat it. Have cocoa with it," said Tanny.

"No, I like to have it in my bedroom."

"You don't eat bread in the night?" said Lilly.

"I do."

25   "What a funny thing to do."

The cottage was in darkness. The Lillys slept soundly. Jim woke up and chewed bread and slept again. In the morning at dawn he rose and went downstairs. Lilly heard him roaming about—heard the woman come in to clean—heard them talking. So he got up to look
30 after his visitor, though it was not seven o'clock, and the woman was busy—But before he went down, he heard Jim come upstairs again.

Mrs. Short was busy in the kitchen when Lilly went down.

"The other gentleman have been down, Sir," said Mrs. Short. "He asked me where the bread and butter were, so I said should I cut
35 him a piece. But he wouldn't let me do it. I gave him a knife and he took it for himself, in the pantry."

"I say, Bricknell," said Lilly at breakfast time, "why do you eat so much bread?"

"I've got to feed up. I've been starved during this damned war."

40   "But hunks of bread won't feed you up."

"Gives the stomach something to work at, and prevents it grinding on the nerves," said Jim.

"But surely you don't want to keep your stomach always full and heavy."

"I do, my boy. I do. It needs keeping solid. I'm losing life, if I don't. I tell you I'm losing life. Let me put something inside me."

"I don't believe bread's any use."

During breakfast Jim talked about the future of the world.

"I reckon Christ's the finest thing time has ever produced," said he; "and will remain it."

"But you don't want crucifixions *ad infinitum*," said Lilly.

"What? Why not?"

"Once is enough—and have done."

"Don't you think love and sacrifice are the finest things in life?" said Jim, over his bacon.

"Depends *what* love, and what sacrifice," said Lilly. "If I really believe in an Almighty God, I am willing to sacrifice for Him. That is, I'm willing to yield my own personal interest to the bigger creative interest.—But it's obvious Almighty God isn't mere Love."

"I think it is. Love and only love," said Jim. "I think the greatest joy is sacrificing oneself to love."

"To *someone* you love, you mean," said Tanny.

"No I don't. I don't mean someone at all. I mean love—love—love. I sacrifice myself to love. I reckon that's the highest man is capable of."

"But you can't sacrifice yourself to an abstract principle," said Tanny.

"That's just what you can do. And that's the beauty of it. Who represents the principle doesn't matter. Christ is the principle of love," said Jim.

"But no!" said Tanny. "It *must* be more individual. It must be *somebody* you love, not abstract love in itself. How can you sacrifice yourself to an abstraction."

"Ha, I think Love and your Christ detestable," said Lilly—"a sheer ignominy."

"Finest thing the world has produced," said Jim.

"No. A thing which sets itself up to be betrayed! No, it's foul. Don't you see it's the Judas principle you really worship. Judas is the real hero. But for Judas the whole show would have been *manqué*."*

"Oh yes," said Jim. "Judas was inevitable. I'm not sure that Judas wasn't the greatest of the disciples—and Jesus knew it. I'm not sure Judas wasn't the disciple Jesus loved."

"Jesus certainly encouraged him in his Judas tricks," said Tanny. Jim grinned knowingly at Lilly.

5 "Then it was a nasty combination. And anything which turns on a Judas climax is a dirty show, to my thinking. I think your Judas is a rotten, dirty worm, just a dirty little self-conscious sentimental twister. And out of all Christianity he is the hero today. When people say Christ they mean Judas. They find him luscious on the palate.
10 And Jesus fostered him—" said Lilly.

"He's a profound figure, is Judas. It's taken two thousand years to begin to understand him," said Jim, pushing the bread and marmalade into his mouth.

"A traitor is a traitor—no need to understand any further. And a
15 system which rests all its weight on a piece of treachery makes that treachery not only inevitable but sacred. That's why I'm sick of Christianity—At any rate this modern Christ-mongery."

"The finest thing the world has produced, or ever will produce—Christ and Judas—" said Jim.

20 "Not to me," said Lilly. "Foul combination."

It was a lovely morning in early March. Violets were out, and the first wild anemones. The sun was quite warm. The three were about to take out a picnic lunch. Lilly however was suffering from Jim's presence.

25 "Jolly nice here," said Jim. "Mind if I stay till Saturday?"

There was a pause. Lilly felt he was being bullied, almost obscenely bullied. Was he going to agree?

Suddenly he looked up at Jim.

"I'd rather you went tomorrow," he said.

30 Tanny, who was sitting opposite Jim, dropped her head in confusion.

"What's tomorrow?" said Jim.

"Thursday," said Lilly.

"Thursday," repeated Jim. And he looked up and got Lilly's eye.
35 He wanted to say "Friday then?"

"Yes, I'd rather you went Thursday," repeated Lilly.

"But Rawdon—!" broke in Tanny, who was suffering. She stopped, however.

"We can walk across country with you some way if you like," said
40 Lilly to Jim. It was a sort of compromise.

"Fine!" said Jim. "We'll do that, then."

It was lovely sunshine, and they wandered through the woods. Between Jim and Tanny was a sort of growing *rapprochement*, which got on Lilly's nerves.

"What the hell do you take that beastly personal tone for?" cried Lilly at Tanny, as the three sat under a leafless great beech-tree.

"But I'm not personal at all, am I Mr. Bricknell?" said Tanny.

Jim watched Lilly, and grinned pleasedly.

"Why shouldn't you be, anyhow?" he said.

"Yes!" she retorted. "Why not!"

"Not while I'm here. I loathe the slimy creepy personal intimacy.— *'Don't you think, Mr. Bricknell, that it's lovely to be able to talk quite simply to somebody? Oh, it's such a relief, after most people——'*" Lilly mimicked his wife's last speech savagely.

"But I *mean* it," cried Tanny. "It *is* lovely."

"Dirty messing," said Lilly angrily.

Jim watched the dark, irascible little man with amusement. They rose, and went to look for an inn, and beer. Tanny still clung rather stickily to Jim's side.

But it was a lovely day, the first of all the days of spring, with crocuses and wall-flowers in the cottage gardens, and white cocks crowing in the quiet hamlet.

When they got back in the afternoon to the cottage, they found a telegram for Jim. He let the Lillys see it—"Meet you for a walk on your return journey Lois." At once Tanny wanted to know all about Lois. Lois was a nice girl, well-to-do middle-class, but also an actress, and she would do anything Jim wanted.

"I must get a wire to her to meet me tomorrow," he said. "Where shall I say?"

Lilly produced the map, and they decided on time and station at which Lois, coming out of London, should meet Jim. Then the happy pair could walk along the Thames valley, spending a night perhaps at Marlow, or some such place.

Off went Jim and Lilly once more to the postoffice. They were quite good friends. Having so inhospitably fixed the hour of departure, Lilly wanted to be nice. Arrived at the postoffice, they found it shut: half-day closing for the little shop.

"Well," said Lilly. "We'll go to the station."

They proceeded to the station—found the station-master—were conducted down to the signal-box. Lilly naturally hung back from

people, but Jim was hob-nob with the station-master and the signal
man, quite officer-and-my-men kind of thing. Lilly sat out on the
steps of the signal-box, rather ashamed, while the long telegram was
shouted over the telephone to the junction-town—first the young
5　lady and her address, then the message "Meet me X. station 3.40
tomorrow walk back great pleasure Jim."

Anyhow that was done. They went home to tea. After tea, as the
evening fell, Lilly suggested a little stroll in the woods, while Tanny
prepared the dinner. Jim agreed, and they set out. The two men
10　wandered through the trees in the dusk, till they came to a bank on
the farther edge of the wood. There they sat down.

And there Lilly said what he had to say. "As a matter of fact," he
said, "it's nothing but love and self-sacrifice which makes you feel
yourself losing life."

15　"You're wrong. Only love brings it back—and wine. If I drink a
bottle of burgundy I feel myself restored at the middle—right here!
I feel the energy back again. And if I can fall in love—But it's
becoming so damned hard—"

"What, to fall in love?" asked Lilly.

20　"Yes."

"Then why not leave off trying! What do you want to poke yourself
and prod yourself into love, for?"

"Because I'm *dead* without it. I'm dead. I'm dying."

"Only because you force yourself. If you drop working yourself
25　up—"

"I shall die. I only live when I can fall in love. Otherwise I'm dying
by inches. Why, man, you don't know what it was like. I used to get
the most grand feelings— like a great rush of force, or light— a great
rush—right here, as I've said, at the solar plexus. And it would come
30　any time—any where—no matter where I was. And then I was all
right."

"All right for what?—for making love?"

"Yes man, I was."

"And now you aren't?—Oh well, leave love alone, as any
35　twopenny doctor would tell you."

"No, you're off it there. It's nothing technical. Technically I can
make love as much as you like. It's nothing a doctor has any say in.
It's what I feel inside me. I feel the life going. I know it's going. I
never get those inrushes now, unless I drink a jolly lot, or if I possibly
40　could fall in love. Technically, I'm potent all right—oh yes!"

"You should leave yourself and your inrushes alone."

"But you can't. It's a sort of ache."

"Then you should stiffen your backbone. It's your backbone that matters. You shouldn't want to abandon yourself. You shouldn't want to fling yourself all loose into a woman's lap. You should stand by yourself and learn to *be* by yourself. Why don't you be more like the Japanese you talk about? Quiet, aloof little devils. They don't bother about being loved. They keep themselves taut in their own selves—there, at the bottom of the spine—the devil's own power they've got there."

Jim mused a bit.

"Think they have?" he laughed. It seemed comic to him.

"Sure! Look at them. Why can't you gather yourself there?"

"At the tail?"

"Yes. Hold yourself firm there."

Jim broke into a cackle of a laugh, and rose. The two went through the dark woods back to the cottage. Jim staggered and stumbled like a drunken man: or worse, like a man with locomotor ataxia:* as if he had no power in his lower limbs.

"Walk there—!" said Lilly, finding him the smoothest bit of the dark path. But Jim stumbled and shambled, in a state of nauseous weak relaxation. However, they reached the cottage: and food and beer—and Tanny, piqued with curiosity to know what the men had been saying privately to each other.

After dinner they sat once more talking round the fire. Lilly sat in a small chair facing the fire, the other two in the arm-chairs on either side the hearth.

"How nice it will be for you, walking with Lois towards London tomorrow," gushed Tanny sentimentally.

"Good God!" said Lilly. "Why the dickens doesn't he walk by himself, without wanting a woman always there, to hold his hand."

"Don't be so spiteful," said Tanny. "*You* see that you have a woman always there, to hold *your* hand."

"My hand doesn't need holding," snapped Lilly.

"Doesn't it! More than most men's! But you're so beastly ungrateful and mannish. Because I hold you safe enough all the time you like to pretend you're doing it all yourself."

"All right. Don't drag yourself in," said Lilly, detesting his wife at that moment. "Anyhow," and he turned to Jim, "it's time you'd done slobbering yourself over a lot of little women, one after the other."

"Why shouldn't I, if I like it?" said Jim.

"Yes, why not?" said Tanny.

"Because it makes a fool of you. Look at you, stumbling and staggering with no use in your legs. I'd be ashamed if I were you."

5   "Would you?" said Jim.

"I would. And it's nothing but your wanting to be loved which does it. A maudlin crying to be loved, which makes your knees all go rickety."

"Think that's it?" said Jim.

10   "What else is it. You haven't been here a day, but you must telegraph for some female to be ready to hold your hand the moment you go away. And before she lets go, you'll be wiring for another. *You want to be loved*, you want to be loved—a man of your years. It's disgusting—"

15   "I don't see it. I believe in love—" said Jim, watching and grinning oddly.

"Bah, love! Messing, that's what it is. It wouldn't matter if it did you no harm. But when you stagger and stumble down a road, out of sheer sloppy relaxation of your will— —"

20   At this point Jim suddenly sprang from his chair at Lilly, and gave him two or three hard blows with his fists, upon the front of the body. Then he sat down in his own chair again, saying sheep-ishly:

"I knew I should have to do it, if he said any more."

25   Lilly sat motionless as a statue, his face like paper. One of the blows had caught him rather low, so that he was almost winded, and could not breathe. He sat rigid, paralysed as a winded man is. But he wouldn't let it be seen. With all his will he prevented himself from gasping. Only through his parted lips he drew tiny gasps, controlled,

30   nothing revealed to the other two. He hated them both far too much.

For some minutes there was dead silence, whilst Lilly silently and viciously fought for his breath. Tanny opened her eyes wide in a sort of pleased bewilderment, and Jim turned his face aside, and hung his clasped hands between his knees.

35   "There's a great silence, suddenly!" said Tanny.

"What is there to say?" ejaculated Lilly rapidly, with a spoonful of breath which he managed to compress and control into speech. Then he sat motionless again, concerned with the business of getting back his wind, and not letting the other two see.

40   Jim jerked in his chair, and looked round.

"It isn't that I don't like the man," he said, in a rather small voice. "But I knew if he went on I should have to do it."

To Lilly, rigid and physically preoccupied, there sounded a sort of self-consciousness in Jim's voice, as if the whole thing had been semi-deliberate. He detected the sort of maudlin deliberateness 5 which goes with hysterics, and he was colder, more icy than ever.

Tanny looked at Lilly, puzzled, bewildered, but still rather pleased, as if she demanded an answer. None being forthcoming, she said:

"Of course, you mustn't expect to say all those things without 10 rousing a man."

Still Lilly did not answer. Jim glanced at him, then looked at Tanny.

"It isn't that I don't like him," he said, slowly. "I like him better than any man I've ever known, I believe." He clasped his hands and 15 turned aside his face.

"Judas!" flashed through Lilly's mind.

Again Tanny looked for her husband's answer.

"Yes Rawdon," she said. "You can't say the things you do without their having an effect. You really ask for it, you know." 20

"It's no matter." Lilly squeezed the words out coldly. "He wanted to do it, and he did it."

A dead silence ensued now. Tanny looked from man to man.

"I could feel it coming on me," said Jim.

"Of course!" said Tanny. "Rawdon doesn't know the things he 25 says." She was pleased that he had had to pay for them, for once.

It takes a man a long time to get his breath back, after a sharp blow in the wind. Lilly was managing by degrees. The others no doubt attributed his silence to deep or fierce thoughts. It was nothing of the kind: merely a cold struggle to get his wind back, without letting 30 them know he was struggling: and a sheer, stock-stiff hatred of the pair of them.

"I like the man," said Jim. "Never liked a man more than I like him." He spoke as if with difficulty.

"The man" stuck safely in Lilly's ears. 35

"Oh well," he managed to say. "It's nothing. I've done my talking and had an answer, for once."

"Yes, Rawdy, you've had an answer, for once. Usually you don't get an answer, you know—and that's why you go so far—in the things you say. Now you'll know how you make people feel." 40

"Quite!" said Lilly.

"*I* don't feel anything. I don't mind what he says," said Jim.

"Yes, but he ought to know the things he *does* say," said Tanny.
"He goes on, without considering the person he's talking to. This
time it's come back on him. He mustn't say such personal things, if
he's not going to risk an answer."

"I don't mind what he says. I don't mind a bit," said Jim.

"Nor do I mind," said Lilly indifferently. "I say what I feel—You
do as you feel—There's an end of it."

A sheepish sort of silence followed this speech. It was broken by a
sudden laugh from Tanny.

"The things that happen to us!" she said, laughing rather shrilly.
"Suddenly, like a thunderbolt, we're all struck into silence!"

"Rum game, eh!" said Jim, grinning.

"Isn't it funny! Isn't life too funny!" She looked again at her
husband. "But Rawdy, you must admit it was your own fault."

Lilly's stiff face did not change.

"Why *fault*!" he said, looking at her coldly. "What is there to talk
about?"

"Usually there's so much," she said sarcastically.

A few phrases dribbled out of the silence. In vain Jim tried to get
Lilly to thaw, and in vain Tanny gave her digs at her husband. Lilly's
stiff, inscrutable face did not change, he was polite and aloof. So they
all went to bed.

In the morning, the walk was to take place, as arranged, Lilly and
Tanny accompanying Jim to the third station across country. The
morning was lovely, the country beautiful. Lilly liked the countryside
and enjoyed the walk. But a hardness inside himself never relaxed.
Jim talked a little again about the future of the world, and a higher
state of Christlikeness in man. But Lilly only laughed. Then Tanny
managed to get ahead with Jim, sticking to his side and talking
sympathetic personalities. But Lilly, feeling it from afar, ran after
them and caught them up. They were silent.

"What was the interesting topic?" he said cuttingly.

"Nothing at all!" said Tanny, nettled. "Why must you interfere?"

"Because I intend to," said Lilly.

And the two others fell apart, as if severed with a knife. Jim walked
rather sheepishly, as if cut out.

So they came at last past the canals to the wayside station: and at
last Jim's train came. They all said goodbye. Jim and Tanny were

both waiting for Lilly to show some sign of real reconciliation. But none came. He was cheerful and aloof.

"Goodbye," he said to Jim. "Hope Lois will be there all right. Third station on. Goodbye! Goodbye!"

"You'll come to Rackham?" said Jim, leaning out of the train.

"We should love to," called Tanny, after the receding train.

"All right," said Lilly, non-commital.

But he and his wife never saw Jim again. Lilly never intended to see him: a devil sat in the little man's breast.

"You shouldn't play at little Jesus, coming so near to people, wanting to help them," was Tanny's last word.

Chapter IX.

Low-water Mark[*]

Tanny went away to Norway to visit her people, for the first time for three years. Lilly did not go: he did not want to. He came to London
5 and settled in a room over Covent Garden market. The room was high up, a fair size, and stood at the corner of one of the streets and the market itself, looking down on the stalls and the carts and the arcade. Lilly would climb out of the window and sit for hours watching the behaviour of the great draught-horses which brought
10 the mountains of boxes and vegetables. Funny half-human creatures they seemed, so massive and fleshy, yet so cockney. There was one which could not bear donkeys, and which used to stretch out its great teeth like some massive serpent after every poor diminutive ass that came with a coster's barrow.[*] Another great horse could not endure
15 standing. It would shake itself and give little starts, and back into the heaps of carrots and broccoli, whilst the driver went into a frenzy of rage.

There was always something to watch. One minute it was two great loads of empty crates, which in passing had got entangled, and
20 reeled, leaning to fall disastrously. Then the drivers cursed and swore and dismounted and stared at their jeopardised loads: till a thin fellow was persuaded to scramble up the airy mountains of cages, like a monkey. And he actually managed to put them to rights. Great sigh of relief when the vans rocked out of the market.

25 Again there was a particular page-boy in buttons, with a round and perky behind, who nimbly carried a tea-tray from somewhere to somewhere, under the arches beside the market. The great brawny porters would tease him, and he would stop to give them cheek. One afternoon a giant lunged after him: the boy darted gracefully among
30 the heaps of vegetables, still bearing aloft his tea-tray, like some young blue-buttoned acolyte fleeing before a false god. The giant rolled after him—when alas, the acolyte of the tea-tray slipped among the vegetables, and down came the tray. Then tears, and a roar of unfeeling mirth from the giants. Lilly felt they were going to
35 make it up to him.

Another afternoon a young swell sauntered persistently among the vegetables, and Lilly, seated in his high little balcony, wondered why. But at last, a taxi, and a very expensive female, in a sort of silver brocade gown and a great fur shawl and ospreys in her bonnet. Evidently an assignation. Yet what could be more conspicuous than this elegant pair, picking their way through the cabbage-leaves.

And then, one cold grey afternoon in early April, a man in a black overcoat and a bowler hat, walking uncertainly. Lilly had risen and was just retiring out of the chill, damp air. For some reason he lingered to watch the figure. The man was walking east. He stepped rather insecurely off the pavement, and wavered across the setts* between the wheels of the standing vans. And suddenly he went down. Lilly could not see him on the floor, but he saw some van-men go forward, and he saw one of them pick up the man's hat.

"I'd better go down," said Lilly to himself.

So he began running down the four long flights of stone stairs, past the many doors of the multifarious business premises, and out into the market. A little crowd had gathered, and a large policeman was just rowing into the centre of the interest. Lilly, always a hoverer on the edge of public commotions, hung now hesitating on the outskirts of the crowd.

"What is it?" he said, to a rather sniffy messenger boy.

"Drunk," said the messenger boy: except that, in unblushing cockney, he pronounced it "Drank."

Lilly hung further back on the edge of the little crowd.

"Come on here. Where d'you want to go?" he heard the hearty tones of the policeman.

"I'm all right. I'm all right," came the testy drunken answer.

"All right, are yer! All right, and *then* some,—Come on, get on your pins."

"I'm all right! I'm all right."

The voice made Lilly peer between the people. And sitting on the granite setts, being hauled up by a burly policeman, he saw our acquaintance Aaron, very pale in the face and a little dishevelled.

"Like me to tuck the sheets round you, shouldn't you! Fancy yourself snug in bed, don't you. You won't believe you're right in the way of traffic, will you now, in Covent Garden Market. Come on, we'll see to you." And the policeman hoisted the bitter and unwilling Aaron.

Lilly was quickly at the centre of the affair, unobtrusive like a shadow, different from the other people.

"Help him up to my room, will you?" he said to the constable. "Friend of mine."

5   The large constable looked down on the bare-headed wispy, unobtrusive Lilly with good-humoured suspicion and incredulity. Lilly could not have borne it if the policeman had uttered any of this cockney suspicion, so he watched him. There was a great gulf between the public official and the odd, quiet little individual—yet
10 Lilly had his way.

"Which room?" said the policeman, dubious.

Lilly pointed quickly round. Then he said to Aaron:

"Were you coming to see me, Sisson? You'll come in, won't you?"

Aaron nodded rather stupidly and testily. His eyes looked angry.
15 Somebody stuck his hat on his head for him, and made him look a fool. Lilly took it off again, and carried it for him. He turned, and the crowd eased. He watched Aaron sharply, and saw that it was with difficulty he could walk. So he caught him by the arm on the other side from the policeman, and they crossed the road to the pavement.
20 "Not so much of this sort of thing these days," said the policeman.

"Not so much opportunity," said Lilly.

"More than there was, though. Coming back to the old days, like. Working round, bit by bit."

They had arrived at the stairs. Aaron stumbled up.
25 "Steady now! Steady does it!" said the policeman, steering his charge. There was a curious breach of distance between Lilly and the constable.

At last Lilly opened his own door. The room was pleasant. The fire burned warm, the piano stood open, the sofa was untidy with
30 cushions and papers. Books and papers covered the big writing desk. Beyond the screen made by the bookshelves and the piano were two beds, with washstand by one of the large windows, the one through which Lilly had climbed.

The policeman looked round curiously.
35 "More cosy here than in the lock-up, sir!" he said.

Lilly laughed. He was hastily clearing the sofa.

"Sit on the sofa, Sisson," he said.

The policeman lowered his charge, with a—

"Right we are, then!"
40 Lilly felt in his pocket, and gave the policeman half a crown. But

he was watching Aaron, who sat stupidly on the sofa, very pale and semi-conscious.

"Do you feel ill, Sisson?" he said sharply.

Aaron looked back at him with heavy eyes, and shook his head slightly.

"I believe you are," said Lilly, taking his hand.

"Might be a bit o' this flu, you know," said the policeman.

"Yes," said Lilly. "Where is there a doctor?" he added, on reflection.

"The nearest?" said the policeman. And he told him. "Leave a message for you, Sir?"

Lilly wrote his address on a card, then changed his mind.

"No, I'll run round myself if necessary," he said.

And the policeman departed.

"You'll go to bed, won't you?" said Lilly to Aaron, when the door was shut. Aaron shook his head sulkily.

"I would if I were you. You can stay here till you're all right. I'm alone, so it doesn't matter."

But Aaron had relapsed into semi-consciousness. Lilly put the big kettle on the gas stove, the little kettle on the fire. Then he hovered in front of the stupefied man. He felt uneasy. Again he took Aaron's hand and felt the pulse.

"I'm sure you aren't well. You must go to bed," he said. And he kneeled and unfastened his visitor's boots. Meanwhile the kettle began to boil, he put a hot-water bottle into the bed.

"Let us get your overcoat off," he said to the stupefied man. "Come along." And with coaxing and pulling and pushing he got off the overcoat and coat and waistcoat.

At last Aaron was undressed and in bed. Lilly brought him tea. With a dim kind of obedience he took the cup and would drink. He looked at Lilly with heavy eyes.

"I gave in, I gave in to her, else I should ha' been all right," he said.

"To whom?" said Lilly.

"I gave in to her—and afterwards I cried, thinking of Lottie and the children. I felt my heart break, you know. And that's what did it. I should have been all right if I hadn't given in to her—"

"To whom?" said Lilly.

"Josephine. I felt, the minute I was loving her, I'd done myself. And I had. Everything came back on me. If I hadn't given in to her, I should ha' kept all right."

"Don't bother now. Get warm and still—"

"I felt it—I felt it go, inside me, the minute I gave in to her. It's perhaps killed me."

"No, not it. Never mind, be still. Be still, and you'll be all right in the morning."

"It's my own fault, for giving in to her. If I'd kept myself back, my liver wouldn't have broken inside me, and I shouldn't have been sick. And I knew—"

"Never mind now. Have you drunk your tea? Lie down. Lie down, and go to sleep."

Lilly pushed Aaron down in the bed, and covered him over. Then he thrust his hands under the bedclothes and felt his feet—still cold. He arranged the water bottle. Then he put another cover on the bed.

Aaron lay still, rather grey and peaked-looking, in a stillness that was not healthy. For some time Lilly went about stealthily, glancing at his patient from time to time. Then he sat down to read.

He was roused after a time by a moaning of troubled breathing and a fretful stirring in the bed. He went across. Aaron's eyes were open, and dark looking.

"Have a little hot milk," said Lilly.

Aaron shook his head faintly, not noticing.

"A little Bovril?"*

The same faint shake.

Then Lilly wrote a note for the doctor, went into the office on the same landing, and got a clerk, who would be leaving in a few minutes, to call with the note. When he came back he found Aaron still watching.

"Are you here by yourself?" asked the sick man.

"Yes. My wife's gone to Norway."

"For good?"

"No," laughed Lilly. "For a couple of months or so. She'll come back here: unless she joins me in Switzerland or somewhere."

Aaron was still for a while.

"You've not gone with her," he said at length.

"To see her people? No, I don't think they want me very badly—And I didn't want very badly to go. Why should I? It's better for married people to be separated sometimes."

"Ay!—" said Aaron, watching the other man with fever-darkened eyes.

"I hate married people who are two in one—stuck together like two jujube lozenges," said Lilly.

"Me an' all. I hate 'em myself," said Aaron.

"Everybody ought to stand by themselves, in the first place—men and women as well. They can come together, in the second place, if they like. But nothing is any good unless each one stands alone, intrinsically."

"I'm with you there," said Aaron. "If I'd kep' myself to myself I shouldn't be bad now—Though I'm not very bad. I s'll be all right in the morning.—But I did myself in when I went with another woman. I felt myself go—as if the bile broke inside me, and I was sick."

"Josephine seduced you?" laughed Lilly.

"Ay, right enough," replied Aaron grimly. "She won't be coming here, will she?"

"Not unless I ask her."

"You won't ask her, though—?"

"No, not if you don't want her."

"I don't."

The fever made Aaron naïve and communicative, unlike himself. And he knew he was being unlike himself, he knew that he was not in proper control of himself, so he was unhappy, uneasy.

"I'll stop here the night then, if you don't mind," he said.

"You'll have to," said Lilly. "I've sent for the doctor. I believe you've got the flu."

"Think I have?" said Aaron frightened.

"Don't be scared," laughed Lilly.

There was a long pause. Lilly stood at the window looking at the darkening market, beneath the street-lamps.

"I s'll have to go to the hospital, if I have," came Aaron's voice.

"No, if it's only going to be a week or a fortnight's business, you can stop here. I've nothing to do," said Lilly.

"There's no occasion for you to saddle yourself with me," said Aaron dejectedly.

"You can go to your hospital if you like—or back to your lodging—if you wish to," said Lilly. "You can make up your mind when you see how you are in the morning."

"No use going back to my lodgings," said Aaron.

"I'll send a telegram to your wife if you like," said Lilly.

Aaron was silent, dead silent, for some time.

"Nay," he said at length, in a decided voice. "Not if I die for it."

Lilly remained still, and the other man lapsed into a sort of semi-sleep, motionless and abandoned. The darkness had fallen over London, and away below the lamps were white. Lilly lit the green-shaded reading lamp over the desk. Then he stood and looked at Aaron, who lay still, looking sick. Rather beautiful the bones of the countenance: but the skull too small for such a heavy jaw and rather coarse mouth. Aaron half-opened his eyes, and writhed feverishly, as if his limbs could not be in the right place. Lilly mended the fire, and sat down to write. Then he got up and went downstairs to unfasten the street-door, so that the doctor could walk up. The business people had gone from their various holes, all the lower part of the tall house was in darkness.

Lilly waited and waited. He boiled an egg and made himself toast. Aaron said he might eat the same. Lilly cooked another egg and took it to the sick man. Aaron looked at it and pushed it away with nausea. He would have some tea. So Lilly gave him tea.

"Not much fun for you, doing this for somebody who is nothing to you," said Aaron.

"I shouldn't if you were unsympathetic to me," said Lilly. "As it is, it's happened so, and so we'll let it be."

"What time is it?"

"Nearly eight o'clock."

"Oh my Lord, the opera."

And Aaron got half out of bed. But as he sat on the bedside he knew he could not safely get to his feet. He remained a picture of dejection.

"Perhaps we ought to let them know," said Lilly.

But Aaron, blank with stupid misery, sat huddled there on the bedside without answering.

"I'll run round with a note," said Lilly. "I suppose others have had flu, beside you. Lie down!"

But Aaron stupidly and dejectedly sat huddled on the side of the bed, wearing old flannel pyjamas of Lilly's, rather small for him. He felt too sick to move.

"Lie down! Lie down!" said Lilly. "And keep still while I'm gone. I shan't be more than ten minutes."

"I don't care if I die," said Aaron.

Lilly laughed.

"You're a long way from dying," said he, "or you wouldn't say it."

But Aaron only looked up at him with queer, far-off, haggard eyes, something like a criminal who is just being executed.

"Lie down!" said Lilly, pushing him gently into the bed. "You won't improve yourself sitting there, anyhow."

Aaron lay down, turned away, and was quite still. Lilly quietly left the room on his errand.

The doctor did not come until ten o'clock: and worn out with work when he did come.

"Isn't there a lift in this establishment?" he said, as he groped his way up the stone stairs. Lilly had heard him, and run down to meet him.

The doctor poked the thermometer under Aaron's tongue and felt the pulse. Then he asked a few questions: listened to the heart and breathing.

"Yes, it's the flu," he said curtly. "Nothing to do but to keep warm in bed and not move, and take plenty of milk and liquid nourishment. I'll come round in the morning and give you an injection. Lungs are all right so far."

"How long shall I have to be in bed?" said Aaron.

"Oh—depends. A week at least."

Aaron watched him sullenly—and hated him. Lilly laughed to himself. The sick man was like a dog that is ill but which growls from a deep corner, and will bite if you put your hand in. He was in a state of black depression.

Lilly settled him down for the night, and himself went to bed. Aaron squirmed with heavy, pained limbs, the night through, and slept and had bad dreams. Lilly got up to give him drinks. The din in the market was terrific before dawn, and Aaron suffered bitterly.

In the morning he was worse. The doctor gave him injections against pneumonia.

"You wouldn't like me to wire to your wife?" said Lilly.

"No," said Aaron abruptly. "You can send me to the hospital. I'm nothing but a piece of carrion."

"Carrion!" said Lilly. "Why?"

"I know it. I feel like it."

"Oh, that's only the sort of nauseated feeling you get with flu."

"I'm only fit to be thrown underground, and made an end of. I can't stand myself—"

He had a ghastly, grey look of self-repulsion.

"It's the germ that makes you feel like that," said Lilly. "It poisons the system for a time. But you'll work it off."

At evening he was no better, the fever was still high. Yet there were no complications—except that the heart was irregular.

"The one thing I wonder," said Lilly, "is whether you hadn't better be moved out of the noise of the market. It's fearful for you in the early morning."

"It makes no difference to me," said Aaron.

5 The next day he was a little worse, if anything. The doctor knew there was nothing to be done. At evening he gave the patient a calomel pill.* It was rather strong, and Aaron had a bad time. His burning, parched, poisoned inside was twisted and torn. Meanwhile carts banged, porters shouted, all the hell of the market went on
10 outside, away down on the cobble setts. But this time the two men did not hear.

"You'll feel better now," said Lilly, "after the operation."

"It's done me harm," cried Aaron fretfully. "Send me to the hospital, or you'll repent it. Get rid of me in time."

15 "Nay," said Lilly. "You get better. Damn it, you're only one among a million."

Again over Aaron's face went the ghastly grimace of self-repulsion.

"My soul's gone rotten," he said.

20 "No," said Lilly. "Only toxin in the blood."

Next day the patient seemed worse, and the heart more irregular. He rested badly. So far, Lilly had got a fair night's rest. Now Aaron was not sleeping, and he seemed to struggle in the bed.

"Keep your courage up, man," said the doctor sharply. "You give
25 way."

Aaron looked at him blackly, and did not answer.

In the night Lilly was up time after time. Aaron would slip down on his back, and go semi-conscious. And then he would awake, as if drowning, struggling to move, mentally shouting aloud, yet making
30 no sound for some moments, mentally shouting in frenzy, but unable to stir or make a sound. When at last he got some sort of physical control he cried: "Lift me up! Lift me up!"

Lilly hurried and lifted him up, and he sat panting with a sobbing motion, his eyes gloomy and terrified, more than ever like a criminal
35 who is just being executed. He drank brandy, and was laid down on his side.

"Don't let me lie on my back," he said, terrified.

"No, I won't," said Lilly.

Aaron frowned curiously on his nurse.

40 "Mind you don't let me," he said, exacting and really terrified.

"No, I won't let you."

And now Lilly was continually crossing over and pulling Aaron on to his side, whenever he found him slipped down on his back.

In the morning the doctor was puzzled. Probably it was the toxin in the blood which poisoned the heart. There was no pneumonia. And yet Aaron was clearly growing worse. The doctor agreed to send in a nurse for the coming night.

"What's the matter with you, man!" he said sharply to his patient. "You give way! You give way! Can't you pull yourself together?"

But Aaron only became more gloomily withheld, retracting from life. And Lilly began to be really troubled. He got a friend to sit with the patient in the afternoon, whilst he himself went out and arranged to sleep in Aaron's room, at his lodging.

The next morning, when he came in, he found the patient lying as ever, in a sort of heap in the bed. Nurse had had to lift him up and hold him up again. And now Aaron lay in a sort of semi-stupor of fear, frustrated anger, misery and self-repulsion: a sort of interlocked depression.

The doctor frowned when he came. He talked with the nurse, and wrote another prescription. Then he drew Lilly away to the door.

"What's the matter with the fellow?" he said. "Can't you rouse his spirit? He seems to be sulking himself out of life. He'll drop out quite suddenly, you know, if he goes on like this. Can't you rouse him up?"

"I think it depresses him partly that his bowels won't work. It frightens him. He's never been ill in his life before," said Lilly.

"His bowels won't work if he lets all his spirit go, like an animal dying of the sulks," said the doctor impatiently. "He might go off quite suddenly—dead before you can turn round— —"

Lilly was properly troubled. Yet he did not quite know what to do. It was early afternoon, and the sun was shining into the room. There were daffodils and anemones in a jar, and freesias and violets. Down below in the market were two stalls of golden and blue flowers, gay.

"The flowers are lovely in the spring sunshine," said Lilly. "I wish I were in the country, don't you? As soon as you are better we'll go. It's been a terrible cold wet spring. But now it's going to be nice. Do you like being in the country?"

"Yes," said Aaron.

He was thinking of his garden. He loved it. Never in his life had he been away from a garden before.

"Make haste and get better, and we'll go."

"Where?" said Aaron.

"Hampshire. Or Berkshire.—Or perhaps you'd like to go home?—Would you?"

Aaron lay still, and did not answer.

"Perhaps you want to, and you don't want to," said Lilly. "You can please yourself, anyhow."

There was no getting anything definite out of the sick man—his soul seemed stuck, as if it would not move.

Suddenly Lilly rose and went to the dressing-table.

"I'm going to rub you with oil," he said. "I'm going to rub you as mothers do their babies whose bowels don't work."

Aaron frowned slightly as he glanced at the dark, self-possessed face of the little man.

"What's the good of that?" he said irritably. "I'd rather be left alone."

"Then you won't be."

Quickly he uncovered the blond lower body of his patient, and began to rub the abdomen with oil, using a slow, rhythmic, circulating motion, a sort of massage. For a long time he rubbed finely and steadily, then went over the whole of the lower body, mindless, as if in a sort of incantation. He rubbed every speck of the man's lower body—the abdomen, the buttocks, the thighs and knees, down to the feet, rubbed it all warm and glowing with camphorated oil, every bit of it, chafing the toes swiftly, till he was almost exhausted. Then Aaron was covered up again, and Lilly sat down in fatigue to look at his patient.

He saw a change. The spark had come back into the sick eyes, and the faint trace of a smile, faintly luminous, into the face. Aaron was regaining himself. But Lilly said nothing. He watched his patient fall into a proper sleep.

And he sat and watched him sleep. And he thought to himself. "I wonder why I do it. I wonder why I bother with him . . . Jim ought to have taught me my lesson. As soon as this man's really better he'll punch me in the wind, metaphorically if not actually, for having interfered with him. And Tanny would say, he was quite right to do it. She says I want power over them. What if I do? They don't care how much power the mob has over them, the nation, Lloyd George and Northcliffe* and the police and money. They'll yield themselves up to that sort of power quickly enough, and immolate themselves *pro bono publico* by the million. And what's the *bonum publicum** but a mob power. Why can't they submit to a bit of healthy individual authority. The fool would die, without me: just as that fool Jim will die in hysterics one day. Why does he last so long!

"Tanny's the same. She does nothing really but resist me: my authority, or my influence, or just *me*. At the bottom of her heart she just blindly and persistently opposes me. God knows what it is she opposes: just me myself. She thinks I want her to submit to me. So I do, in a measure natural to our two selves. Somewhere, she ought to submit to me. But they all prefer to kick against the pricks.* Not that *they* get many pricks. I get them. Damn them all, why don't I leave them alone. They only grin and feel triumphant when they've insulted one and punched one in the wind.

"This Aaron will do just the same. I like him, and he ought to like me. And he'll be another Jim: he *will* like me, if he can knock the wind out of me. A lot of little Stavrogins coming up to whisper affectionately, and biting one's ear.*

"But anyhow I can soon see the last of this chap: and him the last of all the rest. I'll be damned for ever if I see their Jims and Roberts and Julias and Scotts any more. Let them dance round their insipid hell-broth. Thin tack it is.

"There's a whole world besides this little gang of Europeans. Except, dear God, that they've exterminated all the peoples worth knowing. I can't do with folk who teem by the billion, like the Chinese and Japs and orientals altogether. Only vermin teem by the billion. Higher types breed slower. I would have loved the Aztecs and the Red Indians. I *know* they hold the element in life which I am looking for—They had living pride. Not like the flea-bitten Asiatics —Even niggers are better than Asiatics, though they are wallowers.—The American races—and the South Sea Islanders—the Marquesans, the Maori blood. That was the true blood. It wasn't frightened. All the rest are craven—Europeans, Asiatics, Africans —everyone at his own individual quick craven and cringing: only conceited in the mass, the mob. How I hate them: the mass-bullies, the individual Judases.

"Well, if one will be a Jesus he must expect his Judas. That's why Abraham Lincoln gets shot. A Jesus makes a Judas inevitable. A man should remain himself, not try to spread himself over humanity. He should pivot himself on his own pride.

"I suppose really I ought to have packed this Aaron off to the hospital. Instead of which here am I rubbing him with oil to rub the life into him. And I *know* he'll bite me, like a warmed snake, the moment he recovers. And Tanny will say 'Quite right too,' I shouldn't have been so intimate. No, I should have left it to mechanical doctors and nurses.

5 "So I should. Everything to its own. And Aaron belongs to this little system, and Jim is waiting to be psychoanalysed, and Tanny is waiting for her own glorification.

"All right, Aaron. Last time I break my bread* for anybody, this is. So get better, my flautist, so I can go away.

10 "It was easy for the Red Indians and the Others to take their hook into death.* They might have stayed a bit longer to help one to defy the white masses.

"I'll make some tea—"

Lilly rose softly and went across to the fire. He had to cross a
15 landing to a sort of little lavatory, with a sink and a tap, for water. The clerks peeped out at him from an adjoining office and nodded. He nodded, and disappeared from their sight as quickly as possible, with his kettle. His dark eyes were quick, his dark hair was untidy, there was something silent and withheld about him. People could
20 never approach him quite ordinarily.

He put on the kettle, and quietly set cups and plates on a tray. The room was clean and cosy and pleasant. He did the cleaning himself, and was as efficient and inobtrusive a housewife as any woman. While the kettle boiled, he sat darning the socks which he had taken
25 off Aaron's feet when the flautist arrived, and which he had washed. He preferred that no outsider should see him doing these things. Yet he preferred also to do them himself, so that he should be independent of outside aid.

His face was dark and hollow, he seemed frail, sitting there in the
30 London afternoon darning the black woollen socks. His full brow was knitted slightly, there was a tension. At the same time, there was an indomitable stillness about him, as it were in the atmosphere about him. His hands, though small, were not very thin. He bit off the wool as he finished his darn.

35 As he was making the tea he saw Aaron rouse up in bed.

"I've been to sleep. I feel better," said the patient, turning round to look what the other man was doing. And the sight of the water steaming in a jet into the teapot seemed attractive.

"Yes," said Lilly. "You've slept for a good two hours."

40 "I believe I have," said Aaron.

"Would you like a little tea?"

"Ay—and a bit of toast."

"You're not supposed to have solid food.—Let me take your temperature."

The temperature was down to a hundred, and Lilly, in spite of the doctor, gave Aaron a piece of toast with his tea, enjoining him not to mention it to the nurse.

In the evening the two men talked.

"You do everything for yourself, then?" said Aaron.

"Yes, I prefer it."

"You like living all alone?"

"I don't know about that. I never have lived alone. Tanny and I have been very much alone in various countries: but that's two, not one."

"You miss her then?"

"Yes, of course. I missed her horribly in the cottage, when she'd first gone. I felt my heart was broken. But here, where we've never been together, I don't notice it so much."

"She'll come back," said Aaron.

"Yes, she'll come back. But I'd rather meet her abroad than here—and get on a different footing."

"Why?"

"Oh, I don't know. There's something with marriage altogether, I think. *Egoïsme à deux*—"

"What's that mean?"

"*Egoïsme à deux?* Two people, one egoism. Marriage is a self-conscious egoistic state, it seems to me."

"You've got no children?" said Aaron.

"No. Tanny wants children badly. I don't. I'm thankful we have none."

"Why?"

"I can't quite say. I think of them as a burden. Besides, there *are* such millions and billions of children in the world. And we know well enough what sort of millions and billions of people they'll grow up into. I don't want to add my quota to the mass—It's against my instinct—"

"Ay—!" laughed Aaron, with a curt acquiescence.

"Tanny's furious. But then, when a woman has got children, she thinks the world wags only for them and her. Nothing else. The whole world wags for the sake of the children—and their sacred mother."

"Ay, that's *damned* true," said Aaron.

"And myself, I'm sick of the children stunt. Children are all right, so long as you just take them for what they are: young immature things like kittens and half-grown dogs, nuisances, sometimes very charming. But I'll be hanged if I can see anything high and holy
5   about children. I should be sorry to, it would be so bad for the children. Young brats, tiresome and amusing in turns."

"When they don't give themselves airs," said Aaron.

"Yes, indeed. Which they do half the time. Sacred children, and sacred motherhood, I'm absolutely fed stiff by it. That's why I'm
10 thankful I have no children. Tanny can't come it over me there."

"It's a fact. When a woman's got her children, by God, she's a bitch in the manger. You can starve while she sits on the hay. It's useful to keep her pups warm."

"Yes."

15 "Why, you know—" Aaron turned excitedly in the bed, "they look on a man as if he was nothing but an instrument to get and rear children. If you have anything to do with a woman, she thinks it's because you want to get children by her.—And I'm damned if it is. I want my own pleasure, or nothing: and children be damned."

20 "Ah women!—*they* must be loved, at any price!" said Lilly. "And if you just don't want to love them—and tell them so—what a crime."

"A crime!" said Aaron. "They make a criminal of you. Them and their children be cursed. Is my life given me for nothing but to get
25 children, and work to bring them up? See them all in hell first. They'd better die while they're children, if childhood's all that important."

"I quite agree," said Lilly. "If childhood is more important than manhood, then why live to be a man at all? Why not remain an
30 infant?"

"Be damned and blasted to women and all their importances," cried Aaron. "They want to get you under, and children is their chief weapon."

"Men have got to stand up to the fact that manhood is more than
35 childhood—and then force women to admit it," said Lilly. "But the rotten whiners, they're all grovelling before a baby's napkin and a woman's petticoat."

"It's a fact," said Aaron. But he glanced at Lilly oddly, as if suspiciously. And Lilly caught the look. But he continued:

40 "And if they think you try to stand on your legs and walk with the

feet of manhood, why, there isn't a blooming father and lover among them but will do his best to get you down and suffocate you—either with a baby's napkin or a woman's petticoat."

Lilly's lips were curling, he was dark and bitter.

"Ay, it is like that," said Aaron, rather subduedly.

"The man's spirit has gone out of the world. Men can't move an inch unless they can grovel humbly at the end of the journey."

"No," said Aaron, watching with keen, half-amused eyes.

"That's why marriage wants readjusting—or extending—to get men on to their own legs once more, and to give them the adventure again. But men won't stick together and fight for it. Because once a woman has climbed up with her children, she'll find plenty of grovellers ready to support her and suffocate any defiant spirit. And women will sacrifice eleven men, fathers, husbands, brothers and lovers, for one baby—or for her own female self-conceit—"

"She will that," said Aaron.

"And can you find two men to stick together, without feeling criminal, and without cringing, and without betraying one another? You can't. One is sure to go fawning round some female, then they both enjoy giving each other away, and doing a new grovel before a woman again."

"Ay," said Aaron.

After which Lilly was silent.

Chapter X.

The War Again

"One is a fool," said Lilly, "to be lachrymose. The thing to do is to get a move on."

Aaron looked up with a glimpse of a smile. The two men were sitting before the fire at the end of a cold, wet April day: Aaron convalescent, somewhat chastened in appearance.

"Ay," he said rather sourly. "A move back to Guilford Street."

"Oh I meant to tell you," said Lilly. "I was reading an old Baden history. They made a law in 1528—not a law, but a regulation—that: if a man forsakes his wife and children, as now so often happens, the said wife and children are at once to be despatched after him.— I thought that would please you. Does it?"

"Yes," said Aaron briefly.

"They would have arrived the next day, like a forwarded letter."

"I should have had to get a considerable move on, at that rate," grinned Aaron.

"Oh no. You might quite like them here." But Lilly saw the white frown of determined revulsion on the convalescent's face.

"Wouldn't you?" he asked.

Aaron shook his head.

"No," he said. And it was obvious he objected to the topic. "What are you going to do about your move on?"

"Me!" said Lilly. "I'm going to sail away next week—or steam dirtily away on a tramp called the Maud Allen Wing."

"Where to?"

"Malta."

"Where from?"

"London Dock. I fixed up my passage this morning for ten pounds. I am cook's assistant, signed on."

Aaron looked at him with a little admiration.

"You can take a sudden jump, can you?" he said.

"The difficulty is to refrain from jumping: overboard or anywhere."

Aaron smoked his pipe slowly.

"And what good will Malta do you?" he asked, envious.

"Heaven knows. I shall cross to Syracuse, and move up Italy."

"Sounds as if you were a millionaire."

"I've got thirty-five pounds in all the world. But something will come along." 5

"I've got more than that," said Aaron.

"Good for you," replied Lilly.

He rose and went to the cupboard, taking out a bowl and a basket of potatoes. He sat down again, paring the potatoes. His busy activity annoyed Aaron. 10

"But what's the good of going to Malta? Shall *you* be any different in yourself, in another place? You'll be the same there as you are here."

"How am I here?"

"Why you're all the time grinding yourself against something 15 inside you. You're never free. You're never content. You never stop chafing."

Lilly dipped his potato into the water, and cut out the eyes carefully. Then he cut it in two, and dropped it in the clean water of the second bowl. He had not expected this criticism. 20

"Perhaps I don't," said he.

"Then what's the use of going somewhere else? You won't change yourself."

"I may in the end," said Lilly.

"You'll be yourself, whether it's Malta or London," said Aaron. 25

"There's a doom for me," laughed Lilly. The water on the fire was boiling. He rose and threw in salt, then dropped in the potatoes with little plops. "But there are lots of mes. I'm not only just one proposition. A new place brings out a new thing in a man. Otherwise you'd have stayed in your old place with your family." 30

"The man in the middle of you doesn't change," said Aaron.

"Do you find it so?" said Lilly.

"Ay. Every time."

"Then what's to be done?"

"Nothing, as far as I can see. You get as much amusement out of 35 life as possible, and there's the end of it."

"All right then, I'll get the amusement."

"Ay, all right then," said Aaron. "But there isn't anything wonderful about it. You talk as if you were doing something special. You aren't. You're no more than a man who drops into a pub for a 40 drink, to liven himself up a bit. Only you give it a lot of names, and make out as if you were looking for the philosopher's stone, or something like that. When you're only killing time like the rest of folks, before time kills you."

5   Lilly did not answer. It was not yet seven o'clock, but the sky was dark. Aaron sat in the firelight. Even the saucepan on the fire was silent. Darkness, silence, the firelight in the upper room, and the two men together.

"It isn't quite true," said Lilly, leaning on the mantel-piece and
10 staring down into the fire.

"Where isn't it?—You talk, and you make a man believe you've got something he hasn't got? But where is it, when it comes to? What have you got, more than me or Jim Bricknell! Only a bigger choice of words, it seems to me."

15   Lilly was motionless and inscrutable like a shadow.

"Does it, Aaron!" he said, in a colourless voice.

"Yes. What else is there to it?" Aaron sounded testy.

"Why," said Lilly at last, "there's something. I agree, it's true what you say about me. But there's a bit of something else. There's just a
20 bit of something in me, I think, which *isn't* a man running into a pub for a drink—"

"And what—?"

The question fell into the twilight like a drop of water falling down a deep shaft into a well.

25   "I think a man may come into possession of his own soul at last—as the Buddhists teach—but without ceasing to love, or even to hate. One loves, one hates—but somewhere beyond it all, one understands, and possesses one's soul in patience and in peace—"

"Yes," said Aaron slowly, "while you only stand and talk about it.
30 But when you've got no chance to talk about it—and when you've got to live—you don't possess your soul, neither in patience nor in peace, but any devil that likes possesses you and does what it likes with you, while you fridge* yourself and fray yourself out like a worn rag."

"I don't care," said Lilly. "I'm learning to possess my soul in
35 patience and in peace, and I know it. And it isn't a negative Nirvana either. And if Tanny possesses her own soul in patience and peace as well—and if in this we understand each other at last—then there we are, together and apart at the same time, and free of each other, and eternally inseparable. I have my Nirvana—and I have it all to myself.
40 But more than that. It coincides with her Nirvana."

"Ah yes," said Aaron. "But I don't understand all that word-splitting."

"I do though. You learn to be quite alone, and possess your own soul in isolation—and at the same time, to be perfectly *with* someone else—that's all I ask."

"Sort of sit on a mountain top, back to back with somebody else, like a couple of idols."

"No—because it isn't a case of sitting—or a case of back to back. It's what you get to after a lot of fighting and a lot of sensual fulfilment. And it never does away with the fighting and with the sensual passion. It flowers on top of them, and it would never flower save on top of them."

"What wouldn't?"

"The possessing one's own soul—and the being together with someone else in silence, beyond speech."

"And you've got them?"

"I've got a *bit* of the real quietness inside me."

"So has a dog on a mat."

"So I believe too."

"Or a man in a pub."

"Which I don't believe."

"You prefer the dog?"

"Maybe."

There was silence for a few moments.

"And I'm the man in the pub," said Aaron.

"You aren't the dog on the mat, anyhow."

"And you're the idol on the mountain top, worshipping your-self."

"You talk to me like a woman, Aaron."

"How do you talk to *me*, do you think?"

"How do I?"

"Are the potatoes done?"

Lilly turned quickly aside, and switched on the electric light. Everything changed. Aaron sat still before the fire, irritated. Lilly went about preparing the supper.

The room was pleasant at night. Two tall dark screens hid the two beds. In front, the piano was littered with music, the desk littered with papers. Lilly went out on to the landing, and set the chops to grill on the gas stove. Hastily he put a small table on the hearth-rug, spread it with a blue-and-white cloth, set plates and glasses. Aaron did not move. It was not his nature to concern himself with domestic matters—and Lilly did it best alone.

The two men had an almost uncanny understanding of one another—like brothers. They came from the same district, from the same class. Each might have been born into the other's circumstance. Like brothers, there was a profound hostility between them. But hostility is not antipathy.

Lilly's skilful housewifery always irritated Aaron: it was so self-sufficient. But most irritating of all was the little man's unconscious assumption of priority. Lilly was actually unaware that he assumed this quiet predominance over others. He mashed the potatoes, he heated the plates, he warmed the red wine, he whisked eggs into the milk pudding, and served his visitor like a housemaid. But none of this detracted from the silent assurance with which he bore himself, and with which he seemed to domineer over his acquaintance.

At last the meal was ready. Lilly drew the curtains, switched off the central light, put the green-shaded electric lamp on the table, and the two men drew up to the meal. It was good food, well cooked and hot. Certainly Lilly's hands were no longer clean: but it was clean dirt, as he said.

Aaron sat in the low arm-chair at table. So his face was below, in the full light. Lilly sat high on a small chair, so that his face was in the green shadow. Aaron was handsome, and always had that peculiar well-dressed look of his type. Lilly was indifferent to his own appearance, and his collar was a rag.

So the two men ate in silence. They had been together alone for a fortnight only: but it was like a small eternity. Aaron was well now—only he suffered from the depression and the sort of fear that follows influenza.

"When are you going?" he asked irritably, looking up at Lilly, whose face hovered in that green shadow above, and worried him.

"One day next week. They'll send me a telegram. Not later than Thursday."

"You're looking forward to going?" The question was half bitter.

"Yes. I want to get a new tune out of myself."

"Had enough of this?"

"Yes."

A flush of anger came on Aaron's face.

"You're easily on, and easily off," he said, rather insulting.

"Am I?" said Lilly. "What makes you think so?"

"Circumstances," replied Aaron sourly.

To which there was no answer. The host cleared away the plates, and put the pudding on the table. He pushed the bowl to Aaron.

"I suppose I shall never see you again, once you've gone," said Aaron.

"It's your choice. I will leave you an address."

After this, the pudding was eaten in silence.

"Besides, Aaron," said Lilly, drinking his last sip of wine, "what do you care whether you see me again or not? What do you care whether you see anybody again or not? You want to be amused. And now you're irritated because you think I am not going to amuse you any more: and you don't know who *is* going to amuse you. I admit it's a dilemma. But it's a hedonistic dilemma of the commonest sort."

"I don't know hedonistic.—And supposing I am as you say—are you any different?"

"No, I'm not very different. But I always persuade myself there's a bit of difference. Do you know what Josephine Ford confessed to me? She had her lovers enough. 'There isn't any such thing as love, Lilly,' she said. 'Men are simply afraid to be alone. That is absolutely all there is in it: fear of being alone.'"

"What by that?"* said Aaron.

"You agree?"

"Yes, on the whole."

"So do I—on the whole. And then I asked her what about woman. And then she said with a woman it wasn't fear, it was just boredom. A woman is like a violinist: any fiddle, any instrument rather than empty hands and no tune going."

"Yes—what I said before: getting as much amusement out of life as possible," said Aaron.

"You amuse me—and I'll amuse you."

"Yes—just about that."

"All right Aaron," said Lilly. "I'm not going to amuse you, or try to amuse you any more."

"Going to try somebody else: and Malta."

"Malta anyhow."

"Oh and somebody else—in the next five minutes."

"Yes—that also."

"Goodbye and good luck to you."

"Goodbye and good luck to you, Aaron."

With which Lilly went aside to wash the dishes. Aaron sat alone under the zone of light, turning over a score of *Pelléas.** Though the noise of London was around them, it was far below, and in the room was a deep silence. Each of the men seemed invested in his own
5   silence.

Aaron suddenly took his flute, and began trying little passages from the opera on his knee. He had not played since his illness. The noise came out a little tremulous, but low and sweet. Lilly came forward with a plate and a cloth in his hand.

10   "Aaron's rod is putting forth again," he said, smiling.

"What?" said Aaron, looking up.

"I said Aaron's rod is putting forth again."

"What rod?"

"Your flute, for the moment."

15   "It's got to put forth my bread and butter."

"Is that all the buds it's going to have?"

"What else!"

"Nay—that's for you to show. What flowers do you imagine came out of the rod of Moses's brother?"

20   "Scarlet runners, I should think, if he'd got to live on them."

"Scarlet enough, I'll bet."

Aaron turned unnoticing back to his music. Lilly finished the wiping of the dishes, then took a book and sat on the other side of the table.

25   "It's all one to you then," said Aaron suddenly, "whether we ever see one another again?"

"Not a bit," said Lilly, looking up over his spectacles. "I very much wish there might be something that held us together."

"Then if you wish it, why isn't there?"

30   "You might wish your flute to put out scarlet-runner flowers at the joints."

"Ay—I might. And it would be all the same."

The moment of silence that followed was extraordinary in its hostility.

35   "Oh, we shall run across one another again some time," said Aaron.

"Sure," said Lilly. "More than that: I'll write you an address that will always find me. And when you write I will answer you."

He took a bit of paper and scribbled an address. Aaron folded it
40   and put it into his waistcoat pocket. It was an Italian address.

"But how can I live in Italy?" he said. "You can shift about. I'm tied to a job."

"You—with your budding rod, your flute—and your charm—you can always do as you like."

"My what?"

"Your flute and your charm."

"What charm?"

"Just your own. Don't pretend you don't know you've got it. I don't really like charm myself: too much of a trick about it. But whether or not, you've got it."

"It's news to me."

"Not it."

"Fact, it is."

"Ha! Somebody will always take a fancy to you. And you can live on that, as well as on anything else."

"Why do you always speak so despisingly?"

"Why shouldn't I?"

"Have you any right to despise another man?"

"When did it go by rights?"

"No, not with you."

"You answer me like a woman, Aaron."

Again there was a space of silence. And again it was Aaron who at last broke it.

"We're in different positions, you and me," he said.

"How?"

"You can live by your writing—but I've got to have a job."

"Is that all?" said Lilly.

"Ay. And plenty. You've got the advantage of me."

"Quite," said Lilly. "But why? I was a dirty-nosed little boy when you were a clean-nosed little boy. And I always had more patches on my breeches than you: neat patches too, my poor mother! So what's the good of talking about advantages. You had the start. And at this very moment you could buy me up, lock, stock and barrel. So don't feel hard done by. It's a lie."

"You've got your freedom."

"I make it and I take it."

"Circumstances make it for you."

"As you like."

"You don't do a man justice," said Aaron.

"Does a man care?"

"He might."

"Then he's no man."

"Thanks again, old fellow."

"Welcome," said Lilly, grimacing.

5   Again Aaron looked at him, baffled, almost with hatred. Lilly grimaced at the blank wall opposite, and seemed to ruminate. Then he went back to his book. And no sooner had he forgotten Aaron, reading the fantasies of a certain Leo Frobenius,* than Aaron must stride in again.

10   "You can't say there isn't a difference between your position and mine," he said pertinently.

Lilly looked darkly over his spectacles.

"No by God," he said. "I should be in a poor way otherwise."

"You can't say you haven't the advantage—your *job* gives you the
15 advantage."

"All right. Then leave it out with my job, and leave me alone."

"That's your way of dodging it."

"My dear Aaron, I agree with you perfectly. There is no difference between us, save the fictitious advantage given to me by my job.
20 Save for my job—which is to write lies—Aaron and I are two identical little men in one and the same little boat. Shall we leave it at that, now?"

"Yes," said Aaron. "That's about it."

"Let us shake hands on it—and go to bed, my dear chap. You are
25 just recovering from influenza, and look paler than I like."

"You mean you want to be rid of me," said Aaron.

"Yes, I do mean that," said Lilly.

"Ay," said Aaron.

And after a few minutes more staring at the score of *Pelléas*, he
30 rose, put the score away on the piano, laid his flute beside it, and retired behind the screen. In silence, the strange dim noise of London sounding from below, Lilly read on about the Kabyles.* His soul had the faculty of divesting itself of the moment, and seeking further, deeper interests. These old Africans! And Atlantis! Strange,
35 strange wisdom of the Kabyles! Old, old dark Africa, and the world before the flood! How jealous Aaron seemed! The child of a jealous God.* A jealous God! Could any race be anything but despicable, with such an antecedent?

But no, persistent as a jealous God himself, Aaron re-appeared in
40 his pyjamas, and seated himself in his chair.

"What is the difference then between you and me, Lilly?" he said.

"Haven't we shaken hands on it—a difference of jobs."

"You don't believe that though, do you?"

"Nay, now I reckon you're trespassing."

"Why am I? I know you don't believe it."

"What do I believe then?" said Lilly.

"You believe you know something better than me—and that you are something better than me. Don't you?"

"Do *you* believe it?"

"What?"

"That I *am* something better than you, and that I *know* something better?"

"No, because I don't see it," said Aaron.

"Then if you don't see it, it isn't there. So go to bed and sleep the sleep of the just and the convalescent. I am not to be badgered any more."

"Am I badgering you?" said Aaron.

"Indeed you are."

"So I'm in the wrong again?"

"Once more, my dear."

"You're a God-Almighty in your way, you know."

"So long as I'm not in anybody else's way—. Anyhow, you'd be much better sleeping the sleep of the just. And I'm going out for a minute or two. Don't catch cold there with nothing on—"

"I want to catch the post," he added, rising.

Aaron looked up at him quickly. But almost before there was time to speak, Lilly had slipped into his hat and coat, seized his letters, and gone.

It was a rainy night. Lilly turned down King Street to walk to Charing Cross. He liked being out of doors. He liked to post his letters at Charing Cross postoffice. He did not want to talk to Aaron any more. He was glad to be alone.

He walked quickly down Villiers Street to the river, to see it flowing blackly towards the sea. It had an endless fascination for him: never failed to soothe him and give him a sense of liberty. He liked the night, the dark rain, the river, and even the traffic. He enjoyed the sense of friction he got from the streaming of people who meant nothing to him. It was like a fox slipping alert among unsuspecting cattle.

When he got back, he saw in the distance the lights of a taxi

standing outside the building where he lived, and heard a thumping
and hallooing. He hurried forward.

It was a man called Herbertson.

"Oh, why, there you are!" exclaimed Herbertson, as Lilly drew
5   near. "Can I come up and have a chat?"

"I've got that man who's had flu. I should think he is gone to bed."

"Oh!" The disappointment was plain. "Well, look here! I'll just
come up for a couple of minutes." He laid his hand on Lilly's arm. "I
heard you were going away. Where are you going?"

10 "Malta."

"Malta! Oh, I know Malta very well. Well now, it'll be all right if I
come up for a minute? I'm not going to see much more of you,
apparently." He turned quickly to the taxi. "What is it on the clock?"

The taxi was paid, the two men went upstairs. Aaron was in bed,
15 but he called as Lilly entered the room.

"Hullo!" said Lilly. "Not asleep? Captain Herbertson has come in
for a minute."

"Hope I shan't disturb you," said Captain Herbertson, laying
down his stick and gloves, and his cap. He was in uniform. He was
20 one of the few surviving officers of the Guards,* a man of about
forty-five, good-looking, getting rather stout. He settled himself in
the chair where Aaron had sat, hitching up his trousers. The gold
identity plate, with its gold chain, fell conspicuously over his wrist.

"Been to *Rosemary*,"* he said. "Rotten play, you know—but
25 passes the time awfully well. Oh, I quite enjoyed it."

Lilly offered him Sauterne—the only thing in the house.

"Oh yes! How awfully nice! Yes, thanks, I shall love it. Can I have
it with soda. Thanks! Do you know, I think that's the very best drink
in the tropics: sweet white wine, with soda. Yes—well!—Well now,
30 why are you going away?"

"For a change," said Lilly.

"You're quite right, one needs a change now the damned thing is
all over. As soon as I get out of khaki I shall be off. Malta! Yes! I've
been in Malta several times. I think Valletta is quite enjoyable,
35 particularly in winter, with the opera. Oh—er—how's your wife? All
right? Yes!—glad to see her people again. Bound to be—Oh, by the
way, I met Jim Bricknell. Sends you a message hoping you'll go down
and stay—down at Captain Bingham's place in Surrey, you know.
Awfully queer lot down there. Not my sort, no. You won't go down?
40 No, I shouldn't. Not the right sort of people."

Herbertson rattled away, rather spasmodic. He had been through the very front hell of the war—and like every man who had, he had the war at the back of his mind, like an obsession. But in the meantime, he skirmished.

"Yes. I was on guard one day* when the Queen gave one of her tea-parties to the blind. Awful affair. But the children are awfully nice children. Prince of Wales awfully nice, almost too nice. Prince Henry smart boy too—oh, a smart boy. Queen Mary poured the tea, and I handed round bread and butter. She told me I made a very good waiter. I said, Thank you, Madam. But I like the children. Very different from the Battenbergs. Oh!—" he wrinkled his nose. "I can't stand the Battenbergs."

"Mount Battens," said Lilly.

"Yes! Awful mistake, changing the royal name. They were Guelfs, why not remain it. Why, I'll tell you what Battenberg* did. He was in the Guards, too—"

The talk flowed on: about royalty and the Guards, Buckingham Palace and St. James.

"Rather a nice story about Queen Victoria. Man named Joyce, something or other, often used to dine at the Palace. And he was an awfully good imitator—really clever, you know. Used to imitate the Queen. 'Mr. Joyce,' she said, 'I hear your imitation is very amusing. Will you do it for us now, and let us see what it is like?'—'Oh no, Madam! I'm afraid I couldn't do it now. I'm afraid I'm not in the humour.' But she would have him do it.—And it was really awfully funny. He had to do it. You know what he did. He used to take a table-napkin, and put it on with one corner over his forehead, and the rest hanging down behind, like her veil thing. And then he sent for the kettle-lid. He always had the kettle-lid, for that little crown of hers. And then he impersonated her. But he was awfully good—so clever. 'Mr. Joyce,' she said. 'We are not amused. Please leave the room.' Yes, that is exactly what she said: '*We* are not amused—please leave the room.' I like the *We*, don't you? And he a man of sixty or so. However, he left the room and for a fortnight or so he wasn't invited—Wasn't she wonderful—Queen Victoria?"

And so, by light transitions, to the Prince of Wales at the front, and thus into the trenches. And then Herbertson was on the subject he was obsessed by. He had come, unconsciously, for this and this only: to talk war to Lilly: or at Lilly. For the latter listened and watched, and said nothing. As a man at night helplessly takes a taxi to find

some woman, some prostitute, Herbertson had almost unthinkingly
got into a taxi and come battering at the door in Covent Garden, only
to talk war to Lilly, whom he knew very little. But it was a driving
instinct—to come and get it off his chest.

5 And on and on he talked, over his wine and soda. He was not
conceited—he was not showing off—far from it. It was the same
thing here in this officer as it was with the privates, and the same with
this Englishman as with a Frenchman or a German or an Italian.
Lilly had sat in a cow-shed listening to a youth in the north country:
10 he had sat on the corn-straw that the oxen had been treading out, in
Calabria, under the moon: he had sat in a farm-kitchen with a
German prisoner: and every time it was the same thing, the same
hot, blind, anguished voice of a man who has seen too much,
experienced too much, and doesn't know where to turn. None of the
15 glamour of returned heroes, none of the romance of war: only a hot,
blind, mesmerised voice, going on and on, mesmerised by a vision
that the soul cannot bear.

In this officer, of course, there was a lightness and an appearance
of bright diffidence and humour. But underneath it all was the same
20 as in the common men of all the combatant nations: the hot, seared
burn of unbearable experience, which did not heal nor cool, and
whose irritation was not to be relieved. The experience gradually
cooled on top: but only with a surface crust. The soul did not heal,
did not recover.

25 "I used to be awfully frightened," laughed Herbertson. "Now you
say, Lilly, you'd never have stood it. But you would. You're
nervous—and it was just the nervous ones that did stand it. When
nearly all our officers were gone, we had a man come out—a man
called Margeritson, from India—big merchant people out there.
30 They all said he was no good—not a bit of good—nervous chap. No
good at all. But when you had to get out of the trench and go for the
Germans he was perfect—perfect—It all came to him then, at the
crisis, and he was perfect.

"Some things frighten one man, and some another. Now shells
35 would never frighten me. But I couldn't stand bombs. You could tell
the difference between our machines and the Germans. Ours was a
steady noise—drrrrrrrr!—but theirs was heavy, drrrr*ruru*drrrr*ruru*
—! My word, that got on my nerves . . . . . .

"No I was never hit. The nearest thing was when I was knocked
40 down by an exploding shell—several times that—you know. When

you shout like mad for the men to come and dig you out, under all the earth. And my word, you do feel frightened then." Herbertson laughed with a twinkling motion to Lilly. But between his brows there was a tension like madness.

"And a funny thing, you know—how you don't notice things.   5
In—let me see—1916—the Germans guns were a lot better than ours. Ours were old, and when they're old you can't tell where they'll hit: whether they'll go beyond the mark, or whether they'll fall short. Well this day our guns were firing short, and killing our own men. We'd had the order to charge, and were running forward, and I   10
suddenly felt hot water spurting on my neck—" He put his hand to the back of his neck and glanced round apprehensively. "It was a chap called Innes—Oh, an awfully decent sort—people were in the Argentine. He'd been calling out to me as we were running, and I was just answering. When I felt this hot water on my neck and saw   15
him running past me with no head—he'd got no head, and he went running past me. I don't know how far, but a long way . . . Blood, you know—Yes—well—

"Oh, I hated Chelsea—I loathed Chelsea—Chelsea was purgatory to me. I had a corporal called Wallace—he was a fine chap   20
—oh, he was a fine chap—six foot two—and about twenty-four years old. He was my stand-back. Oh, I hated Chelsea, and parades, and drills. You know, when it's drill, and you're giving orders, you forget what order you've just given—in front of the Palace there the crowd don't notice—but it's awful for *you*. And you know you daren't look   25
round to see what the men are doing. But Wallace was splendid. He was just behind me, and I'd hear him, quite quiet you know, 'It's right wheel, sir.' Always perfect, always perfect—yes—well . . .

"You know you don't get killed if you don't think you will. Now I never thought I should get killed. And I never knew a man get killed   30
if he hadn't been thinking he would. I said to Wallace I'd rather be out here, at the front, than at Chelsea. I hated Chelsea—I can't tell you how much. 'Oh no, sir!' he said. 'I'd rather be at Chelsea than here. I'd rather be at Chelsea. There isn't hell like this at Chelsea.' We'd had orders that we were to go back to the real camp the next   35
day. 'Never mind, Wallace,' I said. 'We shall be out of this hell-on-earth tomorrow.' And he took my hand. We weren't much for showing feeling or anything in the Guards. But he took my hand. And we climbed out to charge—Poor fellow, he was killed—" Herbertson dropped his head, and for some moments seemed to go   40

unconscious, as if struck. Then he lifted his face, and went on in the same animated chatty fashion: "You see, he had a presentiment. I'm sure he had a presentiment. None of the men got killed unless they had a presentiment—like that, you know ..."

5   Herbertson nodded keenly at Lilly, with his sharp, twinkling, yet obsessed eyes. Lilly wondered why he made the presentiment responsible for the death—which he obviously did—and not *vice versa*. Herbertson implied every time, that you'd never get killed if you could keep yourself from having a presentiment. Perhaps there
10   was something in it. Perhaps the soul issues its own ticket of death, when it can stand no more. Surely life controls life: and not accident.

      "It's a funny thing what shock will do. We had a sergeant and he shouted to me. Both his feet were off—both his feet, clean at the ankle. I gave him morphia. You know officers aren't allowed to use
15   the needle—might give the man blood poisoning. You give those tabloids. They say they act in a few minutes, but they *don't*. It's a quarter of an hour. And nothing is more demoralising than when you have a man, wounded, you know, and crying out. Well this man I gave him the morphia before he got over the stunning, you know. So
20   he didn't feel the pain. Well, they carried him in. I always used to like to look after my men. So I went next morning and I found he hadn't been removed to the Clearing Station. I got hold of the doctor and I said, 'Look here! Why hasn't this man been taken to the Clearing Station?' I used to get excited. But after some years they'd got used to
25   me. 'Don't get excited, Herbertson, the man's dying.' 'But,' I said, 'he's just been talking to me as strong as you are.' And he had—he'd talk as strong and well as you or me, then go quiet for a bit. I said I gave him the morphia before he came round from the stunning. So he'd felt nothing. But in two hours he was dead. The doctor says that
30   the shock does it like that sometimes. You can do nothing for them. Nothing vital is injured—and yet the life is broken in them. Nothing can be done—funny thing—Must be something in the brain—"

      "It's obviously not the brain," said Lilly. "It's deeper than the brain."

35   "Deeper," said Herbertson, nodding.

      "Funny thing where life is. We had a lieutenant. You know we all buried our own dead. Well, he looked as if he was asleep. Most of the chaps looked like that." Herbertson closed his eyes and laid his face aside, like a man asleep and dead peacefully. "You very rarely see a
40   man dead with any other look on his face—you know the other

look.—" And he clenched his teeth with a sudden, momentaneous, ghastly distortion.—"Well, you'd never have known this chap was dead. He had a wound here—in the back of the head—and a bit of blood on his hand—and nothing else, nothing. Well, I said we'd give him a decent burial. He lay there waiting—and they'd wrapped him in a filthy blanket—you know. Well I said he should have a proper blanket. He'd been dead lying there a day and a half you know. So I went and got a blanket, a beautiful blanket, out of his private kit—his people were Scotch, well-known family—and I got the pins, you know, ready to pin him up properly, for the Scots Guards to bury him. And I thought he'd be stiff, you see. But when I took him by the arms, to lift him on, he sat up. It gave me an awful shock. 'Why he's alive!' I said. But they said he was dead. I couldn't believe it. It gave me an awful shock. He was as flexible as you or me, and looked as if he was asleep. You couldn't believe he was dead. But we pinned him up in his blanket. It was an awful shock to me. I couldn't believe a man could be like that after he'd been dead two days …

"The Germans were wonderful with the machine guns—it's a wicked thing, a machine gun. But they couldn't touch us with the bayonet. Every time the men came back they had bayonet practice, and they got awfully good. You know when you thrust at the Germans—so—if you miss him, you bring your rifle back sharp, with a round swing, so that the butt comes up and hits up under the jaw. It's one movement, following on with the stab, you see, if you miss him. It was too quick for them—But bayonet charge was worst, you know. Because your man cries out when you catch him, when you get him, you know. That's what does you …

"No, oh no, this was no war like other wars. All the machinery of it. No, you couldn't stand it, but for the men. The men are wonderful, you know. They'll be wiped out … No, it's your men who keep you going, if you're an officer … But there'll never be another war like this. Because the Germans are the only people who could make a war like this—and I don't think they'll ever do it again, do you?

"Oh, they were wonderful, the Germans. They were amazing. It was incredible, what they invented and did. We had to learn from them, in the first two years. But they were too methodical. That's why they lost the war. They were too methodical. They'd fire their guns every ten minutes—regular: Think of it. Of course we knew when to run, and when to lie down. You got so that you knew almost

exactly what they'd do—if you'd been out long enough. And then you
could time what you wanted to do yourselves.

"They were a lot more nervous than we were, at the last. They
sent up enough light at night from their trenches—you know, those
5   things that burst in the air like electric light—we had none of that to
do—they did it all for us—lit up everything. They were more
nervous than we were . . ."

It was nearly two o'clock when Herbertson left. Lilly, depressed,
remained before the fire. Aaron got out of bed and came uneasily to
10 the fire.

"It gives me the belly-ache, that damned war," he said.

"So it does me," said Lilly. "All unreal."

"Real enough for those that had to go through it."

"No, least of all for them," said Lilly sullenly. "Not as real as a
15 bad dream. Why the hell don't they wake up and realise it!"

"That's a fact," said Aaron. "They're hypnotised by it."

"And they want to hypnotise me. And I won't be hypnotised. The
war was a lie and is a lie and will go on being a lie till somebody busts
it."

20 "It was a fact—you can't bust that. You can't bust the fact that it
happened."

"Yes you can. It never happened. It never happened to me. No
more than my dreams happen. My dreams don't happen: they only
seem."

25 "But the war did happen, right enough," smiled Aaron palely.

"No it didn't. Not to me or to any man, in his own self. It took
place in the automatic sphere, like dreams do. But the *actual man* in
every man was just absent—asleep—or drugged—inert—dream-
logged. That's it."

30 "You tell 'em so," said Aaron.

"I do. But it's no good. Because they won't wake up now
even—perhaps never. They'll all kill themselves in their sleep."

"They wouldn't be any better if they did wake up and be
themselves—that is, supposing they are asleep, which I can't see.
35 They are what they are—and they're all alike—and never very
different from what they are now."

Lilly stared at Aaron with black eyes.

"Do you believe in them less than I do, Aaron?" he asked slowly.

"I don't even want to believe in them."

40 "But in yourself?" Lilly was almost wistful—and Aaron uneasy.

"I don't know that I've any more right to believe in myself than in them," he replied. Lilly watched and pondered.

"No," he said. "That's not true—I *knew* the war was false: humanly quite false. I always knew it was false. The Germans were false, we were false, everybody was false."

"And not you?" asked Aaron shrewishly.

"There was a wakeful, self-possessed bit of me which knew that the war and all that horrible movement was false for me. And so I wasn't going to be dragged in. The Germans could have shot my mother or me or what they liked: I wouldn't have joined the *war*. I would like to kill my enemy. But become a bit of that huge obscene machine they called the war, that I never would, no, not if I died ten deaths and had eleven mothers violated. But I would like to kill my enemy: oh yes, more than one enemy. But not as a unit in a vast obscene mechanism. That never: no, never."

Poor Lilly was too earnest and vehement. Aaron made a fine nose. It seemed to him like a lot of words and a bit of wriggling out of a hole.

"Well," he said, "you've got men and nations, and you've got the machines of war—so how are you going to get out of it? League of Nations?"

"Damn all leagues. Damn all masses and groups, anyhow. All I want is to get *myself* out of their horrible heap: to get out of the swarm. The swarm to me is nightmare and nullity—horrible helpless writhing in a dream. I want to get myself awake, out of it all—all that mass-consciousness, all that mass-activity—it's the most horrible nightmare to me. No man is awake and himself. No man who was awake and in possession of himself would use poison gases: no man. His own awake self would scorn such a thing. It's only when the ghastly mob-sleep, the dream helplessness of the mass-psyche overcomes him, that he becomes completely base and obscene."

"Ha—well," said Aaron. "It's the wide-awake ones that invent the poison gas, and use it. Where should we be without it?"

Lilly started, went stiff and hostile.

"Do you mean that, Aaron?" he said, looking into Aaron's face with a hard, inflexible look.

Aaron turned aside half sheepishly.

"That's how it looks on the face of it, isn't it?" he said.

"Look here, my friend, it's too late for you to be talking to me about the face of things. If that's how you feel, put your things on and

follow Herbertson. Yes—go out of my room. I don't put up with the
face of things here."

Aaron looked at him in cold amazement.

"It'll do tomorrow morning, won't it?" he asked, rather mocking.

5   "Yes," said Lilly coldly. "But please go tomorrow morning."

"Oh, I'll go all right," said Aaron. "Everybody's got to agree with
you—that's your price."

But Lilly did not answer. Aaron turned into bed, his satirical smile
under his nose. Somewhat surprised, however, at this sudden turn of
10   affairs.

As he was just going to sleep, dismissing the matter, Lilly came
once more to his bedside, and said, in a hard voice:

"I'm *not* going to pretend to have friends on the face of things. No,
and I *don't* have friends who don't fundamentally agree with me. A
15   friend means one who is at one with me in matters of life and death.
And if you're at one with all the rest, then you're their friend, not
mind. So be *their* friend. And please leave me in the morning. You
owe me nothing, you have nothing more to do with me. I have had
enough of these friendships where I pay the piper and the mob calls
20   the tune.

"Let me tell you, moreover, your heroic Herbertsons lost us more
than ever they won. A brave ant is a damned cowardly individual.
Your heroic officers are a sad sight *afterwards*, when they come
home. Bah, your Herbertson! The only justification for war is what
25   we learn from it. And what have they learnt?—Why did so many of
them have presentiments, as he called it? Because they could feel
inside them, there was nothing to come after. There was no
life-courage: only death-courage. Nothing beyond this hell—only
death or love-languishing—"

30   "What could they have seen, anyhow," said Aaron.

"It's not what you see, actually. It's the kind of spirit you keep
inside you: the life-spirit. When Wallace had presentiments,
Herbertson, being officer, should have said: None of that, Wallace.
You and I, we've got to live and make life smoke.—Instead of which
35   he let Wallace be killed, and his own heart be broken. Always the
death-choice—And we won't, we simply will not face the world as
we've made it, and our own souls as we find them, and take the
responsibility. We'll never get anywhere till we stand up man to man
and face *everything* out, and break the old forms, but never let our
40   own pride and courage of life be broken."

Lilly broke off, and went silently to bed: Aaron turned over to sleep, rather resenting the sound of so many words. What difference did it make, anyhow. In the morning, however, when he saw the other man's pale, closed, rather haughty face, he realised that something *had* happened. Lilly was courteous and even affable: but with a curious cold space between him and Aaron. Breakfast passed, and Aaron knew that he must leave. There was something in Lilly's bearing which just showed him the door. In some surprise and confusion, and in some anger, not unmingled with humorous irony, he put his things in his bag. He put on his hat and coat. Lilly was seated rather stiffly writing.

"Well," said Aaron. "I suppose we shall meet again."

"Oh sure to," said Lilly, rising from his chair. "We are sure to run across one another."

"When are you going?" asked Aaron.

"In a few days' time."

"Oh well, I'll run in and see you before you go, shall I?"

"Yes, do."

Lilly escorted his guest to the top of the stairs, shook hands, and then returned into his own room, closing the door on himself.

Aaron did not find his friend at home when he called. He took it rather as a slap in the face. But then he knew quite well that Lilly had made a certain call on his, Aaron's soul: a call which he, Aaron, did not at all intend to obey. If in return the soul-caller chose to shut his street-door in the face of the world-friend—well, let it be quits. He was not sure whether he felt superior to his unworldly enemy or not. He rather thought he did.*

Chapter XI.

More Pillar of Salt

The opera season ended, Aaron was invited by Cyril Scott to join a group of musical people in a village by the sea. He accepted, and spent a pleasant month. It pleased the young men musically-inclined and bohemian by profession to patronise the flautist, whom they declared marvellous. Bohemians with well-to-do parents, they could already afford to squander a little spasmodic and self-gratifying patronage. And Aaron did not mind being patronised. He had nothing else to do.

But the party broke up early in September. The flautist was detained a few days at a country house, for the amusement of the guests. Then he left for London.

In London he found himself at a loose end. A certain fretful dislike of the patronage of indifferent young men, younger than himself, and a certain distaste for regular work in the orchestra made him look round. He wanted something else. He wanted to disappear again. Qualms and emotions concerning his abandoned family overcame him. The early, delicate autumn affected him. He took a train to the Midlands.

And again, just after dark, he strolled with his little bag across the field which lay at the end of his garden. It had been mown, and the grass was already growing long. He stood and looked at the line of back windows, lighted once more. He smelled the scents of autumn, phlox and moist old vegetation and corn in sheaf. A nostalgia which was half at least revulsion affected him. The place, the home, at once fascinated and revolted him.

Sitting in his shed, he scrutinised his garden carefully, in the starlight. There were two rows of beans, rather dishevelled. Near at hand the marrow plants sprawled from their old bed. He could detect the perfume of a few carnations. He wondered who it was had planted the garden, during his long absence. Anyhow, there it was, planted and fruited and waning into autumn.

The blind was not drawn. It was eight o'clock. The children were going to bed. Aaron waited in his shed, his bowels stirred with violent but only half-admitted emotions. There was his wife, slim and graceful, holding a little mug to the baby's mouth. And the baby was drinking. She looked lonely. Wild emotions attacked his heart. There was going to be a wild and emotional reconciliation.

Was there? It seemed like something fearful and imminent. A passion arose in him, a craving for the violent emotional reconciliation. He waited impatiently for the children to be gone to bed, gnawed with restless desire.

He heard the clock strike nine, then half-past, from the village behind. The children would be asleep. His wife was sitting sewing some little frock. He went lingering down the garden path, stooping to lift the fallen carnations, to see how they were. There were many flowers, but small. He broke one off, then threw it away. The golden rod was out. Even in the little lawn there were asters, as of old.

His wife started to listen, hearing his step. He was filled with a violent conflict of tenderness, like a sickness. He hesitated, tapping at the door, and entered. His wife started to her feet, at bay.

"What have you come for!" was her involuntary ejaculation.

But he, with the familiar old* jerk of his head towards the garden, asked with a faint smile:

"Who planted the garden?"

And he felt himself dropping into the twang of the vernacular, which he had discarded.

Lottie only stood and stared at him, objectively. She did not think to answer. He took his hat off, and put it on the dresser. Again the familiar act maddened her.

"What have you come for?" she cried again, with a voice full of hate. Or perhaps it was fear and doubt and even hope as well. He heard only hate.

This time he turned to look at her. The old dagger was drawn in her.

"I wonder," he said, "myself."

Then she recovered herself, and with trembling hand picked up her sewing again. But she still stood at bay, beyond the table. She said nothing. He, feeling tired, sat down on the chair nearest the door. But he reached for his hat, and kept it on his knee. She, as she stood there unnaturally, went on with her sewing. There was silence for some time. Curious sensations and emotions went through the man's frame, seeming to destroy him. They were like electric shocks, which he felt she emitted against him. And an old sickness came in

him again. He had forgotten it. It was the sickness of the un-
recognised and incomprehensible strain between him and her.

After a time she put down her sewing, and sat again in her chair.

"Do you know how vilely you've treated me?" she said, staring
5   across the space at him. He averted his face.

Yet he answered, not without irony:

"I suppose so."

"And why?" she cried. "I should like to know why."

He did not answer. The way she rushed in made him go vague.
10   "Justify yourself. Say why you've been so vile to me. Say what you
had against me," she demanded.

"What I *had* against her," he mused to himself: and he wondered
that she used the past tense. He made no answer.

"Accuse me," she insisted. "Say what I've done to make you treat
15   me like this. Say it. You must *think* it hard enough."

"Nay," he said. "I don't think it."

This speech, by which he merely meant that he did not trouble to
formulate any injuries he had against her, puzzled her.

"Don't come pretending you love me, *now*. It's too late," she said
20   with contempt. Yet perhaps also hope.

"You might wait till I start pretending," he said.

This enraged her.

"You vile creature!" she exclaimed. "Go! What have you come
for?"
25   "To look at *you*," he said sarcastically.

After a few minutes she began to cry, sobbing violently into her
apron. And again his bowels stirred and boiled.

"What have I done! What have I done! I don't know what I've
done that he should be like this to me," she sobbed, into her apron. It
30   was childish, and perhaps true. At least it was true from the childish
part of her nature. He sat gloomy and uneasy.

She took the apron from her tear-stained face, and looked at him.
It was true, in her moments of roused exposure she was a beautiful
woman—a beautiful woman. At this moment, with her flushed,
35   tear-stained, wilful distress, she was beautiful.

"Tell me," she challenged. "Tell me! Tell me what I've done.
Tell me what you have against me. Tell me."

Watching like a lynx, she saw the puzzled, hurt look in his face.
Telling isn't so easy—especially when the trouble goes too deep for
40   conscious comprehension. He couldn't *tell* what he had against her.

And he had not the slightest intention of doing what she would have liked him to do, starting to pile up detailed grievances. He knew the detailed grievances were nothing in themselves.

"You *can't*," she cried vindictively. "You *can't*. You *can't* find anything real to bring against me, though you'd like to. You'd like to be able to accuse me of something, but you *can't* because you know there isn't anything."

She watched him, watched. And he sat in the chair near the door, without moving.

"You're unnatural, that's what you are," she cried. "You're unnatural. You're not a man. You haven't got a man's feelings. You're nasty, and cold, and unnatural. And you're a coward. You're a coward. You ran away from me, without telling me what you've got against me."

"When you've had enough, you go away and you don't care what you do," he said, epigrammatic.

She paused a moment.

"Enough of what?" she said. "What have you had enough of? Of me and your children? It's a nice manly thing to say. Haven't I loved you? Haven't I loved you for twelve years, and worked and slaved for you and tried to keep you right? Heavens knows where you'd have been but for me, evil as you are at the bottom. You're evil, that's what it is—and weak. You're too weak to love a woman and give her what she wants: too weak. Unmanly and cowardly, he runs away."

"No wonder," he said.

"No," she cried. "It *is* no wonder, with a nature like yours: weak and unnatural and evil. It *is* no wonder."

She became quiet—and then started to cry again, into her apron. Aaron waited. He felt physically weak.

"And who knows what you've been doing all these months," she wept. "Who knows all the vile things you've been doing. And you're the father of my children—the father of my little girls—and who knows what vile things he's guilty of, all these months."

"I shouldn't let my imagination run away with me," he answered. "I've been playing the flute in the orchestra of one of the theatres in London."

"Ha!" she cried. "It's more than that. Don't think I'm going to believe you. I know you, with your smooth-sounding lies. You're a liar, as you know. And I know you've been doing other things besides play a flute in an orchestra. You!—as if I don't know you. And then coming crawling back to me with your lies and your pretence. Don't think I'm taken in."

"I should be sorry," he said.

"Coming crawling back to me, and expecting to be forgiven," she
5 went on. "But no—I don't forgive—and I can't forgive—never—not as long as I live shall I forgive what you've done to me."

"You can wait till you're asked, anyhow," he said.

"And you can wait," she said. "And you *shall* wait." She took up her sewing, and stitched steadily, as if calmly. Anyone glancing in
10 would have imagined a quiet domestic hearth at that moment. He, too, feeling physically weak, remained silent, feeling his soul absent from the scene.

Again she suddenly burst into tears, weeping bitterly.

"And the children," she sobbed, rocking herself with grief and
15 chagrin. "What have I been able to say to the children—what have I been able to tell them."

"What *have* you told them?" he asked coldly.

"I told them you'd gone away to work," she sobbed, laying her head on her arms on the table. "What else could I tell them? I
20 couldn't tell them the vile truth about their father. I couldn't tell *them* how evil you are." She sobbed and moaned.

He wondered what exactly the vile truth would have been, had she *started* to tell it. And he began to feel, coldly and cynically, that among all her distress there was a luxuriating in the violent emotions
25 of the scene in hand, and the situation altogether.

Then again she became quiet, and picked up her sewing. She stitched quietly, wistfully, for some time. Then she looked up at him—a long look of reproach, and sombre accusation, and wifely tenderness. He turned his face aside.

30 "You know you've been wrong to me, don't you?" she said, half wistfully, half menacing.

He felt her wistfulness and her menace tearing him in his bowels and loins.

"You do know, don't you?" she insisted, still with the wistful
35 appeal, and the veiled threat.

"You do, or you would answer," she said. "You've still got enough that's right in you, for you to know."

She waited. He sat still, as if drawn by hot wires.

Then she slipped across to him, put her arms round him, sank on
40 her knees at his side, and sank her face against his thigh.

"Say you know how wrong you are. Say you know how cruel you've been to me," she pleaded. But under her female pleading and appeal he felt the iron of her threat.

"You *do* know it," she murmured, looking up into his face as she crouched by his knee. "You *do* know it. I can see in your eyes that you know it. And why have you come back to me, if you don't know it! Why have you come back to me? Tell me!" Her arms gave him a sharp, compulsory little clutch round the waist. "Tell me! Tell me!" she murmured, with all her appeal liquid in her throat.

But him, it half overcame, and at the same time, horrified. He had a certain horror of her. The strange, liquid sound of her appeal seemed to him like the swaying of a serpent which mesmerises the fated, fluttering, helpless bird. She clasped her arms round him, she drew him to her, she half roused his passion. At the same time she coldly horrified and repelled him. He had not the faintest feeling, at the moment, of his own wrong. But she wanted to win his own self-betrayal out of him. He could see himself as the fascinated victim, falling to this cajoling, awful woman, the wife of his bosom. But as well, he had a soul outside himself, which looked on the whole scene with cold revulsion, and which was as unchangeable as time.

"No," he said. "I don't feel wrong."

"You *do*!" she said, giving him a sharp, admonitory clutch. "You *do*. Only you're silly, and obstinate, babyish and silly and obstinate. An obstinate little boy—you *do* feel wrong. And you *are* wrong. And you've got to say it."

But quietly he disengaged himself and got to his feet, his face pale and set, obstinate as she said. He put his hat on, and took his little bag. She watched him curiously, still crouching by his chair.

"I'll go," he said, putting his hand on the latch.

Suddenly she sprang to her feet and clutched him by the shirt-neck, her hand inside his soft collar, half strangling him.

"You villain," she said, and her face was transfigured with passion as he had never seen it before, horrible. "You villain!" she said thickly. "What have you come here for?"

His soul went black as he looked at her. He broke her hand away from his shirt collar, bursting the stud-holes. She recoiled in silence. And in one black, unconscious movement he was gone, down the garden and over the fence and across the country, swallowed in a black unconsciousness.

She, realising, sank upon the hearth-rug and lay there curled upon herself. She was defeated. But she too would never yield. She lay quite motionless for some time. Then she got up, feeling the draught on the floor. She closed the door, and drew down the blind. Then she looked at her wrist, which he had gripped, and which 5 pained her. Then she went to the mirror and looked for a long time at her white, strained, determined face. Come life, come death, she too would never yield. And she realised now that he would never yield.

She was faint with weariness, and would be glad to get to bed and sleep.

10 Aaron meanwhile had walked across the country and was looking for a place to rest. He found a cornfield with a half-built stack, and sheaves in stook. Ten to one some tramp would have found the stack. He threw a dozen sheaves together and lay down, looking at the stars in the September sky. He too would never yield. The illusion of love 15 was gone for ever. Love was a battle in which each party strove for the mastery of the other's soul. So far, man had yielded the mastery to woman. Now he was fighting for it back again. And too late, for the woman would never yield.

But whether woman yielded or not, he would keep the mastery of 20 his own soul and conscience and actions. He would never yield himself up to her judgment again. He would hold himself forever beyond her jurisdiction.

Henceforth, life single, not life double.

He looked at the sky, and thanked the universe for the blessedness 25 of being alone in the universe. To be alone, to be oneself, not to be driven or violated into something which is not oneself, surely it is better than anything. He thought of Lottie, and knew how much more truly herself she was when she was alone, with no man to distort her. And he was thankful for the division between them. Such 30 scenes as the last were too horrible and unreal.

As for future unions, too soon to think about it. Let there be clean and pure division first, perfected singleness. That is the only way to final, living unison: through sheer, finished singleness.

Chapter XII.

Novara*

Having no job for the autumn, Aaron fidgetted in London. He played at some concerts and some private shows. He was one of an odd quartette, for example, which went to play to Lady Artemis Hooper, when she lay in bed after her famous escapade of falling through the window of her taxi-cab.* Aaron had that curious knack, which belongs to some people, of getting into the swim without knowing he was doing it. Lady Artemis thought his flute lovely, and had him again to play for her. Aaron looked at her, and she at him. She, as she reclined there in bed in a sort of half-light, well made-up, smoking her cigarettes and talking in a rather raucous voice, making her slightly rasping witty comments to the other men in the room—of course there were other men, the audience—was a shock to the flautist. This was the bride of the moment! Curious how raucous her voice sounded out of the cigarette smoke. Yet he liked her—the reckless note of the modern, social freebooter. In himself was a touch of the same quality.

"Do you love playing?" she asked him.

"Yes—" he said, with that shadow of irony which seemed like a smile on his face.

"Live for it, so to speak," she said.

"I make my living by it," he said.

"But that's not really how you take it?" she said. He eyed her. She watched him over her cigarette. It was a personal moment.

"I don't think about it," he said.

"I'm sure you don't. You wouldn't be so good if you did. You're awfully lucky, you know, to be able to pour yourself down your flute."

"You think I go down easy?" he laughed.

"Ah!" she replied, flicking her cigarette broadcast. "That's the point. What should you say, Jimmy?" she turned to one of the men. He screwed his eyeglass nervously and stiffened himself to look at her.

"I—I shouldn't like to say, off-hand," came the small-voiced,

self-conscious answer. And Jimmy bridled himself and glanced at
Aaron.

"Do you find it a tight squeeze, then?" she said, turning to Aaron
once more.

5   "No, I can't say that," he answered. "What of me goes down goes
down easy enough. It's what doesn't go down."

"And how much is that?" she asked, eying him.

"A good bit maybe," he said.

"Slops over, so to speak," she retorted sarcastically. "And which
10   do you enjoy more, trickling down your flute or slopping over on to
the lap of Mother Earth—of Miss, more probably!"

"Depends," he said.

Having got him a few steps too far upon the personal ground, she
left him to get off by himself.

15   So he found London got on his nerves. He felt it rubbed him the
wrong way. He was flattered, of course, by his own success—and felt
at the same time irritated by it. This state of mind was by no means
acceptable. Wherever he was he liked to be given, tacitly, the first
place—or a place among the first. Among the musical people he
20   frequented, he found himself on a callow kind of equality with
everybody, even the stars and aristocrats, at one moment, and a
backstairs outsider the next. It was all just as the moment demanded.
There was a certain excitement in slithering up and down the social
scale, one minute chatting in a personal *tête-à-tête* with the most
25   famous, or notorious, of the society beauties: and the next walking
in the rain, with his flute in a bag, to his grubby lodging in Bloomsbury. Only the excitement roused all the savage sarcasm that lay at
the bottom of his soul, and which burned there like an unhealthy
bile.

30   Therefore he determined to clear out—to disappear. He had a
letter from Lilly, from Novara. Lilly was drifting about. Aaron wrote
to Novara, and asked if he should come to Italy, having no money to
speak of. "Come if you want to. Bring your flute. And if you've no
money, put on a good suit of clothes and a big black hat, and play
35   outside the best café in any Italian town, and you'll collect enough to
get on with."

It was a sporting chance. Aaron packed his bag and got a passport,
and wrote to Lilly to say he would join him, as invited, at Sir William
Franks'.* He hoped Lilly's answer would arrive before he left
40   London. But it didn't.

Therefore behold our hero alighting at Novara, two hours late, on a wet dark evening. He hoped Lilly would be there: but nobody. With some slight dismay he faced the big, crowded station. The stream of people carried him automatically through the barrier, a porter having seized his bag, and volleyed various unintelligible questions at him. Aaron understood not one word. So he just wandered after the blue blouse of the porter.

The porter deposited the bag on the steps of the station front, fired off more questions and gesticulated into the half-illuminated space of darkness outside the station. Aaron decided it meant a cab, so he nodded and said "Yes." But there were no cabs. So once more the blue-bloused porter slung the big bag and the little bag on the strap over his shoulder, and they plunged into the night, towards some lights and a sort of theatre place.

One carriage stood there in the rain—yes, and it was free.

"Keb? yes—or-right—sir. Whe'to? Where you go? Sir William Franks. Yes, I know. Long way go—go long way. Sir William Franks."

The cabman spattered his few words of English. Aaron gave the porter an English shilling. The porter let the coin lie in the middle of his palm, as if it were a live beetle, and darted to the light of the carriage to examine the beast, exclaiming volubly. The cabman, wild with interest, peered down from the box into the palm of the porter, and carried on an impassioned dialogue. Aaron stood with one foot on the step.

"What you give—he? One franc?" asked the driver.

"A shilling," said Aaron.

"One sheeling. Yes. I know that. One sheeling English"—and the driver went off into impassioned exclamations in Torinese.* The porter, still muttering and holding his hand as if the coin might sting him, filtered away.

"Or-right. He know—sheeling—or-right. English moneys, eh? Yes, he know. You get up, sir."

And away went Aaron, under the hood of the carriage, clattering down the wide darkness of Novara, over a bridge apparently, past huge rain-wet statues, and through more rainy half-lit streets.

They stopped at last outside a sort of park wall* with trees above. The big gates were just beyond.

"Sir William Franks—there—" in a mixture of Italian and English the driver told Aaron to get down and ring the bell on the right.

Aaron got down and in the darkness was able to read the name on the plate.

"How much?" said Aaron to the driver.

"Ten franc," said the fat driver.

5 But it was his turn now to screw down and scrutinise the pink ten-shilling note. He waved it in his hand.

"Not good, eh? Not good moneys?"

"Yes," said Aaron, rather indignantly. "Good English money. Ten shillings. Better than ten francs, a good deal. Better—better—"

10 "Good—you say? Ten sheeling—" The driver muttered and muttered, as if dissatisfied. But as a matter of fact he stowed the note in his waistcoat pocket with considerable satisfaction, looked at Aaron curiously, and drove away.

Aaron stood there in the dark outside the big gates, and wished

15 himself somewhere else. However, he rang the bell. There was a huge barking of dogs on the other side. Presently a light switched on, and a woman, followed by a man, appeared cautiously, in the half-opened doorway.

"Sir William Franks?" said Aaron.

20 "Si, signore."

And Aaron stepped with his two bags inside the gate. Huge dogs jumped round. He stood in the darkness under the trees at the foot of the park. The woman fastened the gate—Aaron saw a door—and through an uncurtained window a man writing at a desk—rather like

25 the clerk in an hotel office. He was going with his two bags to the open door, when the woman stopped him, and began talking to him in Italian. It was evident he must not go on. So he put down the bags. The man stood a few yards away, watchfully.

Aaron looked down at the woman and tried to make out something

30 of what she was saying, but could not. The dogs still barked spasmodically, drops fell from the tall dark trees that rose overhead.

"Is Mr. Lilly here? Mr. Lilly?" he asked.

"Signor Lillee. No signore—"

And off the woman went in Italian. But it was evident Lilly was not

35 at the house. Aaron wished more than ever he had not come, but had gone to an hotel.

He made out that the woman was asking him for his name—"Meester—? Meester—?" she kept saying, with a note of interrogation.

"Sisson. Mr. Sisson," said Aaron, who was becoming impatient. And he found a visiting card to give her. She seemed appeased—said something about telephone—and left him standing.

The rain had ceased, but big drops were shaken from the dark high trees. Through the uncurtained window he saw the man at the desk reach the telephone. There was a long pause. At length the woman came back and motioned to him to go up—up the drive which curved and disappeared under the dark trees.

"Go up there?" said Aaron, pointing.

That was evidently the intention. So he picked up his bags and strode forward, from out of the circle of electric light, up the curved drive in the darkness. It was a steep incline. He saw trees and the grass slopes. There was a tang of snow in the air.

Suddenly, up ahead, a brilliant light switched on. He continued uphill through the trees along the path, towards it, and at length emerged at the foot of a great flight of steps, above which was a wide glass entrance, and an Italian manservant in white gloves hovering as if on the brink.

Aaron emerged from the drive and climbed the steps. The manservant came down two steps and took the little bag. Then he ushered Aaron and the big bag into a large, pillared hall, with thick turkish carpet on the floor, and handsome appointments. It was spacious, comfortable and warm; but somewhat pretentious; rather like the imposing hall into which the heroine suddenly enters on the film.

Aaron dropped his heavy bag, with relief, and stood there, hat in hand, in his damp overcoat in the circle of light, looking vaguely at the yellow marble pillars, the gilded arches above, the shadowy distances and the great stairs. The butler disappeared—re-appeared in another moment—and through an open doorway came the host. Sir William was a small, clean old man with a thin white beard and a courtly deportment, wearing a black velvet dinner-jacket faced with purple silk.

"How do you do, Mr. Sisson. You come straight from England?"

Sir William held out his hand courteously and benevolently, smiling an old man's smile of hospitality.

"Mr. Lilly has gone away?" said Aaron.

"Yes. He left us several days ago."

Aaron hesitated.

"You didn't expect me, then?"

"Yes, oh yes. Yes, oh yes. Very glad to see you—Well now, come in and have some dinner—"

At this moment Lady Franks appeared—short, rather plump, but
5 erect and definite, in a black silk dress and pearls round her throat.

"How do you do? We are just at dinner," she said. "You haven't eaten? No—well then—would you like a bath now, or—?"

It was evident the Franks had dispensed much hospitality: much of it charitable. Aaron felt it.

10 "No," he said. "I'll wash my hands and come straight in, shall I?"

"Yes, perhaps that would be better—"

"I'm afraid I am a nuisance—"

"Not at all—Beppe—" and she gave instructions in Italian.

Another footman appeared, and took the big bag. Aaron took the
15 little one this time. They climbed the broad, turning stairs, crossed another handsome lounge, gilt and ormolu and yellow silk chairs and scattered copies of *The Graphic* or of *Country Life,** then they disappeared through a doorway into a much narrower flight of stairs. Man can so rarely keep it up all the way, the grandeur.

20 Two black and white chamber-maids appeared. Aaron found himself in a blue silk bedroom, and a footman unstrapping his bag, which he did not want unstrapped. Next minute he was beckoned and allured by the Italian servants down the corridor, and presented to the handsome, spacious bathroom, which was warm and creamy-
25 coloured and glittering with massive silver and mysterious with up-to-date conveniences. There he was left to his own devices, and felt like a small boy finding out how it works. For even the mere turning on of the taps was a problem in silver mechanics.

In spite of all the splendours and the elaborated convenience, he
30 washed himself in good hot water, and wished he were having a bath, chiefly because of the wardrobe of marvellous turkish towels. Then he clicked his way back to his bedroom, changed his shirt and combed his hair in the blue silk bedroom with the Greuze* picture, and felt a little dim and superficial surprise. He had fallen into
35 country house parties before, but never into quite such a plushy sense of riches. He felt he ought to have his breath taken away. But alas, the cinema has taken our breath away so often, investing us in all the splendours of the splendidest American millionaire, or all the heroics and marvels of the Somme* or the North Pole, that life has
40 now no magnate richer than we, no hero nobler than we have been,

on the film. *Connu! Connu!** Everything life has to offer is known
to us, couldn't be known better, from the film.

So Aaron tied his tie in front of a big Venice mirror, and nothing
was a surprise to him. He found a footman hovering to escort him to
the dining-room—a real Italian footman, uneasy because milady's   5
dinner was unsettled. He entered the rather small dining-room, and
saw the people at table.

He was told various names: bowed to a young slim woman with big
blue eyes and dark hair like a photograph, then to a smaller rather
colourless young woman with a large nose: then to a stout, rubicund,   10
bald colonel, and to a tall, thin, Oxford-looking major with a black
patch over his eye—both these men in khaki: finally to a good-
looking, well-nourished young man in a dinner-jacket, and he sat
down to his soup, on his hostess' left hand. The colonel sat on her
right, and was confidential. Little Sir William, with his hair and his   15
beard white like spun glass, his manner very courteous and animated, the purple facings of his velvet jacket very impressive, sat at
the far end of the table jesting with the ladies and showing his teeth
in an old man's smile, a little bit affected, but pleasant, wishing
everybody to be happy.   20

Aaron ate his soup, trying to catch up. Milady's own confidential
Italian butler, fidelity itself, hovered quivering near, spiritually
helping the new-comer to catch up. Two nice little entrée dishes,
specially prepared for Aaron to take the place of the bygone fish and
vol-au-vents of the proper dinner, testified to the courtesy and   25
charity of his hostess.

Well, eating rapidly, he had more or less caught up by the time the
sweets came. So he swallowed a glass of wine and looked round. His
hostess with her pearls, and her diamond star in her grey hair, was
speaking of Lilly and then of music to him.   30

"I hear you are a musician. That's what I should have been if I had
had my way."

"What instrument?" asked Aaron.

"Oh, the piano. Yours is the flute, Mr. Lilly says. I think the flute
can be so attractive. But I feel, of course, you have more range with   35
the piano. I love the piano—and orchestra."

At that moment, the colonel and hostess-duties distracted her.
But she came back in snatches. She was a woman who reminded him
a little of Queen Victoria; so assured in her own room, a large part of
her attention always given to the successful issue of her duties, the   40

remainder at the disposal of her guests. It was an old-fashioned, not
unpleasant feeling: like retrospect. But she had beautiful big, smooth
emeralds and sapphires on her fingers. Money! What a curious thing
it is! Aaron noticed the deference of all the guests at table: a touch of
5 obsequiousness: before the money! And the host and hostess
accepted the deference, nay, expected it, as their due. Yet both Sir
William and Lady Franks *knew* that it was only money and success.
They had both a certain afterthought, knowing dimly that the game
was but a game, and that they were the helpless leaders in the game.
10 They had a certain basic ordinariness which prevented their making
any great hits, and which kept them disillusioned all the while. They
remembered their poor and insignificant days.

"And I hear you were playing in the orchestra at Covent Garden.
We came back from London last week. I enjoyed Beecham's operas
15 so much."

"Which do you like best?" said Aaron.

"Oh, the Russian. I think *Ivan.** It is such fine music."

"I find *Ivan* artificial."

"Do you? Oh, I don't think so. No, I don't think you can say that."

20 Aaron wondered at her assurance. She seemed to put him just a
tiny bit in his place, even in an opinion on music. Money gave her
that right too. Curious—the only authority left. And he deferred to
her opinion: that is, to her money. He did it almost deliberately.
Yes—what did he believe in, besides money? What does any man?

25 He looked at the black patch over the major's eye. What had he given
his eye for?—the nation's money. Well, and very necessary too;
otherwise we might be where the wretched Austrians are.* Instead of
which—how smooth his hostess' sapphires!

"Of course I myself prefer Moussorgsky," said Aaron. "I think he
30 is a greater artist. But perhaps it is just personal preference."

"Yes. *Boris* is wonderful. Oh, some of the scenes in *Boris*!"

"And even more *Kovantchina*,"* said Aaron. "I wish we could go
back to melody pure and simple. Yet I find *Kovantchina*, which is all
mass music practically, gives me more satisfaction than any other
35 opera."

"Do you really. I shouldn't say so: oh no—But you can't mean
that you would like all music to go back to melody pure and simple!
Just a flute—just a pipe! Oh, Mr. Sisson, you are bigoted for your
instrument. I just *live* in harmony—chords, chords!" She struck
40 imaginary chords on the white damask, and her sapphires swam

blue. But at the same time she was watching to see if Sir William had still got beside his plate the white medicine *cachet** which he must swallow at every meal. Because if so, she must remind him to swallow it. However, at that very moment, he put it on his tongue. So that she could turn her attention again to Aaron and the imaginary chord on the white damask; the thing she just lived in. But the rubicund bald colonel, more rubicund after wine, most rubicund now the marsala was going, snatched her attention with a burly homage to her femininity, and shared his fear with her with a boyish gallantry.

When the women had gone up, Sir William came near and put his hand on Aaron's shoulder. It was evident the charm was beginning to work. Sir William was a self-made man, and not in the least a snob. He liked the fundamental ordinariness in Aaron, the commonness of the common man.

"Well now, Mr. Sisson, we are very glad to see you: very glad indeed. I count Mr. Lilly one of the most interesting men it has ever been my good fortune to know. And so for your own sake, and for Mr. Lilly's sake, we are very glad to see you. Arthur, my boy, give Mr. Sisson some marsala—and take some yourself."

"Thank you, Sir," said the well-nourished young man in nice evening clothes. "You'll take another glass yourself, Sir?"

"Yes, I will, I will. I will drink a glass with Mr. Sisson. Major, where are you wandering off to? Come and take a glass with us, my boy."

"Thanks, Sir William," drawled the young major with the black patch.

"Now Colonel—I hope you are in good health and spirits."

"Never better, Sir William, never better."

"I'm very glad to hear it: very glad indeed. Try my marsala—I think it is quite good. Port is beyond us for the moment—for the moment—"

And the old man sipped his brown wine, and smiled again. He made quite a handsome picture: but he was frail.

"And where are you bound, Mr. Sisson? Towards Rome?"

"I came to meet Lilly," said Aaron.

"Ah! But Lilly has fled over the borders by this time. Never was such a man for crossing frontiers. Wonderful person, to be able to do it."

"Where has he gone?" said Aaron.

"I think to Geneva for the moment. But he certainly talked of Venice. You yourself have no definite goal?"

"No."

"Ah! You have not come to Italy to practice your art?"

"I shall *have* to practice it: or else—no, I haven't come for that."

"Ah, you will *have* to practice it. Ah yes! We are all under the necessity to eat. And you have a family in England? Am I not right?"

"Quite. I've got a family depending on me."

"Yes, then you must practice your art: you must practice your art. Well—shall we join the ladies? Coffee will no doubt be served."

"Will you take my arm, Sir?" said the well-nourished Arthur.

"Thank you, thank you," the old man motioned him away.

So they went upstairs to where the three women were sitting in the library round the fire: chattering not very interested. The entry of Sir William at once made a stir.

The girl in white, with the biggish nose, fluttered round him. She was Arthur's wife. The girl in soft blue spread herself on the couch; she was the young Major's wife: and she had a blue band round her hair. The Colonel hovered stout and fidgetty round Lady Franks and the liqueur stand. He and the Major were both in khaki—belonging to the service on duty in Italy still.

Coffee appeared—and Sir William doled out *crème de menthe*. There was no conversation—only tedious words. The little party was just commonplace and dull—boring. Yet Sir William, the self-made man, was a study. And the young, Oxford-like Major, with his English diffidence and his one dark, pensive, baffled eye was only waiting to be earnest, poor devil.

The girl in white had been a sort of companion to Lady Franks, so that Arthur was more or less a son-in-law. In this capacity he acted. Aaron strayed round uneasily looking at the books, bought but not read, and at the big pictures above. It was Arthur who fetched out the little boxes containing the orders conferred on Sir William for his war-work: and perhaps more, for the many thousands of pounds he had spent on his war-work.

There were three orders: one British, and quite important, a large silver star for the breast: one Italian, smaller, and silver and gold; and one from the State of Ruritania,* in silver and red-and-green enamel, smaller than the others.

"Come now, William," said Lady Franks, "you must try them all on. You must try them all on together, and let us see how you look."

The little, frail old man, with his strange old man's blue eyes and his old man's perpetual laugh, swelled out his chest and said:

"What, am I to appear in all my vanities?" And he laughed shortly.

"Of course you are. We want to see you," said the white girl.

"Indeed we do! We shouldn't mind all appearing in such vanities—what, Lady Franks!" boomed the Colonel.

"I should think not," replied his hostess. "When a man has honours conferred on him, it shows a poor spirit if he isn't proud of them."

"Of course I am proud of them!" said Sir William.

"Well then, come and have them pinned on. I think it's wonderful to have got so much in one life-time—wonderful—" said Lady Franks.

"Oh, Sir William is a wonderful man," said the Colonel.

"Well—we won't say so before him. But let us look at him in his orders."

Arthur, always ready on these occasions, had taken the large and shining British star from its box, and drew near to Sir William, who stood swelling his chest, pleased, proud, and a little wistful.

"This one first, Sir," said Arthur.

Sir William stood very still, half tremulous, like a man undergoing an operation.

"And it goes just here—the level of the heart. This is where it goes." And carefully he pinned the large, radiating ornament on the black velvet dinner-jacket of the old man.

"That is the first—and very becoming," said Lady Franks.

"Oh very becoming! Very becoming!" said the tall wife of the Major—she was a handsome young woman of the tall frail type.

"Do you think so, my dear?" said the old man, with his eternal smile: the curious smile of old people when they are dead.

"Not only becoming, Sir," said the Major, bending his tall slim figure forwards. "But a reassuring sign that a nation knows how to distinguish her valuable men."

"Quite!" said Lady Franks. "I think it is a very great honour to have got it. The king was most gracious, too—Now the other. That goes beside it—the Italian—"

Sir William stood there undergoing the operation of the pinning-on. The Italian star being somewhat smaller than the British, there was a slight question as to where exactly it should be placed.

However, Arthur decided it: and the old man stood before the company with his two stars on his breast.

"And now the Ruritanian," said Lady Franks eagerly.

"That doesn't go on the same level with the others, Lady Franks," said Arthur. "That goes much lower down—about here."

"Are you sure?" said Lady Franks. "Doesn't it go more here?"

"No no, no no, not at all. Here! Isn't it so, Sybil?"

"Yes, I think so," said Sybil.

Old Sir William stood quite silent, his breast prepared, peering over the facings of his coat to see where the star was going. The Colonel was called in, and though he knew nothing about it, he agreed with Arthur, who apparently did know something. So the star was pinned quite low down. Sir William, peeping down, exclaimed:

"Well, that is most curious now! I wear an order over the pit of my stomach! I think that is very curious: a curious place to wear an order."

"Stand up! Stand up and let us look!" said Lady Franks. "There now, isn't it handsome? And isn't it a great deal of honour for one man? Could he have expected so much, in one life-time? I call it wonderful. Come and look at yourself dear"—and she led him to a mirror.

"What's more, all thoroughly deserved," said Arthur.

"I should think so," said the Colonel, fidgetting.

"Ah yes, nobody has deserved them better," cooed Sybil.

"Nor on more humane and generous grounds," said the Major, *sotto voce*.

"The effort to save life, indeed," returned the Major's young wife: "Splendid!"

Sir William stood naïvely before the mirror and looked at his three stars on his black velvet dinner-jacket.

"Almost directly over the pit of my stomach," he said. "I hope that is not a decoration for my greedy *appetite*." And he laughed at the young women.

"I assure you it is in position, Sir," said Arthur. "Absolutely correct. I will read it out to you later."

"Aren't you satisfied? Aren't you a proud man! Isn't it wonderful?" said Lady Franks. "Why what more could a man want from life? He could never *expect* so much."

"Yes, my dear. I *am* a proud man. Three countries have honoured me—" There was a little breathless pause.

"And not more than they ought to have done," said Sybil.

"Well! Well! I shall have my head turned. Let me return to my own humble self. I am too much in the stars at the moment."

Sir William turned to Arthur to have his decorations removed. Aaron, standing in the background, felt the whole scene strange, childish, a little touching. And Lady Franks was so obviously trying to *console* her husband: to console the frail excitable old man with his honours. But why console him? Did he need consolation? And did she? It was evident that only the hard-money-woman in her put any price on the decorations.

Aaron came forward and examined the orders, one after the other. Just metal playthings of curious shiny silver and gilt and enamel. Heavy the British one—but only like some heavy buckle, a piece of metal merely when one turned it over. Somebody dropped the Italian cross, and there was a moment of horror. But the lump of metal took no hurt. Queer to see the things stowed in their boxes again. Aaron had always imagined these mysterious decorations as shining by nature on the breasts of heroes. Pinned on pieces of metal were a considerable come-down.

The orders were put away, the party sat round the fire in the comfortable library, the men sipping more *crème de menthe*, since nothing else offered, and the couple of hours in front promising the tedium of small-talk of tedious people who had really nothing to say and no particular originality in saying it.

Aaron, however, had reckoned without his host. Sir William sat upright in his chair, with all the determination of a frail old man who insists on being level with the young. The new guest sat in a lower chair, smoking, that curious glimmer on his face which made him so attractive, and which only meant that he was looking on the whole scene from the outside, as it were from beyond a fence. Sir William came almost directly to the attack.

"And so, Mr. Sisson, you have no definite purpose in coming to Italy!"

"No, none," said Aaron. "I wanted to join Lilly."

"But when you had joined him—?"

"Oh nothing—stay here a time, in this country, if I could earn my keep."

"Ah!—earn your keep? So you hope to earn your keep here? May I ask how?"

"By my flute."

"Italy is a poor country."

"I don't want much."

"You have a family to provide for."

"They are provided for—for a couple of years."

5   "Oh indeed! Is that so?"

The old man got out of Aaron the detailed account of his circumstances—how he had left so much money to be paid over to his wife, and had received only a small amount for himself.

"I see you are like Lilly—you trust to Providence," said Sir
10   William.

"Providence or fate," said Aaron.

"Lilly calls it Providence," said Sir William. "For my own part, I always advise Providence plus a banking account. I have every belief in Providence, plus a banking account. Providence and no banking
15   account I have observed to be almost invariably fatal. Lilly and I have argued it. He believes in casting his bread upon the waters.* I sincerely hope he won't have to cast himself after his bread, one of these days. Providence with a banking account. Believe in Providence once you have secured enough to live on. I should consider it
20   disastrous to believe in Providence *before*. One can never be *sure* of Providence."

"What can you be sure of, then?" said Aaron.

"Well, in moderation, I can believe in a little hard cash, and in my own ability to earn a little hard cash."

25   "Perhaps Lilly believes in his own ability too."

"No. Not so. Because he will never directly work to earn money. He works—and works quite well, I am told: but only as the spirit moves him, and never with any eye to the market. Now I call that *tempting* Providence, myself. The spirit may move him in quite an
30   opposite direction to the market—then where is Lilly? I have put it to him more than once."

"The spirit generally does move him dead against the market," said Aaron. "But he manages to scrape along."

"In a state of jeopardy: all the time in a state of jeopardy," said the
35   old man. "His whole existence, and that of his wife, is completely precarious. I found, in my youth, the spirit moved me to various things which would have left me and my wife starving. So I realised in time, this was no good. I took my spirit in hand, therefore, and made him pull the cart which mankind is riding in. I harnessed him
40   to the work of productive labour. And so he brought me my reward."

"Yes," said Aaron. "But every man according to his belief."

"I don't see," said Sir William, "how a man can *believe* in a Providence unless he sets himself definitely to the work of earning his daily bread, and making provision for future needs. That's what Providence means to me—making provision for oneself and one's family. Now Mr. Lilly—and you yourself—you say you believe in a Providence that does *not* compel you to earn your daily bread, and make provision. I confess myself I cannot see it: and Lilly has never been able to convince me."

"I don't believe in a kindhearted Providence," said Aaron, "and I don't believe Lilly does. But I believe in chance. I believe, if I go my own way, without tying my nose to a job, chance will always throw something in my way: enough to get along with."

"But on what do you base such a very unwarrantable belief?"

"I just feel like that."

"And if you are ever quite without success—and nothing to fall back on?"

"I can work at something."

"In case of illness for example?"

"I can go to hospital—or die."

"Dear me!—However, you are more logical than Lilly. He seems to believe that he has the Invisible—call it Providence if you will—on his side, and that this Invisible will never leave him in the lurch, or let him down, so long as he sticks to his own side of the bargain, and *never* works for his own ends. I don't quite see how he works. Certainly he seems to me a man who squanders a great deal of talent unworthily. Yet for some reason or other he calls this true, genuine activity, and has a contempt for actual work by which a man makes provision for his years and for his family.— In the end, he will have to fall back on charity. But when I say so, he denies it, and says that in the end we, the men who work and make provision, will have to fall back on him. Well, all I can say is, that *so far* he is in far greater danger of having to fall back on me, than I on him."

The old man sat back in his chair with a little laugh of triumph. But it smote almost devilishly on Aaron's ears, and for the first time in his life he felt that there existed a necessity for taking sides.

"I don't suppose he will do much falling back," he said.

"Well, he is young yet. You are both young. You are squandering your youth. I am an old man, and I see the end."

"What end, Sir William?"

"Charity—and poverty—and some not very congenial 'job,' as you call it, to put bread in your mouth. No, no, I would not like to trust myself to your Providence, or to your Chance. Though I admit your Chance is a sounder proposition than Lilly's Providence. You speculate with your life and your talent. I admit the nature which is a born speculator. After all, with your flute you will speculate in other people's taste for luxury, as a man may speculate in theatres or *trains de luxe*. You are the speculator. That may be your way of wisdom. But Lilly does not even speculate. I cannot see his point. I cannot see his point. Yet I have the greatest admiration for his mentality."

The old man had fired up during this conversation—and all the others in the room had gone silent. Lady Franks was palpably uneasy. She alone knew how frail the old man was—frailer by far than his years. She alone knew what fear of his own age, what fear of death haunted him now: fear of his own non-existence. His own old age was an agony to him: worse than an agony, a horror. He wanted to be young—to live, to live. And he was old, he was breaking up. The glistening youth of Aaron, the impetuousness of Lilly fascinated him. And both these men seemed calmly to contradict his own wealth and honours.

Lady Franks tried to turn off the conversation to the trickles of normal chit-chat. The Colonel was horribly bored—so were all the women—Arthur was indifferent. Only the young Major was implicated, troubled in his earnest and philosophic spirit.

"What I can't see," he said, "is the place that others have in your scheme."

"It isn't a scheme," said Aaron.

"Well then, your way of life. Isn't it pretty selfish, to marry a woman and then expect her to live on very little indeed, and that always precarious, just because you happen to believe in Providence or in Chance: which I think worse. What I don't see is where others come in. What would the world be like if everybody lived that way?"

"Other people can please themselves," said Aaron.

"No they can't—because you take first choice, it seems to me. Supposing your wife—or Lilly's wife—asks for security and for provision, as Sir William says. Surely she has a right to it."

"If I've no right to it myself—and I *have* no right to it, if I don't want it—then what right has she?"

"Every right, I should say. All the more since you are improvident."

"Then she must manage her rights for herself. It's no good her foisting her rights on to me."

"Isn't that pure selfishness?"

"It may be. I shall send my wife money as long as I've money to send."

"And supposing you have none?"

"Then I can't send it—and she must look out for herself."

"I call that almost criminal selfishness."

"I can't help it."

The conversation with the young Major broke off.

"It is certainly a good thing for society that men like you and Mr. Lilly are not common," said Sir William, laughing.

"Becoming commoner every day, you'll find," interjaculated the Colonel.

"Indeed! Indeed! Well. May we ask you another question, Mr. Sisson? I hope you don't object to our catechism?"

"No. Nor your judgment afterwards," said Aaron, grinning.

"Then upon what grounds did you abandon your family? I know it is a tender subject. But Lilly spoke of it to us, and as far as I could see ..."

"There were no grounds," said Aaron. "No, there weren't. I just left them."

"Mere caprice?"

"If it's a caprice to be begotten—and a caprice to be born—and a caprice to die—then that was a caprice, for it was the same."

"Like birth or death?—I don't follow."

"It happened to me: as birth happened to me once—and death will happen. It was a sort of death too: or a sort of birth. But as undeniable as either. And without any more grounds."

The old, tremulous man, and the young man, were watching one another.

"A natural event," said Sir William.

"A natural event," said Aaron.

"Not that you loved any other woman?"

"God save me from it."

"You just left off loving?"

"Not even that. I went away."

"What from?"

"From it all."

"From the woman in particular?"

"Oh yes. Yes. Yes, that."

"And you couldn't go back?"

Aaron shook his head.

"Yet you can give no reasons?"

5   "Not any reasons that would be any good. It wasn't a question of reasons. It was a question of her and me and what must be. What makes a child be born out of its mother, to the pain and trouble of both of them? I don't know."

"But that is a natural process."

10   "So is this—or nothing."

"No," interposed the Major. "Because birth is a universal process—and yours is a specific, almost unique event."

"Well, unique or not, it so came about. I didn't even leave off loving her—not as far as I know. I left her as I shall leave the earth 15 when I die—because it has to be."

"Do you know what I think it is, Mr. Sisson?" put in Lady Franks. "I think you are just in a wicked state of mind: just that. Mr. Lilly too. And you must be very careful, or some great misfortune will happen to you."

20   "It may," said Aaron.

"And it will, mark my word it will."

"You almost wish it might, as a judgment on me," smiled Aaron.

"Oh no indeed. I should only be too sorry. But I feel it will, unless you are careful."

25   "I'll be careful then."

"Yes, and you can't be too careful."

"You make me frightened."

"I would like to make you very frightened indeed, so that you went back humbly to your wife and family."

30   "It would *have* to be a big fright then, I assure you."

"Ah, you are really heartless. It makes me angry."

She turned angrily aside.

"Well, well! Well, well! Life! Life! Young men are a new thing to me!" said Sir William, shaking his head. "Well, well! What do you 35 say to whiskey and soda, Colonel?"

"Why delighted, Sir William," said the Colonel, bouncing up.

"A night-cap, and then we retire," said Lady Franks.

Aaron sat thinking. He knew Sir William liked him: and that Lady Franks didn't. One day he might have to seek help from Sir 40 William. So he had better placate milady. Wrinkling the fine, half mischievous smile on his face, and trading on his charm, he turned to his hostess.

"You wouldn't mind, Lady Franks, if I said nasty things about my wife and found a lot of fault with her. What makes you angry is that I know it is not a bit more her fault than mine, that we come apart. It can't be helped."

"Oh yes, indeed. I disapprove of your way of looking at things altogether. It seems to me altogether cold and unmanly and inhuman. Thank goodness my experience of a man has been different."

"We can't all be alike, can we? And if I don't choose to let you see me crying, that doesn't prove I've never had a bad half hour, does it? I've had many—ay, and a many."

"Then why are you so *wrong*, so wrong in your behaviour?"

"I suppose I've got to have my bout out: and when it's out, I can alter."

"Then I hope you've almost had your bout out," she said.

"So do I," said he, with a half repentant, half depressed look on his attractive face. The corners of his mouth grimaced slightly under his moustache.

"The best thing you can do is to go straight back to England, and to her."

"Perhaps I'd better ask her if she wants me, first," he said drily.

"Yes, you might do that too." And Lady Franks felt she was quite getting on with her work of reform, and the restoring of woman to her natural throne. Best not go too fast, either.

"Say when" shouted the Colonel, who was manipulating the syphon.

"When," said Aaron.

The men stood up to their drinks.

"Will you be leaving in the morning, Mr. Sisson?" asked Lady Franks.

"May I stay till Monday morning?" said Aaron. They were at Saturday evening.

"Certainly. And you will take breakfast in your room: we all do. At what time? Half-past eight?"

"Thank you very much."

"Then at half-past eight the man will bring it in. Goodnight."

Once more in his blue silk bedroom, Aaron grimaced to himself and stood in the middle of the room grimacing. His hostess' admonitions were like vitriol in his ears. He looked out of the window. Through the darkness of trees, the lights of a city below. Italy! The air was cold with snow. He came back into his soft warm room. Luxurious it was. And luxurious the deep warm bed.

5 He was still asleep when the man came noiselessly in with the tray: and it was morning. Aaron woke and sat up. He felt that the deep warm bed, and the soft warm room had made him sleep too well: robbed him of his night, like a narcotic. He preferred to be more uncomfortable and more aware of the flight of the dark hours. It 10 seemed numbing.

The footman in his grey house-jacket was neat and Italian and sympathising. He gave good-morning in Italian—then softly arranged the little table by the bedside, and put out the toast and coffee and butter and boiled egg and honey, with silver and delicate 15 china. Aaron watched the soft, catlike motions of the man. The dark eyes glanced once at the blond man, leaning on his elbow on the pillow. Aaron's face had that watchful, half-amused expression. The man said something in Italian. Aaron shook his head, laughed, and said:

20 "Tell me in English."

The man went softly to the window curtains, and motioned them with his hand.

"Yes do," said Aaron.

So the man drew the buff-coloured silk curtains: and Aaron, 25 sitting in bed, could see away beyond red roofs of a town, and in the further heaven great snowy mountains.

"The Alps," he said in surprise.

"Gli Alpi—si signore."* The man bowed, gathered up Aaron's clothes, and silently retired.

30 Aaron watched through the window. It was a frosty morning at the end of September,* with a clear blue morning-sky, Alpine, and the watchful, snow-streaked mountain tops bunched in the distance, as if waiting. There they were, hovering round, circling, waiting. They reminded him of marvellous striped skypanthers circling round a 35 great camp: the red-roofed city. Aaron looked, and looked again. In the near distance, under the house elm-tree tops were yellowing. He felt himself changing inside his skin.

So he turned away to his coffee and eggs. A little silver egg-cup with a curious little frill round it: honey in a frail, iridescent glass 40 bowl, gold-iridescent: the charm of delicate and fine things. He smiled half mockingly to himself. Two instincts played in him: the one, an instinct for fine delicate things: he had attractive hands; the other, an inclination to throw the dainty little table with all its niceties out of the window. It evoked a sort of devil in him.

He took his bath: the man had brought back his things: he dressed 5 and went downstairs. No one in the lounge: he went down to the ground floor: no one in the big hall with its pillars of yellow marble and its gold arches, its enormous, dark, bluey-red carpet. He stood before the great glass doors. Some red flowers still were blooming in the tubs on the steps, handsome: and beautiful chrysanthemums in 10 the wide portico. Beyond, yellow leaves were already falling on the green grass and the neat drive. Everywhere was silent and empty. He climbed the wide stairs, sat in the long upper lounge where the papers were. He wanted his hat and coat, and did not know where to find them. The windows looked on to a terraced garden, the hill 15 rising steeply behind the house. He wanted to go out.

So he opened more doors, and in a long drawing-room came upon five or six menservants, all in the grey house-jackets, all clean-shaven, neat, with neat black hair, all with dusters or brushes or feather brooms, and all frolicking, chattering, playing like so many 20 monkeys. They were all of the same neat, smallish size. They were all laughing. They rolled back a great rug as if it were some football game, one flew at the curtains. And they merely looked at Aaron and went on chattering, and laughing and dusting.

Surprised, and feeling that he trespassed, he stood at the window a 25 moment looking out. The noise went on behind him. So he turned, smiling, and asked for his hat, pointing to his head. They knew at once what he wanted. One of the fellows beckoned him away, down to the hall and to the long cupboard place where hats and coats and sticks were hung. There was his hat; he put it on, while the man 30 chattered to him pleasantly and unintelligibly, and opened for him the back door, into the garden.

Chapter XIII.

Wie es Ihnen Gefällt*

The fresh morning air comes startling after a central-heated house.
So Aaron found it. He felt himself dashing up the steps into the
garden like a bird dashing out of a trap where it has been caught: that
warm and luxurious house. Heaven bless us, we who want to save
civilisation. We had better make up our minds what of it we want to
save. The kernel may be all well and good. But there is precious little
kernel, to a lot of woolly stuffing and poisonous rind.

The gardens to Sir William's place were not imposing, and still
rather war-neglected. But the pools of water lay smooth in the bright
air, the flowers showed their colours beside the walks. Many birds
dashed about, rather bewildered, having crossed the Alps in their
migration southwards. Aaron noted with gratification a certain big
magnificence, a certain reckless powerfulness in the still-blossom-
ing, harsh-coloured, autumn flowers. Distinct satisfaction he
derived from it.

He wandered upwards, up the succeeding flights of steps, till he
came to the upper rough hedge, and saw the wild copse on the
hill-crest just above. Passing through a space in the hedge, he
climbed the steep last bit of Sir William's land. It was a little
vineyard, with small vines and yellowing leaves. Everywhere the
place looked neglected—but as if man had just begun to tackle it
once more.

At the very top, by the wild hedge where spindle-berries hung
pink, seats were placed, and from here the view was very beautiful.
The hill dropped steep beneath him. A river wound on the near side
of the city, crossed by a white bridge. The city lay close clustered,
ruddy on the plains, glittering in the clear air with its flat roofs and
domes and square towers, strangely naked-seeming in the clear,
clean air. And massive in the further nearness, snow-streaked
mountains, the tiger-like Alps. Tigers prowling between the north
and the south. And this beautiful city lying nearest exposed. The
snow-wind brushed her this morning like the icy whiskers of a tiger.
And clear in the light lay Novara, wide, fearless, violent Novara.

Beautiful the perfect air, the perfect and unblemished Alp-sky. And like the first southern flower, Novara.

Aaron sat watching in silence. Only the uneasy birds rustled. He watched the city and the winding river, the bridges, and the imminent Alps. He was on the south side. On the other side of the time barrier. His old sleepy English nature was startled in its sleep. He felt like a man who knows it is time to wake up, and who doesn't want to wake up, to face the responsibility of another sort of day.

To open his darkest eyes and wake up to a new responsibility. Wake up and enter on the responsibility of a new self in himself. Ach, the horror of responsibility! He had all his life slept and shelved the burden. And he wanted to go on sleeping. It was so hateful to have to get a new grip on his own bowels, a new hard recklessness into his heart, and new and responsible consciousness into his mind and soul. He felt some finger prodding, prodding, prodding him awake out of the sleep of pathos and tragedy and spasmodic passion, and he wriggled, unwilling, oh most unwilling to undertake the new business.

In fact he ran away again. He gave a last look at the town and its white-fanged mountains, and descended through the garden, round the way of the kitchen garden and garage and stables and pecking chickens, back to the house again. In the hall still no one. He went upstairs to the long lounge. There sat the rubicund, bald, boy-like Colonel reading *The Graphic.* Aaron sat down opposite him, and made a feeble attempt at conversation. But the Colonel wasn't having any. It was evident he didn't care for the fellow—Mr. Aaron that is. Aaron therefore dried up, and began to sit him out, with the aid of *The Queen.** Came a servant, however, and said that the Signor Colonello was called up from the hospital, on the telephone. The Colonel once departed, Aaron fled again, this time out of the front doors, and down the steep little park to the gates.

Huge dogs and little dogs came bounding forward. Out of the lodge came the woman with the keys, smiling very pleasantly this morning. So, he was in the street. The wide road led him inevitably to the big bridge, with the violent, physical stone statue-groups. Men and women were moving about, and he noticed for the first time the littleness and the momentaneousness of the Italians in the street. Perhaps it was the wideness of the bridge and the subsequent big open boulevard. But there it was: the people seemed little upright brisk figures moving in a certain isolation, like tiny figures on a big stage. And he felt himself moving in the space between. All the northern cosiness gone. He was set down with a space round him.

Little trams flitted down the boulevard in the bright sweet light. The barbers' shops were all busy, half the Novaresi at that moment ambushed in lather, full in the public gaze. A shave is nothing if not a public act, in the south. At the little outdoor tables of the cafés a very few drinkers sat before empty coffee-cups. Most of the shops were shut. It was too soon after the war for life to be flowing very fast. The feeling of emptiness, of neglect, of lack of supplies was evident everywhere.

Aaron strolled on, surprised himself at his gallant feeling of liberty: a feeling of bravado and almost swaggering carelessness which is Italy's best gift to an Englishman. He had crossed the dividing line, and the values of life, though ostensibly and verbally the same, were dynamically different. Alas, however, the verbal and the ostensible, the accursed mechanical ideal gains day by day over the spontaneous life-dynamic, so that Italy becomes as idea-bound and as automatic as England: just a business proposition.

Coming to the station, he went inside. There he saw a money-changing window which was open, so he planked down a five-pound note and got two-hundred-and-ten Lire. Here was a start. At a bookstall he saw a man buy a big time-table with a large railway map in it. He immediately bought the same. Then he retired to a corner to get his whereabouts.

In the morning he must move: where? He looked on the map. The map seemed to offer two alternatives, Milan and Genoa. He chose Milan, because of its musical associations and its cathedral. Milano then. Strolling and still strolling, he found the boards announcing Arrivals and Departures. As far as he could make out, the train for Milan left at 9.00 in the morning.

So much achieved, he left the big desolating caravanserai of the station. Soldiers were camped in every corner, lying in heaps asleep. In their grey-green uniform, he was surprised at their sturdy limbs and uniformly short stature. For the first time he saw the cock-feathers of the Bersaglieri.* There seemed a new life-quality every-where. Many worlds, not one world. But alas, the one world triumphing more and more over the many worlds, the big oneness swallowing up the many small diversities in its insatiable gnawing appetite, leaving a dreary sameness throughout the world, that means at last complete sterility.

Aaron however was too new to the strangeness, he had no eye for the horrible sameness that was spreading like a disease over Italy from England and the north. He plunged into the space in front of the station, and took a new wide boulevard. To his surprise he ran towards a big and over-animated statue that stood resolutely with its back to the magnificent snow-domes of the wild Alps. Wolves in the street could not have startled him more than those magnificent fierce-gleaming mountains of snow at the street-end, beyond the statue. He stood and wondered, and never thought to look who the gentleman was. Then he turned right round, and began to walk home.

Luncheon was at one o'clock. It was half-past twelve when he rang at the lodge gates. He climbed through the leaves of the little park, on a side-path, rather reluctantly towards the house. In the hall Lady Franks was discussing with Arthur a fat Pekinese who did not seem very well. She was sure the servants did not obey her orders concerning the Pekinese bitch. Arthur, who was more than indifferent, assured her they did. But she seemed to think that the whole of the male human race was in league against the miserable specimen of a she-dog. She almost cried, thinking her Queenie *might* by some chance meet with, perhaps, a harsh word or look. Queenie apparently fattened on the secret detestation of the male human species.

"I can't bear to think that a dumb creature might be ill-treated," she said to Aaron. "Thank Goodness the Italians are better than they used to be."

"Are they better than they used to be?"

"Oh much. They have learnt it from us."

She then enquired if her guest had slept, and if he were rested from his journey. Aaron, into whose face the faint snow-wind and the sun had brought a glow, replied that he had slept well and enjoyed the morning, thank you. Whereupon Lady Franks knitted her brows and said Sir William had had such a bad night. He had not been able to sleep, and had got up and walked about the room. The least excitement, and she dreaded a break-down. He must have absolute calm and restfulness.

"There's one for you and your jawing last night, Aaron my boy!" said our hero to himself.

"I thought Sir William seemed so full of life and energy," he said, aloud.

"Ah did you! No, he *wants* to be. But he can't do it. He's very much upset this morning. I have been very anxious about him."

"I am sorry to hear that."

Lady Franks departed to some duty. Aaron sat alone before the fire. It was a huge fire-place, like a dark chamber shut in by tall, finely-wrought iron gates. Behind these iron gates of curly iron the logs burned and flickered like leopards slumbering and lifting their heads within their cage. Aaron wondered who was the keeper of the savage element, who it was that would open the iron grille and throw on another log, like meat to the lions. To be sure the fire was only to be looked at: like wild beasts in the Zoo. For the house was warm from roof to floor. It was strange to see the blue air of sunlight outside, the yellow-edged leaves falling in the wind, the red flowers shaking.

The gong sounded softly through the house. The Colonel came in heartily from the garden, but did not speak to Aaron. The Major and his wife came pallid down the stairs. Lady Franks appeared, talking domestic-secretarial business with the wife of Arthur. Arthur, well-nourished and half at home, called down the stairs. And then Sir William descended, old and frail now in the morning, shaken: still he approached Aaron heartily, and asked him how he did, and how he had spent his morning. The old man who had made a fortune: how he expected homage: and how he got it! Homage, like most things, is just a convention and a social trick. Aaron found himself paying homage too to the old man who had made a fortune. But also, exacting a certain deference in return, from the old man who had made a fortune. Getting it too. On what grounds? Youth, maybe. But mostly, scorn for fortunes and fortune-making. Did he scorn fortunes and fortune-making? Not he, otherwise whence this homage for the old man with much money. Aaron, like everybody else, was rather paralysed by a million sterling, personified in one old man. Paralysed, fascinated, overcome. All those three. Only having no final control over his own make-up, he could not drive himself into the money-making or even into the money-having habit. And he had just wit enough to threaten Sir William's golden king with his own ivory queen and knights of wilful life. And Sir William quaked.

"Well, and how have you spent your morning?" asked the host.

"I went first to look at the garden."

"Ah, not much to see now. They have been beautiful with flowers, once. But for two and a half years the house has been a hospital for officers—and even tents in the park and garden—as many as two hundred wounded and sick at a time. We are only just returning to civil life. And flowers need time. Yes—yes—British officers—for two and a half years.—But did you go up, now, to the belvedere?"

"To the top—where the vines are? I never expected the mountains." 5

"You never expected the mountains? Pray, why not? They are always there?"

"But I was never there before. I never knew they were there, round the town. I didn't expect it like that." 10

"Ah! So you found our city impressive?"

"Very! Ah very! A new world to me. I feel I've come out of myself."

"Yes, it is a wonderful sight—a wonderful sight—But you have not been *into* the town?" 15

"Yes. I saw the men being shaved, and all the soldiers at the station: and a statue, and mountains behind it. Oh, I've had a full morning."

"A full morning! That is good, that is good!" The old man looked again at the younger man, and seemed to get life from him, to live in 20 him vicariously.

"Come," said the hostess. "Luncheon."

Aaron sat again on his hostess' left hand. The Colonel was more affable now it was meal-time. Sir William was again in a good-humour, chaffing the young ladies with an old man's gallantry. But 25 now he insisted on drawing Aaron into the play. And Aaron did not want to be drawn. He did not one bit want to chaffer gallantries with the young women. Between him and Sir William there was a curious rivalry—unconscious on both sides. The old knight had devoted an energetic, adventurous, almost an artistic nature to the making of his 30 fortune and the developing of later philanthropies. He had no children. Aaron was devoting a similar nature to anything but fortune-making and philanthropy. The one held life to be a storing-up of produce and a conservation of energy: the other held life to be a sheer spending of energy and a storing-up of nothing but experi- 35 ence. There they were, in opposition, the old man and the young. Sir William kept calling Aaron into the chaffer at the other end of the table: and Aaron kept on refusing to join. He hated long distance answers, anyhow. And in his mood of the moment he hated the young women. He had a conversation with Arthur about statues: 40

concerning which Aaron knew nothing, and Arthur less than nothing. Then Lady Franks turned the conversation to the soldiers at the station, and said how Sir William had equipped rest-huts for the Italian privates, near the station: but that such was the jealousy
5 and spite of the Italian Red Cross—or some such body, locally—that Sir William's huts had been left empty—standing unused—while the men had slept on the stone floor of the station, night after night, in icy winter.—There was evidently much bitter feeling as a result of Sir William's philanthropy. Apparently even the honey of lavish
10 charity had turned to gall in the Italian mouth: at least the official mouth. Which gall had been spat back at the charitable, much to his pain. It is in truth a difficult world, particularly when you have another race to deal with. After which came the beef-olives.

"Oh," said Lady Franks, "I had such a dreadful dream last night,
15 such a dreadful dream. It upset me so much. I have not been able to get over it all day."

"What was it?" said Aaron. "Tell it, and break it."

"Why," said his hostess, "I dreamed I was asleep in my room—just as I actually was—and that it was night, yet with a terrible sort of
20 light, like the dead light before dawn, so that one could see. And my maid Giuseppina came running into my room saying: 'Signora! Signora! Si alza! Subito! Signora! Vengono su!'—and I said, 'Chi? Chi sono chi vengono? Chi?'—'I Novaresi! I Novaresi vengono su. Vengono qui!'*—I got out of bed and went to the window. And
25 there they were, in the dead light, rushing up to the house, through the trees. It was so awful, I haven't been able to forget it all day."

"Tell me what the words are in English," said Aaron.

"Why, she said 'Get up, get up—the Novaresi, the people of Novara are coming up—vengono su—they are coming up—the
30 Novara people—work-people.' I can't forget it. It was so real, I can't believe it didn't actually happen."

"Ah," said Aaron. "It will never happen. I know, that whatever one foresees, and *feels* has happened, never happens in real life. It sort of works itself off through the imagining of it."

35 "Well, it was almost more real to me than real life," said his hostess.

"Then it will never happen in real life," he said.

Luncheon passed, and coffee. The party began to disperse—Lady Franks to answer more letters, with the aid of Arthur's wife—some
40 to sleep, some to walk. Aaron escaped once more through the big

gates. This time he turned his back on the town and the mountains, and climbed up the hill into the country. So he went between the banks and the bushes, watching for unknown plants and shrubs, hearing the birds, feeling the influence of a new soil. At the top of the hill he saw over into vineyards, and a new strange valley with a 5 winding river, and jumbled, entangled hills. Strange wild country so near the town. It seemed to keep an almost virgin wildness—yet he saw the white houses dotted here and there.

Just below him was a peasant house: and on a little loggia in the sun two peasants in white shirt sleeves and black Sunday suits were 10 sitting drinking wine, and talking, talking. Peasant youths in black hats, their sweethearts in dark stuff dresses, wearing no hat, but a black silk or a white silk scarf, passed slowly along the little road just below the ridge. None looked up to see Aaron sitting there alone. From some hidden place somebody was playing an accordion, a jerky 15 sound in the still afternoon. And away beyond lay the unchanging, mysterious valley, and the infolding, mysterious hills of Italy.

Returning back again another way, he lost himself at the foot of the hill in new and deserted suburb streets—unfinished streets of seemingly unfinished houses. Then a sort of boulevard where 20 bourgeois families were taking the Sunday afternoon walk: stout papas, stout, pallid mamas in rather cheap black fur, little girls very much dressed, and long lads in short socks and round sailor caps, ribbons fluttering. Alien they felt, alien, alien, as a bourgeois crowd always does, but particularly a foreign, Sunday-best bourgeois 25 crowd. Aaron wandered and wandered, finding the tram terminus and trying blank, unfinished street after street. He had a great disinclination to ask his way.

At last he recognised the bank and the little stream of water that ran along the street side. So he was back in time for tea. A hospital 30 nurse was there, and two other strange women. Arthur played the part of host. Sir William came in from a walk with the dogs, but retired to his room without taking tea.

And so the evening fell. Aaron sat in the hall at some distance from the fire, which burned behind its wrought iron gates. He was tired 35 now with all his impressions, and dispirited. He thought of his wife and children at home: of the church-bells ringing so loudly across the field beyond his garden end: of the dark-clad people trailing unevenly across the two paths, one to the left, one to the right, forking their way towards the houses of the town, to church or to 40 chapel: mostly to chapel. At this hour he himself would be dressed in his best clothes, tying his bow, ready to go out to the public house. And his wife would be resenting his holiday departure, whilst she was left fastened to the children.

5   Rather tired and dispirited in this alien place, he wondered if he wished himself back. But the moment he actually *realised* himself at home, and felt the tension of barrenness which it meant, felt the curious and deadly opposition of his wife's will against his own nature, the almost nauseating ache which it amounted to, he pulled
10   himself together and rejoiced again in his new surroundings. Her will, her will, her terrible, implacable, cunning will! What was there in the female will so diabolical, he asked himself, that it could press like a flat sheet of iron against a man all the time? The female will! He realised now that he had a horror of it. It was flat and inflexible as
15   a sheet of iron. But also it was cunning as a snake that could sing treacherous songs.

    Of two people at a deadlock, he always reminded himself, there is not one only wholly at fault. Both must be at fault. Having a detached and logical soul, he never let himself forget this truth. Take Lottie!
20   He had loved her. He had never loved any other woman. If he had had his other affairs—it was out of spite or defiance or curiosity. They meant nothing. He and Lottie had loved one another. And the love had developed almost at once into a kind of combat. Lottie had been the only child of headstrong, well-to-do parents. He also had
25   been the only child of his widowed mother. Well then, both he and Lottie had been brought up to consider themselves the first in whatsoever company they found themselves. During the early months of the marriage he had, of course, continued the spoiling of the young wife. But this never altered the fact that, by his very nature,
30   he considered himself as first and almost as single in any relation-ship. First and single he felt, and as such he bore himself. It had taken him years to realise that Lottie also felt herself first and single: under all her whimsicalness and fretfulness was a conviction as firm as steel: that she, as woman, was the centre of creation, the man was
35   but an adjunct. She, as woman, and particularly as mother, was the first great source of life and being, and also of culture. The man was but the instrument and the finisher. She was the source and the substance.

    Sure enough, Lottie had never formulated this belief inside
40   herself. But it was formulated for her in the whole world. It is the

substantial and professed belief of the whole white world. She did but inevitably represent what the whole world around her asserted: the life-centrality of woman. Woman, the life-bearer, the life-source.

Nearly all men agree to the assertion. Practically all men, even while demanding their selfish rights as superior males, tacitly agree to the fact of the sacred life-bearing priority of woman. Tacitly, they yield the worship to that which is female. Tacitly, they conspire to agree that all that is productive, all that is fine and sensitive and most essentially noble, is woman. This, in their productive and religious souls, they believe. And however much they may react against the belief, loathing their women, running to prostitutes, or beer or *anything*, out of reaction against this great and ignominious dogma of the sacred priority of women, still they do but profane the god they worship. Profaning woman, they still inversely worship her.

But in Aaron was planted another seed. He did not know it. He started off on the good old tack of worshipping his woman while his heart was honest, and profaning her in his fits of temper and revolt. But he made a bad show. Born in him was a spirit which could not worship woman: no, and would not. Could not and would not. It was not in him. In early days, he tried to pretend it was in him. But through his plaintive and homage-rendering love of a young husband was always, for the woman, discernible the arrogance of self-unyielding male. He never yielded himself: never. All his mad loving was only an effort. Afterwards, he was as devilishly unyielded as ever. And it was an instinct in her, that her man must yield to her, so that she should envelop him, yielding, in her all-beneficent love. She was quite sure that her love was all-beneficent. Of this no shadow of doubt. She was quite sure that the highest her man could ever know or ever reach, was to be perfectly enveloped in her all-beneficent love. This was her idea of marriage. She held it not as an idea, but as a profound impulse and instinct: an instinct developed in her by the age in which she lived. All that was deepest and most sacred in her feeling centred in this belief.

And he outraged her! Oh, from the first day and the first night, she felt he outraged her. True, for some time she had been taken in by his manifest love. But though you can deceive the conscious mind, you can never deceive the deep unconscious instinct. She could never understand whence arose in her, almost from the first days of marriage with him, her terrible paroxysms of hatred for him. She was

in love with him: ah heaven, how maddeningly she was in love with him: a certain unseizable beauty that was his, and which fascinated her as a snake a bird. But in revulsion, how she hated him! How she abhorred him! How she despised and shuddered at him! He seemed
5 a horrible thing to her.

And then again, oh God, the agony of her desire for him. The agony of her long, long desire for him. He was a passionate lover. He gave her, ostensibly, all she asked for. He withheld from her nothing, no experience, no degree of intimacy. She was his initiate, or he hers.
10 And yet, oh horror for a woman, he withheld everything from her. He withheld the very centre of himself. For a long time, she never realised. She was dazed and maddened only. But as months of married experience passed into years of married torment, she began to understand. It was that, after their most tremendous and, it
15 seemed to her, heaven-rending passion—yea, when for her every veil seemed rent and a terrible and sacred creative darkness covered the earth*—then—after all this wonder and miracle—in crept a poisonous grey snake of disillusionment, a poisonous grey snake of disillusion that bit her to madness, so that she really was a mad
20 woman, demented.

Why? Why? He never gave himself. He never came to her, *really*. He withheld himself. Yes, in those supreme and sacred times which for her were the whole culmination of life and being, the ecstasy of unspeakable passional conjunction, he was not really hers. He was
25 withheld. He withheld the central core of himself, like the devil and hell-fiend he was. He cheated and made play with her tremendous passional soul, her sacred sex passion, most sacred of all things for a woman. All the time, some central part of him stood apart from her, aside, looking on.
30 Oh, agony and horror for a passionate, fierce-hearted woman! She who loved him. She who loved him to madness. She who would have died for him. She who did die with him, many terrible and magnificent connubial deaths, in his arms, her husband.

Her husband! How bitter the word grew to her! Her husband! and
35 him never once given, given wholly to her! Her husband—and in all the frenzied finality of desire, she never *fully* possessed him, not once. No, not once. As time went on, she learned it for inevitable. Not once!

And then, how she hated him! Cheated, foiled, betrayed, forced to
40 love him or to hate him: never able to be at peace near him nor away

from him: poor Lottie, no wonder she was as a mad woman. She was strictly as a woman demented, after the birth of her second child. For all her instinct, all her impulse, all her desire, and above all, all her *will*, was to possess her man in very fulness once: just once: and once and for all. Once, just once: and it would be once and for all. 5

But never! Never! Not once! Never! Not for one single solitary second! Was it not enough to send a woman mad. Was it not enough to make her demented! Yes, and mad she was. She made his life a hell for him. She bit him to the bone with her frenzy of rage, chagrin, and agony. She drove him mad too: mad, so that he beat her: mad so 10 that he longed to kill her. But even in his greatest rages it was the same: he never finally lost himself: he remained, somewhere in the centre, in possession of himself. She sometimes wished he would kill her: or that she would kill him. Neither event happened.

And neither of them understood what was happening. How 15 should they? They were both dazed, horrified, and mortified. He took to leaving her alone as much as was possible. But when he *had* to come home, there was her terrible will, like a flat cold snake coiled round his soul and squeezing him to death. Yes, she did not relent. She was a good wife and mother. All her duties she fulfilled. But she 20 was not one to yield. *He* must yield. That was written in eternal letters, on the iron tablet* of her will. *He* must yield. She the woman, the mother of his children, how should she ever even think to yield? It was unthinkable. He, the man, the weak, the false, the treacherous, the half-hearted, it was he who must yield. Was not hers the 25 divine will and the divine right? Ha, she would be less than woman if she ever capitulated, abandoned her divine responsibility as woman! No, *he* must yield.

So, he was unfaithful to her. Piling reproach after reproach upon himself, he added adultery to his brutality. And this was the 30 beginning of the end. She was more than maddened: but he began to grow silent, unresponsive, as if he did not hear her. He was unfaithful to her: and oh, in such a low way. Such shame, such shame! But he only smiled carelessly now, and asked her what she wanted. She had asked for all she got. That he reiterated. And that 35 was all he would do.

Terrible was, that she found even his smile of insolent indifference half-beautiful. Oh bitter chain to bear! But she summoned up all her strange woman's will. She fought against his fascination, the fascination he exerted over her. With fearful efforts of will she fought 40 against it, and mastered it. And then, suddenly, horror and agony of it, up it would rush in her again, her unbearable desire for him, the longing for his contact, his quality of beauty.

That was a cross hard to bear. Yet even that she bore. And
5 schooled herself into a fretful, petulant manner of indifference. Her odd, whimsical petulance hid a will which he, and he alone, knew to be stronger than steel, strong as a diabolical, cold grey snake that presses and presses and cannot relax: nay, cannot relax. She became the same as he. Even in her moments of most passionate desire for
10 him, the cold and snake-like tension of her will never relaxed, and the cold, snake-like eye of her intention never closed.

So, till it reached a deadlock. Each will was wound tense, and so fixed. Fixed! There was neither any relaxing or any increase of pressure. Fixed. Hard like a numbness, a grip that was solidifying
15 and turning to stone.

He realised, somehow, that at this terrible passive game of fixed tension she would beat him. Her fixed female soul, her wound-up female will would solidify into stone—whereas his must break. In him something must break. It was a cold and fatal deadlock,
20 profitless. A life-automatism of fixed tension that suddenly, in him, did break. His will flew loose in a recoil: a recoil away from her. He left her, as inevitably as a broken spring flies out from its hold.

Not that he was broken. He would not do her even that credit. He had only flown loose from the old centre-fixture. His will was still
25 entire and unabated. Only he did not know: he did not understand. He swung wildly about from place to place, as if he were broken.

Then suddenly, on this Sunday evening in the strange country, he realised something about himself. He realised that he had never intended to yield himself fully to her or to anything: that he did not
30 intend ever to yield himself up entirely to her or to anything: that his very being pivoted on the fact of his isolate self-responsibility, aloneness. His intrinsic and central aloneness was the very centre of his being. Break it, and he broke his being. Break this central aloneness, and he broke everything. It was the great temptation, to
35 yield himself: and it was the final sacrilege. Anyhow, it was something which, from his profoundest soul, he did not intend to do. By the innermost isolation and singleness of his own soul he would abide though the skies fell on top of one another, and seven heavens collapsed.

40 Vaguely he realised this. And vaguely he realised that this had

been the root cause of his strife with Lottie: Lottie, the only person who had mattered at all to him in all the world: save perhaps his mother. And his mother had not mattered, no, not one-half nor one-fifth what Lottie had mattered. So it was: there was, for him, only her significant in the universe. And between him and her 5 matters were as they were.

He coldly and terribly hated her, for a moment. Then no more. There was no solution. It was a situation without a solution. But at any rate, it was now a defined situation. He could rest in peace.

Thoughts something in this manner ran through Aaron's sub- 10 conscious mind as he sat still in the strange house. He could not have fired it all off at any listener, as these pages are fired off at any chance reader. Nevertheless there it was, risen to half consciousness in him. All his life he had *hated* knowing what he felt. He had wilfully, if not consciously, kept a gulf between his passional soul and his open 15 mind. In his mind was pinned up a nice description of himself, and a description of Lottie, sort of authentic passports to be used in the conscious world. These authentic passports, self-describing: nose short, mouth normal, etc; he had insisted that they should do all the duty of the man himself. This ready-made and very banal idea of 20 himself as a really quite nice individual: eyes blue, nose short, mouth normal, chin normal: this he had insisted was really himself. It was his conscious mask.

Now at last, after years of struggle, he seemed suddenly to have dropped his mask on the floor, and broken it. His authentic 25 self-describing passport, his complete and satisfactory idea of himself suddenly became a rag of paper, ridiculous. What on earth did it matter if he was nice or not, if his chin was normal or abnormal?

His mask, his idea of himself dropped and was broken to bits. 30 There he sat now maskless and invisible. That was how he strictly felt: invisible and undefined, rather like Wells' *Invisible Man*.* He had no longer a mask to present to people: he was present and invisible: they *could* not really think anything about him, because they could not really see him. What did they see when they looked at him? 35 Lady Franks, for example. He neither knew nor cared. He only knew he was invisible to himself and everybody, and that all thinking about what he was like was only a silly game of Mrs. Mackenzie's Dead.*

So there. The old Aaron Sisson was as if painfully transmuted, as 40 the Invisible Man when he underwent his transmutations. Now he was gone, and no longer to be seen. His visibility lost for ever.

And then what? Sitting there as an invisible presence, the preconceived world melted also and was gone. Lady Franks, Sir William, all the guests, they talked and manoeuvred with their visible personalities, manipulating the masks of themselves. And underneath there was something invisible and dying—something fading, wilting: the essential plasm of themselves: their invisible being.

Well now, and what next? Having in some curious manner tumbled from the tree of modern knowledge, and cracked and rolled out from the shell of the preconceived idea of himself like some dark, night-lustrous chestnut from the green ostensibility of the burr, he lay as it were exposed but invisible on the floor, knowing, but making no conceptions: knowing, but having no idea. Now that he was finally unmasked and exposed, the accepted idea of himself cracked and rolled aside like a broken chestnut-burr, the mask split and shattered, he was at last quiet and free. He had dreaded exposure: and behold, we cannot be exposed, for we are invisible. We cannot be exposed to the looks of others, for our very being is night-lustrous and unseeable. Like the Invisible Man, we are only revealed through our clothes and our masks.

In his own powerful but subconscious fashion Aaron realised this. He was a musician. And hence even his deepest *ideas* were not word-ideas, his very thoughts were not composed of words and ideal concepts. They too, his thoughts and his ideas, were dark and invisible, as electric vibrations are invisible no matter how many words they may purport. If I, as a word-user, must translate his deep conscious vibrations into finite words, that is my own business. I do but make a translation of the man. He would speak in music. I speak with words.

The inaudible music of his conscious soul conveyed his meaning in him quite as clearly as I convey it in words: probably much more clearly. But in his own mode only: and it was in his own mode only he realised what I must put into words. These words are my own affair. His mind was music.

Don't grumble at me then, gentle reader, and swear at me that this damned fellow wasn't half clever enough to think all these smart things, and realise all these fine-drawn-out subtleties. You are quite right, he wasn't, yet it all resolved itself in him as I say, and it is for you to prove that it didn't.

In his now silent, maskless state of wordless comprehension, he knew that he had never wanted to surrender himself utterly to Lottie: nor to his mother: nor to anybody. The last extreme of self-abandon in love was for him an act of false behaviour. His own nature inside him fated him not to take this last false step, over the edge of the 5 abyss of selflessness. Even if he wanted to, he could not. He might struggle on the edge of the precipice like an assassin struggling with his own soul, but he could not conquer. For, according to all the current prejudice and impulse in one direction, he too had believed that the final achievement, the consummation of human life, was this 10 flinging oneself over the precipice, down the bottomless pit of love. Now he realised that love, even in its intensest, was only an attribute of the human soul: one of its incomprehensible gestures. And to fling down the whole soul in one gesture of finality in love was as much a criminal suicide as to jump off a church-tower or a mountain-peak. 15 Let a man give himself as much as he liked in love, to seven thousand extremities, he must never give himself *away*. The more generous and the more passionate the soul, the more it *gives* itself. But the more absolute remains the law, that it shall never give itself away. Give thyself, but give thyself not away. That is the lesson written at 20 the end of the long strange lane of love.

The *idée fixe* of today is that every individual shall not only give himself, but shall achieve the last glory of giving himself away. And since this takes two—you can't even make a present of yourself unless you've got somebody to receive the present—; since this last 25 extra-divine act takes two people to perform it, you've got to take into count not only your giver but your receiver. Who is going to be the giver and who the receiver.

Why, of course, in our long-drawn-out Christian day, man is given and woman is recipient. Man is the gift, woman the receiver. 30 This is the sacrament we live by; the holy Communion we live for. That man give himself to woman in an utter and sacred abandon, all, all, all himself given, and taken. Woman, eternal woman, she is the communicant. She receives the sacramental body and spirit of the man. And when she's got it, according to her passionate and 35 all-too-sacred desire, completely, when she possesses her man at last finally and ultimately, without blemish or reservation in the perfection of the sacrament: then, also, poor woman, the blood and the body of which she has partaken become insipid or nauseous to her, she is driven mad by the endless meal of the marriage 40 sacrament, poisoned by the sacred communion which was her goal and her soul's ambition.

We have pushed a process into a goal. The aim of any process is not the perpetuation of that process, but the completion thereof. Love is a process of the incomprehensible human soul: love also incomprehensible, but still only a process. The process should work to a completion, not to some horror of intensification and extremity wherein the soul and body ultimately perish. The completion of the process of love is the arrival at a state of simple, pure self-possession, for man and woman. Only that. Which isn't exciting enough for us sensationalists. We prefer abysses and maudlin self-abandon and self-sacrifice, the degeneration into a sort of slime and merge.

Perhaps, truly, the process of love is never accomplished. But it moves in great stages, and at the end of each stage a true goal, where the soul possesses itself in simple and generous singleness. Without this, love is a disease.

So Aaron, crossing a certain border-line and finding himself alone completely, accepted his loneliness or single-ness as a fulfilment, a state of fulfilment. The long fight with Lottie had driven him at last to himself, so that he was quiet as a thing which has its root deep in life, and has lost its anxiety. As for considering the lily, it is not a matter of consideration. The lily toils and spins hard enough,* in her own way. But without that strain and that anxiety with which we try to weave ourselves a life. The lily is life-rooted, life-central. She *cannot* worry. She is life itself, a little, delicate fountain playing creatively, for as long or as short a time as may be, and unable to be anxious. She may be sad or sorry, if the north wind blows. But even then, anxious she cannot be. Whether her fountain play or cease to play, from out the cold, damp earth, she cannot be anxious. She may only be glad or sorry, and continue her way. She is perfectly herself, whatever befall! even if frosts cut her off. Happy lily, never to be saddled with an *idée fixe*, never to be in the grip of a monomania for happiness or love or fulfilment. It is not *laisser aller*. It is life-rootedness. It is being by oneself, life-living, like the much-mooted lily. One toils, one spins, one strives: just as the lily does. But like her, taking one's own life-way amidst everything, and taking one's own life-way alone. Love too. But there also, taking one's way alone, happily alone in all the wonders of communion, swept up on the winds, but never swept away from one's very self. Two eagles in mid-air, maybe, like Whitman's "Dalliance of Eagles."* Two eagles in mid-air, grappling, whirling, coming to their intensification of love-oneness there in mid-air. In mid-air the love consummation. But all the time each lifted on its own wings: each bearing itself up on its own wings at every moment of the mid-air love consummation. That is the splendid love-way. 5

———————————

The party was festive at dinner-time, the women in their finest dresses, new flowers on the table, the best wine going. It was Sunday evening. Aaron too was dressed—and Lady Franks, in black lace and pearls, was almost gay. There were quails for dinner. The Colonel 10 was quite happy. An air of conviviality gathered round the table during the course of the meal.

"I hope," said Aaron, "that we shall have some music tonight."

"I want so much to hear your flute," said his hostess.

"And I your piano," he said. 15

"I am very weak—very out of practice. I tremble at the thought of playing before a musician. But you must not be too critical."

"Oh," said Aaron. "I am not a man to be afraid of."

"Well, we will see," said Lady Franks. "But I am afraid of music itself." 20

"Yes," said Aaron. "I think it is risky."

"Risky! I don't see that! Music risky?* Bach? Beethoven! No, I don't agree. On the contrary, I think it is most elevating—most morally inspiring. No, I tremble before it because it *is* so wonderful and elevating." 25

"I often find it makes me feel diabolical," said he.

"That is your misfortune, I am sure," said Lady Franks. "Please do take another—but perhaps you don't like mushrooms?"

Aaron quite liked mushrooms, and helped himself to the entrée.

"But perhaps," said she, "you are too modern. You don't care for 30 Bach or Beethoven or Chopin—dear Chopin."

"I find them all quite as modern as I am."

"Is that so. Yes. For myself I am quite old-fashioned—though I can appreciate Strauss and Stravinsky as well, some things. But my old things—ah, I don't think the moderns are so fine. They are not so 35 deep. They haven't fathomed life so deeply." Lady Franks sighed faintly.

"They don't care for depths," said Aaron.

"No, they haven't the capacity. But I like big, deep music. Oh, I love orchestra. But my instrument is the piano. I like the great 40 masters, Bach, Beethoven. They have such faith. You were talking of faith—believing that things would work out well for you in the end. Beethoven inspires that in me too."

"He makes you feel that all will be well with you at last?"

"Yes, he does. He makes me feel faith in my *personal* destiny. And I do feel that there is something in one's special fate. I feel that I myself have a special kind of fate, that will always look after me."

"And you can trust to it?"

"Yes, I can. It *always* turns out right. I think something has gone wrong—and then, it always turns out right. Why when we were in London—when we were at lunch one morning it suddenly struck me, haven't I left my fur cloak somewhere? It was rather cold, so I had taken it with me, and then never put it on.—And I hadn't brought it home. I had left it somewhere. But whether in a taxi, or in a shop, or in a little show of pictures I had been to, I couldn't remember. I *could not* remember. And I thought to myself: have I lost my cloak? I went round to everywhere I could think of: no trace of it. But I didn't give it up. Something prompted me not to give it up: quite distinctly, I felt something telling me that I should get it back. So I called at Scotland Yard and gave the information.—Well, two days later I had a notice from Scotland Yard, so I went. And there was my cloak. I had it back.—And that has happened to me almost every time. I almost *always* get my things back. And I always feel that something looks after me, do you know: almost takes care of me."

"But do you mean when you lose things—or in your life?"

"I mean when I lose things—or when I want to get something I want—I am very nearly always successful. And I always feel there is some sort of higher power which does it for me."

"Finds your cloak for you."

"Yes. Wasn't it extraordinary? I felt when I saw my cloak in Scotland Yard: There, I *knew* I should recover you. And I always feel, as I say, that there is some higher power which helps me.—Do you feel the same?"

"No, not that way, worse luck. I lost a batch of music a month ago which didn't belong to me—and which I couldn't replace. But I never could recover it: though I'm sure nobody wanted it."

"How very unfortunate! Whereas my fur cloak was just the thing that gets stolen most."

"I wished some power would trace my music: but apparently we aren't all gifted alike with guardian angels."

"Apparently not. And that is how I regard it: almost as a gift, you know, that my fairy godmother gave me in my cradle."

"For always recovering your property?"

"Yes—and succeeding in my undertakings."

"I'm afraid I had no fairy godmother."

"Well—I think I had. And very glad I am of it."

"Why yes," said Aaron, looking at his hostess.

So the dinner sailed merrily on.

"But does Beethoven make you feel," said Aaron as an after-thought, "in the same way—that you will always find the things you have lost?"

"Yes—he makes me feel the same faith: that what I lose will be returned to me. Just as I found my cloak. And that if I enter into an undertaking, it will be successful."

"And your life has been always successful?"

"Yes—almost always. We have succeeded with almost everything."

"Why yes," said Aaron, looking at her again.

But even so, he could see a good deal of hard wornness under her satisfaction. She had had her suffering, sure enough. But none the less, she was in the main satisfied. She sat there, a good hostess, and expected the homage due to her success. And of course she got it. Aaron himself did his little share of shoe-licking, and swallowed the taste of boot-polish with a grimace, knowing what he was about.

The dinner wound gaily to an end. The ladies retired. Sir William left his seat of honour at the end of the table and came and sat next to Aaron, summoning the other three men to cluster near.

"Now Colonel," said the host, "send round the bottle."

With a flourish of the elbow and shoulder, the Colonel sent on the port: actually port, in those bleak, post-war days!

"Well, Mr. Sisson," said Sir William, "we will drink to your kind Providence: providing, of course, that we shall give no offence by so doing."

"No Sir—No Sir! The Providence belonged to Mr. Lilly. Mr. Sisson put his money on kindly fortune, I believe," said Arthur, who, rosy and fresh with wine, looked as if he would make a marvellous *bonne bouche* for a finely-discriminating cannibal.

"Ah yes indeed! A much more ingratiating lady to lift our glasses to. Mr. Sisson's kindly fortune. *Fortuna gentilissima!** Well, Mr. Sisson, and may your Lady Fortune ever smile on you."

Sir William lifted his glass with an odd little smirk, some touch of a strange, prim old satyr lurking in his oddly inclined head. Nay, more than satyr: that curious, rather terrible iron demon that has fought with the world and wrung wealth from it, and which knows all about 5 it. The devilish spirit of iron itself, and iron machines. So, with his strange, old smile showing his teeth rather terribly, the old knight glowered sightlessly over his glass at Aaron. Then he drank: the strange, careful, old-man's gesture in drinking.

"But," said Aaron, "if Fortune is a female——"

10 "Fortune! Fortune! Why, Fortune is a lady. What do you say, Major?"

"She has all the airs of one, Sir William," said the Major, with the wistful grimness of his age and culture. And the young fellow stared like a crucified cyclop from his one eye: the black shutter being over 15 the other.

"And all the graces," capped Sir William, delighted with himself.

"Oh quite!" said the Major. "For some, all the airs, and for others, all the graces."

"Faint heart ne'er won fair lady, my boy," said Sir William. "Not 20 that your heart is faint. On the contrary—as we know, and your country knows. But with Lady Fortune you need another kind of stout heart—oh quite another kind."

"I believe it, Sir: and the kind of stout heart which I am afraid I haven't got," said the Major.

25 "What!" said the old man. "Show the white feather before you've tackled the lady! Fill the Major's glass, Colonel. I am quite sure we will none of us ever say die."

"Not likely. Not if we know it," said the Colonel, stretching himself heartily inside his tunic. He was becoming ruddier than the 30 cherry.* All he cared about at the moment was his gay little portglass. But the Major's young cheek was hollow and sallow, his one eye terribly pathetic.

"And you, Mr. Sisson," said Sir William, "mean to carry all before you by taking no thought for the morrow.* Well now, we can 35 only wish you success."

"I don't want to carry all before me," said Aaron. "I should be sorry. I want to walk past most of it."

"Can you tell us where to? I am intrigued, as Sybil says, to know where you will walk to. Come now. Enlighten us."

40 "Nowhere, I suppose."

"But is that satisfactory? Can you find it satisfactory?"

"Is it even true?" said the Major. "Isn't it quite as positive an act to walk away from a situation as to walk towards it?"

"My dear boy, you can't merely walk away from a situation. Believe that. If you walk away from Rome, you walk into the Maremma, or into the Alban Hills, or into the sea—but you walk into something. Now if I am going to walk away from Rome, I prefer to choose my direction, and therefore my destination."

"But you can't," said the Major.

"What can't you?"

"Choose. Either your direction or your destination—" The Major was obstinate.

"Really!" said Sir William. "I have not found it so. I have not found it so. I have had to keep myself hard at work, all my life, choosing between this or that."

"And we," said the Major, "have no choice, except between this or nothing."

"Really! I am afraid," said Sir William, "I am afraid I am too old—or too young—which shall I say?—to understand."

"Too young, Sir," said Arthur sweetly. "The child was always father to the man,* I believe."

"I confess the Major makes me feel childish," said the old man. "The choice between this or nothing is a puzzler to me. Can you help me out, Mr. Sisson? What do you make of this this-or-nothing business? I can understand neck-or-nothing—"

"I prefer the *nothing* part of it to the *this* part of it," said Aaron grinning.

"Colonel," said the old man, "throw a little light on this nothingness."

"No, Sir William," said the Colonel. "I am all right as I am."

"As a matter of fact, so are we all, perfectly A.1.," said Arthur. Aaron broke into a laugh.

"That's the top and bottom of it," he laughed, flushed with wine, and handsome. "We're all as right as ninepence. Only it's rather nice to talk."

"There!" said Sir William. "We're all right as ninepence! We're all as right as ninepence. So there we'll leave it, before the Major has time to say he is twopence short." Laughing his strange old soundless laugh, Sir William rose and made a little bow. "Come up and join the ladies in a minute or two," he said. Arthur opened the door for him and he left the room.

The four men were silent for a moment—then the Colonel

whipped up the decanter and filled his glass. Then he stood up and clinked glasses with Aaron, like a real old sport.

"Luck to you," he said.

"Thanks," said Aaron.

5 "You're going in the morning?" said Arthur.

"Yes," said Aaron.

"What train?" said Arthur.

"Eight-forty."

"Oh—then we shan't see you again. Well—best of luck."

10 "Best of luck—" echoed the Colonel.

"Same to you," said Aaron, and they all peered over their glasses and quite loved one another for a rosy minute.

"I should like to know, though," said the hollow-cheeked young Major with the black flap over his eye, "whether you do really mean you are all right—that it is all right with you—or whether you only say so to get away from the responsibility."

"I mean I don't really care—I don't a damn—let the devil take it all."

"The devil doesn't want it, either," said the Major.

20 "Then let him leave it. I don't care one single little curse about it all."

"Be damned! What is there to care about?" said the Colonel.

"Ay, what?" said Aaron.

"It's all the same, whether you care or don't care. So I say it's much easier not to care," said Arthur.

"Of course it is," said the Colonel gaily.

"And I think so too," said Aaron.

"Right you are! We're all as right as ninepence—what? Good old sport! Here's yours!" cried the Colonel.

30 "We shall have to be going up," said Arthur, wise in his generation.

As they went into the hall, Arthur suddenly put one arm round Aaron's waist, and one arm round the Colonel's and the three did a sudden little barn-dance towards the stairs. Arthur was feeling himself quite let loose again, back in his old regimental mess.

Approaching the foot of the stairs, he let go again. He was in that rosy condition when united-we-stand.* But unfortunately it is a complicated job to climb the stairs in unison. The whole lot tends to fall backwards. Arthur, therefore, rosy, plump, looking so good to eat, stood still a moment in order to find his own neatly-slippered feet. Having found them, he proceeded to put them carefully one before the other, and to his enchantment found that this procedure was carrying him magically up the stairs. The Colonel, like a drowning man, clutched feebly for the straw of the great stair-rail— and missed it. He would have gone under, but that Aaron's hand gripped his arm. So, orientating once more like a fragile tendril, he reached again for the banister rail, and got it. After which, lifting his feet as if they were little packets of sand tied to his trouser-buttons, he manipulated his way upwards. Aaron was in that pleasant state when he saw what everybody else was doing and was unconscious of what he did himself. Whilst tall, gaunt, erect, like a murdered Hamlet resurrected in khaki, with the terrible black shutter over his eye, the young Major came last.

Arthur was making a stern fight for his composure. His whole future depended on it. But do what he would, he could not get the flushed, pleased, mess-happy look off his face. The Colonel, oh awful man, did a sort of plump roly-poly cake-walk, like a fat boy, right to the very door of the sanctum-sanctorum, the library. Aaron was inwardly convulsed. Even the Major laughed.

But Arthur stiffened himself militarily and cleared his throat. All four started to compose themselves, like actors going on the stage, outside that library door. And then Arthur softly, almost wistfully, opened and held the door for the others to pass. The Colonel slunk meekly in, and sat in a chair in the background. The Major stalked in expressionless, and hovered towards the sofa where his wife sat.

There was rather a cold-water-down-your-back feeling in the library. The ladies had been waiting for coffee: Sir William was waiting too. Therefore in a little tension, half silent, the coffee was handed round. Lady Franks was discussing something with Arthur's wife. Arthur's wife was in a cream lace dress, and looking what is called lovely. The Major's wife was in amethyst chiffon with dark-red roses, and was looking blindingly beautiful. The Colonel was looking into his coffee-cup as wistfully as if it contained the illusion of tawny port. The Major was looking into space, as if there and there alone etc. Arthur was looking for something which Lady Franks had asked for, and which he was much too flushed to find. Sir William was looking at Aaron, and preparing for another *coeur à coeur.**

"Well," he said, "I doubt if you will care for Milan. It is one of the least Italian of all the towns, in my opinion. Venice of course is a thing apart. I cannot stand, myself, that miserable specimen the modern Roman. He has most of the vices of the old Romans and none of the virtues. The most congenial town, perhaps, for a stranger, is Florence. But it has a very bad climate."

5   Lady Franks rose significantly and left the room, accompanied by Arthur's wife. Aaron, knew, silently, that he was summoned to follow. His hostess had her eye on him this evening. But always postponing his obedience to the cool commands of women, he remained talking with his host in the library, and sipping *crème de*
10 *menthe.* Came the ripple of the pianoforte from the open doorway down at the further end of the room. Lady Franks was playing, in the large drawing-room. And the ripple of the music contained in it the hard insistence of the little woman's will. Coldly, and decidedly, she intended there should be no more unsettling conversations for the
15 old Sir William. Aaron was to come forthwith into the drawing-room. Which Aaron plainly understood—and so he didn't go. No, he didn't go, though the pianoforte rippled and swelled in volume. No, and he didn't go even when Lady Franks left off playing and came into the library again. There he sat, talking with Sir William. Let us
20 do credit to Lady Franks' will-power, and admit that the talk was quite empty and distracted—none of the depths and skirmishes of the previous occasions. None the less, the talk continued. Lady Franks retired, discomfited, to her piano again. She would never break in upon her lord.

25 So now Aaron relented. He became more and more distracted. Sir William wandered away like some restless, hunted soul. The Colonel still sat in his chair, nursing his last drop of *crème de menthe* resentfully. He did not care for the green toffee-stuff. Arthur was busy. The Major lay sprawled in the last stages of everything on the
30 sofa, holding his wife's hand. And the music came pathetically through the open folding-doors. Of course, she played with feeling—it went without saying. Aaron's soul felt rather tired. But she had a touch of discrimination also.

He rose and went to the drawing-room. It was a large, vacant-
35 seeming, Empire sort of drawing-room, with yellow silk chairs along the walls and yellow silk panels upon the walls, and a huge, vasty crystal chandelier hanging from a far-away-above ceiling. Lady Franks sat at a large black Bechstein piano at one end of this vacant yellow state-room. She sat, a little plump elderly lady in black lace,
40 for all the world like Queen Victoria in Max Beerbohm's drawing of

Alfred Tennyson reading to her Victorian Majesty,* with space
before her. Arthur's wife was bending over some music in a remote
corner of the big room.

Aaron seated himself on one of the chairs by the wall, to listen.
Certainly it was a beautiful instrument. And certainly, in her way, 5
she loved it. But Aaron remembered an anthem in which he had
taken part as a boy.

> His eye is on the sparrow
> So I know He watches me.*

For a long time he had failed to catch the word *sparrow*, and had 10
heard:

> His eye is on the spy-hole
> So I know He watches me.

Which was just how it had all seemed to him, as a boy.

Now, as ever, he felt the eye was on the spy-hole. There sat the 15
woman playing music. But her inward eye was on the spy-hole of her
vital affairs—her domestic arrangements, her control of her household, guests and husband included. The other eye was left for the
music, don't you know.

Sir William appeared hovering in the doorway, not at all liking the 20
defection of Mr. Aaron. Then he retreated. He seemed not to care
for music. The major's wife hovered—felt it her duty to aude, or play
audience—and entered, seating herself in a breath of lilac and
amethyst again at the near distance. The Major, after a certain
beating about the bush, followed and sat rapt in dim contemplation 25
near his wife. Arthur luckily was still busy with something.

Aaron of course made proper musical remarks in the intervals—
Arthur's wife sorted out more pieces. Arthur appeared—and then
the Colonel. The Colonel tip-toed beautifully across the wide blank
space of the Empire room, and seated himself on a chair, rather in 30
the distance, with his back to the wall, facing Aaron. When Lady
Franks finished her piece, to everybody's amazement the Colonel
clapped gaily to himself and said Bravo!, as if at a Café Chantant,*
looking around for his glass. But there was no glass. So he crossed
his neatly-khakied legs, and looked rapt again. 35

Lady Franks started with a *vivace* Schumann* piece. Everybody
listened in sanctified silence, trying to seem to like it. When suddenly
our Colonel began to spring and bounce in his chair, slinging his

loose leg with a kind of rapture up and down in the air, and capering upon his posterior, doing a sitting-down jig to the Schumann *vivace*. Arthur, who had seated himself at the farthest extremity of the room, winked with wild bliss at Aaron. The Major tried to look as if he noticed nothing, and only succeeded in looking agonised. His wife studied the point of her silver shoe minutely, and peeped through her hair at the performance. Aaron grimly chuckled, and loved the Colonel with real tenderness.

And the game went on while the *vivace* lasted. Up and down bounced the plump Colonel on his chair, kicking with his bright, black-patent toe higher and higher, getting quite enthusiastic over his jig. Rosy and unabashed, he was worthy of the great nation he belonged to. The broad-seated Empire chair showed no signs of giving way. Let him enjoy himself, away there across the yellow Sahara of this silk-panelled salon. Aaron felt quite cheered up.

"Well now," he thought to himself, "this man is in entire command of a very important branch of the British Service in Italy. We are a great race still."

But Lady Franks must have twigged. Her playing went rather stiff. She came to the end of the *vivace* movement, and abandoned her piece.

"I always prefer Schumann in his *vivace* moods," said Aaron.

"Do you?" said Lady Franks. "Oh, I don't know."

It was now the turn of Arthur's wife to sing. Arthur seemed to get further away: if it was possible, for he was at the remotest remote end of the room, near the gallery doors. The Colonel became quiet, pensive. The Major's wife eyed the young woman in white lace, and seemed not to care for lace. Arthur seemed to be trying to push himself backwards through the wall. Lady Franks switched on more lights into the vast and voluminous crystal chandelier which hung like some glory-cloud above the room's centre. And Arthur's wife sang—sweet little French songs, and "Ye Banks and Braes," and *Caro mio ben,** which goes without saying: and so on. She had quite a nice voice and was quite adequately trained. Which is enough said. Aaron had all his nerves on edge.

Then he had to play the flute. Arthur strolled upstairs with him, arm-in-arm, where he went to fetch his instrument.

"I find music in the home rather a strain, you know," said Arthur.

"Cruel strain. I quite agree," said Aaron.

"I don't mind it so much in the theatre—or even a concert—

where there are a lot of other people to take the edge off—But after a good dinner—"

"It's medicine," said Aaron.

"Well, you know, it really is, to me. It affects my inside."

Aaron laughed. And then, in the yellow drawing-room, blew into 5 his pipe and played. He knew so well that Arthur, the Major, the Major's wife, the Colonel, and Sir William thought it merely an intolerable bore. However, he played. His hostess even accompanied him in a Mozart bit.

Chapter XIV.

XX Settembre[*]

Aaron was wakened in the morning by the soft entrance of the butler with the tray: it was just seven o'clock. Lady Franks' household was punctual as the sun itself.

But our hero roused himself with a wrench. The very act of lifting himself from the pillow was like a fight this morning. Why? He recognised his own wrench, the pain with which he struggled under the necessity to move. Why shouldn't he want to move? Why not? Because he didn't want the day in front—the plunge into a strange country, towards nowhere, with no aim in view. True, he said that ultimately he wanted to join Lilly. But this was hardly more than a sop, an excuse for his own irrational behaviour. He was breaking loose from one connection after another: and what for? Why break every tie? Snap, snap, snap went the bonds and ligatures which bound him to the life that had formed him, the people he had loved or liked. He found all his affections snapping off, all the ties which united him with his own people coming asunder. And why? In God's name, why? What was there instead?

There was nothingness. There was just himself, and blank nothingness. He had perhaps a faint sense of Lilly ahead of him: an impulse in that direction: or else merely an illusion. He could not persuade himself that he was seeking for love, for any kind of unison or communion. He knew well enough that the thought of any loving, any sort of real coming together between himself and anybody or anything, was just objectionable to him. No—he was not moving *towards* anything: he was moving almost violently away from everything. And that was what he wanted. Only that. Only let him *not* run into any sort of embrace with anything or anybody—this was what he asked. Let no new connection be made between himself and anything on earth. Let all old connections break. This was his craving.

Yet he struggled under it this morning as under the lid of a tomb. The terrible sudden weight of inertia! He knew the tray stood ready by the bed: he knew the automobile would be at the door at eight o'clock, for Lady Franks had said so, and he half divined that the servant had also said so: yet there he lay, in a kind of paralysis in this bed. He seemed for the moment to have lost his will. Why go forward into more nothingness, away from all that he knew, all he was accustomed to and all he belonged to?

However, with a click he sat up. And the very instant he had poured his coffee from the little silver coffee-pot into his delicate cup, he was ready for anything and everything. The sense of silent adventure took him, the exhilarated feeling that he was fulfilling his own inward destiny. Pleasant to taste was the coffee, the bread, the honey—delicious.

The man brought his clothes, and again informed him that the automobile would be at the door at eight o'clock: or at least so he made out.

"I can walk," said Aaron.

"Milady ha comandato l'automobile," said the man softly.

It was evident that if Milady had ordered it, so it must be.

So Aaron left the still-sleeping house, and got into the soft and luxurious car. As he dropped through the park he wondered that Sir William and Lady Franks should be so kind to him: a complete stranger. But so it was. There he sat in their car. He wondered, also, as he ran over the bridge and into the city, whether this soft-running automobile would ever rouse the socialistic bile of the work-people. For the first time in his life, as he sat among the snug cushions, he realised what it might be to be rich and uneasy: uneasy, even if not afraid, lurking there inside an expensive car.—Well, it wasn't much of a sensation anyhow: and riches were stuffy, like wadded upholstery on everything. He was glad to get out into the fresh air of the common crowd. He was glad to be in the bleak, not-very-busy station. He was glad to be part of common life. For the very atmosphere of riches seems to be stuffed and wadded, never any real reaction. It was terrible, as if one's very body, shoulders and arms, were upholstered and made cushiony. Ugh, but he was glad to shake off himself the atmosphere of wealth and motor-cars, to get out of it all. It was like getting out of quilted clothes.

"Well," thought Aaron, "if this is all it amounts to, to be rich, you can have riches. They talk about money being power. But the only sort of power it has over me is to bring on a kind of numbness, which I fairly hate. No wonder rich people don't seem to be really alive."

The relief of escaping quite took away his self-conscious embarrassment at the station. He carried his own bags, bought a third class ticket, and got into the train for Milan without caring one straw for the comments or the looks of the porters.

It began to rain. The train ran across the great plain of north Italy. Aaron sat in his wood-seated carriage and smoked his pipe in silence, looking at the thick, short Lombards opposite him without heeding them. He paid hardly any outward attention to his surroundings, but sat involved in himself.

In Milan he had been advised to go to the Hotel Britannia, because it was not expensive, and English people went there. So he took a carriage, drove round the green space in front of Milan station, and away into the town. The streets were busy, but only half-heartedly so.

It must be confessed that every new move he made was rather an effort. Even he himself wondered why he was struggling with foreign porters and foreign cabmen, being talked at and not understanding a word. But there he was. So he went on with it.

The hotel was small and congenial. The hotel porter answered in English. Aaron was given a little room with a tiny balcony, looking on to a quiet street. So, he had a home of his own once more. He washed, and then counted his money. Thirty-seven pounds he had: and no more. He stood on the balcony and looked at the people going by below. Life seems to be moving so quick, when one looks down on it from above.

Across the road was a large stone house with its green shutters all closed. But from the flagpole under the eaves, over the central window of the uppermost floor—the house was four storeys high— waved the Italian flag in the melancholy damp air. Aaron looked at it—the red, white and green tricolor, with the white cross of Savoy* in the centre. It hung damp and still. And there seemed a curious vacancy in the city—something empty and depressing in the great human centre. Not that there was really a lack of people. But the spirit of the town seemed depressed and empty. It was a national holiday. The Italian flag was hanging from almost every housefront.

It was about three o'clock in the afternoon. Aaron sat in the restaurant of the hotel drinking tea, for he was rather tired, and looking through the thin curtains at the little square outside, where people passed: little groups of dark, aimless-seeming men, a little bit poorer looking—perhaps rather shorter in stature—but very much like the people in any other town. Yet the feeling of the city was so different from that of London. There seemed a curious emptiness.

The rain had ceased, but the pavements were still wet. There was a tension.

Suddenly there was a noise of two shots, fired in rapid succession. Aaron turned startled to look into the quiet piazza. And to his amazement, the pavements were empty, not a soul was in sight. Two minutes before the place was busy with passers-by, and a newspaper man selling the *Corriere*,* and little carriages rattling through. Now, as if by magic, nobody, nothing. It was as if they had all melted into thin air.

The waiter too was peeping behind the curtain. A carriage came trotting into the square—an odd man took his way alone—the traffic began to stir once more, and people re-appeared as suddenly as they had disappeared. Then the waiter ran hastily and furtively out and craned his neck, peering round the square. He spoke with two youths—rather loutish youths. Then he returned to his duty in the hotel restaurant.

"What was it? What were the shots?" Aaron asked him.

"Oh—somebody shooting at a dog," said the man negligently.

"At a dog!" said Aaron, with round eyes.

He finished his tea, and went out into the town. His hotel was not far from the cathedral square. Passing through the arcade, he came in sight of the famous cathedral with its numerous spines pricking into the afternoon air. He was not as impressed as he should have been. And yet there was something in the northern city—this big square with all the trams threading through, the little yellow Continental trams: and the spiny bulk of the great cathedral, like a grey-purple sea-urchin with many spines, on the one side, the ornamental grass-plots and flower-beds on the other: the big shops going all along the further strands, all round: and the endless restless nervous drift of a north Italian crowd, so nervous, so twitchy; nervous and twitchy as the slipping past of the little yellow tram-cars; it all affected him with a sense of strangeness, nervousness, and approaching winter. It struck him the people were afraid of themselves: afraid of their own souls, and that which was in their own souls.

Turning up the broad steps of the cathedral, he entered the famous building. The sky had cleared, and the freshened light shone coloured in living tablets round the wonderful, towering, rose-hearted dusk of the great church. At some altars lights flickered uneasily. At some unseen side altar mass was going on, and a strange

ragged music fluttered out on the incense-dusk of the great and lofty
interior, which was all shadow, all shadow, hung round with jewel
tablets of light. Particularly beautiful the great east bay, above the
great altar. And all the time, over the big-patterned marble floor, the
5   faint click and rustle of feet coming and going, coming and going,
like shallow uneasy water rustled back and forth in a trough. A white
dog trotted pale through the under-dusk, over the pale, big-
patterned floor. Aaron came to the side altar where mass was going
on, candles ruddily wavering. There was a small cluster of kneeling
10 women—a ragged handful of on-looking men—and people
wandering up and wandering away, young women with neatly
dressed black hair, and shawls, but without hats; fine young women
in very high heels; young men with nothing to do; ragged men with
nothing to do. All strayed faintly clicking over the slabbed floor, and
15 glanced at the flickering altar where the white-surpliced boys were
curtseying and the white-and-gold priest was bowing, his hands over
his breast, in the candle-light. All strayed, glanced, lingered, and
strayed away again, as if the spectacle were not sufficiently holding.
The bell chimed for the elevation of the Host. But the thin trickle of
20 people trickled the same, uneasily, over the slabbed floor of the
vastly-upreaching shadow-foliaged cathedral.

The smell of incense in his nostrils, Aaron went out again by a side
door, and began to walk along the pavements of the cathedral square,
looking at the shops. Some were closed, and had little notices pinned
25 on them. Some were open, and seemed half-stocked with half-
elegant things. Men were crying newspapers. In the cafés a few men
were seated drinking vermouth. In the doorway of the restaurants
waiters stood inert, looking out on the streets. The curious heart-
eating *ennui* of the big town on a holiday came over our hero. He felt
30 he must get out, whatever happened. He could not bear it.

So he went back to his hotel and up to his room. It was still only
five o'clock. And he did not know what to do with himself. He lay
down on the bed, and looked at the painting on his bedroom ceiling.
It was a terrible business in reckitt's blue* and browny gold, with
35 awful heraldic beasts, rather worm-wriggly, displayed in a blue field.

As he lay thinking of nothing and feeling nothing except a certain
weariness, or dreariness, or tension, or God-knows-what, he heard a
loud hoarse noise of humanity in the distance, something frightening. Rising, he went on to his little balcony. It was a sort of
40 procession, or march of men, here and there a red flag fluttering

from a man's fist. There had been a big meeting, and this was the issue. The procession was irregular, but powerful: men four abreast. They emerged irregularly from the small piazza into the street, calling and vociferating. They stopped before a shop and clotted into a crowd, shouting, becoming vicious. Over the shop-door hung a tricolor, a national flag. The shop was closed, but the men began to knock at the door. They were all workmen, some in railway-men's caps, mostly in black felt hats. Some wore red cotton neck-ties. They lifted their faces to the national flag, and as they shouted and gesticulated Aaron could see their strong teeth in their jaws. There was something frightening in their lean, strong Italian jaws, something inhuman and possessed-looking in their foreign, southern-shaped faces, so much more formed and demon-looking than northern faces. They had a demon-like set purpose, and the noise of their voices was like a jarring of steel weapons. Aaron wondered what they wanted. There were no women—all men—a strange male, slashing sound. Vicious it was—the head of the procession swirling like a little pool, the thick wedge of the procession beyond, flecked with red flags.

A window opened above the shop, and a frowsty looking man, yellow-pale, was quickly and nervously hauling in the national flag. There were shouts of derision and mockery—a great overtone of acrid derision—the flag and its owner ignominiously disappeared. And the procession moved on. Almost every shop had a flag flying. And every one of these flags now disappeared, quickly or slowly, sooner or later, in obedience to the command of the vicious, derisive crowd, that marched and clotted slowly down the street, having its own way. Only one flag remained flying—the big tricolor that floated from the top storey of the house opposite Aaron's hotel. The ground floor of this house consisted of shop-premises—now closed. There was no sign of any occupant. The flag floated inert aloft.

The whole crowd had come to a stop immediately below the hotel, and all were now looking up at the green and white and red tricolor which stirred damply in the early evening light, from under the broad eaves of the house opposite. Aaron looked at the long flag, which drooped almost unmoved from the eaves-shadow, and he half expected it to furl itself up of its own accord, in obedience to the will of the masses. Then he looked down at the packed black shoulders of the mob below, and at the curious clustering pattern of a sea of black hats. He could hardly see anything but hats and shoulders, uneasily

moving like boiling pitch away beneath him. But the shouts began to come up hotter and hotter. There had been a great ringing of a door-bell and battering on the shop-door. The crowd—the swollen head of the procession—talked and shouted, occupying the centre of
5　the street but leaving the pavement clear. A woman in a white blouse appeared in the shop-door. She came out and looked up at the flag and shook her head and gesticulated with her hands. It was evidently not her flag—she had nothing to do with it. The leaders again turned to the large house-door, and began to ring all the bells and to knock
10　with their knuckles. But no good—there was no answer. They looked up again at the flag. Voices rose ragged and ironical. The woman explained something again. Apparently there was nobody at home in the upper floors—all entrance was locked—there was no caretaker. Nobody owned the flag. There it hung under the broad
15　eaves of the strong stone house, and didn't even know that it was guilty. The woman went back into her shop and drew down the iron shutter from inside.

The crowd, nonplussed, now began to argue and shout and whistle. The voices rose in pitch and derision. Steam was getting up.
20　There hung the flag. The procession crowded forward and filled the street in a mass below. All the rest of the street was empty and shut up. And still hung the showy rag, red and white and green, up aloft.

Suddenly there was a lull—then shouts, half-encouraging, half-derisive. And Aaron saw a smallish-black figure of a youth, fair-
25　haired, not more than seventeen years old, clinging like a monkey to the front of the house, and by the help of the heavy drain-pipe and the stone-work ornamentation climbing up to the stone ledge that ran under ground-floor windows, up like a sudden cat on to the projecting footing. He did not stop there, but continued his race like
30　some frantic lizard running up the great wall-front, working away from the noise below, as if in sheer fright. It was one unending wriggling movement, sheer up the front of the impassive, heavy stone house.

The flag hung from a pole under one of the windows of the top
35　storey—the third floor. Up went the wriggling figure of the pos-sessed youth. The cries of the crowd below were now wild, ragged ejaculations of excitement and encouragement. The youth seemed to be lifted up, almost magically on the intense upreaching excite-ment of the massed men below. He passed the ledge of the first floor,
40　like a lizard he wriggled up and passed the ledge or coping of the

second floor, and there he was, like an upward-climbing shadow, scrambling on to the coping of the third floor. The crowd was for a second electrically still as the boy rose there erect, cleaving to the wall with the tips of his fingers.

But he did not hesitate for one breath. He was on his feet and running along the narrow coping that went across the house under the third floor windows, running there on that narrow footing away above the street, straight to the flag. He had got it—he had clutched it in his hand, a handful of it. Exactly like a great flame rose the simultaneous yell of the crowd as the boy jerked and got the flag loose. He had torn it down. A tremendous prolonged yell, touched with a snarl of triumph, and searing like a puff of flame, sounded as the boy remained for one moment with the flag in his hand looking down at the crowd below. His face was odd and elated and still. Then with the slightest gesture he threw the flag from him, and Aaron watched the gaudy remnant falling towards the many faces, whilst the noise of yelling rose up unheard.

There was a great clutch and hiss in the crowd. The boy still stood unmoved, holding by one hand behind him, looking down from above, from his dangerous elevation, in a sort of abstraction.

And the next thing Aaron was conscious of was the sound of trumpets. A sudden startling challenge of trumpets, and out of nowhere a sudden rush of grey-green carabinieri* battering the crowd wildly with truncheons. It was so sudden that Aaron *heard* nothing any more. He only saw.

In utmost amazement he saw the greeny-grey uniformed carabinieri rushing thick and wild and indiscriminate on the crowd: a sudden new excited crowd in uniforms attacking the black crowd, beating them wildly with truncheons. There was a seething moment in the street below. And almost instantaneously the original crowd burst in a terror of frenzy. The mob broke as if something had exploded inside it. A few black-hatted men fought furiously to get themselves free of the hated soldiers; in the confusion bunches of men staggered, reeled, fell, and were struggling among the legs of their comrades and of the carabinieri. But the bulk of the crowd just burst and fled—in every direction. Like drops of water they seemed to fly up at the very walls themselves. They darted into any entry, any doorway. They sprang up the walls and clambered into the ground-floor windows. They sprang up the walls on to window-ledges, and then jumped down again and ran—clambering, wriggling, darting,

running in every direction; some cut, blood on their faces, terror or
frenzy of flight in their hearts. Not so much terror as the frenzy of
running away. In a breath the street was empty.

And all the time, there above on the stone coping stood the
5   long-faced, fair-haired boy, while four stout carabinieri in the street
below stood with uplifted revolvers and covered him, shouting that if
he moved they would shoot. So there he stood, still looking down,
still holding with his left hand behind him, covered by the four
revolvers. He was not so much afraid as twitchily self-conscious
10   because of his false position.

Meanwhile down below the crowd had dispersed—melted
momentaneously. The carabinieri were busy arresting the men who
had fallen and been trodden underfoot, or who had foolishly let
themselves be taken: perhaps half a dozen men, half a dozen
15   prisoners; less rather than more. The sergeant ordered these to be
secured between soldiers. And last of all the youth up above, still
covered by the revolvers, was ordered to come down. He turned
quite quietly, and quite humbly, cautiously picked his way along the
coping towards the drain-pipe. He reached this pipe and began, in
20   humiliation, to climb down. It was a real climb down.

Once in the street he was surrounded by the grey uniforms. The
soldiers formed up. The sergeant gave the order. And away they
marched, the dejected youth a prisoner between them.*

Then were heard a few scattered yells of derision and protest, a
25   few shouts of anger and derision against the carabinieri. There were
once more gangs of men and groups of youths along the street. They
sent up an occasional shout. But always over their shoulders, and
pretending it was not they who shouted. They were all cowed and
hang-dog once more, and made not the slightest effort to save the
30   youth. Nevertheless they prowled and watched, ready for the next
time.

So, away went the prisoner and the grey-green soldiers, and the
street was left to the little gangs and groups of hang-dog, discontented men, all thoroughly out of countenance. The scene was ended.*

35   Aaron looked round, dazed. And then for the first time he noticed,
on the next balcony to his own, two young men:* young gentlemen,
he would have said. The one was tall and handsome and well-
coloured, might be Italian. But the other, with his pale thin face and
his rimless monocle in his eye, he was surely an Englishman. He was
40   surely one of the young officers shattered by the war. A look of

strange, arch, bird-like pleasure was on his face at this moment: if
one could imagine the gleaming smile of a white owl over the events
that had just passed, this was the impression produced on Aaron by
the face of the young man with the monocle. The other youth, the
ruddy handsome one, had knitted his brows in mock distress, and 5
was glancing with a look of shrewd curiosity at Aaron, and with a look
of almost self-satisfied excitement first to one end of the street, then
to the other.

"But imagine, Angus, it's all over!" he said, laying his hand on the
arm of the monocled young man, and making great eyes—not 10
without a shrewd glance in Aaron's direction.

"Did you see him fall!" replied Angus, with another strange
gleam.

"Yes! But was he *hurt*—?"

"*I* don't know. I should think so. He fell right back out of that 15
window on to those stones!"

"But how perfectly *awful*! Did you ever see anything like it?"

"No. It's one of the funniest things I ever did see. I saw nothing
quite like it, even in the war—"

Here Aaron withdrew into his room. His mind and soul were in a 20
whirl. He sat down in his chair, and did not move again for a great
while. When he did move, he took his flute and played he knew not
what. But strange, strange his soul passed into his instrument. Or
passed half into his instrument. There was a big residue left, to go
bitter, or to ferment into good old wine of wisdom. 25

He did not notice the dinner gong, and only the arrival of the
chamber-maid, to put the wash-table in order, sent him down to the
restaurant. The first thing he saw, as he entered, was the two young
Englishmen seated at a table in a corner just behind him. Their hair
was brushed straight back from their foreheads, making the sweep of 30
the head bright and impeccable, and leaving both the young faces
clear as if in cameo. Angus had laid his monocle on the table, and
was looking round the room with wide, light-blue eyes, looking hard,
like some bird-creature, and seeming to see nothing. He had
evidently been very ill: was still very ill. His cheeks and even his jaw 35
seemed shrunken, almost withered. He forgot his dinner: or he did
not care for it. Probably the latter.

"What do you think, Francis," he said, "of making a plan to see
Florence and Siena* and Orvieto on the way down, instead of going
straight to Rome?" He spoke in precise, particularly-enunciated 40

words, in a public-school manner, but with a strong twang of South Wales.

"Why Angus," came the graceful voice of Francis, "I thought we had settled to go straight through via Pisa." Francis was graceful in everything—in his tall, elegant figure, in the poses of his handsome head, in the modulation of his voice.

"Yes, but I see we can go either way—either Pisa or Florence. And I thought it might be nice to look at Florence and Siena and Orvieto. I believe they're very lovely," came the soft, precise voice of Angus, ending in a touch of odd emotion on the words "very lovely," as if it were a new experience to him to be using them.

"I'm *sure* they're marvellous. I'm quite sure they're marvellously beautiful," said Francis, in his assured, elegant way. "Well then, Angus—suppose we do that, then?—When shall we start?"

Angus was the nervous insister. Francis was quite occupied with his own thoughts and calculations and curiosity. For he was very curious, not to say inquisitive. And at the present moment he had a new subject to ponder.

This new subject was Aaron, who sat with his back to our new couple, and who, with his fine sharp ears, caught every word that they said. Aaron's back was broad enough, and his shoulders square, and his head rather small and fairish and well-shaped—and Francis was intrigued. He wanted to know, was the man English. He *looked* so English—yet he might be—he might perhaps be Danish, Scandinavian, or Dutch. Therefore the elegant young man watched and listened with all his ears.

The waiter who had brought Aaron his soup now came very free and easy, to ask for further orders.

"What would you like to drink? Wine? Chianti? Or white wine? Or beer?"—The old-fashioned "Sir" was dropped. It is too old-fashioned now, since the war.

"What *should* I drink?" said Aaron, whose acquaintance with wines was not very large.

"Half-litre of Chianti: that is very good," said the waiter, with the air of a man who knew only too well how to bring up his betters, and train them in the way they should go.

"All right," said Aaron.

The welcome sound of these two magic words, All Right! was what the waiter most desired. "All Right! Yes! All Right!" This is the pith, the marrow, the sum and essence of the English language to a southerner. Of course it is not *all right*. It is *Or-rye*—and one word at that. The blow that would be given to most foreign waiters, if they were forced to realise that the famous *orye* was really composed of two words, and spelt *all right*, would be too cruel, perhaps.

"Half-litre Chianti. Orye," said the waiter. And we'll let him say it.

"*English!*" whispered Francis melodramatically in the ear of Angus. "I *thought* so. The flautist."

Angus put in his monocle, and stared at the oblivious shoulders of Aaron, without apparently seeing anything.

"Yes. Obviously English," said Angus, pursing like a bird.

"Oh but I *heard* him," whispered Francis emphatically.

"Quite," said Angus. "But quite inoffensive."

"Oh but Angus, my dear—he's the *flautist*. Don't you remember? The divine bit of Scriabin.* At least I believe it was Scriabin—But *perfectly divine*!!! I adore the flute above all things—" And Francis placed his hand on Angus' arm, and rolled his eyes—Lay this to the credit of a bottle of Lacrimae Cristi,* if you like.

"Yes. So do I," said Angus, again looking archly through the monocle, and seeing nothing. "I wonder what he's doing here."

"Don't you think we might *ask* him?" said Francis, in a vehement whisper. "After all, we are the only three English people in the place."

"For the moment, apparently we are," said Angus. "But the English are all over the place wherever you go, like bits of orange peel in the street. Don't forget that, Francesco."

"No Angus, I don't. The point is, his flute is *perfectly divine*—and he seems quite attractive in himself. Don't you think so?"

"Oh quite," said Angus, whose observations had got no further than the black cloth of the back of Aaron's jacket. That there was a man inside he had not yet paused to consider.

"Quite a musician," said Francis.

"The hired sort," said Angus, "most probably."

"But he *plays*—he *plays* most marvellously. *That* you can't get away from, Angus."

"I quite agree," said Angus.

"Well then? Don't you think we might hear him again? Don't you think we might get him to play for us?—But I should love it more than anything."

"Yes, I should too," said Angus. "You might ask him to coffee and a liqueur."

"I should like to—most awfully. But do you think I might?"

"Oh yes. He won't mind being offered a coffee and liqueur. We can give him something decent—Where's the waiter?" Angus lifted his pinched, ugly bare face and looked round with weird command for the waiter. The waiter, having not much to do, and feeling ready

5   to draw these two weird young birds, allowed himself to be summoned.

"Where's the wine list? What liqueurs have you got?" demanded Angus abruptly.

The waiter rattled off a list, beginning with *Strega** and ending

10 with cherry brandy.

"Grand Marnier," said Angus. "And leave the bottle."

Then he looked with arch triumph at Francis, like a wicked bird. Francis bit his finger moodily, and glowered with handsome, dark-blue, uncertain eyes at Mr. Aaron, who was just surveying the

15 *Frutta*: which consisted of two rather old pomegranates and various pale yellow apples, with a sprinkling of withered dried figs. At the moment, they all looked like a *Natura Morta** arrangement.

"But do you think I might—?" said Francis moodily. Angus pursed his lips with a reckless brightness.

20 "Why not? I see no reason why you shouldn't," he said. Whereupon Francis cleared his throat, disposed of his serviette, and rose to his feet, slowly but gracefully. Then he composed himself, and took on the air he wished to assume at the moment. It was a nice dégagé air, half naïve and half enthusiastic. Then he crossed to Aaron's

25 table, and stood on one lounging hip, gracefully, and bent forward in a confidential manner, and said:

"*Do* excuse me. But I *must* ask you if it was you we heard playing the flute so perfectly wonderfully, just before dinner."

The voice was confidential and ingratiating. Aaron, relieved from

30 the world's stress and seeing life anew in the rosy glow of half a litre of good old Chianti—the war was so near, but gone by—looked up at the dark-blue, ingenuous, well-adapted eyes of our friend Francis, and smiling, said:

"Yes. I saw you on the balcony as well."

35 "Oh, did you notice us?" plunged Francis. "But wasn't it an extraordinary affair?"

"Very," said Aaron. "I couldn't make it out, could you?"

"Oh," cried Francis. "I never try. It's all much too new and complicated for me.—But perhaps you know Italy?"

40 "No, I don't," said Aaron.

"Neither do we. And we feel rather stunned. We had only just arrived—and then—Oh!" Francis put up his hand to his comely brow and rolled his eyes. "I feel perfectly overwhelmed with it still."

He here allowed himself to sink friendlily into the vacant chair opposite Aaron's.

"Yes, I thought it was a bit exciting," said Aaron. "I wonder what will become of him—"

"—Of the one who climbed for the flag, you mean? No!—But wasn't it perfectly marvellous! Oh incredible, quite incredible!—And then your flute to finish it all! Oh! I felt it only wanted that.—I haven't got over it yet. But your playing was *marvellous*, really marvellous. Do you know, I can't forget it. You are a professional musician, of course?"

"If you mean I play for a living," said Aaron. "I have played in orchestras in London."

"Of course! Of course! I knew you must be a professional. But don't you give private recitals too?"

"No, I never have."

"Oh!" cried Francis, catching his breath. "I can't believe it. But you play *marvellously*! Oh, but I just loved it, it simply swept me away, after that scene in the street. It seemed to sum it all up, you know."

"Did it," said Aaron, rather grimly.

"But won't you come and have coffee with us at our table?" said Francis. "We should like it most awfully if you would."

"Yes, thank you," said Aaron, half rising.

"But you haven't had your dessert," said Francis, laying a fatherly detaining hand on the arm of the other man. Aaron looked at the detaining hand.

"The dessert isn't much to stop for," he said. "I can take with me what I want." And he picked out a handful of dried figs.

The two went across to Angus' table.

"We're going to take coffee together," said Francis complacently, playing the host with a suave assurance that was rather amusing and charming in him.

"Yes. I'm very glad," said Angus. Let us give the show away: he was being wilfully nice. But he *was* quite glad: to be able to be so nice. Anything to have a bit of life going: especially a bit of pleased life. He looked at Aaron's comely, wine-warmed face with gratification.

"Have a Grand Marnier," he said. "I don't know how bad it is.

Everything is bad now. They lay it down to the war as well. It used to be quite a decent drink. What the war had got to do with bad liqueurs, I don't know."

Aaron sat down in a chair at their table.

5   "But let us introduce ourselves," said Francis. "I am Francis—or really Franz Dekker—And this is Angus Guest, my friend."

"And my name is Aaron Sisson."

"What! What did you say?" said Francis, leaning forward. He too had sharp ears.

10   "Aaron Sisson."

"Aaron Sisson! Oh, but how amusing! What a *nice* name!"

"No better than yours, is it?"

"Mine! Franz Dekker! Oh, much more amusing, *I* think," said Francis archly.

15   "Oh well, it's a matter of opinion. You're the double decker, not me."

"The double decker!" said Francis archly. "Why, what do you mean!—" He rolled his eyes significantly. "But may I introduce my friend Angus Guest."

20   "You've introduced me already, Francesco," said Angus.

"So sorry," said Francis.

"Guest!" said Aaron.

Francis suddenly began to laugh.

"May he not be Guest?" he asked, fatherly.

25   "Very likely," said Aaron. "Not that I was ever good at guessing."

Francis tilted his eyebrows. Fortunately the waiter arrived with the coffee.

"Tell me," said Francis, "will you have your coffee black, or with milk?" He was determined to restore a tone of sobriety.

30   The coffee was sipped in sober solemnity.

"Is music your line as well, then?" asked Aaron.

"No, we're painters. We're going to work in Rome."

"To earn your living?"

"Not yet."

35   The amount of discretion, modesty, and reserve which Francis put into these two syllables gave Aaron to think that he had two real young swells to deal with.

"No," continued Francis. "I was only *just* down from Oxford when the war came—and Angus had been about ten months at the

40   Slade—But I have always painted.—So now we are going to work,

really hard, in Rome, to make up for lost time.—Oh, one has lost so much time, in the war. And such *precious* time! I don't know if ever one will even be able to make it up again." Francis tilted his handsome eyebrows and put his head on one side with a wise-distressed look.

"No," said Angus. "One will never be able to make it up. What is more, one will never be able to start again where one left off. We're shattered old men, now, in one sense. And in another sense, we're just pre-war babies."

The speech was uttered with an odd abruptness and didacticism which made Aaron open his eyes. Angus had that peculiar manner: he seemed to be haranguing himself in the circle of his own thoughts, not addressing himself to his listener. So his listener listened on the outside edge of the young fellow's crowded thoughts. Francis put on a distressed air, and let his attention wander. Angus pursed his lips and his eyes were stretched wide with a kind of pleasure, like a wicked owl which has just joyfully hooted an ill omen.

"Tell me," said Francis to Aaron. "Where were *you* all the time during the war?"

"I was doing my job," said Aaron. Which led to his explaining his origins.

"Really! So your music is quite new! But how interesting!" cried Francis.

Aaron explained further.

"And so the war hardly affected you? But what did you *feel* about it, privately?"

"I didn't feel much. I didn't know what to feel. Other folks did such a lot of feeling, I thought I'd better keep my mouth shut."

"Yes, quite!" said Angus. "Everybody had such a lot of feelings on somebody else's behalf, that nobody ever had time to realise what they felt themselves. I know I was like that. The feelings all came on to me from the outside: like flies settling on meat. Before I knew where I was I was eaten up with a swarm of feelings, and I found myself in the trenches. God knows what for. And ever since then I've been trying to get out of my swarm of feelings, which buzz in and out of me and have nothing to do with me. I realised it in hospital. It's exactly like trying to get out of a swarm of nasty dirty flies. And every one you kill makes you sick, but doesn't make the swarm any less."

Again Angus pursed and bridled and looked like a pleased, wicked

white owl. Then he polished his monocle on a very choice silk
handkerchief, and fixed it unseeing in his left eye.

But Francis was not interested in his friend's experiences. For
Francis had had a job in the War Office—whereas Angus was a war
5 hero with shattered nerves. And let him depreciate his own experiences as much as he liked, the young man with the monocle kept
tight hold on his prestige as a war hero. Only for himself, though. He
by no means insisted that anyone else should be war-bitten.

Francis was one of those men who, like women, can set up the
10 sympathetic flow and make a fellow give himself away without
realising what he is doing. So there sat our friend Aaron, amusingly
unbosoming himself of all his history and experiences, drawn out by
the arch, subtle attentiveness of the handsome Francis. Angus
listened too with pleased amusedness on his pale, emaciated face,
15 pursing his shrunken jaw. And Aaron sipped various glasses of the
liqueur, and told all his tale as if it was a comedy. A comedy it
seemed, too, at that hour. And a comedy no doubt it was. But mixed,
like most things in this life. Mixed.

It was quite late before this séance broke up: and the waiter itching
20 to get rid of the fellows.

"Well now," said Francis as he rose from the table and settled his
elegant waist, resting on one hip, as usual. "We shall see you in the
morning, I hope. You say you are going to Venice. Why? Have you
some engagement in Venice?"

25   "No," said Aaron. "I only was going to look for a friend—
Rawdon Lilly."

"Rawdon Lilly! Why, is he in Venice? Oh, I've heard *such* a lot
about him. I should like *so* much to meet him. But I heard he was in
Germany—"

30   "I don't know where he is."

"Angus! Didn't we hear that Lilly was in Germany?"

"Yes, in Munich, being psychoanalysed, I believe it was."

Aaron looked rather blank.

"But have you anything to take you to Venice? It's such a bad
35 climate in the winter. Why not come with us to Florence?" said
Francis.

Aaron wavered. He really did not know what to do.

"Think about it," said Francis, laying his hand on Aaron's arm.
"Think about it tonight. And we'll meet you in the morning. At what
40 time?"

"Any time," said Aaron.

"Well, say eleven. We'll meet in the lounge here at eleven. Will that suit you? All right then. It's so awfully nice meeting you. That marvellous flute.—And think about Florence. But do come. Don't disappoint us."

The two young men went elegantly upstairs.

5

Chapter XV.

A Railway Journey

The next day but one, the three set off for Florence. Aaron had made
an excursion from Milan with the two young heroes, and dined with
them subsequently at the most expensive restaurant in the town.
Then they had all gone home—and had sat in the young men's
bedroom drinking tea, whilst Aaron played the flute. Francis was
really musical, and enchanted. Angus enjoyed the novelty, and the
moderate patronage he was able to confer. And Aaron felt amused
and pleased, and hoped he was paying for his treat.

So behold them setting off for Florence in the early morning.
Angus and Francis had first class tickets: Aaron took a third class.

"Come and have lunch with us on the train," said Angus. "I'll
order three places, and we can lunch together."

"Oh, I can buy a bit of food at the station," said Aaron.

"No, come and lunch with us. It will be much nicer. And we shall
enjoy it as well," said Angus.

"Of course! Ever so much nicer! Of course!" cried Francis. "Yes,
why not indeed! Why should you hesitate?"

"All right then," said Aaron, not without some feeling of con-
straint.

So they separated. The young men settled themselves amidst the
red plush and crochet-work, looking, with their hair plastered
smoothly back, quite as first class as you could wish, creating quite
the right impression on the porters and the travelling Italians. Aaron
went to his third class, further up the train.

"Well then, *au revoir*, till luncheon," cried Francis.

The train was fairly full in the third and second classes. However,
Aaron got his seat, and the porter brought on his bags, after
disposing of the young men's luggage. Aaron gave the tip uneasily.
He always hated tipping—it seemed humiliating both ways. And the
airy aplomb of the two young cavaliers, as they settled down among
the red plush and the obsequiousness, and said "Well then, *au revoir*
till luncheon," was peculiarly unsettling: though they did not intend
it so.

"The porter thinks I'm their servant—their valet," said Aaron to himself, and a curious half-amused, half-contemptuous look flickered on his face. It annoyed him. The falsity occasioned by the difference in the price of the tickets was really humiliating. Aaron had lived long enough to know that as far as manhood and intellect went—nay, even education—he was not the inferior of the two young "gentlemen." He knew quite well that, as far as intrinsic nature went, they did not imagine him an inferior: rather the contrary. They had rather an exaggerated respect for him and his life-power, and even his origin. And yet—they had the inestimable cash advantage—and they were going to keep it. They knew it was nothing more than an artificial cash superiority. But they gripped it all the more intensely. They were the upper middle classes. They were Eton and Oxford. And they were going to hang on to their privileges. In these days, it is a fool who abdicates before he's forced to. And therefore:

"Well then—*au revoir* till luncheon."

They were being so awfully nice. And inwardly they were *not* condescending. But socially, they just had to be. The world is made like that. It wasn't their own private fault. It was no fault at all. It was just the mode in which they were educated, the style of their living. And as we know, *le style, c'est l'homme.**

Angus came of very wealthy iron people near Merthyr.* Already he had a very fair income of his own. As soon as the law-business concerning his father's and his grandfather's will was settled, he would be well off. And he knew it, and valued himself accordingly. Francis was the son of a highly-esteemed barrister and politician of Sydney, and in his day would inherit his father's lately-won baronetcy. But Francis had not very much money: and was much more class-flexible than Angus. Angus had been born in a house with a park, and of awful hard-willed, money-bound people. Francis came of a much more adventurous, loose, excitable family, he had the colonial newness and adaptability. He knew, for his own part, that class superiority was just a trick, nowadays. Still, it was a trick that paid. And a trick he was going to play as long as it did pay.

While Aaron sat, a little pale at the gills, immobile, ruminating these matters, a not very pleasant look about his nose-end, he heard a voice:

"Oh there you *are*! I thought I'd better come and see, so that we can fetch you at lunch time.—You've got a seat? Are you quite comfortable? Is there anything I could get you? Why, you're in a non-smoker!—But that doesn't matter, everybody will smoke. Are you sure you have everything? Oh, but wait just one moment—"

5 It was Francis, long and elegant, with his straight shoulders and his coat buttoned to show his waist, and his face so well-formed and so modern. So modern, altogether. His voice was pleasantly modulated, and never hurried. He now looked as if a thought had struck him. He put a finger to his brow, and hastened back to his own carriage. In a minute he returned with a new London literary

10 magazine.

"Something to read—I shall have to *fly*—See you at lunch," and he had turned and elegantly hastened, but not too fast, back to his carriage. The porter was holding the door for him. So Francis looked pleasantly hurried, but by no means rushed. Oh dear no. He

15 took his time. It was not for him to bolt and scramble like a mere Italian.

The people in Aaron's carriage had watched the apparition of the elegant youth intently. For them, he was a being from another sphere—no doubt a young milordo with power, wealth, and glamor-

20 ous life behind him. Which was just what Francis intended to convey. So handsome—so very, very impressive in all his elegant calm showiness. He made such a *bella figura.*[*] It was just what the Italians loved. Those in the first class regions thought he might even be an Italian, he was so attractive.

25 The train in motion, the many Italian eyes in the carriage studied Aaron. He too was good-looking. But by no means fascinating as the young milordo. Not half as sympathetic. No good at all at playing a rôle. Probably a servant of the young signori.

Aaron stared out of the window, and played the one single British

30 rôle left to him, that of ignoring his neighbours, isolating himself in their midst, and minding his own business. Upon this insular trick our greatness and our predominance depends—such as it is. Yes, they might look at him. They might think him a servant or what they liked. But he was inaccessible to them. He isolated himself upon

35 himself, and there remained.

It was a lovely day, a lovely, lovely day of early autumn. Over the great plain of Lombardy a magnificent blue sky glowed like midsummer, the sun shone strong. The great plain, with its great stripes of cultivation—without hedges or boundaries—how beautiful it was!

40 Sometimes he saw oxen ploughing. Sometimes, oh so beautiful,

teams of eight, of ten, even of twelve pale, great soft oxen in
procession, ploughing the dark velvety earth, a driver with a great
whip at their head, a man far behind holding the plough-shafts.
Beautiful the soft, soft plunging motion of oxen moving forwards.
Beautiful the strange, snaky lifting of the muzzles, the swaying of the
sharp horns. And the soft, soft crawling motion of a team of oxen, so
invisible, almost, yet so inevitable. Now and again straight canals of
water flashed blue. Now and again the great lines of grey-silvery
poplars rose and made avenues or lovely grey airy quadrangles
across the plain. Their top boughs were spangled with gold and
green leaf. Sometimes the vine-leaves were gold and red, a pattern-
ing. And the great square farm-homesteads, white, red-roofed, with
their out-buildings, stood naked amid the lands, without screen or
softening. There was something big and exposed about it all. No
more the cosy English ambushed life: no longer the cosy littleness of
the landscape. A bigness—and nothing to shelter the unshrinking
spirit. It was all exposed, exposed to the sweep of plain, to the high
strong sky, and to human gaze. A kind of boldness, an indifference.
Aaron was impressed and fascinated. He looked with a new interest
at the Italians in the carriage with him—for this same boldness and
indifference and exposed gesture. And he found it in them too. And
again it fascinated him. It seemed so much bigger, as if the walls of
life had fallen.—Nay, the walls of English life will have to fall.

Sitting there in the third class carriage, he became happy again.
The *presence* of his fellow-passengers was not so hampering as in
England. In England, everybody seems held tight and gripped,
nothing is left free. Every passenger seems like a parcel holding his
string as fast as he can about him, lest one corner of the wrapper
should come undone and reveal what is inside. And every other
passenger is forced, by the public will, to hold himself as tight-
bound also. Which in the end becomes a sort of self-conscious
madness.

But here, in the third class carriage, there was no tight string
round every man. They were not all trussed with self-conscious
string as tight as capons. They had a sufficient amount of callousness
and indifference and natural equanimity. True, one of them spat
continually on the floor, in large spits. And another sat with his boots
all unlaced and his collar off, and various important buttons undone.
They did not seem to care if bits of themselves did show, through the
gaps in the wrapping. Aaron winced—but he preferred it to English

tightness. He was pleased, he was happy with the Italians. He thought how generous and natural they were.

So the towns passed by, and the hours, and he seemed at last to have got outside himself and his old conditions. It seemed like a great escape. There was magic again in life—real magic. Was it illusion, or was it genuine. He thought it was genuine, and opened his soul as if there was no danger.

Lunch time came. Francis summoned Aaron down the rocking train. The three men had a table to themselves, and all felt they were enjoying themselves very much indeed. Of course Francis and Angus made a great impression again. But in the dining car were mostly middle-class, well-to-do Italians. And these did not look upon our two young heroes as two young wonders. No, rather with some criticism, and some class-envy. But they were impressed: oh, they were impressed! How should they not be, when our young gentlemen had such an air! Aaron was conscious all the time that the fellow-diners were being properly impressed by the flower of civilisation and the salt of the earth, namely, young, well-to-do Englishmen. And he had a faint premonition, based on experience perhaps, that fellow-passengers in the end never forgive the man who has "impressed" them. Mankind loves being impressed. It asks to be impressed. It almost forces those whom it can force to play a rôle and to make an impression. And afterwards, never forgives.

When the train ran into Bologna Station, they were still in the restaurant car. Nor did they go at once to their seats. Angus had paid the bill. There was three-quarters-of-an-hour's wait in Bologna.

"You may as well come down and sit with us," said Francis. "We've got nobody in our carriage, so why shouldn't we all stay together during the wait. You kept your own seat, I suppose."

No, he had forgotten. So when he went to look for it, it was occupied by a stout man who was just taking off his collar and wrapping a white kerchief round his neck. The third class carriages were packed. For those were early days after the war, while men still had pre-war notions and were poor. Ten months would steal imperceptibly by, and the mysterious revolution would be effected.* Then, the second class and the first class would be packed, indescribably packed, crowded, on all great trains: and the third class carriages, lo and behold, would be comparatively empty. Oh marvellous days of bankruptcy, when nobody will condescend to travel third!

However, these were still modest, sombre months immediately after the peace. So a large man with a fat neck and a white kerchief, and his collar over his knee, sat in Aaron's seat. Aaron looked at the man, and at his own luggage overhead. The fat man saw him looking and stared back: then stared also at the luggage overhead: and with his almost invisible north-Italian gesture said much plainer than words could have said it: "Go to hell. I'm here and I'm going to stop here."

There was something insolent and unbearable about the look—and about the rocky fixity of the large man. He sat as if he had insolently taken root in his seat. Aaron flushed slightly. Francis and Angus strolled along the train, outside, for the corridor was already blocked with the mad Bologna rush, and the baggage belonging. They joined Aaron as he stood on the platform.

"But where is your seat?" cried Francis, peering into the packed and jammed compartments of the third class.

"That man's sitting in it."

"Which?" cried Francis, indignant.

"The fat one there—with the collar on his knee."

"But it was *your seat*—!"

Francis' gorge rose in indignation. He mounted into the corridor. And in the doorway of the compartment he bridled like an angry horse rearing, bridling his head. Poising himself on one hip, he stared fixedly at the man with the collar on his knee, then at the baggage aloft. He looked down at the fat man as a bird looks down from the eaves of a house. But the man looked back with a solid, rock-like impudence, before which an Englishman quails: a jeering, immovable insolence, with a sneer round the nose and a solid-seated posterior.

"But," said Francis in English—none of them had any Italian yet. "But," said Francis, turning round to Aaron: "that was *your seat?*" and he flung his long fore-finger in the direction of the fat man's thighs.

"Yes!" said Aaron.

"And he's *taken* it—!" cried Francis in indignation.

"And knows it too," said Aaron.

"But—!" and Francis looked round imperiously, as if to summon his bodyguard. But bodyguards are no longer forthcoming, and train-guards are far from satisfactory. The fat man sat on, with a sneer-grin, very faint but very effective, round his nose, and a

solidly-planted posterior. He quite enjoyed the pantomime of the young foreigners. The other passengers said something to him, and he answered laconic. Then they all had the faint sneer-grin round their noses. A woman in the corner grinned jeeringly straight in
5　Francis' face. His charm failed entirely this time: and as for his commandingness, that was ineffectual indeed. Rage came up in him.

"Oh well—something must be done," said he decisively. "But didn't you put something in the seat to *reserve* it?"

"Only that *New Statesman**—but he's moved it."

10　The man still sat with the invisible sneer-grin on his face, and that peculiar and immovable plant of his Italian posterior.

"Mais—cette place était *réservée*—"* said Francis, moving to the direct attack.

The man turned aside and ignored him utterly—then said
15　something to the men opposite, and they all began to show their teeth in a grin.

Francis was not so easily foiled. He touched the man on the arm. The man looked round threateningly, as if he had been struck.

"Cette place est réservée—par ce Monsieur—" said Francis with
20　hauteur, though still in an explanatory tone, and pointing to Aaron.

The Italian looked him, not in the eyes, but between the eyes, and sneered full in his face. Then he looked with contempt at Aaron. And then he said, in Italian, that there was room for such snobs in the first class, and that they had not any right to come occupying the
25　place of honest men in the third.

"Già! Già!" barked the other passengers in the carriage.

"Loro possono andare [in] prima classe—*prima classe*!" said the woman in the corner, in a very high voice, as if talking to deaf people, and pointing at Aaron's luggage, then along the train to the first class
30　carriages.

"C'è posto là,"* said one of the men, shrugging his shoulders.

There was a jeering quality in the hard insolence which made Francis go very red and Angus very white. Angus stared like a death's-head behind his monocle, with death-blue eyes.

35　"Oh, never mind. Come along to the first class. I'll pay the difference. We shall be much better all together. Get the luggage down, Francis. It wouldn't be possible to travel with this lot, even if he gave up the seat. There's plenty of room in our carriage—and I'll pay the extra," said Angus.

40　He knew there was one solution—and only one—Money.

But Francis bit his finger. He felt almost beside himself—and quite powerless. For he knew the guard of the train would jeer too. It is not so easy to interfere with honest third class Bolognesi in Bologna station, even if they *have* taken another man's seat. Powerless, his brow knitted, and looking just like Mephistopheles with his high forehead and slightly arched nose, Mephistopheles in a rage, he hauled down Aaron's bag and handed it to Angus. So they transferred themselves to the first class carriage, while the fat man and his party in the third class watched in jeering, triumphant silence. Solid, planted, immovable, in static triumph.

So Aaron sat with the others amid the red plush, whilst the train began its long slow climb of the Apennines, stinking sulphureous through tunnels innumerable. Wonderful the steep slopes, the great chestnut woods, and then the great distances glimpsed between the heights, Firenzuola* away and beneath, Turneresque hills far off, built of heaven-bloom, not of earth. It was cold at the summit-station, ice and snow in the air, fierce. Our travellers shrank into the carriage again, and wrapped themselves round.

Then the train began its long slither downhill, still through a whole necklace of tunnels, which fortunately no longer stank. So down and down, till the plain appears in sight once more, the Arno valley. But then began the inevitable hitch that always happens in Italian travel. The train began to hesitate—to falter to a halt, whistling shrilly as if in protest: whistling pip-pip-pip in expostulation as it stood forlorn among the fields: then stealing forward again and stealthily making pace, gathering speed, till it had got up a regular spurt: then suddenly the brakes came on with a jerk, more faltering to a halt, more whistling and pip-pip-pipping, as the engine stood jingling with impatience: after which another creep and splash, and another choking off. So on till they landed in Prato station: and there they sat. A fellow-passenger told them, there was an hour to wait here: an hour. Something had happened up the line.

"Then I propose we make tea," said Angus, beaming.

"Why not! Of course. Let us make tea. And I will look for water."

So Aaron and Francis went to the restaurant bar and filled the little pan at the tap. Angus got down the red picnic case, of which he was so fond, and spread out the various arrangements on the floor of the coupé. He soon had the spirit-lamp burning, the water heating. Francis proposed that he and Aaron should dash into Prato and see what could be bought, whilst the tea was in preparation. So off they

went, leaving Angus like a busy old wizard manipulating his arrangements on the floor of the carriage, his monocle beaming with bliss.
The one fat fellow-passenger with a lurid striped rug over his knees
watched with acute interest. Everybody who passed the doorway
5 stood to contemplate the scene with pleasure. Officials came and
studied the situation with appreciation. Then Francis and Aaron
returned with a large supply of roast chestnuts, piping hot, and
hard dried plums, and good dried figs, and rather stale rusks. They
found the water just boiling, Angus just throwing in the tea-egg,
10 and the fellow-passenger just poking his nose right in, he was so
thrilled.

Nothing pleased Angus so much as thus pitching camp in the
midst of civilisation. The scrubby newspaper packets of chestnuts,
plums, figs and rusks were spread out: Francis flew for salt to the
15 man at the bar, and came back with a little paper of rock-salt: the
brown tea was dispensed in the silver-fitted glasses from the
immortal luncheon-case: and the picnic was in full swing. Angus,
being in the height of his happiness, now sat on the seat cross-
legged, with his feet under him, in the authentic Buddha fashion,
20 and on his face the queer rapt alert look, half a smile, also somewhat
Buddhistic, holding his glass of brown tea in his hand. He was as rapt
and immobile as if he really were in a mystic state. Yet it was only his
delight in the tea-party. The fellow-passenger peered at the tea, and
said in broken French, was it good. In equally fragmentary French
25 Francis said very good, and offered the fat passenger some. He,
however, held up his hand in protest, as if to say not for any money
would he swallow the hot-watery stuff. And he pulled out a flask of
wine. But a handful of chestnuts he accepted.

The train-conductor, ticket-collector, and the heavy green soldier
30 who protected them, swung open the door and stared attentively.
The fellow-passenger addressed himself to these new-comers, and
they all began to smile good-naturedly. Then the fellow-passenger
—he was stout and fifty and had a brilliant striped rug always over
his knees—pointed out the Buddha-like position of Angus, and the
35 three in-starers smiled again. And so the fellow-passenger thought
he must try too. So he put aside his rug, and lifted his feet from the
floor, and took his toes in his hands, and tried to bring his legs up
and his feet under him. But his knees were fat, his trousers in the
direst extreme of peril, and he could no more manage it than if he
40 had tried to swallow himself. So he desisted suddenly, rather scared,

whilst the three bunched and official heads in the doorway laughed and jested at him, showing their teeth and teasing him. But on our gipsy party they turned their eyes with admiration. They loved the novelty and the fun. And on the thin, elegant Angus in his new London clothes they looked really puzzled, as he sat there immobile, gleaming through his monocle like some Buddha going wicked, perched cross-legged and ecstatic on the red velvet seat. They marvelled that the lower half of him could so double up, like a foot-rule. So they stared till they had seen enough. When they suddenly said "Buon' appetito,"* withdrew their heads and shoulders, slammed the door, and departed.

Then the train set off also—and shortly after six arrived in Florence. It was debated what should Aaron do in Florence. The young men had engaged a room at Bertolini's hotel, on the Lungarno. Bertolini's was not expensive—but Aaron knew that his friends would not long endure hotel life. However, he went along with the other two, trusting to find a cheaper place on the morrow.

It was growing quite dark as they drove to the hotel, but still was light enough to show the river rustling, the Ponte Vecchio* spanning its little storeys across the flood, on its low, heavy piers: and some sort of magic of the darkening, varied houses facing, on the other side of the stream. Of course they were all enchanted.

"I knew," said Francis, "we should love it."

Aaron was told he could have a little back room and pension terms for fifteen Liras a day, if he stayed at least fifteen days. The exchange was then at forty-five. So fifteen Liras meant just six-shillings-and-sixpence a day, without extras. Extras meant wine, tea, butter, and light. It was decided he should look for something cheaper next day.

By the tone of the young men, he now gathered that they would prefer it if he took himself off to a cheaper place. They wished to be on their own.

"Well then," said Francis, "you will be in to lunch here, won't you? Then we'll see you at lunch."

It was as if both the young men had drawn in their feelers now. They were afraid of finding the new man an incubus. They wanted to wash their hands of him. Aaron's brow darkened.

> "Perhaps it was right your love to dissemble
> But why did you kick me down the stairs ..."*

Then morning found him out early, before his friends had arisen.
It was sunny again. The magic of Florence at once overcame him,
and he forgot the bore of limited means and hotel costs. He went
straight out of the hotel door, across the road, and leaned on the river
5 parapet. There ran the Arno: not such a flood after all, but a green
stream with shoals of pebbles in its course. Across, and in the
delicate shadow of the early sun, stood the opposite Lungarno, the
old flat houses, pink, or white, or grey stone, with their green
shutters, some closed, some opened. It had a flowery effect, the
10 skyline irregular against the morning light. To the right the delicate
Trinita bridge, to the left, the old bridge with its little shops over the
river. Beyond, towards the sun, glimpses of green, sky-bloomed
country: Tuscany.

There was a noise and clatter of traffic: boys pushing handbarrows
15 over the cobble stones, slow bullocks stepping side by side, and
shouldering one another affectionately, drawing a load of country
produce, then horses in great brilliant scarlet cloths, like vivid palls,
slowly pulling the long narrow carts of the district: and men
hu-huing!—and people calling: all the sharp, clattering morning
20 noise of Florence.

"Oh Angus! Do come and look! *Oh* so lovely!"

Glancing up, he saw the elegant figure of Francis, in fine
coloured-silk pyjamas, perched on a small upper balcony, turning
away from the river towards the bedroom again, his hand lifted to his
25 lips, as if to catch there his cry of delight. The whole pose was classic
and effective: and very amusing. How the Italians would love it!

Aaron slipped back across the road, and walked away under the
houses towards the Ponte Vecchio. He passed the bridge—and
passed the Uffizi—watching the green hills opposite, and San
30 Miniato.* Then he noticed the over-dramatic group of statuary in the
Piazza Mentana*—male and physical and melodramatic— and then
the corner house. It was a big old Florentine house, with many green
shutters and wide eaves. There was a notice-plate by the door—
"Pension Nardini."*

35 He came to a full stop. He stared at the notice-plate, stared at the
glass door, and turning round, stared at the over-pathetic dead
soldier on the arm of his over-heroic pistol-firing comrade; *Mentana*
—and the date! Aaron wondered what and where Mentana was.
Then at last he summoned his energy, opened the glass door, and
40 mounted the first stairs.

He waited some time before anybody appeared. Then a maid-servant.

"Can I have a room?" said Aaron.

The bewildered, wild-eyed servant maid opened a door and showed him into a heavily-gilt, heavily-plush drawing-room with a great deal of frantic grandeur about it. There he sat and cooled his heels for half an hour. Arrived at length a stout young lady—handsome, with big dark-blue Italian eyes—but anaemic and too stout.

"Oh!" she said as she entered, not knowing what else to say.

"Good-morning," said Aaron awkwardly.

"Oh Good-morning! English! Yes! Oh, I am so sorry to keep you, you know, to make you wait so long. I was upstairs, you know, with a lady. Will you sit?"

"Can I have a room?" said Aaron.

"A room! Yes, you can."

"What terms?"

"Terms! Oh! Why, ten francs a day, you know, pension—if you stay—How long will you stay?"

"At least a month, I expect."

"A month! Oh yes. Yes, ten francs a day."

"For everything?"

"Everything. Yes, everything. Coffee, bread, honey or jam in the morning: lunch at half-past twelve; tea in the drawing-room, half-past four: dinner at half-past seven: all very nice. And a warm room with the sun—Would you like to see?"

So Aaron was led up the big, rambling old house to the top floor—then along a long old corridor—and at last into a big bedroom with two beds and a red tiled floor—a little dreary, as ever—but the sun just beginning to come in, and a lovely view on to the river, towards the Ponte Vecchio, and at the hills with their pines and villas and verdure opposite.

Here he would settle. The signorina would send a man for his bags, at half-past two in the afternoon.

At luncheon Aaron found the two friends, and told them of his move.

"How very nice for you! Ten francs a day—but that is nothing. I am so pleased you've found something. And when will you be moving in?" said Francis.

"At half-past two."

"Oh, so soon. Yes, just as well.—But we shall see you from time to time, of course. What did you say the address was? Oh yes—just near the awful statue. Very well. We can look you up any time—and you will find us here. Leave a message if we should happen not to be
5   in—we've got lots of engagements—"

Chapter XVI.

Florence

The very afternoon after Aaron's arrival in Florence the sky became dark, the wind cold, and rain began steadily to fall. He sat in his big, bleak room above the river, and watched the pale green water fused with yellow, the many-threaded streams fuse into one, as swiftly the surface flood came down from the hills. Across, the dark green hills looked darker in the wet, the umbrella pines held up in vain above the villas. But away below, on the Lungarno, traffic rattled as ever.

Aaron went down at five o'clock to tea, and found himself alone next a group of women, mostly Swedes or Danish or Dutch, drinking a peculiar brown herb-brew which tasted like nothing else on earth, and eating two thick bits of darkish bread smeared with a brown smear which hoped it was jam, but hoped in vain. Unhappily he sat in the gilt and red, massively ornate room, while the foreign women eyed him. Oh bitter to be a male under such circumstances.

He escaped as soon as possible back to his far-off regions, lonely and cheerless, away above. But he rather liked the far-off remoteness in the big old Florentine house: he did not mind the peculiar dark, uncosy dreariness. It was not really dreary: only indifferent. Indifferent to comfort, indifferent to all homeliness and cosiness. The over-big furniture trying to be impressive, but never to be pretty or bright or cheerful. There it stood, ugly and apart. And there let it stand.—Neither did he mind the lack of fire, the cold sombreness of his big bedroom. At home, in England, the bright grate and the ruddy fire, the thick hearth-rug and the man's arm-chair, these had been inevitable. And now he was glad to get away from it all. He was glad not to have a cosy hearth, and his own arm-chair. He was glad to feel the cold, and to breathe the unwarmed air. He preferred the Italian way of no fires, no heating. If the day was cold, he was willing to be cold too. If it was dark, he was willing to be dark. The cosy brightness of a real home—it had stifled him till he felt his lungs would burst. The horrors of real domesticity. No, the Italian brutal way was better.

So he put his overcoat over his knee, and studied some music he had bought in Milan: some Pergolesi and the Scarlatti he liked, and some Corelli.* He preferred frail, sensitive, abstract music, with not much feeling in it, but a certain limpidity and purity. Night fell as he

5 sat reading the scores. He would have liked to try certain pieces on his flute. But his flute was too sensitive, it winced from the new strange surroundings, and would not blossom.

Dinner sounded at last—at eight o'clock, or something after. He had to learn to expect the meals always forty minutes late. Down he

10 went, down the long, dark, lonely corridors and staircases. The dining-room was right downstairs. But he had a little table to himself near the door, the elderly women were at some distance. The only other men were Agostino, the unshapely waiter, and an Italian duke, with wife and child and nurse, the family sitting all together at a table

15 halfway down the room, and utterly preoccupied with a little yellow dog.

However, the food was good enough, and sufficient, and the waiter and the maidservant cheerful and bustling. Everything felt happy-go-lucky and informal, there was no particular atmosphere.

20 Nobody put on any airs, because nobody in the Nardini took any notice if they did. The little ducal dog yapped, the ducal son shouted, the waiter dropped half a dozen spoons, the old women knitted during the waits, and all went off so badly that it was quite pleasant. Yes, Aaron preferred it to Bertolini's, which was trying to be efficient

25 and correct: though not making any strenuous effort. Still, Bertolini's was much more up to the scratch, there was the tension of proper standards. Whereas here at Nardini's, nothing mattered very much.

It was November. When he got up to his far-off room again, Aaron felt almost as if he were in a castle with the drawbridge drawn

30 up. Through the open window came the sound of the swelling Arno, as it rushed and rustled along over its gravel-shoals. Lights spangled the opposite side. Traffic sounded deep below. The room was not really cold, for the summer sun so soaks into these thick old buildings, that it takes a month or two of winter to soak it out.—The

35 rain still fell.

In the morning it was still November, and the dawn came slowly. And through the open window was the sound of the river's rushing. But the traffic started before dawn, with a bang and a rattle of carts, and a bang and jingle of tram-cars over the not-distant bridge. Oh

40 noisy Florence! At half-past seven Aaron rang for his coffee: and got

it at a few minutes past eight. The signorina had told him to take his
coffee in bed.

Rain was still falling. But towards nine o'clock it lifted, and he
decided to go out. A wet, wet world. Carriages going by, with huge
wet shiny umbrellas, black and with many points, erected to cover   5
the driver and the tail of the horse and the box-seat. The hood of the
carriage covered the fare. Clatter-clatter through the rain. Peasants
with long wagons and slow oxen, and pale-green huge umbrellas
erected for the driver to walk beneath. Men tripping along in cloaks,
shawls, umbrellas, anything, quite unconcerned. A man loading   10
gravel in the river-bed, in spite of the wet. And innumerable bells
ringing: but innumerable bells. The great soft trembling of the
cathedral bell felt in all the air.

Anyhow it was a new world. Aaron went along close to the tall
thick houses, following his nose. And suddenly he caught sight of the   15
long slim neck of the Palazzo Vecchio up above, in the air. And in
another minute he was passing between massive buildings, out into
the Piazza della Signoria.* There he stood still and looked round him
in real surprise, and real joy. The flat, empty square with its stone
paving was all wet. The great buildings rose dark. The dark, sheer   20
front of the Palazzo Vecchio went up like a cliff, to the battlements,
and the slim tower soared dark and hawk-like, crested, high above.
And at the foot of the cliff stood the great naked David, white and
stripped in the wet, white against the dark, warm-dark cliff of the
building—and near, the heavy naked men of Bandinelli.*   25

The first thing he had seen, as he turned into the square, was the
back of one of these Bandinelli statues: a great naked man of marble,
with a heavy back and strong naked flanks over which the water was
trickling. And then to come immediately upon the David, so much
whiter, glistening skin-white in the wet, standing a little forward, and   30
shrinking.

He may be ugly, too naturalistic, too big, and anything else you
like. But the David in the Piazza della Signoria, there under the dark
great Palace, in the position Michelangelo* chose for him, there,
standing forward stripped and exposed and eternally half-shrinking,   35
half-wishing to expose himself, he is the genius of Florence. The
adolescent, the white, self-conscious, physical adolescent: enormous, in keeping with the stark, grim, enormous palace, which is
dark and bare as he is white and bare. And behind, the big, lumpy
Bandinelli men are in keeping too. They may be ugly—but they are   40

there in their place, and they have their own lumpy reality. And this morning in the rain, standing unbroken, with the water trickling down their flanks and along the inner side of their great thighs, they were real enough, representing the undaunted physical nature of the heavier Florentines.

Aaron looked and looked at the three great naked men. David so much white, and standing forward, self-conscious: then at the great splendid front of the Palazzo Vecchio: and at the fountain splashing water upon its wet, wet figures; and the distant equestrian statue;* and the stone-flagged space of the grim square. And he felt that here he was in one of the world's living centres, here, in the Piazza della Signoria. The sense of having arrived—of having reached a perfect centre of the human world: this he had.

And so, satisfied, he turned round to look at the bronze Perseus which rose just above him. Benvenuto Cellini's dark hero looked female, with his plump hips and his waist, female and rather insignificant: graceful, and rather vulgar. The clownish Bandinellis were somehow more to the point.—Then all the statuary in the Loggia!* But that is a mistake. It looks too much like the yard of a monumental mason.

The great, naked men in the rain, under the dark-grey November sky, in the dark, strong, inviolable square! The wonderful hawk-head of the old palace! The physical, self-conscious adolescent, Michelangelo's David, shrinking and exposing himself, with his white, slack limbs! Florence, passionate, fearless Florence had spoken herself out.—Aaron was fascinated by the Piazza della Signoria. He never went into the town, nor returned from it to his lodging, without contriving to pass through the square. And he never passed through it without satisfaction. Here men had been at their intensest, most naked pitch, here, at the end of the old world and the beginning of the new. Since then, always rather puling and apologetic.

Aaron felt a new self, a new life-urge rising inside himself. Florence seemed to start a new man in him. It was a town of men. On Friday morning, so early, he heard the traffic. Early, he watched the rather low, two-wheeled traps of the peasants spanking recklessly over the bridge, coming in to town. And then, when he went out, he found the Piazza della Signoria packed with men: but all, all men. And all farmers, land-owners and land-workers. The curious, fine-nosed Tuscan farmers, with their half-sardonic, amber-

coloured eyes. Their curious individuality, their clothes worn so easy
and reckless, their hats with the personal twist. Their curious full
oval cheeks, their tendency to be too fat, to have a belly and heavy
limbs. Their close-sitting dark hair. And above all, their sharp,
almost acrid, mocking expression, the silent curl of the nose, the 5
eternal challenge, the rock-bottom unbelief, and the subtle fearlessness. The dangerous, subtle, never-dying fearlessness, and the acrid
unbelief. But men! Men! A town of men, in spite of everything. The
one manly quality, undying, acrid fearlessness. The eternal challenge of the unquenched human soul. Perhaps too acrid and 10
challenging today, when there is nothing left to challenge. But
men—who existed without apology and without justification. Men
who would neither justify themselves nor apologise for themselves.
Just men. The rarest thing left in our sweet Christendom.

Altogether Aaron was pleased with himself, for being in Florence. 15
Those were early days after the war, when as yet very few foreigners
had returned, and the place had the native sombreness and intensity.
So that our friend did not mind being alone.

The third day, however, Francis called on him. There was a tap at
the bedroom door, and the young man entered, all eyes of curiosity. 20

"Oh there you *are*!" he cried, flinging his hand and twisting his
waist and then laying his hand on his breast. "Such a *long* way up to
you! But *miles*—! Well, how are you? Are you quite all right here?
You are? I'm so glad—we've been so *rushed*, seeing people, that we
haven't had a *minute*. But not a *minute*! People! People! People! Isn't 25
it amazing how many there are, and how many one knows, and gets
to know! But amazing! Endless acquaintances!—oh, and such quaint
people here! so *odd*!! So *more* than odd! Oh extraordinary—!"
Francis chuckled to himself over the extraordinariness. Then he
seated himself gracefully at Aaron's table. "Oh, *music*! What? 30
Corelli! So interesting! So very *clever*, these people, weren't they!—
Corelli and the younger Scarlatti and all that crowd." Here he closed
the score again. "But now—*look*! Do you want to know anybody
here, or don't you? I've told them about you, and of course they're
dying to meet you and hear you play. But I thought it best not to 35
mention anything about—about your being hard-up, and all that. I
said you were just here on a visit. You see with this kind of people I'm
sure it's much the best not to let them start off by thinking you will
need them at all—or that you *might* need them. Why give yourself
away, anyhow? Just meet them and take them for what they're 40

worth—and then you can see. If they like to give you an engagement
to play at some show or other—well, you can decide when the time
comes whether you will accept. Much better that these kind of
people shouldn't get it into their heads at once that they can hire your
services. It doesn't do. They haven't enough discrimination for that.
Much best make rather a favour of it, than sort of *ask* them to hire
you.— Don't you agree? Perhaps I'm wrong."

Aaron sat and listened and wondered at the wisdom and the
genuine kindness of the young *beau*. And more still, he wondered at
the profound social disillusionment. This handsome collie dog was
something of a social wolf, half showing his fangs at the moment. But
with genuine kindheartedness for another wolf. Aaron was touched.

"Yes, I think that's the best way," he said.

"You do! Yes, so do I. Oh, they are such queer people! Why is it,
do you think, that English people abroad go so very *queer*—so
ultra-English—*incredible!*—and at the same time so perfectly impossible? But impossible! Pathological, I assure you.—And as for their
sexual behaviour—oh dear, don't mention it. I assure you it doesn't
bear mention.—And all quite flagrant, quite unabashed—under the
cover of this fanatical Englishness. But I couldn't begin *to tell* you all
the things. It's just incredible."

Aaron wondered how on earth Francis had been able to discover
and bear witness to so much that was incredible, in a bare two days.
But a little gossip, and an addition of lurid imagination will carry you
anywhere.

"Well now," said Francis. "What are you doing today?"

Aaron was not doing anything in particular.

"Then will you come and have dinner with us—?"

Francis fixed up the time and the place—a small restaurant at the
other end of the town. Then he leaned out of the window.

"Fascinating place! Oh, fascinating place!" he said, soliloquy.
"And you've got a superb view. Almost better than ours, I think.—
Well then, half-past seven. We're meeting a few other people, mostly
residents or people staying some time. We're not inviting them. Just
dropping in, you know—a little restaurant. We shall see you then!
Well then, *a rivederci* till this evening.—So glad you like Florence!
I'm simply loving it—revelling. And the pictures!—Oh—"

The party that evening consisted all of men: Francis and Angus,
and a writer, James Argyle, and little Algy Constable, and tiny Louis

Mee, and deaf Walter Rosen.* They all snapped and rattled at one another, and were rather spiteful but rather amusing. Francis and Angus had to leave early. They had another appointment. And James Argyle got quite tipsy, and said to Aaron:

"But my boy, don't let yourself be led astray by the talk of such people as Algy. Beware of them, my boy, if you've a soul to save. If you've a soul to save!" And he swallowed the remains of his litre.

Algy's nose trembled a little, and his eyes blinked.

"And if you've a soul to *lose*," he said, "I would warn you very earnestly against Argyle." Whereupon Algy shut one eye and opened the other so wide, that Aaron was almost scared.

"Quite right, my boy. Ha! Ha! Never a truer thing said! Ha-Ha-Ha." Argyle laughed his Mephistophelian tipsy laugh. "They'll teach you to save. Never was such a lot of ripe old savers! Save their old trouser-buttons! Go to them if you want to learn to save. Oh yes, I advise it seriously. You'll lose nothing—not even a reputation.—You may lose your *soul*, of course. But that's a detail, among such a hoard of banknotes and trouser-buttons. Ha-ha! What's a soul, to them—?"

"What is it to you, is perhaps the more pertinent question," said Algy, flapping his eyelids like some crazy owl. "It is you who specialise in the matter of soul, and we who are in need of enlightenment—"

"Yes, very true, you *are*! You *are* in need of enlightenment. A set of benighted wise virgins. Ha-ha-ha! That's good, that—benighted wise virgins! What—" Argyle put his red face near to Aaron's, and made a *moue*, narrowing his eyes quizzically as he peered up from under his level grey eyebrows. "Sit in the dark to save the lamp-oil!—And all no good to them.—When the bridegroom cometh—!* Ha-ha!—Good that! Good, my boy!—The bridegroom—" he giggled to himself. "What about the bridegroom, Algy, my boy? Eh? What about him? Better trim your wick, old man, if it's not too late—"

"We were talking of souls, not wicks, Argyle," said Algy.

"Same thing. Upon my soul it all amounts to the same thing. Where's the soul in a man that hasn't got a bedfellow—eh?—answer me that! Can't be done, you know. Might as well ask a virgin chicken to lay you an egg.— I don't know what cock-bird committed adultery with the holy dove, before it laid the Easter egg, I'm sure. But there must have been one, you know. There must have been one. Ha! Ha! Ha!—I'd give a lot to have seen him at it. Soul is born of—, believe me. Of nothing but—."

We cannot print the word used by Argyle, though it is a quite common one, often chalked on walls by little boys.

"Then there ought to be a good deal of it about," said Algy.

"Of what? Of soul? There ought to be a good deal of soul about?—Ah, because there's a good deal of—, you mean.— Ah, I wish it were so. I wish it were so. But believe me, there's far more damned chastity in the world, than anything else. Even in this town.— Call it chastity, if you like. I see nothing in it but sterility. It takes a rat to praise long tails. Impotence set up the praise of chastity—believe me or not—but that's the bottom of it. The virtue is made out of the necessity.—Ha-ha-ha!—They can't do it, and so they make a virtue of not doing it. Like them! Like them! Ha-ha! Saving their souls! Why they'd save their urine if they could. Grieves them to part with it.—ha!—ha!—ha!"

There was a pause. Argyle was in his cups, which left no more to be said. Algy, quivering and angry, looked disconcertingly round the room as if he were quite calm and collected. The deaf Jewish Rosen was smiling down his nose and saying: "What was that last? I didn't catch that last," cupping his ear with his hand in the frantic hope that someone would answer. No one paid any heed.

"I shall be going," said Algy, looking round. Then to Aaron he said, "You play the flute, I hear. May we hear you some time?"

"Yes," said Aaron, non-committal.

"Well look here—come to tea tomorrow. I shall have some friends, and Del Torre will play the piano. Come to tea tomorrow, will you?"

"Thank you, I will."

"And perhaps you'll bring your flute along."

"Don't you do any such thing, my boy. Make them entertain *you*, for once.—They're always squeezing an entertainment out of somebody—" and Argyle desperately emptied the remains of Algy's wine into his own glass: whilst Algy stood as if listening to something far-off, and blinking terribly.

"Anyhow," he said at length, "you'll come, won't you? And bring the flute if you feel like it."

"Don't you take that flute, my boy," persisted Argyle. "Don't think of such a thing. If they want a concert, let them buy their tickets and go to the Teatro Diana. Or to Marchesa del Torre's Saturday morning. She can afford to treat them."

Algy looked at Argyle, and blinked.

"Well," he said. "I hope you'll get home all right, Argyle."

"Thank you for your courtesy, Algy. Won't you lend me your arm?"

As Algy was small and frail, somewhat shaky: and as Argyle was a finely built, heavy man of fifty or more, the slap was unkind.

"Afraid I can't tonight. Goodnight—"

Algy departed, so did little Mee, who had sat with a little delighted disapproval on his tiny, bird-like face, without saying anything. And even the Jew Rosen put away his deaf-machine and began awkwardly to take his leave. His long nose was smiling to itself complacently at all the things Argyle had been saying.

When he too had gone, Argyle arched his brows at Aaron, saying:

"Oh, my dear fellow, what a lot they are!—Little Mee—looking like an innocent little boy. He's over seventy if he's a day. Well over seventy. Well, you don't believe me. Ask his mother—ask his mother. She's ninety-five. Old lady of ninety-five—" Argyle even laughed himself at his own preposterousness.

"And then Algy—Algy's not a fool, you know. Oh, he can be most entertaining, most witty, and amusing. But he's out of place here. He should be in Kensington, dandling round the ladies' drawing-rooms and making his *mots*.* They're rich, you know, the pair of them. Little Mee used to boast that he lived on eleven-and-threepence a week. Had to, poor chap. But then what does a white mouse like that need? Makes a heavy meal on a cheese-paring. Luck, you know—but of course he's come into money as well. Rich as Croesus,* and still lives on nineteen-and-twopence a week. Though it's nearly double, of course, what it used to be. No wonder he looks anxious. They disapprove of me—oh, quite right, quite right from their own point of view. Where would their money be otherwise? It wouldn't last long if I laid hands on it—" he made a devilish quizzing face. "But you know, they get on my nerves. Little old maids, you know, little old maids. I'm sure I'm surprised at their patience with me.—But when people are patient with you, you want to spit gall at them. Don't you? Ha-ha-ha! Poor old Algy.—Did I lay it on him, tonight, or did I miss him?"

"I think you got him," said Aaron.

"He'll never forgive me. Depend on it, he'll never forgive me.

Ha-ha! I like to be unforgiven. It adds *zest* to one's intercourse with people, to know that they'll never forgive one. Ha-ha-ha! Little old maids, who do their knitting with their tongues. Poor old Algy—he drops his stitches now. Ha-ha-ha!—Must be eighty, I should say."

5 Aaron laughed. He had never met a man like Argyle before—and he could not help being charmed. The other man had a certain wicked whimsicality that was very attractive, when levelled against someone else, and not against oneself. He must have been very handsome in his day, with his natural dignity, and his clean-shaven

10 strong square face. But now his face was all red and softened and inflamed, his eyes had gone small and wicked under his bushy grey brows. Still he had a presence. And his grey hair, almost gone white, was still handsome.

"And what are you going to do in Florence?" asked Argyle.

15 Aaron explained.

"Well," said Argyle, "make what you can out of them, and then go. Go before they have time to do the dirty on you. If they think you want anything from them, they'll treat you like a dog, like a dog. Oh, they're very frightened of anybody who wants anything of them:

20 frightened to death. I see nothing of them.— Live by myself—see nobody. Can't stand it, you know: their silly little tea-parties—simply can't stand it. No, I live alone—and shall die alone.—At least, I sincerely hope so. I should be sorry to have any of them hanging round."

25 The restaurant was empty, the pale, malarial waiter—he had of course contracted malaria during the war—was looking purple round the eyes. But Argyle callously sat on. Aaron therefore rose to his feet.

"Oh, I'm coming, I'm coming," said Argyle.

30 He got unsteadily to his feet. The waiter helped him on with his coat: and he put a disreputable-looking little curly hat on his head. Then he took his stick.

"Don't look at my appearance, my dear fellow," said Argyle. "I am frayed at the wrists—Look here!" He showed the cuffs of his

35 overcoat, just frayed through. "I've got a trunkful of clothes in London, if only somebody would bring it out to me.—Ready then! Avanti!"*

And so they passed out into the still rainy street. Argyle lived in the very centre of the town: in the cathedral square. Aaron left him at his

40 hotel door.

"But come and see me," said Argyle. "Call for me at twelve
o'clock—or just before twelve—and let us have luncheon together.
What! Is that all right?—Yes, come just before twelve—When?—
tomorrow? Tomorrow morning? Will you come tomorrow?"

Aaron said he would come on Monday.

"Monday, eh! You say Monday! Very well then. Don't you forget
now. Don't you forget. For I've a memory like a vice. *I* shan't
forget—Just before twelve then. And come right up. I'm right under
the roof. In Paradise, as the porter always says. Siamo nel paradiso.*
But he's a *crétin*. As near Paradise as I care for, for it's devilish hot in
summer, and damned cold in winter. Don't you forget now—
Monday, twelve o'clock."

And Argyle pinched Aaron's arm fast, then went unsteadily up the
steps to his hotel door.

The next day at Algy's there was a crowd. Algy had a very pleasant
flat indeed, kept more scrupulously neat and finicking than ever any
woman's flat was kept.* So today, with its bowls of flowers and its
pictures and books and old furniture, and Algy, very nicely dressed,
fluttering and blinking and making really a charming host, it was all
very delightful to the little mob of visitors. They were a curious lot, it
is true: everybody rather exceptional. Which though it may be
startling, is so very much better fun than everybody all alike. Aaron
talked to an old, old Italian elegant in side-curls, who peeled off his
grey gloves and studied his formalities with a delightful Mid-
Victorian dash, and told stories about a *plaint* which Lady Surry had
against Lord Marsh, and was quite incomprehensible. Out rolled the
English words, like plums out of a burst bag, and all completely
unintelligible. But the old *beau* was supremely satisfied. He loved
talking English, and holding his listeners spell-bound.

Next to Aaron on the sofa sat the Marchesa Del Torre,* an
American woman from the Southern States, who had lived most of
her life in Europe. She was about forty years of age, handsome,
well-dressed, and quiet in the buzz of the tea-party. It was evident
she was one of Algy's lionesses. Now she sat by Aaron, eating
nothing, but taking a cup of tea and keeping still. She seemed
sad—or not well perhaps. Her eyes were heavy. But she was very
carefully made up, and very well-dressed, though simply: and sitting
there, full-bosomed, rather sad, remote-seeming, she suggested to
Aaron a modern Cleopatra brooding, Anthony-less.

Her husband, the Marchese, was a little intense Italian in a

Colonel's grey uniform, cavalry,* leather gaiters. He had blue eyes,
his hair was cut very short, his head looked hard and rather military:
he would have been taken for an Austrian officer, or even a German,
had it not been for the peculiar Italian sprightliness and touch of
5   grimace in his mobile countenance. He was rather like a gnome—
not ugly, but odd.

Now he came and stood opposite to Signor di Lanti, and quizzed
him in Italian. But it was evident, in quizzing the old buck, the little
Marchese was hovering near his wife, in earshot. Algy came up with
10 cigarettes, and she at once began to smoke, with that peculiar heavy
intensity of a nervous woman.

Aaron did not say anything—did not know what to say. He was
peculiarly conscious of the woman sitting next to him, her arm near
his. She smoked heavily, in silence, as if abstracted, a sort of cloud on
15 her level, dark brows. Her hair was dark, but a softish brown, not
black, and her skin was fair. Her bosom would be white—Why
Aaron should have had this thought, he could not for the life of him
say.

Manfredi, her husband, rolled his blue eyes and grimaced as he
20 laughed at old Lanti. But it was obvious that his attention was
diverted sideways, towards his wife. Aaron, who was tired of nursing
a tea-cup, placed it on a table and resumed his seat in silence. But
suddenly the little Marchese whipped out his cigarette-case, and
making a little bow, presented it to Aaron, saying:

25 "Won't you smoke?"

"Thank you," said Aaron.

"Turkish that side—Virginian there—you see."

"Thank you, Turkish," said Aaron.

The little officer in his dove-grey and yellow uniform snapped his
30 box shut again, and presented a light.

"You are new in Florence?" he said, as he presented the match.

"Four days," said Aaron.

"And I hear you are musical."

"I play the flute—no more."

35 "Ah yes—but then you play it as an artist, not as an accomplishment."

"But how do you know?" laughed Aaron.

"I was told so—and I believe it."

"That's nice of you, anyhow—But you are a musician too."

40 "Yes—we are both musicians—my wife and I."

Manfredi looked at his wife. She flicked the ash off her cigarette.

"What sort?" said Aaron.

"Why how do you mean, what sort? We are dilettanti, I suppose."

"No—what is your instrument? The piano?"

"Yes—the pianoforte. And my wife sings. But we are very much out of practice. I have been at the war four years, and we have had our home in Paris. My wife was in Paris, she did not wish to stay in Italy alone. And so—you see—everything goes—"

"But you will begin again?"

"Yes. We have begun already. We have music on Saturday mornings. Next Saturday a string quartette, and violin solos by a young Florentine woman—a friend—very good indeed, daughter of our Professor Tortoli, who composes—as you may know—"

"Yes," said Aaron.

"Would you care to come and hear—?"

"Awfully nice if you would—" suddenly said the wife, quite simply, as if she had merely been tired, and not talking before.

"I should like to very much—"

"Do come then."

While they were making the arrangements, Algy came up in his blandest manner.

"Now Marchesa—might we hope for a song?"

"No—I don't sing any more," came the slow, contralto reply.

"Oh, but you can't mean you say that deliberately—"

"Yes, quite deliberately—" She threw away her cigarette and opened her little gold case to take another.

"But what can have brought you to such a disastrous decision?"

"I can't say," she replied, with a little laugh. "The war, probably."

"Oh, but don't let the war deprive us of this, as of everything else."

"Can't be helped," she said. "I have no choice in the matter. The bird has flown—" She spoke with a certain heavy languor.

"You mean the bird of your voice? Oh, but that is quite impossible. One can hear it calling out of the leaves every time you speak."

"I'm afraid you can't get him to do any more than call out of the leaves."

"But—but—pardon me—is it because you don't intend there should be any more song? Is that your intention?"

"That I couldn't say," said the Marchesa, smoking, smoking.

"Yes," said Manfredi. "At the present time it is because she *will* not—not because she cannot. It is her will, as you say."

"Dear me! Dear me!" said Algy. "But this is really another
5 disaster added to the war list.—But—but—will none of us ever be able to persuade you?" He smiled half cajoling, half pathetic, with a prodigious flapping of his eyes.

"I don't know," said she. "That will be as it must be."

"Then can't we say it must be *song* once more?"

10   To this sally she merely laughed, and pressed out her half-smoked cigarette.

"How very disappointing! How very cruel of—of fate—and the war—and—and all the sum total of evils," said Algy.

"Perhaps—" here the little and piquant host turned to Aaron.
15 "Perhaps Mr. Sisson, your flute might call out the bird of song. As thrushes call each other into challenge, you know. Don't you think that is very probable?"

"I have no idea," said Aaron.

"But you, Marchesa. Won't you give us hope that it might be
20 so?"

"I've no idea, either," said she. "But I should very much like to hear Mr. Sisson's flute. It's an instrument I like extremely."

"There now. You see you may work the miracle, Mr. Sisson. Won't you play to us?"

25   "I'm afraid I didn't bring my flute along," said Aaron. "I didn't want to arrive with a little bag."

"Quite!" said Algy. "What a pity it wouldn't go in your pocket."

"Not music and all," said Aaron.

"Dear me! What a *comble** of disappointment. I never felt so
30 strongly, Marchesa, that the old life and the old world had collapsed—Really—I shall soon have to try to give up being cheerful at all."

"Don't do that," said the Marchesa. "It isn't worth the effort."

"Ah! I am glad you find it so. Then I have hope."

35   She merely smiled, indifferent.

The tea-party began to break up—Aaron found himself going down the stairs with the Marchesa and her husband. They descended all three in silence, husband and wife in front. Once outside the door, the husband asked:

40   "How shall we go home, dear? Tram or carriage—?" It was evident he was economical.

"Walk," she said, glancing over her shoulder at Aaron. "We are all going the same way, I believe."

Aaron said where he lived. They were just across the river. And so all three proceeded to walk through the town.

"You are sure it won't be too much for you—too far?" said the little officer, taking his wife's arm solicitously. She was taller than he. But he was a spirited fellow.

"No, I feel like walking."

"So long as you don't have to pay for it afterwards."

Aaron gathered that she was not well. Yet she did not look ill—unless it were nerves. She had that peculiar heavy remote quality of pre-occupation and neurosis.

The streets of Florence were very full this Sunday evening, almost impassable, crowded particularly with gangs of grey-green soldiers. The three made their way brokenly, and with difficulty. The Italian was in a constant state of returning salutes. The grey-green, sturdy, unsoldierly soldiers looked at the woman as she passed.

"I am sure you had better take a carriage," said Manfredi.

"No—I don't mind it."

"Do you feel at home in Florence?" Aaron asked her.

"Yes—as much as anywhere. Oh yes—quite at home."

"Do you like it as well as anywhere?" he asked.

"Yes—for a time. Paris for the most part."

"Never America?"

"No, never America. I came when I was quite a little girl to Europe—Madrid—Constantinople—Paris. I hardly knew America at all."

Aaron remembered that Francis had told him, the Marchesa's father had been Ambassador to Paris.

"So you feel you have no country of your own?"

"I have Italy. I am Italian now, you know."

Aaron wondered why she spoke so muted, so numbed. Manfredi seemed really attached to her—and she to him. They were so simple with one another.

They came towards the bridge where they should part.

"Won't you come and have a cocktail?" she said.

"Now?" said Aaron.

"Yes. This is the right time for a cocktail. What time is it, Manfredi?"

"Half-past six. Do come and have one with us," said the Italian. "We always take one about this time."

Aaron continued with them over the bridge. They had the first floor of an old palazzo opposite, a little way up the hill. A manservant opened the door.

"If only it will be warm," she said. "The apartment is almost
5 impossible to keep warm. We will sit in the little room."

Aaron found himself in a quite warm room with shaded lights and a mixture of old Italian stiffness and deep soft modern comfort. The Marchesa went away to take off her wraps, and the Marchese chatted with Aaron. The little officer was amiable and kind, and it was
10 evident he liked his guest.

"Would you like to see the room where we have music?" he said. "It is a fine room for the purpose—we used before the war to have music every Saturday morning, from ten to twelve: and all friends might come. Usually we had fifteen or twenty people. Now we are
15 starting again. I myself enjoy it so much. I am afraid my wife isn't so enthusiastic as she used to be. I wish something would rouse her up, you know. The war seemed to take her life away. Here in Florence are so many amateurs. Very good indeed. We can have very good chamber-music indeed. I hope it will cheer her up and make her
20 quite herself again. I was away for such long periods, at the front.—And it was not good for her to be alone.—I am hoping now all will be better."

So saying, the little, odd officer switched on the lights of the long salon. It was a handsome room in the Italian mode of the Empire
25 period—beautiful old faded tapestry panels—reddish—and some ormolu furniture—and other things mixed in—rather conglomerate, but pleasing, all the more pleasing. It was big, not too empty, and seemed to belong to human life, not to show and shut-upedness. The host was happy showing it.

30 "Of course the flat in Paris is more luxurious than this," he said. "But I prefer this. I prefer it here." There was a certain wistfulness as he looked round, then began to switch off the lights.

They returned to the little salotta.* The Marchesa was seated in a low chair. She wore a very thin white blouse, that showed her arms
35 and her throat. She was a full-breasted, soft-skinned woman, though not stout.

"Make the cocktails then, Manfredi," she said. "Do you find this room very cold?" she asked of Aaron.

"Not a bit cold," he said.

40 "The stove goes all the time," she said, "but without much effect."

"You wear such thin clothes," he said.

"Ah no, the stove should give heat enough. Do sit down. Will you smoke? There are cigarettes—and cigars, if you prefer them."

"No, I've got my own, thanks.

She took her own cigarette from her gold case. 5

"It is a fine room, for music, the big room," said he.

"Yes, quite. Would you like to play for us some time, do you think?"

"Do you want me to? I mean does it interest you?"

"What—the flute?" 10

"No—music altogether—"

"Music altogether—! Well! I used to love it. Now—I'm not sure. Manfredi lives for it, almost."

"For that and nothing else?" asked Aaron.

"No, no! No no! Other things as well." 15

"But you don't like it much any more?"

"I don't know. Perhaps I don't. I'm not sure."

"You don't look forward to the Saturday mornings?" he asked.

"Perhaps I don't—But for Manfredi's sake, of course, I do.—But for his sake more than my own, I admit. And I think he knows it." 20

"A crowd of people in one's house—" said Aaron.

"Yes, the people. But it's not only that. It's the music itself—I think I can't stand it any more.—I don't know."

"Too emotional? Too much feeling for you?"

"Yes, perhaps. But no. What I can't stand is chords, you know: 25 harmonies. A number of sounds all sounding together. It just makes me ill. It makes me feel so sick."

"What—do you want discords?—dissonances?"

"No—they are nearly as bad.—No, it's just when any number of musical notes, different notes, come together, harmonies or dis- 30 cords. Even a single chord struck on the piano. It makes me feel sick. I just feel as if I should retch.—Isn't it strange? Of course, I don't tell Manfredi. It would be too cruel to him. It would cut his life in two."

"But then why do you have the music—the Saturdays— then?" 35

"Oh, I just keep out of the way as much as possible. I'm sure you feel there is something wrong with me, that I take it as I do," she added, as if anxious: but half ironical.

"No—I was just wondering—I believe I feel something the same myself.—I know orchestra makes me blind with hate or I don't know 40 what. But I want to throw bombs."

"There now. It does that to me too. Only now it has fairly got me down, and I feel nothing but helpless nausea. You know, like when you are seasick."

Her dark-blue, heavy, haunted-looking eyes were resting on him as if she hoped for something. He watched her face steadily, a curious intelligence flickering on his own.

"Yes," he said. "I understand it.—And I know, *at the bottom*, I'm like that. But I keep myself from realising, don't you know. Else perhaps, where should I be? Because I make my life and my living at it, as well."

"At music! Do you! But how bad for you.—But perhaps the flute is different. I have a feeling that it is.—I can think of one single pipe-note—yes, I can think of it quite, quite calmly. And I can't even think of the piano, or of the violin with its tremolo, or of orchestra, or of a string quartette—or even a military band—I can't think of it without a shudder. I can only bear drum-and-fife. Isn't it crazy of me—But from the other, from what we call music proper, I've endured too much. But bring your flute one day. Bring it, will you. And let me hear it quite alone. Quite, quite alone. I think it might do me an awful lot of good. I do really. I can imagine it." She closed her eyes, and her strange, sing-song lapsing voice came to an end. She spoke almost like one in a trance—or a sleep-walker.

"I've got it now in my overcoat pocket," he said, "if you like."

"Have you? Yes!" She was never hurried: always slow and resonant, so that the echoes of her voice seemed to linger. "Yes—do get it. Do get it.—And play in the other room—quite—quite without accompaniment. Do—and try me."

"And you will tell me what you feel?"

"Yes."

Aaron went out to his overcoat. When he returned with his flute, which he was screwing together, Manfredi had come with the tray and the three cocktails. The Marchesa took her glass.

"Listen Manfredi," she said. "Mr. Sisson is going to play, quite alone in the sala. And I am going to sit here and listen."

"Very well," said Manfredi. "Drink your cocktail first.—Are you going to play without music?"

"Yes," said Aaron.

"I'll just put on the lights for you."

"No—leave it dark. Enough light will come in from here."

"Sure?" said Manfredi.

"Yes."

The little soldier was an intruder at the moment. Both the others felt it so. But they bore him no grudge. They knew it was they who were exceptional, not he. Aaron swallowed his drink, and looked towards the door.

"Sit down, Manfredi. Sit still," said the Marchesa.

"Won't you let me try some accompaniment?" said the soldier.

"No. I shall just play a little thing from memory," said Aaron.

"Sit down, dear. Sit down," said the Marchesa to her husband. He seated himself obediently. The flash of bright yellow on the grey of his uniform seemed to make him like a chaffinch or a gnome.

Aaron retired to the other room, and waited awhile, to get back the spell which connected him with the woman, and gave the two of them this strange isolation, beyond the bounds of life, as it seemed.

He caught it again. And there, in the darkness of the big room, he put his flute to his lips, and began to play. It was a clear, sharp, lilted run-and-fall of notes, not a tune in any sense of the word, and yet a melody: a bright, quick sound of pure animation: a bright, quick, animate noise, running and pausing. It was like a bird's singing, in that it had no human emotion or passion or intention or meaning—a ripple and poise of animate sound. But it was unlike a bird's singing, in that the notes followed clear and single one after the other, in their subtle gallop. A nightingale is rather like that—a wild sound. To read all the human pathos into nightingales' singing is nonsense.* A wild, savage, non-human lurch and squander of sound, beautiful, but entirely unaesthetic.

What Aaron was playing was not of his own invention. It was a bit of mediaeval phrasing written for the pipe and the viol. It made the piano seem a ponderous, nerve-wracking steam-roller of noise, and the violin, as we know it, a hateful wire-drawn nerve-torturer.

After a little while, when he entered the smaller room again, the Marchesa looked full into his face.

"Good!" she said. "Good!"

And a gleam almost of happiness seemed to light her up. She seemed like one who had been kept in a horrible enchanted castle—for years and years. Oh, a horrible enchanted castle, with wet walls of emotions and ponderous chains of feelings and a ghastly atmosphere of must-be. She felt she had seen through the opening door a crack of sunshine, and thin, pure, light outside air, outside, beyond this dank and beastly dungeon of feelings and moral necessity. Ugh!—she shuddered convulsively at what had been. She looked at her little husband. Chains of necessity all round him: a little jailor. Yet she was fond of him. If only he would throw away the castle-keys. He was a little gnome. What did he clutch the castle-keys so tight for?

Aaron looked at her. He knew that they understood one another, he and she. Without any moral necessity or any other necessity.— Outside—they had got outside of the castle of so-called human life. Outside the horrible, stinking human castle of life. A bit of true, limpid freedom. Just a glimpse.

"Charming!" said the Marchese. "Truly charming! But what was it you played?"

Aaron told him.

"But truly delightful.—I say, won't you play for us one of these Saturdays?—And won't you let me take the accompaniment?—I should be charmed, charmed if you would."

"All right," said Aaron.

"Do drink another cocktail," said his hostess.

He did so. And then he rose to leave.

"Will you stay to dinner?" said the Marchesa. "We have two people coming—two Italian relatives of my husband. But—"

No, Aaron declined to stay to dinner.

"Then won't you come on—let me see—on Wednesday? Do come on Wednesday. We are alone. And do bring the flute. Come at half-past six, as today, will you? Yes?"

Aaron promised—and then he found himself in the street. It was half-past seven. Instead of returning straight home, he crossed the Ponte Vecchio and walked straight into the crowd. The night was fine now. He had his overcoat over his arm, and in a sort of trance or frenzy, whirled away by his evening's experience, and by the woman, he strode swiftly forward, hardly heeding anything, but rushing blindly on through all the crowd, carried away by his own feelings, as much as if he had been alone, and all these many people merely trees.

Leaving the Piazza Vittorio Emanuele a gang of soldiers suddenly rushed round him, buffeting him in one direction, whilst another gang, swinging round the corner, threw him back helpless again into the midst of the first gang. For some moments he struggled among the rude, brutal little mob of grey-green coarse uniforms that smelt so strong of soldiers. Then, irritated, he found himself free again, shaking himself and passing on towards the cathedral. Irritated, he now put on his overcoat and buttoned it to the throat, closing himself in, as it were, from the brutal insolence of the Sunday night mob of men. Before, he had been walking through them in a rush of naked feeling, all exposed to their tender mercies. He now gathered himself 5 together.

As he was going home, suddenly, just as he was passing the Bargello,* he stopped. He stopped, and put his hand to his breast pocket. His letter-case was gone. He had been robbed.* It was as if lightning ran through him at that moment, as if a fluid electricity 10 rushed down his limbs, through the sluice of his knees, and out at his feet, leaving him standing there almost unconscious. For a moment unconscious and superconscious he stood there. He had been robbed. They had put their hand in his breast and robbed him. If they had stabbed him it could hardly have had a greater effect on 15 him.

And he had known it. He had known it. When the soldiers jostled him so evilly they robbed him. And he knew it. He had known it as if it were fate. Even as if it were fated beforehand.

Feeling quite weak and faint, as if he had really been struck by 20 some evil electric fluid, he walked on. And as soon as he began to walk, he began to reason. Perhaps his letter-case was in his other coat. Perhaps he had not had it with him at all. Perhaps he was feeling all this, just for nothing. Perhaps it was all folly.

He hurried forward. He wanted to make sure. He wanted relief. It 25 was as if the power of evil had suddenly seized him and thrown him, and he wanted to say it was not so, that he had imagined it all, conjured it up. He did not want to admit the power of evil—particularly at that moment. For surely a very ugly evil spirit had struck him, in the midst of that gang of Italian soldiers. He knew it—it had 30 pierced him. It had *got* him.

But he wanted to say it was not so. Reaching the house, he hastened upwards to his far-off, lonely room, through the dark corridors. Once in his own apartment, he shut the door and switched on the light, a sensation like fear at his heart. Then he searched his 35 other pockets. He looked everywhere. In vain.

In vain, truly enough. For he *knew* the thing was stolen. He had known it all along. The soldiers had deliberately plotted, had deliberately rushed him and taken his purse. They must have watched him previously. They must have grinned, and jeered at him. 40

He sat down in a chair, to recover from the shock. The pocket-book contained four hundred francs, three one-pound notes, and various letters and private effects—Well, these were lost.—But it was not so much the loss as the assault on his person that caused him to feel so stricken. He felt the jeering, gibing blows they had given as they jostled him.

And now he sat, weak in every limb, and said to himself: "Yes—and if I hadn't rushed along so full of feeling: if I hadn't exposed myself: if I hadn't got worked up with the Marchesa, and then rushed all kindled through the streets, without reserve: it would never have happened. I gave myself away: and there was someone ready to snatch what I gave. I gave myself away. It is my own fault. I should have been on my guard. I should be always on my guard: always, always. With God and the devil both, I should be on my guard. Godly or devilish, I should hold fast to my reserve and keep on the watch. And if I don't, I deserve what I get."

But still he sat in his chair in his bedroom, dazed. One part of his soul was saying emphatically: "It serves you right. It is nothing but right. It serves everybody right who rushes enkindled through the street, and trusts implicitly in mankind and in the life-spirit, as if mankind and the life-spirit were a playground for enkindled indi-viduals. It serves you right. You have paid about twelve pounds sterling for your lesson. Fool, you might have known beforehand, and then you needn't have paid at all. You can ill afford twelve pounds sterling, you fool. But since paid you have, then mind, mind the lesson is learned. Never again. Never expose yourself again. Never again absolute trust. It is a blasphemy against life, is absolute trust. Has a wild creature ever absolute trust? It minds itself. Sleeping or waking it is on its guard. And so must you be, or you'll go under. Sleeping or waking, man or woman, God or the devil, keep your guard over yourself. Keep your guard over yourself, lest worse befall you.—No man is robbed unless he incites a robber. No man is murdered unless he attracts a murderer. Then be not robbed: it lies within your own power. And be not murdered. Or if you are, you deserve it. Keep your guard over yourself, now, always and forever. Yes, against God quite as hard as against the devil. He's fully as dangerous to you..."

Thus thinking, not in his mind but in his soul, his active living soul, he gathered his equanimity once more, and accepted the fact. So he rose and tidied himself for dinner. His face was now set, and still. His heart also was still—and fearless. Because its sentinel was stationed. Stationed, stationed forever.

And Aaron never forgot. After this, it became essential to him to feel that the sentinel stood guard in his own heart. He felt a strange unease the moment he was off his guard. Asleep or awake, in the 5 midst of the deepest passion or the suddenest love, or in the throes of greatest excitement or bewilderment, somewhere, some corner of himself was awake to the fact that the sentinel of the soul must not sleep: no, never, not for one instant.

Chapter XVII.

High Up over the Cathedral Square*

Aaron and Lilly sat on Argyle's little loggia, high up under the eaves
of the small hotel, a sort of long attic-terrace just under the roof,
where no one would have suspected it. It was level with the grey
conical roof of the Baptistery.* Here sat Aaron and Lilly in the
afternoon, in the last of the lovely autumn sunshine. Below, the
square was already cold in shadow, the pink and white and green
Baptistery rose lantern-shaped as from some sea-shore, cool, cold
and wan now the sun was gone. Black figures, innumerable black
figures, curious because they were all on end, up on end—Aaron
could not say why he expected them to be horizontal—little black
figures up on end, like fishes that swim on their tails, wiggled
endlessly across the piazza, little carriages on natural all-fours
rattled tinily across, the yellow little tram-cars, like dogs slipped
round the corner. The balcony was so high up, that the sound was
ineffectual. The upper space, above the houses, was nearer than the
under-currents of the noisy town. Sunlight, lovely full sunlight,
lingered warm and still on the balcony. It caught the façade of the
cathedral sideways, like the tips of a flower, and sideways lit up the
stem of Giotto's tower,* like a lily stem, or a long, lovely pale pink and
white and green pistil of the lily of the cathedral. Florence, the
flowery town. Firenze—Fiorenze—the flowery town: the red lilies.
The Fiorentini,* the flower-souled. Flowers with good roots in the
mud and muck, as should be: and fearless blossoms in air, like the
cathedral and the tower and the David.

"I love it," said Lilly. "I love this place. I love the cathedral and the
tower. I love its pinkness and its paleness. The gothic souls find fault
with it, and say it is gimcrack and tawdry and cheap. But I love it, it is
delicate and rosy, and the dark stripes are as they should be, like the
tiger marks on a pink lily. It's a lily, not a rose: a pinky white lily with
dark tigery marks. And heavy too, in its own substance: earth-
substance, risen from earth into the air: and never forgetting the
dark, black-fierce earth—I reckon here men for a moment were
themselves, as a plant in flower is for the moment completely itself.

Then it goes off. As Florence has gone off. No flowers now. But it
has flowered. And I don't see why a race should be like an aloe tree,
flower once and die. Why should it? Why not flower again? Why
not?"

"If it's going to, it will," said Aaron. "Our deciding about it won't
alter it."

"The decision is part of the business."

Here they were interrupted by Argyle, who put his head through
one of the windows. He had flecks of lather on his reddened face.

"Do you think you're wise now," he said, "to sit in that sun?"

"In November?" laughed Lilly.

"Always fear the sun when there's an 'r' in the month," said
Argyle. "Always fear it 'r' or no 'r,' *I* say. I'm frightened of it. I've
been in the south, I know what it is. I tell you I'm frightened of it. But
if you think you can stand it—well—"

"It won't last much longer, anyhow," said Lilly.

"Too long for me, my boy. I'm a shady bird, in all senses of the
word, in all senses of the word.—Now are you comfortable? What?
Have another cushion? A rug for your knees? You're quite sure now?
Well, wait just one moment till the waiter brings up a syphon, and
you shall have a whiskey and soda. Precious—oh yes, very precious
these days—like drinking gold. Thirty-five Liras a bottle, my boy!"
Argyle pulled a long face, and made a noise with his lips. "But I had
this bottle given me, and luckily you've come while there's a drop
left. Very glad you have! Very glad you have."

Here he poked a little table through the window, and put a bottle
and two glasses, one a tooth-glass, upon it. Then he withdrew again
to finish shaving. The waiter presently hobbled up with the syphon
and third glass. Argyle pushed his head through the window, that
was only a little higher than the balcony. He was soon neatly shaved,
and was brushing his hair.

"Go ahead, my boys, go ahead with that whiskey!" he said.

"We'll wait for you," said Lilly.

"No, no, don't think of it. However, if you will, I shall be one
minute only—one minute only. I'll put on the water for the tea now.
Oh, damned bad methylated spirit they sell now! And six francs a
litre! Six francs a litre! I don't know what I'm going to do, the air I
breathe costs money nowadays—Just one moment and I'll be with
you! Just one moment—"

In a very little while he came from the tiny attic bedroom, through the tiniest cupboard of a sitting-room under the eaves, where his books were, and where he had hung his old red India tapestries—or silk embroideries—and he emerged there up above the world on the loggia.

"Now then—siamo nel Paradiso, eh? Paradisal enough for you, is it?"

"The devil looking over Lincoln,"* said Lilly laughing, glancing up into Argyle's face.

"The devil looking over *Florence* would feel sad," said Argyle. "The place is fast growing respectable—Oh, piety makes the devil chuckle. But respectability, my boy, argues a serious diminution of spunk. And when the spunk diminishes we-ell—it's enough to make the most sturdy devil look sick. What? No doubt about it, no doubt whatever.—There—!" he had just finished settling his tie and buttoning his waistcoat. "How do I look, eh? Presentable?—I've just had this suit turned. Clever little tailor across the way there. But he charged me a hundred and twenty francs." Argyle pulled a face, and made the little trumping noise with his lips. "However—not bad, is it?—He had to let in a bit at the back of the waistcoat, and a gusset, my boy, a gusset in the trousers back. Seems I've grown in the arsal region. Well, well, might do worse.—Is it all right?"

Lilly eyed the suit.

"Very nice. Very nice indeed. Such a good cloth! That makes all the difference."

"Oh, my dear fellow, all the difference! This suit is eleven years old—eleven years old. But beautiful English cloth—before the war, before the war!"

"It looks quite wonderfully expensive and smart now," said Lilly.

"Expensive and smart, eh! Ha-ha-ha! Well, it cost me a hundred and twenty francs to have it turned, and I found that expensive enough. Well now, come—" here Argyle's voice took on a new gay cheer. "A whiskey and soda, Lilly? Say when! Oh, nonsense, nonsense! You're going to have double that. You're no lily of the valley here, remember. Not with me. Not likely. *Siamo nel paradiso*, remember."

"But why should we drink your whiskey. Tea would do for us just as well."

"Not likely! Not likely! When I have the pleasure of your company, my boy, we drink a glass of something, unless I am utterly stripped. Say when, Aaron."

"When," said Aaron.

Argyle at last seated himself heavily in a small chair. The sun had left the loggia, but was glowing still on Giotto's tower and the top of the cathedral façade, and on the remoter great red tiled dome.

"Look at my little red monthly rose," said Argyle. "Wonderful little fellow! I wouldn't have anything happen to him for the world. Oh, a bacchic little chap. I made Pasquale wear a wreath of them on his hair. Very becoming they were, very.—Oh, I've had a charming show of flowers. Wonderful creatures sunflowers are. They got up and put their heads over the balcony, looking down on the square below. Oh great fun, great fun! The Blessed Damosel looked down*—what?—Lucky thing for her she wasn't on my balcony. I'd have turned up her skirts while she was looking down. Ha-ha-ha! Oh, you never know, she might have enjoyed it. Never believe a woman when she says she's chaste, nor a man when he says he's a— —. Yes, I had a charming show of flowers, charming.—Zinnias, petunias, ranunculus, sunflowers, white stocks—oh charming. Look at that bit of honey-suckle. You see the berries where his flowers were! Delicious scent, I assure you."

Under the little balcony wall Argyle had put square red tiled pots, all round, and in these still bloomed a few pansies and asters, whilst in a corner a monthly rose hung flowers like round blood-drops. Argyle was as tidy and scrupulous in his tiny rooms and his balcony as if he were a first-rate sea-man on a yacht. Lilly remarked on this.

"Do you see signs of the old maid coming out in me? Oh, I don't doubt it. I don't doubt it. We all end that way. Age makes old maids of us all. And Tanny is all right, you say? Bring her to see me. Why didn't she come today?"

"You know you don't like people unless you expect them."

"Oh, but my dear fellow!—You and Tanny; you'd be welcome if you came at my busiest moment. Of course you would. I'd be glad to see you if you interrupted me at my crucial moment with my bedfellow: and *that*'s saying *something*, considering how long I have to sleep alone, these days. I am alone now till August. Then we shall go away together somewhere. But you and Tanny! why, there's the world, and there's Lilly: that's how I put it, my boy."

"All right, Argyle.—Höflichkeiten."

"What, Gar keine Höflichkeiten. Wahrhaftiger Kerl bin ich.*— When am I going to see Tanny? When are you coming to dine with me?"

"After you've dined with us—say the day after tomorrow—"

"Right you are. Delighted—. Let me look if that water's boiling."
He got up and poked half himself inside the bedroom. "Not yet.
Damned filthy methylated spirit they sell. I asked the man if he peed
5 in it. Ha-ha-ha!"

"Probably he does. It seems the chief occupation of the Florentines," said Lilly.

"Without a doubt! Without a doubt! I tell them they can do
nothing more violent than make water. Give them a corner, and
10 they're at it. Town of Peabodys and piss-en-lits—"*

"Look," said Lilly. "There's Del Torre!"

"Like some sort of midge, in that damned grey-and-yellow
uniform. I can't stand it, I tell you. I can't stand the sight of any more
of these uniforms. Like a blight on the human landscape. Like a
15 blight. Like green-flies on rose-trees, smother-flies. Europe's got
the smother-fly in these infernal shoddy militarists."

"Del Torre's coming out of it as soon as he can," said Lilly.

"I should think so too."

"I like him myself—very much. Look, he's seen us! He wants to
20 come up, Argyle."

"What, in that uniform! I'll see him in his grandmother's crinoline
first."

"Don't be fanatical, it's bad taste. Let him come up a minute."

"Not for my sake. But for yours, he shall." Argyle stood at the
25 parapet of the balcony and waved his arm. "Yes, come up," he said,
"come up, you little mistkäfer*—what the Americans call a bug.
Come up and be damned."

Of course Del Torre was too far off to hear this exhortation. Lilly
also waved to him—and watched him pass into the doorway far
30 below.

"I'll rinse one of these glasses for him," said Argyle.

The Marchese's step was heard on the stone stairs: then his
knock.

"Come in! Come in!" cried Argyle from the bedroom, where he
35 was rinsing the glass. The Marchese entered, grinning with his
curious, half courteous greeting. "Go through—go through," cried
Argyle. "Go on to the loggia—and mind your head. Good heavens,
mind your head in that doorway."

The Marchese just missed the top of the doorway as he climbed
40 the abrupt steps on to the loggia—There he greeted Lilly and Aaron
with hearty handshakes.

"Very glad to see you—very glad indeed!" he cried, grinning with excited courtesy and pleasure, and covering Lilly's hand with both his own gloved hands. "When did you come to Florence?"

There was a little explanation. Argyle shoved the last chair—it was a luggage stool—through the window.

"All I can do for you in the way of a chair," he said.

"Ah, that is all right," said the Marchese. "Well, it is very nice up here—and very nice company. Of the very best, the very best in Florence."

"The highest, anyhow," said Argyle grimly, as he entered with the glass. "Have a whiskey and soda, Del Torre. It's the bottom of the bottle, as you see."

"The bottom of the bottle! Then I start with the tail-end, yes!" He stretched his blue eyes so that the whites showed all round, and grinned a wide, gnome-like grin.

"You made that start long ago, my dear fellow. Don't play the *ingénu* with me, you know it won't work. Say when, my man, say when!"

"Yes, when," said Del Torre. "When did I make that start, then?"

"At some unmentionably young age. Chickens such as you soon learn to cheep."

"Chickens such as I soon learn to cheap," repeated Del Torre, pleased with the verbal play. "What is cheap, please? What is *to cheap?*"

"Cheep! Cheep!" Squeaked Argyle, making a face at the little Italian, who was perched on one strap of the luggage stool. "It's what chickens say when they're poking their little noses into new adventures—naughty ones."

"Are chickens naughty? Oh! I thought they could only be good!"

"Featherless chickens like yourself, my boy."

"Oh, as for featherless—Then there is no saying what they will do.—" And here the Marchese turned away from Argyle with the inevitable question to Lilly:

"Well, and how long will you stay in Florence?"

Lilly did not know: but he was not leaving immediately.

"Good! Then you will come and see us at once ..."

Argyle rose once more, and went to make the tea. He shoved a lump of cake—or rather panettone,* good current loaf—through the window, with a knife to cut it.

"Help yourselves to the panettone," he said. "Eat it up. The tea is coming at once. You'll have to drink it in your glasses, there's only one old cup."

The Marchese cut the cake, and offered pieces. The two men took and ate.

5 "So you have already found Mr. Sisson!" said Del Torre to Lilly.

"Ran straight into him in the Via Nazionale," said Lilly.

"Oh, one always runs into everybody in Florence. We are all already acquainted: also with the flute. That is a great pleasure."

"So I think.—Does your wife like it too?"

10 "Very much indeed! She is quite *éprise.** I too shall have to learn to play it."

"And run the risk of spoiling the shape of your mouth—like Alcibiades."*

"Is there a risk? Yes! Then I shan't play it. My mouth is too

15 beautiful.—But Mr. Sisson has not spoilt his mouth."

"Not yet," said Lilly. "Give him time."

"Is he also afraid—like Alcibiades?"

"Are you Aaron?" said Lilly.

"What?"

20 "Afraid of spoiling your beauty by screwing your mouth to the flute?"

"I look a fool, do I, when I'm playing?" said Aaron.

"Only the least little bit in the world," said Lilly. "The way you prance your head, you know, like a horse."

25 "Ah well," said Aaron. "I've nothing to lose."

"And were you surprised, Lilly, to find your friend here?" asked Del Torre.

"I ought to have been. But I wasn't really."

"Then you expected him?"

30 "No. It came naturally though.—But why did you come, Aaron? What exactly brought you?"

"Accident," said Aaron.

"Ah no! No! There is no such thing as accident," said the Italian. "A man is drawn by his fate, where he goes."

35 "You are right," said Argyle, who came now with the teapot. "A man is drawn—or driven. Driven, I've found it. Ah, my dear fellow, what is life but a search for a friend? A search for a friend—that sums it up."

"Or a lover," said the Marchese, grinning.

40 "Same thing. Same thing. My hair is white—but that is the sum of

my whole experience. The search for a friend." There was something at once real and sentimental in Argyle's tone.

"And never finding?" said Lilly, laughing.

"Oh, what would you? Often finding. Often finding. And losing, of course.—A life's history. Give me your glass. Miserable tea, but nobody has sent me any from England—"

"And will you go on till you die, Argyle?" said Lilly. "Always seeking a friend—and always a new one?"

"If I lose the friend I've got. Ah, my dear fellow, in that case I shall go on seeking. I hope so, I assure you. Something will be very wrong with me, if ever I sit friendless and make no search."

"But Argyle, there is a time to leave off."

"To leave off what, to leave off what?"

"Having friends: or a friend, rather: or seeking to have one."

"Oh no! Not at all, my friend. Not at all! Only death can make an end of that, my friend. Only death. And I should say, not even death. Not even death ends a man's search for a friend. That is my belief. You may hang me for it, but I shall never alter."

"Nay," said Lilly. "There is a time to love, and a time to leave off loving."*

"All I can say to that is that my time to leave off hasn't come yet," said Argyle, with obstinate feeling.

"Ah yes, it has. It is only a habit and an idea you stick to."

"Indeed it is no such thing. Indeed it is no such thing. It is a profound desire and necessity: and what is more, a belief."

"An obstinate persistency, you mean," said Lilly.

"Well, call it so if it pleases you. It is by no means so to me." There was a brief pause. The sun had left the cathedral dome and the tower, the sky was full of light, the square swimming in shadow.

"But can a man live," said the Marchese, "without having something he lives for: something he wishes for, or longs for, and tries that he may get?"

"Impossible! Completely impossible!" said Argyle. "Man is a seeker, and except as such, he has no significance, no importance."

"He bores me with his seeking," said Lilly. "He should learn to possess himself—to be himself—and keep still."

"Ay, perhaps so," said Aaron. "Only—"

"But my dear boy, believe me, a man is never himself save in the supreme state of love: or perhaps hate too, which amounts to the same thing. Never really himself.—Apart from this he is a tram-

driver or a money-shoveller or an idea-machine. Only in the state of
love is he really a man, and really himself. I say so, because I know,"
said Argyle.

"Ah yes. That is one side of the truth. It is quite true, also. But it is
5 just as true to say, that a man is never less himself, than in the
supreme state of love. Never less himself, than then."

"Maybe! Maybe! But what could be better? What could be better
than to lose oneself with someone you love, entirely, and so find
yourself. Ah, my dear fellow, that is my creed, that is my creed, and
10 you can't shake me in it. Never in that. Never in that."

"Yes, Argyle," said Lilly. "I know you're an obstinate love-
apostle."

"I am! I am! And I have certain standards, my boy, and certain
ideals which I never transgress. Never transgress. And never
15 abandon."

"All right then, you are an incurable love-maker."

"Pray God I am," said Argyle.

"Yes," said the Marchese. "Perhaps we are all so. What else do
you give? Would you have us make money? Or do you give the centre
20 of your spirit to your work? How is it to be?"

"I don't vitally care either about money or my work or—" Lilly
faltered.

"Or what then?"

"Or anything. I don't really care about anything. Except that—"

25   "You don't care about anything? But what is that for a life?" cried
the Marchese, with a hollow mockery.

"What do *you* care for?" asked Lilly.

"Me? I care for several things. I care for my wife. I care for love.
And I care to be loved. And I care for some pleasures. And I care for
30 music. And I care for Italy."

"You are well off for cares," said Lilly.

"And you seem to me so very poor," said Del Torre.

"I should say so—if he cares for nothing," interjaculated Argyle.
Then he clapped Lilly on the shoulder with a laugh. "Ha! Ha!
35 Ha!—But he only says it to tease us," he cried, shaking Lilly's
shoulder. "He cares more than we do for his own way of loving.
Come along, don't try and take us in. We are old birds, old birds,"
said Argyle. But at the moment he seemed a bit doddering.

"A man can't live," said the Italian, "without an object."

40   "Well—and that object?" said Lilly.

"Well—it may be many things. Mostly it is two things—love, and money. But it may be many things: ambition, patriotism, science, art—many things. But it is some objective. Something outside the self. Perhaps many things outside the self."

"I have had only one objective all my life," said Argyle. "And that was love. For that I have spent my life."

"And the lives of a number of other people too," said Lilly.

"Admitted. Oh, admitted. It takes two to make love: unless you're a miserable—"

"Don't you think," said Aaron, turning to Lilly, "that however you try to get away from it, if you're not after money, and can't fit yourself into a job—you've got to, you've got to try and find something else—somebody else—somebody. You can't really be alone."

"No matter how many mistakes you've made—you can't really be alone—?" asked Lilly.

"You can be alone for a minute. You can be alone just in that minute when you've broken free, and you feel heart thankful to be alone, because the other thing wasn't to be borne. But you can't keep on being alone—No matter how many times you've broken free, and feel, Thank God to be alone—nothing on earth is so good as to breathe fresh air and be alone—no matter how many times you've felt this—it wears off every time, and you begin to look again—and you begin to roam round. And even if you won't admit it to yourself, still you are seeking—seeking. Aren't you? Aren't you yourself seeking?"

"Oh that's another matter," put in Argyle. "Lilly is happily married and on the shelf. With such a fine woman as Tanny I should think so—*rather*! But his is an exceptional nature, and an exceptional case. As for me, I made a hell of my marriage, and I swear it nearly sent me to hell. But I didn't forswear love, when I forswore marriage and woman. Not by *any* means."

"Are you not seeking any more, Lilly?" asked the Marchese. "Do you seek nothing?"

"We married men who haven't left our wives, are we supposed to seek anything?" said Lilly. "Aren't we perfectly satisfied and in bliss with the wonderful women who honour us as wives?"

"Ah yes, yes!" said the Marchese. "But now we are not speaking to the world. Now we try to speak of that which we have in our centre of our hearts."

"And what have we there?" said Lilly.

"Well—shall I say? We have unrest. We have another need. We have something that hurts and eats us, yes, eats us inside. Do I speak the truth?"

"Yes. But what is the something?"

5 "I don't know. I don't know. But it is something in love, I think. It is love itself which gnaws us inside, like a cancer," said the Italian.

"But why should it? Is that the nature of love?" said Lilly.

"I don't know. Truly, I don't know.—But perhaps it *is* in the nature of love—I don't know.—But I tell you. I love my wife—she is 10 very dear to me. I admire her, I trust her, I believe her. She is to me much more than any woman, more even than my mother.—And so, I am very happy. I am very happy, she is very happy, in our love and our marriage.—But wait. Nothing has changed—the love has not changed: it is the same.—And yet we are *not* happy. No, we are not 15 happy. I know she is not happy, I know I am not—"

"Why should you be?" said Lilly.

"Yes—and it is not even happiness," said the Marchese, screwing up his face in a painful effort of confession. "It is not even happiness. No, I do not ask to be happy. Why should I? It is childish—But there 20 is for both of us, I know it, something which bites us, which eats us within, and drives us, drives us, somewhere, we don't know where. But it drives us, and eats away the life—and yet we love each other, and we must not be separate—Do you know what I mean? Do you understand me at all in what I say? I speak what is true—"

25 "Yes, I understand. I'm in the same dilemma myself.—But what I want to hear, is *why* you think it is so. Why is it?"

"Shall I say what I think? Yes? And you can tell me if it is foolish to you.—Shall I tell you? Well. Because a woman, she now first wants the man, and he must go to her because he is wanted. Do you 30 understand?—You know—supposing I go to a woman—supposing she is my wife—and I go to her, yes, with my blood all ready, because it is I who want. Then she puts me off. Then she says, not now, not now, I am tired, I am not well. I do not feel like it. She puts me off—till I am angry or sorry or whatever I am—but till my blood has 35 gone down again, you understand, and I don't want her any more. And then she puts her arms round me, and caresses me, and makes love to me—till she rouses me once more. So, and so she rouses me—and so I come to her. And I love her, it is very good, very good. But it was she who began, it was her initiative, you know.—I do not 40 think, in all my life, my wife has loved me from *my* initiative, you

know. She will yield to me—because I insist, or because she wants to
be a good submissive wife who loves me. So she will yield to me. But
ah, what is it, you know? What is it, a woman who allows me, and who
has no answer? It is something worse than nothing—worse than
nothing. And so it makes me very discontented and unbelieving—If I   5
say to her, she says it is not true—not at all true. Then she says, all
she wants is that I should desire her, that I should love her and desire
her. But even that is putting *her* will first. And if I come to her so, if I
come to her of my own desire, then she puts me off. She puts me off,
or she only allows me to come to her. Even now it is the same, after   10
ten years, as it was at first. But now I know, and for many years I did
not know—"

The little man was intense. His faced was strained, his blue eyes
so stretched that they showed the whites all round. He gazed into
Lilly's face."But does it matter?" said Lilly slowly, "in which of you   15
the desire initiates? Isn't the result the same?"

"It matters. It matters—" cried the Marchese.

"Oh, my dear fellow, how *much* it matters—" interrupted Argyle
sagely.

"Ay!" said Aaron.   20

The Marchese looked from one to the other of them.

"It matters!" he cried. "It matters life or death. It used to be, that
desire started in the man, and the woman answered. It used to be so
for a long time in Italy. For this reason the women were kept away
from the men. For this reason our Catholic religion tried to keep the   25
young girls in convents, and innocent, before marriage. So that with
their minds they should not know, and should not start this terrible
thing, this woman's desire over a man, beforehand. This desire
which starts in a woman's head, when she knows, and which takes a
man for her use, for her service. This is Eve. Ah, I hate Eve. I hate   30
her, when she knows, and when she *wills*. I hate her when she will
make of me that which serves her desire.—She may love me, she
may be soft and kind to me, she may give her life for me. But why?
Only because I am *hers*. I am that thing which does her most intimate
service. She can see no other in me. And I may be no other to her—"   35

"Then why not let it be so, and be satisfied?" said Lilly.

"Because I cannot. I cannot. I would. But I cannot. The Bor-
ghesia—the citizens—the bourgeoisie, they are the ones who can.
Oh yes. The bourgeoisie, the shopkeepers, these serve their wives
so, and their wives love them. They are the marital maquereaux*—   40

the husband-maquereaux, you know. Their wives are so stout and
happy, and they dote on their husbands and always betray them. So it
is with the bourgeoise. She loves her husband so much, and is
always seeking to betray him. Or she is a Madame Bovary,* seeking
5　for a scandal. But the bourgeois husband, he goes on being the same.
He is the horse, and she the driver. When she says gee-up, you
know—then he comes ready, like a hired maquereau. Only he feels
so good, like a good little boy at her breast. And then there are the
nice little children. And so they keep the world going—But for
10　me—" he spat suddenly and with frenzy on the floor.

"You are quite right, my boy," said Argyle. "You are quite right.
They've got the start of us, the women: and we've got to canter when
they say gee-up. I—oh, I went through it all. But I broke the shafts
and smashed the matrimonial cart, I can tell you, and I didn't care
15　whether I smashed her up along with it or not. I didn't care one
single bit, I assure you.—And here I am. And she is dead and buried
these dozen years. Well—well! Life, you know, life. And Women.
Oh, they are the very hottest hell once they get the start of you.
There's *nothing* they won't do to you, once they've got you. Nothing
20　they won't do to you. Especially if they love you. Then you may as
well give up the ghost: or smash the cart behind you, and her in it.
Otherwise she will just harry you into submission, and make a dog of
you, and cuckold you under your nose. And you'll submit. Oh, you'll
submit, and go on calling her my darling. Or else, if you won't
25　submit, she'll do for you. Your only chance is to smash the shafts,
and the whole matrimonial cart. Or she'll do for you. For a woman
has an uncanny, hellish strength—she's a she-bear and a wolf, is a
woman when she's got the start of you. Oh, it's a terrible experience,
if you're not a bourgeois, and not one of the knuckling-under
30　money-making sort."

"Knuckling-under sort. Yes. That is it," said the Marchese.

"But can't there be a balancing of wills?" said Lilly.

"My dear boy, the balance lies in that, that when one goes up, the
other goes down. One acts, the other takes. It is the only way in
35　love—And the women are nowadays the active party. Oh yes, not a
shadow of doubt about it. They take the initiative, and the man plays
up. That's how it is. The man just plays up.—Nice manly proceed-
ing, what!" cried Argyle.

"But why can't man accept it as the natural order of things?" said
40　Lilly. "Science makes it the natural order."

"All my—to science," said Argyle. "No man with one drop of real spunk in him can stand it long."

"Yes! Yes! Yes!" cried the Italian. "Most men want it so. Most men want only, that a woman shall want them, and they shall then play up to her when she has roused them. Most men want only this: that a woman shall choose one man out, to be her man, and he shall worship her and come up when she shall provoke him. Otherwise he is to keep still. And the woman, she is quite sure of her part. She must be loved and adored, and above all, obeyed: particularly in her sex desire. There she must not be thwarted, or she becomes a devil. And if she is obeyed, she becomes a misunderstood woman with nerves, looking round for the next man whom she can bring under. So it is."

"Well," said Lilly. "And then what?"

"Nay," interrupted Aaron. "But do you think it's true what he says? Have you found it like that? You're married. Has your experience been different, or the same?"

"What was yours?" asked Lilly.

"Mine was the same. Mine was the same, if ever it was," said Aaron.

"And mine was *extremely* similar," said Argyle with a grimace.

"And yours, Lilly?" asked the Marchese anxiously.

"Not very different," said Lilly.

"Ah!" cried Del Torre, jerking up erect as if he had found something.

"And what's your way out?" Aaron asked him.

"I'm not out—so I won't holloa," said Lilly. "But Del Torre puts it best.—What do you say is the way out, Del Torre?"

"The way out is that it should change: that the man should be the asker and the woman the answerer. It *must* change."

"But it *doesn't*. Prrr!" Argyle made his trumping noise.

"Does it?" asked Lilly of the Marchese.

"No. I think it does not."

"And will it ever again?"

"Perhaps never."

"And then what?"

"Then? Why then man seeks a *pis-aller.** Then he seeks something which will give him answer, and which will not only draw him, draw him, with a terrible sexual will.—So he seeks young girls, who know nothing, and so can not force him. He thinks he will possess them while they are young, and they will be soft and responding to his wishes.—But in this too he is mistaken. Because now a baby of one year, if it be a female, is like a woman of forty, so is its will made up, so it will force a man."

5 "And so young girls are no good, even as a *pis-aller.*"

"No good—because they are all modern women. Every one, a modern woman. Not one who isn't."

"Terrible thing, the modern woman," put in Argyle.

"And then—?"

10 "Then man seeks other forms of loves, always seeking the loving response, you know, of one gentler and tenderer than himself, who will wait till the man desires, and then will answer with full love.—But it is all *pis-aller*, you know."

"Not by any means, my boy," cried Argyle.

15 "And then a man naturally loves his own wife too, even if it is not bearable to love her."

"Or one leaves her, like Aaron," said Lilly.

"And seeks another woman, so," said the Marchese.

"Does he seek another woman?" said Lilly. "Do you, Aaron?"

20 "I don't *want* to," said Aaron. "But—I can't stand by myself in the middle of the world and in the middle of people, and know I am quite by myself, and nowhere to go, and nothing to hold on to. I can for a day or two—But then, it becomes unbearable as well. You get frightened. You feel you might go funny—as you would if you stood

25 on this balcony wall with all the space beneath you."

"Can't one be alone—quite alone?" said Lilly.

"But no—it is absurd. Like Saint Simeon Stylites on a pillar.* But it is absurd!" cried the Italian.

"I don't mean like Simeon Stylites.—I mean can't one live with

30 one's wife, and be fond of her: and with one's friends, and enjoy their company: and with the world and everything, pleasantly: and yet *know* that one is alone? Essentially, at the very core of me, alone. Eternally alone. And choosing to be alone. Not sentimental or *lonely*. Alone, choosing to be alone, because by one's own nature one is

35 alone. The being with another person is secondary," said Lilly.

"One is alone," said Argyle, "in all but love. In all but love, my dear fellow. And then I agree with you."

"No," said Lilly, "in love most intensely of all, alone."

"Completely incomprehensible," said Argyle. "Amounts to

40 nothing."

"One man is but a part. How can he be so alone?" said the Marchese.

"In so far as he is a single individual soul, he *is* alone—ipso facto. In so far as I am I, and only I am I, and I am only I, in so far, I am inevitably and eternally alone, and it is my last blessedness to know it, and to accept it, and to live with this as the core of my self-knowledge."

"My dear boy, you are becoming metaphysical, and that is as bad as softening of the brain," said Argyle.

"All right," said Lilly.

"And," said the Marchese, "it may be so by *reason*. But in the heart—? Can the heart ever beat quite alone? Plop! Plop!— Can the heart beat quite alone, alone in all the atmosphere, all the space of the universe? Plop! Plop! Plop!—Quite alone in all the space?" A slow smile came over the Italian's face. "It is impossible. It may beat *against* the heart of other men, in anger, all in pressure against the others. It may beat hard, like iron, saying it is independent. But this is only beating against the heart of mankind, not alone.—But either with or against the heart of mankind, or the heart of someone, mother, wife, friend, children—so must the heart of every man beat. It is so."

"It beats alone in its own silence," said Lilly.

The Italian shook his head.

"We'd better be going inside, anyhow," said Argyle. "Some of you will be taking cold."

"Aaron," said Lilly. "Is it true for you?"

"Nearly," said Aaron, looking into the quiet, half-amused, yet frightening eyes of the other man. "Or it has been."

"A miss is as good as a mile," laughed Lilly, rising and picking up his chair to take it indoors. And the laughter of his voice was so like a simple, deliberate amiability, that Aaron's heart really stood still for a second. He knew that Lilly *was* alone—as far as he, Aaron was concerned. Lilly was alone—and out of his isolation came his words, indifferent as to whether they came or not. And he left his friends utterly to their own choice. Utterly to their own choice. Aaron felt that Lilly was *there*, existing in life, yet neither asking for connection nor preventing any connection. He was present, he was the real centre of the group. And yet he asked nothing of them, and he imposed nothing. He left each to himself, and he himself remained just himself: neither more nor less. And there was a finality about it, which was at once maddening and fascinating. Aaron felt angry, as if he were half insulted by the other man's placing the gift of friendship or connection so quietly back in the giver's hands. Lilly would receive no gift of friendship in equality. Neither would he violently

5 refuse it. He let it lie unmarked. And yet at the same time Aaron knew that he could depend on the other man for help, nay, almost for life itself—so long as it entailed no breaking of the intrinsic isolation of Lilly's soul. But this condition was also hateful. And there was also a great fascination in it.

Chapter XVIII.

The Marchesa

So Aaron dined with the Marchesa and Manfredi. He was quite startled when his hostess came in: she seemed like somebody else. She seemed like a demon, her hair on her brows, her terrible modern elegance. She wore a wonderful gown of thin blue velvet, of a lovely colour, with some kind of gauzy gold-threaded filament down the sides. It was terribly modern, short, and showed her legs and her shoulders and breast and all her beautiful white arms. Round her throat was a collar of dark-blue sapphires. Her hair was done low, almost to the brows, and heavy, like an Aubrey Beardsley* drawing. She was most carefully made up—yet with that touch of exaggeration, lips slightly too red, which was quite intentional, and which frightened Aaron. He thought her wonderful, and sinister. She affected him with a touch of horror. She sat down opposite him, and her beautifully shapen legs, in frail, goldish stockings, seemed to glisten metallic naked, thrust from out of the wonderful, wonderful skin, like periwinkle-blue velvet. She had tapestry shoes, blue and gold: and almost one could see her toes: metallic naked. The gold-threaded gauze slipped at her side. Aaron could not help watching the naked-seeming arch of her foot. It was as if she were dusted with dark gold-dust upon her marvellous nudity.

She must have seen his face, seen that he was *ébloui.**

"You brought the flute?" she said, in that toneless, melancholy, unstriving voice of hers. Her voice alone was the same: direct and bare and quiet.

"Yes."

"Perhaps I shall sing later on, if you'll accompany me. Will you?"

"I thought you hated accompaniments."

"Oh no—not just unison. I don't mean accompaniment. I mean unison. I don't know how it will be. But will you try?"

"Yes, I'll try."

"Manfredi is just bringing the cocktails. Do you think you'd prefer orange in yours?"

"I'll have mine as you have yours."

"I don't take orange in mine.—Won't you smoke?"

The strange, naked, remote-seeming voice! And then the beautiful firm limbs thrust out in that dress, and nakedly dusky as with gold dust. Her beautiful woman's legs, slightly glistening, duskily. His one abiding instinct was to touch them, to kiss them.—He had never known a woman exercise such power over him. It was a bare, occult force, something he could not cope with.

Manfredi came in with the little tray. He was still in uniform.

"Hello!" cried the little Italian. "Glad to see you—Well, everything all right? Glad to hear it.—How is the cocktail, Nan?"

"Yes," she said. "All right."

"One drop too much peach, eh?"

"No, all right."

"Ah," and the little officer seated himself, stretching his gaitered legs as if gaily. He had a curious smiling look on his face, that Aaron thought also diabolical—and almost handsome. Suddenly the odd, laughing, satanic beauty of the little man was visible.

"Well, and what have you been doing with yourself?" said he. "What did you do yesterday?"

"Yesterday?" said Aaron. "I went to the Uffizi."

"To the Uffizi? Well! And what did you think of it?"

"Very fine."

"I think it is. I think it is.—What pictures did you look at?"

"I was with Dekker. We looked at most, I believe."

"And what do you remember best?"

"I remember Botticelli's Venus on the shell."*

"Yes!—Yes!—" said Manfredi. "I like her. But I like others better.—You thought her a pretty woman, yes?"

"No—not particularly pretty. But I like her body. And I like the fresh air. I like the fresh air, the summer sea-air all through it—through her as well."

"And her face?" asked the Marchesa, with a slow, ironic smile.

"Yes—she's a bit baby-faced," said Aaron.

"Trying to be more innocent than her own common-sense will let her," said the Marchesa.

"I don't agree with you, Nan," said her husband. "I think it is just that wistfulness and innocence which makes her the true Venus: the true modern Venus. She chooses *not* to know too much. And that is her attraction. Don't you agree, Aaron?—Excuse me, but everybody speaks of you as Aaron. It seems to come naturally. Most people speak of me as Manfredi too, because it is easier, perhaps, than Del

Torre. So if you find it easier, use it.—Do you mind that I call you Aaron?"

"Not at all. I hate Misters, always."

"Yes, so do I. I like one name only."

The little officer seemed very winning and delightful to Aaron this evening—and Aaron began to like him extremely. But the dominating consciousness in the room was the woman's.

"*Do* you agree, Mr. Sisson?" said the Marchesa. "Do you agree that the mock-innocence and the sham wistfulness of Botticelli's Venus are her great charm?"

"I don't think she is at all charming, as a person," said Aaron. "As a particular woman, she makes no impression on me at all. But as a picture—and the fresh air, particularly the fresh air. She doesn't seem so much a woman, you know, as the kind of out-of-doors morning-feeling at the sea-side."

"Quite! A sort of sea-scape of a woman. With a perfectly sham innocence. Are you as keen on innocence as Manfredi is?"

"Innocence?" said Aaron. "It's the sort of thing I don't have much feeling about."

"Ah, I know you," laughed the soldier wickedly. "You are the sort of man who wants to be Anthony to Cleopatra. Ha-ha!"

Aaron winced as if struck. Then he too smiled, flattered. Yet he felt he had been struck. Did he want to be Anthony to Cleopatra? Without knowing, he was watching the Marchesa. And she was looking away, but knew he was watching her. And at last she turned her eyes to his, with a slow, dark smile, full of pain and fuller still of knowledge. A strange, dark, silent look of knowledge she gave him: from so far away, it seemed. And he felt all the bonds that held him melting away. His eyes remained fixed and gloomy, but with his mouth he smiled back at her. And he was terrified. He knew he was sinking towards her—sinking towards her. And he was terrified. But at the back of his mind, also, he knew there was Lilly, whom he might depend on. And also, he wanted to sink towards her. The flesh and blood of him simply melted out, in desire towards her. Cost what may, he must come to her. And yet he knew at the same time that, cost what may, he must keep the power to recover himself from her. He must have his cake and eat it.

And she became Cleopatra to him. "Age cannot wither her, nor custom stale—"* To his instinctive, unwilled fancy, she was Cleopatra.

They went in to dinner, and he sat on her right hand. It was a

smallish table, with a very few daisy-flowers: everything rather frail, and sparse. The food the same—nothing very heavy, all rather exquisite. They drank hock. And he was aware of her beautiful arms, and her bosom; her low-crowded, thick hair, parted in the centre:
5 the sapphires on her throat, the heavy rings on her fingers: and the paint on her lips, the fard. Something deep, deep at the bottom of him hovered upon her, cleaved to her. Yet he was as if sightless, in a stupor. Who was she, what was she? He had lost all his grasp. Only he sat there, with his face turned to hers, or to her, all the time. And
10 she talked to him. But she never looked at him.

Indeed she said little. It was the husband who talked. His manner towards Aaron was almost caressive. And Aaron liked it. The woman was silent mostly, and seemed remote. And Aaron felt his life ebb towards her. He felt the marvellousness, the rich beauty of her arms
15 and breast. And the thought of her gold-dusted smooth limbs beneath the table made him feel almost an idiot.

The second wine was a gold-coloured Moselle, very soft and rich and beautiful. She drank this with pleasure, as one who understands. And for dessert there was a dish of cacchi—that orange-coloured,
20 pulpy Japanese fruit—persimmons. Aaron had never eaten these before. Soft, almost slimy, of a wonderful colour, and of a flavour that had sunk from harsh astringency down to that first decay-sweetness which is all autumn-rich. The Marchese loved them, and scooped them out with his spoon. But she ate none.

25 Aaron did not know what they talked about, what was said. If someone had taken his mind away altogether, and left him with nothing but a body and a spinal consciousness, it would have been the same.

But at coffee the talk turned to Manfredi's duties. He would not be
30 free from the army for some time yet. On the morrow, for example, he had to be out and away before it was day. He said he hated it, and wanted to be a free man once more. But it seemed to Aaron he would be a very bored man, once he was free.—And then they drifted on to talk of the palazzo in which was their apartment.

35 "We've got such a fine terrace—you can see it from your house where you are," said Manfredi. "Have you noticed it?"

"No," said Aaron.

"Near that tuft of palm-trees. Don't you know?"

"No," said Aaron.

40 "Let us go out and show it him," said the Marchesa.

Manfredi fetched her cloak, and they went through various doors, then up some steps. The terrace was broad and open. It looked straight across the river at the opposite Lungarno: and there was the thin-necked tower of the Palazzo Vecchio, and the great dome of the cathedral in the distance, in shadow-bulk in the cold-aired night of stars. Little trams were running brilliant over the flat new bridge on the right. And from a garden just below rose a tuft of palm-trees.

"You see," said the Marchesa, coming and standing close to Aaron, so that she just touched him, "you can know the terrace, just by these palm-trees. And you are in the Nardini just across there, are you? On the top floor, you said?"

"Yes, the top floor—one of the middle windows, I think."

"One that is always open now—and the others are shut. I have noticed it, not connecting it with you."

"Yes, my window is always open."

She was leaning very slightly against him, as he stood. And he knew, with the same kind of inevitability with which he knew he would one day die, that he would be the lover of this woman. Nay, that he *was* her lover already.

"Don't take cold," said Manfredi.

She turned at once indoors. Aaron caught a faint whiff of perfume from the little orange trees in tubs round the wall.

"Will you get the flute?" she said as they entered.

"And will you sing?" he answered.

"Play first," she said.

He did as she wished. As the other night, he went into the big music-room to play. And the stream of sound came out with the quick wild imperiousness of the pipe. It had an immediate effect on her. She seemed to relax the peculiar, drug-like tension which was upon her at all ordinary times. She seemed to go still, and yielding. Her red mouth looked as if it might moan with relief. She sat with her chin dropped on her breast, listening. And she did not move. But she sat softly, breathing rather quick, like one who has been hurt, and is soothed. A certain womanly naturalness seemed to soften her.

And the music of the flute came quick, rather brilliant like a call-note, or like a long quick message, half command. To her it was like a pure male voice—as a blackbird's when he calls: a pure male voice, not only calling, but telling her something, telling her something, and soothing her soul to sleep. It was like the fire-music putting Brunnhild to sleep.* But the pipe did not flicker and sink. It seemed to cause a natural relaxation in her soul, a peace. Perhaps it was more like waking to a sweet, morning-awakening, after a night of tormented, painful tense sleep. Perhaps more like that.

When Aaron came in, she looked at him with a gentle, fresh smile that seemed to make the fard on her face look like a curious tiredness, which now she might recover from. And as the last time, it was difficult for her to identify this man with the voice of the flute. It was rather difficult. Except that, perhaps, between his brows was something of a doubt, and in his bearing an aloofness that made her dread he might go away and not come back. She could see it in him, that he might go away and not come back.

She said nothing to him, only just smiled. And the look of knowledge in her eyes seemed, for the moment, to be contained in another look: a look of faith, and at last happiness. Aaron's heart stood still. No, in her moment's mood of faith and at last peace, life-trust, he was perhaps more terrified of her than in her previous sinister elegance. His spirit started and shrank. What was she going to ask of him?

"I am so anxious that you should come to play one Saturday morning," said Manfredi. "With an accompaniment, you know. I should like so much to hear you with the piano accompaniment."

"Very well," said Aaron.

"Will you really come? And will you practice with me, so that I can accompany you?" said Manfredi eagerly.

"Yes. I will," said Aaron.

"Oh good! Oh good! Look here, come in on Friday morning and let us both look through the music."

"If Mr. Sisson plays for the public," said the Marchesa, "he must not do it for charity. He must have the proper fee."

"No, I don't want it," said Aaron.

"But you must earn money, mustn't you?" said she.

"I must," said Aaron. "But I can do it somewhere else."

"No. If you play for the public, you must have your earnings. When you play for me, it is different."

"Of course," said Manfredi. "Every man must have his wage. I have mine from the Italian government—"

After a while, Aaron asked the Marchesa if she would sing.

"Shall I?" she said.

"Yes, do."

"Then I will sing alone first, to let you see what you think of it—I shall be like Trilby—I won't say like Yvette Guilbert, because I daren't. So I will be like Trilby, and sing a little French song. Though not Malbrouk, and without a Svengali to keep me in tune."*

She went near the door, and stood with her hands by her side. There was something wistful, almost pathetic now, in her elegance.

> "Derrière chez mon père
> *Vole vole mon coeur, vole!*
> Derrière chez mon père
> Il y a un pommier doux.
> *Tout doux, et iou*
> *Et iou, tout doux.*
> *Il y a un pommier doux.*
>
> Trois belles princesses
> *Vole vole mon coeur, vole!*
> Trois belles princesses
> Sont assis dessous.
> *Tout doux, et iou*
> *Et iou, tout doux*
> *Sont assis dessous.*"*

She had a beautiful, strong, sweet voice. But it was faltering, stumbling and sometimes it seemed to drop almost to speech. After three verses she faltered to an end, bitterly chagrined.

"No," she said. "It's no good. I can't sing." And she dropped in her chair.

"A lovely little tune," said Aaron. "Haven't you got the music?"

She rose, not answering, and found him a little book.

"What do the words mean?" he asked her.

She told him. And then he took his flute.

"You don't mind if I play it, do you?" he said.

So he played the tune. It was so simple. And he seemed to catch the lilt and the timbre of her voice.

"Come and sing it while I play—" he said.

"I can't sing," she said, shaking her head rather bitterly.

"But let us try," said he, disappointed.

"I know I can't," she said. But she rose.

He remained sitting at the little table, the book propped up under the reading lamp. She stood at a little distance, unhappy.

"I've always been like that," she said. "I could never sing music, unless I had a thing drilled into me, and then it wasn't singing any more."

But Aaron wasn't heeding. His flute was at his mouth, he was watching her. He sounded the note, but she did not begin. She was twisting her handkerchief. So he played the melody alone. At the end of the verse, he looked up at her again, and a half mocking smile
5   played in his eyes. Again he sounded the note, a challenge. And this time, as at his bidding, she began to sing. The flute instantly swung with a lovely soft firmness into the song, and she wavered only for a minute or two. Then her soul and her voice got free, and she sang—she sang as she wanted to sing, as she had always wanted to
10   sing, without that awful scotch, that impediment inside her own soul, which prevented her.

She sang free, with the flute gliding along with her. And oh, how beautiful it was for her! How beautiful it was to sing the little song in the sweetness of her own spirit. How sweet it was to move pure and
15   unhampered at last in the music! The lovely ease and lilt of her own soul in its motion through the music! She wasn't aware of the flute. She didn't know there was anything except her own pure lovely song-drift. Her soul seemed to breathe as a butterfly breathes, as it rests on a leaf and slowly breathes its wings. For the first time! For
20   the first time her soul drew its own deep breath. All her life, the breath had caught half-way. And now she breathed full, deep, to the deepest extent of her being.

And oh, it was so wonderful, she was dazed. The song ended, she stood with a dazed, happy face, like one just coming awake. And the
25   fard on her face seemed like the old night-crust, the bad sleep. New and luminous she looked out. And she looked at Aaron with a proud smile.

"Bravo Nan! That was what you wanted," said her husband.

"It was, wasn't it?" she said, turning a wondering, glowing face to
30   him.

His face looked strange and withered and gnome-like, at the moment.

She went and sat in her chair, quite silent, as if in a trance. The two men also sat quite still. And in the silence a little drama played
35   itself between the three, of which they knew definitely nothing. But Manfredi knew that Aaron had done what he himself never could do, for this woman. And yet the woman was his own woman, not Aaron's. And so, he was displaced. Aaron, sitting there, glowed with a sort of triumph. He had performed a little miracle, and felt himself
40   a little wonder-worker, to whom reverence was due. And as in a

dream the woman sat, feeling what a joy it was to float and move like a swan in the high air, flying upon the wings of her own spirit. She was as a swan which never before could get its wings quite open, and so which never could get up into the open, where alone it can sing. For swans, and storks make their music only when they are high, high up in the air. Then they can give sound to their strange spirits. And so she.

Aaron and Manfredi kept their faces averted from one another and hardly spoke to one another. It was as if two invisible hands pushed their faces apart, away, averted. And Aaron's face glimmered with a little triumph, and a little grimace of obstinacy. And the Italian's face looked old, rather monkey-like, and of a deep, almost stone-bare bitterness. The woman looked wondering from one man to the other—wondering. The glimmer of the open flower, the wonder-look, still lasted. And Aaron said in his heart, what a goodly woman, what a woman to taste and enjoy. Ah, what a woman to enjoy! And was it not his privilege? Had he not gained it?

His manhood, or rather his maleness, rose powerfully in him, in a sort of mastery. He felt his own power, he felt suddenly his own virile title to strength and reward. Suddenly, and newly flushed with his own male super-power, he was going to have his reward. The woman was his reward. So it was, in him. And he cast it over in his mind. He wanted her—ha, didn't he! But the husband sat there, like a soap-stone Chinese monkey, greyish-green. So, it would have to be another time.

He rose, therefore, and took his leave.

"But you'll let us do that again, won't you?" said she.

"When you tell me, I'll come," said he.

"Then I'll tell you soon," said she.

So he left, and went home to his own place, and there to his own remote room. As he laid his flute on the table he looked at it and smiled. He remembered that Lilly had called it Aaron's Rod.

"So you blossom, do you?—and thorn as well," said he.

For such a long time he had been gripped inside himself, and withheld. For such a long time it had been hard and unyielding, so hard and unyielding. He had wanted nothing, his desire had kept itself back, fast back. For such a long time his desire for woman had withheld itself, hard and resistant. All his deep, desirous blood had been locked, he had wanted nobody, and nothing. And it had been hard to live, so. Without desire, without any movement of passionate love, only gripped back in recoil! That was an experience to endure.

And now came his desire back. But strong, fierce as iron. Like the strength of an eagle with the lightning in its talons. Something to glory in, something overweening, the powerful male passion, arrogant, royal, Jove's thunderbolt. Aaron's black rod of power, blossoming again with red Florentine lilies and fierce thorns. He moved about in the splendour of his own male lightning, invested in the thunder of the male passion-power. He had got it back, the male godliness, the male godhead.

So he slept, and dreamed violent dreams of strange, black strife, something like the street-riot in Milan, but more terrible. In the morning, however, he cared nothing about his dreams. As soon as it was really light, he rose, and opened his window wide. It was a grey, slow morning. But he saw neither the morning nor the river nor the woman walking on the gravel river-bed with her goose nor the green hill up to San Miniato. He watched the tuft of palm-trees, and the terrace beside it. He could just distinguish the terrace clearly, among the green of foliage. So he stood at his window for a full hour, and did not move. Motionless, planted, he stood and watched that terrace across above the Arno. But like a statue.

After an hour or so, he looked at his watch. It was nine o'clock. So he rang for his coffee, and meanwhile still stood watching the terrace on the hill. He felt his turn had come. The phoenix had risen in fire again, out of the ashes.

Therefore at ten o'clock he went over the bridge. He wrote on the back of his card a request, would she please let him have the little book of songs, that he might practice them over. The manservant went, and came back with the request that Aaron should wait. So Aaron entered, while the man took his hat.

The manservant spoke only French and Spanish, no English. He was a Spaniard, with greyish hair and stooping shoulders and dark, mute-seeming eyes. He spoke as little as possible. The Marchesa had inherited him from her father.

Aaron sat in the little sitting-room and waited. After a rather long time the Marchesa came in—wearing a white, thin blouse and a blue skirt. She was hardly made up at all. She had an odd pleased, yet brooding look on her face as she gave Aaron her hand. Something brooded between her brows. And her voice was strange, with a strange, secret undertone, that he could not understand. He looked up at her. And his face was bright, and his knees, as he sat, were like the knees of the gods.

"You wanted the book of *chansons?*"* she said.

"I wanted to learn your tunes," he replied.

"Yes. Look—here it is!" And she brought him the little yellow book. It was just a hand-book, with melody and words only, no accompaniment. So she stood offering him the book, but waiting as if for something else, and standing as if with another meaning.

He opened the leaves at random.

"But I ought to know which ones you sing," said he, rising and standing by her side with the open book.

"Yes," she said, looking over his arm. He turned the pages one by one. "*Trois jeunes tambours,*" said she. "Yes, that ... Yes, *En passant par la Lorraine ... Auprès de ma blonde ...** Oh, I like that one so much—" He stood and went over the tune in his mind.

"Would you like me to play it?" he said.

"Very much," said she.

So he got his flute, propped up the book against a vase, and played the tune, whilst she hummed it fragmentarily. But as he played, he felt that he did not cast the spell over her. There was no connection. She was in some mysterious way withstanding him. She was withstanding him, and his male super-power, and his thunderbolt desire. She was, in some indescribable way, throwing cold water over his phoenix newly risen from the ashes of its nest in flames.

He realised that she did not want him to play. She did not want him to look at the songs. So he put the book away, and turned round, rather baffled, not quite sure what was happening, yet feeling she was withstanding him. He glanced at her face: it was inscrutable: it was her Cleopatra face once more, yet with something new and warm in it. He could not understand it. What was it in her face that puzzled him? Almost angered him? But she could not rob him of his male power, she could not divest him of his concentrated force.

"Won't you take off your coat?" she said, looking at him with strange, large dark eyes. A strange woman, he could not understand her. Yet, as he sat down again, having removed his overcoat, he felt her looking at his limbs, his physical body. And this went against him, he did not want it. Yet quite fixed in him too was the desire for her, her beautiful white arms, her whole soft white body. And such desire he would not contradict or allow to be contradicted. It was his will also. Her whole soft white body—to possess it in its entirety, its fulness.

"What have you to do this morning?" she asked him.

"Nothing," he said. "Have you?" He lifted his head and looked at her.

"Nothing at all," said she.

And then they sat in silence, he with his head dropped. Then again he looked at her.

"Shall we be lovers?" he said.

She sat with her face averted, and did not answer. His heart struck heavily, but he did not relax.

"Shall we be lovers?" came his voice once more, with the faintest touch of irony.

Her face gradually grew dusky. And he wondered very much to see it.

"Yes," said she, still not looking at him. "If you wish."

"I do wish," he said. And all the time he sat with his eyes fixed on her face, and she sat with her face averted.

"Now?" he said. "And where?"

Again she was silent for some moments, as if struggling with herself. Then she looked at him—a long, strange, dark look, incomprehensible, and which he did not like.

"You don't want emotions? You don't want me to say things, do you?" he said.

A faint ironic smile came on her face.

"I know what all that is worth," she said, with curious calm equanimity. "No, I want none of that."

"Then—?"

But now she sat gazing on him with wide, heavy, incomprehensible eyes. It annoyed him.

"What do you want to see in me?" he asked, with a smile, looking steadily back again.

And now she turned aside her face once more, and once more the dusky colour came in her cheek. He waited.

"Shall I go away?" he said at length.

"Would you rather?" she said, keeping her face averted.

"No," he said.

Then again she was silent.

"Where shall I come to you?" he said.

She paused a moment still, then answered:

"I'll go to my room."

"I don't know which it is," he said.

"I'll show it you," she said.

"And then I shall come to you in ten minutes. In ten minutes," he reiterated.

So she rose, and led the way out of the little salon. He walked with her to the door of her room, bowed his head as she looked at him, holding the door handle; and then he turned and went back to the drawing-room, glancing at his watch.

In the drawing-room he stood quite still, with his feet apart, and waited. He stood with his hands behind him, and his feet apart, quite motionless, planted and firm. So the minutes went by unheeded. He looked at his watch. The ten minutes were just up. He had heard footsteps and doors. So he decided to give her another five minutes. He wished to be quite sure that she had had her own time for her own movements.

Then at the end of the five minutes he went straight to her room, entered, and locked the door behind him. She was lying in bed, with her back to him.

He found her strange, not as he had imagined her. Not powerful, as he had imagined her. Strange, in his arms she seemed almost small and childish, whilst in daily life she looked a full, womanly woman. Strange, the naked way she clung to him! Almost like a sister, a younger sister! Or like a child! It filled him with a curious wonder, almost a bewilderment. In the dark sightlessness of passion, she seemed almost like a clinging child in his arms. And yet, at the crucial moment of passion, like a child who in some deep and essential way mocked him. Even as the electric tension broke from him and passed into her, he felt it. In some strange and incomprehensible way, as a girl-child blindly obstinate in her deepest nature, she was against him. And again, even in the crucial flash of liberation, he felt she was not his woman. Through him went the feeling, "This is not my woman."

But afterwards her fingers traced him and touched him with a strange fine timidity, and a strange, strange curiosity and he felt somewhere beyond himself—as it were shipwrecked. He was acutely sensible to the delicate, inordinate curiosity of her finger-tips, and the stealth, and the innermost secrecy of the approach of her power. —Nay, nay, was this the woman he had known as Cleopatra, with the rouge on her lips and the fard on her face, and the elegant, frightening Paris gown?

He slept for a very little while, and woke suddenly, and his desire

had an element of cruelty in it: something rather brutal. He took *his*
way with her now, and she had no chance now of the curious
opposition, because of the way he took her. And afterwards, she
clung suddenly to his breast, and curled her head there, as if hiding,
5 and as if suddenly convulsed with shyness or shame of what had
been: but still pleased. And so curled, with her head on his breast
and her hair tangling about his throat, it was she who slept now. And
after a long while, he slept too.

And when he woke, and still the desire came back, with something
10 dogged in its persistence, she seemed to wince a little. But perhaps
she was pleased too. But this time she took no part, really.

When he came fully to himself, with that click of awakedness
which is the end, the first shades were closing on the afternoon. He
got up, and even before he reached for his shirt he reached for his
15 watch.

"Quarter past four," he said.

Her eyes stretched wide with surprise as she looked at him. But
she said nothing. The same strange and wide, perhaps insatiable
child-like curiosity was in her eyes as she watched him. He dressed
20 very quickly. And her eyes were wide, and she said no single word.

But when he was dressed, and bent over her to say goodbye, she
put her arms round him, that seemed such frail and childish arms
now, yet withal so deadly in power. Her soft arms round his neck, her
tangle of hair over his face. And yet, even as he kissed her, he felt her
25 deadly. He wanted to be gone. He wanted to get out of her arms and
her clinging and her tangle of hair and her curiosity and her strange
and hateful power.

"You'll come again. We'll be like this again?" she whispered.

And it was hard for him to realise that this was that other woman,
30 who had sat so silently on the sofa, so darkly and reservedly, at the
tea at Algy's.

"Yes! I will!—Goodbye now!" And he kissed her, and walked
straight out of the room. Quickly he took his coat and his hat,
quickly, and left the house. In his nostrils was still the scent with
35 which the bedlinen was faintly scented—he did not know what it
was. But now he wiped his face and his mouth, to wipe it away.

He had eaten nothing since coffee that morning, and was hungry,
faint feeling. And his face, and his mind, felt withered. Curiously he
felt blasted—as if blighted by some electricity. And he knew, he
40 knew quite well he was only in possession of a tithe of his natural

faculties. And in his male spirit he felt himself hating her: hating her deeply, damnably. But he said to himself: "No, I won't hate her. I won't hate her."

So he went on, over the Ponte Vecchio, where the jeweller's windows on the bridge were already blazing with light, on into the town. He wanted to eat something, so he decided to go to a shop he knew, where one could stand and eat good tiny rolls split into truffle or salami sandwiches, and drink marsala. So one after the other he ate little truffle rolls, and drank a few glasses of marsala. And then he did not know what to do. He did not want to eat any more. He had had what he wanted. His hunger had been more nervous than sensual.

So he went into the street. It was just growing dark and the town was lighting up. He felt curiously blazed, as if some flame or electric power had gone through him and withered his vital tissue. Blazed, as if some kind of electric flame had run over him and withered him. His brain felt withered, his mind had only one of its many-sighted eyes left open and unscorched. So many of the eyes of his mind were scorched now and sightless.

Yet a restlessness was in his nerves. What should he do? He remembered he had a letter in his pocket from Sir William Franks. Sir William had still teased him about his fate and his providence, in which he, Aaron, was supposed to trust. "I shall be very glad to hear from you, and to know how your benevolent Providence—or was yours a Fate—has treated you since we saw you—"

So, Aaron turned away, and walked to the postoffice. There he took paper, and sat down at one of the tables in the writing room, and wrote his answer. It was very strange, writing thus when most of his mind's eyes were scorched, and it seemed he could hardly see to hold the pen, to drive it straight across the paper. Yet write he must. And most of his faculties being quenched or blasted for the moment, he wrote perhaps his greatest, or his innermost truth.—"I don't want my Fate or my Providence to treat me well. I don't want kindness or love. I don't believe in harmony and people loving one another. I believe in the fight and in nothing else. I believe in the fight which is in everything. And if it is a question of women, I believe in the fight of love, even if it blinds me. And if it is a question of the world, I believe in fighting it and in having it hate me, even if it breaks my legs. I want the world to hate me, because I can't bear the thought that it might love me. For of all things love is the most deadly to me, and especially from such a repulsive world as I think this is…"

Well, here was a letter for a poor old man to receive. But, in the dryness of his withered mind, Aaron got it out of himself. When a man writes a letter to himself, it is a pity to post it to somebody else. Perhaps the same is true of a book.

His letter written, however, he stamped it and sealed it and put it in the box. That made it final. Then he turned towards home. One fact remained unbroken in the débris of his consciousness: that in the town was Lilly: and that when he needed, he could go to Lilly: also, that in the world was Lottie, his wife: and that against Lottie, his heart burned with a deep, deep, almost unreachable bitterness.— Like a deep burn on his deepest soul, Lottie. And like a fate which he resented, yet which steadied him, Lilly.

He went home and lay on his bed. He had enough self-command to hear the gong and go down to dinner. White and abstract-looking, he sat and ate his dinner. And then, thank God, he could go to bed, alone, in his own cold bed, alone, thank God. To be alone in the night! For this he was unspeakably thankful.

Chapter XIX.

Cleopatra, but not Anthony*

Aaron awoke in the morning feeling better, but still only a part himself. The night alone had restored him. And the need to be alone still was his greatest need. He felt an intense resentment against the Marchesa. He felt that somehow, she had given him a scorpion. And his instinct was to hate her. And yet he avoided hating her. He remembered Lilly—and the saying that one must possess oneself, and be alone in possession of oneself. And somehow, under the influence of Lilly, he refused to follow the reflex of his own passion. He refused to hate the Marchesa. He *did* like her. He *did* esteem her. And after all, she too was struggling with her fate. He had a genuine sympathy with her. Nay, he was not going to hate her.

But he could not see her. He could not bear the thought that she might call and see him. So he took the tram to Settignano,* and walked away all day into the country, having bread and sausage in his pocket. He sat for long hours among the cypress trees of Tuscany. And never had any trees seemed so like ghosts, like soft, strange, pregnant presences. He lay and watched tall cypresses breathing and communicating, faintly moving and as it were walking in the small wind. And his soul seemed to leave him and to go far away, far back, perhaps, to where life was all different and time passed otherwise than time passes now. As in clairvoyance he perceived it: that our life is only a fragment of the shell of life. That there has been and will be life, human life such as we do not begin to conceive. Much that is life has passed away from men, leaving us all mere bits. In the dark, mindful silence and inflection of the cypress trees, lost races, lost language, lost human ways of feeling and of knowing. Men have known as we can no more know, have felt as we can no more feel. Great life-realities gone into the darkness. But the cypresses commemorate. In the afternoon, Aaron felt the cypresses rising dark about him, like so many high visitants from an old, lost, lost subtle world, where men had the wonder of demons about them, the aura of demons, such as still clings to the cypresses, in Tuscany.*

All day, he did not make up his mind what he was going to do. His first impulse was never to see her again. And this was his intention all day. But as he went home in the tram he softened, and thought, Nay, that would not be fair. For how had she treated him, otherwise than generously.

5 She had been generous, and the other thing, that he felt blasted afterwards, which was his experience, that was fate, and not her fault. So he must see her again. He must not act like a churl. But he would tell her—he would tell her that he was a married man, and that though he had left his wife, and though he had no dogma of fidelity,
10 still, the years of marriage had made a married man of him, and any other woman than his wife was a strange woman to him, a violation. "I will tell her," he said to himself, "that at the bottom of my heart I love Lottie still, and that I can't help it. I believe that is true. It isn't love, perhaps. But it is marriage. I am married to Lottie. And that
15 means I can't be married to another woman. It isn't my nature. And perhaps I can't bear to live with Lottie now, because I am married and not in love. When a man is married, he is not in love. A husband is not a lover. Lilly told me that: and I know it's true now. Lilly told me that a husband cannot be a lover, and a lover cannot be a
20 husband. And that women will only have lovers now, and never a husband. Well, I am a husband, if I am anything. And I shall never be a lover again, not while I live. No, not to anybody. I haven't it in me. I am a husband, and so it is finished with me as a lover. I can't be a lover any more, just as I can't be aged twenty any more. I am a man
25 now, not an adolescent. And to my sorrow I am a husband to a woman who wants a lover: always a lover. But all women want lovers. And I can't be it any more. I don't want to. I have finished that. Finished for ever: unless I became senile—"

Therefore next day he gathered up his courage. He would not
30 have had courage unless he had known that he was not alone. The other man was in the town, and from this fact he derived his strength: the fact that Lilly was there. So at teatime he went over the river, and rang at her door. Yes, she was at home, and she had other visitors. She was wearing a beautiful soft afternoon dress, again of a blue like
35 chicory-flowers, a pale, *warm* blue. And she had corn-flowers in her belt: heaven knows where she had got them.

She greeted Aaron with some of a childish shyness. He could tell that she was glad he had come, and that she had wondered at his not coming sooner. She introduced him to her visitors: two young ladies
40 and one old lady and one elderly Italian count. The conversation was mostly in French or Italian, so Aaron was rather out of it.

However, the visitors left fairly early, so Aaron stayed them out. When they had gone, he asked:

"Where is Manfredi?"

"He will come in soon. At about seven o'clock."

Then there was a silence again.

"You are dressed fine today," he said to her.

"Am I?" she smiled.

He was never able to make out quite what she felt, what she was feeling. But she had a quiet little air of proprietorship in him, which he did not like.

"You will stay to dinner tonight, won't you?" she said.

"No,—not tonight," he said. And then, awkwardly, he added: "You know. I think it is better if we are friends—not lovers. You know—I don't feel free. I feel my wife, I suppose, somewhere inside me. And I can't help it—"

She bent her head and was silent for some moments. Then she lifted her face and looked at him oddly.

"Yes," she said. "I am sure you love your wife."

The reply rather staggered him—and to tell the truth, annoyed him.

"Well," he said. "I don't know about love. But when one has been married for ten years—and I did love her—then—some sort of bond or something grows. I think some sort of connection grows between us, you know. And it isn't natural, quite, to break it.—Do you know what I mean?"

She paused a moment. Then, very softly, almost gently, she said: "Yes, I do. I know so well what you mean."

He was really surprised at her soft acquiescence. What *did* she mean?

"But we can be friends, can't we?" he said.

"Yes, I hope so. Why yes! Goodness yes! I should be sorry if we couldn't be friends."

After which speech he felt that everything was all right—everything was A.1. And when Manfredi came home, the first sound he heard was the flute and his wife's singing.

"I'm so glad you've come," his wife said to him. "Shall we go into the sala and have real music? Will you play?"

"I should love to," replied the husband.

Behold them then in the big drawing-room, and Aaron and the Marchese practicing together, and the Marchesa singing an Italian folk-song while her husband accompanied her on the pianoforte.

But her singing was rather strained and forced. Still, they were quite a little family, and it seemed quite nice. As soon as she could, the Marchesa left the two men together, whilst she sat apart. Aaron and Manfredi went through old Italian and old German music, tried one
5 thing and then another, and seemed quite like brothers. They arranged a piece which they should play together on a Saturday morning, eight days hence.

The next day, Saturday, Aaron went to one of the Del Torre music mornings. There was a string quartette—and a violin soloist
10 —and the Marchese at the piano. The audience, some dozen or fourteen friends, sat at the near end of the room, or in the smaller salotta, whilst the musicians performed at the further end of the room. The Lillys were there, both Tanny and her husband. But apart from these, Aaron knew nobody, and felt uncomfortable. The
15 Marchesa gave her guests little sandwiches and glasses of wine or marsala or vermouth, as they chose. And she was quite the hostess: the well-bred and very simple, but still the conventional hostess. Aaron did not like it. And he could see that Lilly too was unhappy. In fact, the little man bolted the moment he could, dragging after him
20 the indignant Tanny, who was so looking forward to the excellent little sandwiches. But no—Lilly just rudely bolted. Aaron followed as soon as he could.

"Will you come to dinner tomorrow evening?" said his hostess to him as he was leaving. And he agreed. He had really resented seeing
25 her as a conventional hostess, attending so charmingly to all the other people, and treating him so merely as one of the guests, among many others. So that when at the last moment she quietly invited him to dinner next day, he was flattered and accepted at once.

The next day was Sunday—the seventh day after his coming
30 together with the Marchesa—which had taken place on the Monday. And already he was feeling much less dramatic in his decision to keep himself apart from her, to be merely friends. Already the memory of the last time was fanning up in him, not as a warning but as a terrible incitement. Again the naked desire was getting hold of
35 him, with that peculiar brutal powerfulness which startled him and also pleased him.

So that by the time Sunday morning came, his recoil had exhausted itself, and he was ready again, eager again, but more wary this time. He sat in his room alone in the morning, playing his flute,
40 playing over from memory the tunes she loved, and imagining how

he and she would get into unison in the evening. His flute, his Aaron's rod would blossom once again with splendid scarlet flowers, the red Florentine lilies. It was curious, the passion he had for her: just unalloyed desire, and nothing else. Something he had not known in his life before. Previously there had been always *some* personal quality, some sort of personal tenderness. But here, none. She did not seem to want it. She seemed to hate it, indeed. No, all he felt was stark, naked desire, without a single pretension. True enough, his last experience had been a warning to him. His desire and himself likewise had broken rather disastrously under the proving. But not finally broken. He was ready again. And with all the sheer powerful insolence of desire he looked forward to the evening. For he almost expected Manfredi would not be there. The officer had said something about having to go to Padua on the Saturday afternoon.

So Aaron went skipping off to his appointment, at seven o'clock. Judge of his chagrin, then, when he found already seated in the salotta an elderly, quite well-known, very cultured and very well connected English authoress. She was charming, in her white hair and dress of soft white wool and white lace, with a long chain of filigree gold beads, like bubbles. She was charming in her old-fashioned manner too, as if the world were still safe and stable, like a garden in which delightful culture, and choice ideas bloomed safe from wind and weather. Alas, never was Aaron more conscious of the crude collapse in the world than when he listened to this animated, young-seeming lady from the safe days of the seventies. All the old culture and choice ideas seemed like blowing bubbles. And dear old Corinna Wade,* she seemed to be blowing bubbles still, as she sat there so charming in her soft white dress, and talked with her bright animation about the influence of woman in Parliament and the influence of woman in the Periclean day.*—Aaron listened spell-bound, watching the bubbles float round his head, and almost hearing them go pop.

To complete the party arrived an elderly littérateur who was more proud of his not-very-important social standing than of his literature. In fact he was one of those English snobs of the old order, living abroad. Perfectly well-dressed for the evening, his grey hair and his prim face was the most well-dressed thing to be met in North Italy.

"Oh, so glad to see you, Mr. ffrench. I didn't know you were in Florence again. You make that journey from Venice so often. I wonder you don't get tired of it," cried Corinna Wade.

"No," he said. "So long as duty to England calls me to Florence, I shall come to Florence. But I can *live* in no town but Venice."

"No, I suppose you can't. Well, there *is* something special about Venice: having no streets and no carriages, and moving about in a gondola. I suppose it is all much more soothing."

"Much less nerve-wracking, yes. And then there is a quality in the whole life—Of course I see few English people in Venice—only the old Venetian families, as a rule."

"Ah yes. That must be very interesting. They are very exclusive still, the Venetian *noblesse?*" said Miss Wade.

"Oh very exclusive," said Mr. ffrench. "That is one of the charms. Venice is really altogether exclusive. It excludes the world, really, and defies time and modern movement. Yes, in spite of the steamers on the canal, and the tourists."

"That is so. That is so. Venice is a strange back-water. And the old families are very proud still, in these democratic days. They have a great opinion of themselves, I am told."

"Well," said Mr. ffrench. "Perhaps you know the rhyme:

> 'Veneziano gran' Signore
> Padovano buon' dottore.
> Vicenzese mangia il gatto
> Veronese tutto matto—' "*

"How very amusing!" said Miss Wade. "*Veneziano* gran' signore." The Venetian is a great gentleman! Yes, I know they are all convinced of it. Really, how very amusing, in these advanced days. To be born a Venetian, is to be born a great gentleman! But this outdoes divine right of kings."

"To be born a Venetian *gentleman* is to be born a great gentleman," said Mr. ffrench, rather fussily.

"You seriously think so?" said Miss Wade. "Well now, what do you base your opinion on?"

Mr. ffrench gave various bases for his opinion.

"Yes—Interesting. Very interesting. Rather like the Byzantines—lingering on into far other ages.* Anna Comnena always charmed me very much. *How* she despised the flower of the north—even Tancred!* And so the lingering Venetian families! And you, in your palazzo on the Grand Canal: you are a northern barbarian civilised into the old Venetian Signoria. But how very romantic a situation!"

It was really amusing to see the old maid, how she skirmished and hit out so gaily, like an old jaunty free lance: and to see the old bachelor, how prim he was, and nervy and fussy and precious, like an old maid.

But need we say that Mr. Aaron felt very much out of it. He sat and listened, with a sardonic small smile on his face and a sardonic gleam in his blue eyes, that looked so very blue on such an occasion. He made the two elderly people uncomfortable with his silence: his democratic silence, Miss Wade might have said.

However, Miss Wade lived out towards Galluzzo,* so she rose early, to catch her tram. And Mr. ffrench gallantly and properly rose to accompany her, to see her safe on board. Which left Aaron and the Marchesa alone.

"What time is Manfredi coming back?" said he.

"Tomorrow," replied she.

There was a pause.

"Why do you have those people?" he asked.

"Who?"

"Those two who were here this evening."

"Miss Wade and Mr. ffrench?—Oh, I like Miss Wade so very much. She is so refreshing."

"Those old people," said Aaron. "They licked the sugar off the pill, and go on as if everything was toffee. And we've got to swallow the pill. It's easy to be refreshing—"

"No, don't say anything against her. I like her so much."

"And him?"

"Mr. ffrench!—Well, he's perhaps a little like the princess who felt the pea through three feather-beds. But he can be quite witty, and an excellent conversationalist too. Oh yes, I like him quite well."

"Matter of taste," said Aaron.

They had not much to say to one another. The time passed, in the pauses. He looked at his watch.

"I shall have to go," he said.

"Won't you stay?" she said, in a small, muted voice.

"Stay all night?" he said.

"Won't you?"

"Yes," he said quietly. Did he not feel the strength of his desire on him.

After which she said no more. Only she offered him whiskey and soda, which he accepted.

"Go then," he said to her. "And I'll come to you.—Shall I come in fifteen minutes?"

She looked at him with strange, slow dark eyes. And he could not understand.

5   "Yes," she said. And she went.

And again, this night as before, she seemed strangely small and clinging in his arms. And this night, in his extreme, he felt his passion drawn from him as if a long, live nerve were drawn out from his body, a long live thread of electric fire, a long, living nerve finely
10   extracted from him, from the very roots of his soul. A long fine discharge of pure, bluish fire, from the core of his soul. It was an excruciating, but also an intensely gratifying sensation. As his passion broke from him to her, he felt the long live hot fire-thread drawn downwards through him, terribly down his legs and through
15   his heels, leaving his heels feeling bruised, and himself feeling vacant. It was like a discharge of lightning, but longer, more terrible.—And this night he slept with a deeper obliviousness than before. But ah, as it grew towards morning, how he wished he could be alone. And then immediately she crept to his breast again.

20   They must stay together till the day was light. And she seemed to love clinging to him and curling strangely on his breast. He could never reconcile it with her who was a hostess entertaining her guests. How could she now in a sort of little ecstasy curl herself and nestle herself on his, Aaron's breast, tangling his face all over with her hair.
25   He verily believed that this was what she really wanted of him: to curl herself on his naked breast, to make herself small, small, to feel his arms round her, and his slow, still, breathing lifting her, while he himself was remote, silent, in some way inaccessible. This seemed almost to make her beside herself with gratification. But why, why?
30   Was it because he was one of her own race, and she, as it were, crept right home to him?

He did not know. He only knew it had nothing to do with him: and that, save out of *complaisance*, he did not want it. Did he not want it?——the magic feeling of phallic immortality!—But at the same
35   time it simply blasted his own central life. It simply blighted him.

And she touched him, and touched him with her strange frail finger-tips, and quivered, and clung to him closer. Strange, she was afraid of him! Of his actual male physique she was afraid as of a fetish. Fetish afraid, and fetish-fascinated! Or was her fear only a
40   delightful game of cat and mouse? Or was the fear genuine, and the

delight the greater: a sort of sacrilege? The fear, the phallic fear: and the dangerous, sacrilegious power over that which she feared.

In some way she was not afraid of him at all. In some other way she used him as a mere magic implement, used him with the most amazing priestess-craft. Himself, the individual man which he was, this she treated with an indifference that was startling to him.

He forgot, perhaps, that this was how he had treated her. His famous desire for her, what had it been but this same attempt to strike a magic fire out of her, for his own ecstasy. They were playing the same game of fire. In him, however, there was all the time something hard and reckless and defiant, which stood apart. She was absolutely gone in her own incantations. She was absolutely gone, like a priestess utterly involved in her terrible rites. And he was part of the ritual only, God and victim in one. God and victim! All the time, God and victim. When his aloof soul realised, amid the welter of incantation, how he was being used,—not as himself but as something quite different—God and victim—then he dilated with intense surprise, and his remote soul stood up tall and knew itself alone. There, as in her incantation she used him to curl herself up against, and again to nestle deeper into! He didn't want it, not at all. He knew he was apart. And he looked back over the whole mystery of their love-contact, and his soul saw himself, saw his own phallic God-and-victim self there lying, with her on his breast. Only his soul apart.

She lay curled on his breast, with her wild hair tangled about him. And he was aware of the strength and beauty and godlikeness that his breast was then to her, the magic male breast with its two nipples. But himself, he stood far-off, like Moses's sister Miriam.* There lay the phallic God, the phallic victim, twined round utterly with this priestess. The breast, the limbs—and then she would drink the one drop of his innermost heart's blood, and he would be carrion. As Cleopatra killed her lovers in the morning. Surely they knew that death was their just climax. They had approached the climax. Accept then.

There was a lust and a temptation: the phallic Godhead. The lust and loveliness of his flesh, his godlike phallic power in the flesh. And the inevitable consummation, the drinking of his innermost drop of heart's blood. Lust and temptation.—And then carrion.

But his soul stood apart and could have nothing to do with it. If he had *really* been tempted, he would have gone on, and she might have

had his central heart's blood. Yes, and thrown away the carrion. He
would have been willing.

But fatally, he was not tempted. His soul stood apart and decided.
At the bottom of his soul he disliked her. Or if not her, then her
5 whole motive. Her whole life-mode. He was neither God nor victim:
neither greater nor less than himself. His soul, in its isolation as she
lay on his breast, chose it so, with the soul's inevitability. So, there
was no temptation.

When it was sufficiently light, he kissed her and left her. Quietly
10 he left the silent flat. He had some difficulty in unfastening the
various locks and bars and catches of the massive door downstairs,
and began, in irritation and anger, to feel he was a prisoner, that he
was locked in. But suddenly the ponderous door came loose, and he
was out in the street. The door shut heavily behind him, with a
15 shudder. He was out in the morning streets of Florence.

Chapter XX.

The Broken Rod

The day was rainy. Aaron stayed indoors alone, and copied music and slept. He felt the same stunned, withered feeling as before, but less intensely, less disastrously, this time. He knew now, without argument or thought that he would never go again to the Marchesa: not as a lover. He would go away from it all. He did not dislike her. But he would never see her again. A great gulf had opened, leaving him alone on the far side.

He did not go out till after dinner. When he got downstairs he found the heavy night-door closed. He wondered: then remembered the Signorina's fear of riots and disturbances. As again he fumbled with the catches, he felt that the doors of Florence were trying to prevent his egress. However, he got out.

It was a very dark night, about nine o'clock, and deserted seeming. He was struck by the strange, deserted feeling of the city's atmosphere. Yet he noticed before him, at the foot of the statue, three men, one with a torch: a long torch with naked flames. The men were stooping over something dark, the man with the torch bending forward too. It was a dark, weird little group, like Mediaeval Florence. Aaron lingered on his doorstep, watching. He could not see what they were doing. But now, the two were crouching down; over a long dark object on the ground, and the one with the torch bending also to look. What was it? They were just at the foot of the statue, a dark little group under the big pediment, the torch-flames weirdly flickering as the torch-bearer moved and stooped lower to the two crouching men, who seemed to be kneeling.

Aaron felt his blood stir. There was something dark and mysterious, stealthy, in the little scene. It was obvious the men did not want to draw attention, they were so quiet and furtive-seeming. And an eerie instinct prevented Aaron's going nearer to look. Instead, he swerved on to the Lungarno, and went along the top of the square, avoiding the little group in the centre. He walked the deserted dark-seeming street by the river, then turned inwards, into the city. He was going to the Piazza Vittorio Emanuele, to sit in the café* which

275

is the centre of Florence at night. There he could sit for an hour, and
drink his vermouth and watch the Florentines.

   As he went along one of the dark, rather narrow streets, he heard a
hurrying of feet behind him. Glancing round, he saw the torch-
5 bearer coming along at a trot, holding his flaming torch up in front of
him as he trotted down the middle of the narrow dark street. Aaron
shrank under the wall. The trotting torch-bearer drew near, and now
Aaron perceived the other two men slowly trotting behind, stealthily,
bearing a stretcher on which a body was wrapped up, completely and
10 darkly covered. The torch-bearer passed, the men with the stretcher
passed too, hastily and stealthily, the flickering flames revealing
them. They took no notice of Aaron, no notice of anything, but
trotted softly on towards the centre of the city. Their queer, quick
footsteps echoed down the distance. Then Aaron too resumed his
15 way.

   He came to the large, brilliantly-lighted café. It was Sunday
evening, and the place was full. Men, Florentines, many, many men
sat in groups and in twos and threes at the little marble tables. They
were mostly in dark clothes or black overcoats. They had mostly
20 been drinking just a cup of coffee—others however had glasses of
wine or liquor. But mostly it was just a little coffee-tray with a tiny
coffee-pot and a cup and saucer. There was a faint film of tobacco
smoke. And the men were all talking: talking, talking with that
peculiar intensity of the Florentines. Aaron felt the intense, com-
25 pressed sound of many half-secret voices. For the little groups and
couples abated their voices, none wished that others should hear
what they said.

   Aaron was looking for a seat—there was no table to himself—
when suddenly someone took him by the arm. It was Argyle.

30 "Come along, now! Come and join us. Here, this way! Come
along!"

   Aaron let himself be led away towards a corner. There sat Lilly
and a strange man: called Levison. The room was warm. Aaron
could never bear to be too hot. After sitting a minute, he rose and
35 took off his coat, and hung it on a stand near the window. As he did
so he felt the weight of his flute—it was still in his pocket. And he
wondered if it was safe to leave it.

   "I suppose no one will steal from the overcoat pockets," he said, as
he sat down.

40 "My dear chap, they'd steal the gold filling out of your teeth, if you

happened to yawn," said Argyle. "Why, have you left valuables in
your overcoat?"

"My flute," said Aaron.

"Oh, they won't steal that," said Argyle.

"Besides," said Lilly, "we should see anyone who touched it." 5
And so they settled down to the vermouth.

"Well," said Argyle, "what have you been doing with yourself, eh?
I haven't seen a glimpse of you for a week. Been going to the dogs,
eh?"

"Or the bitches," said Aaron. 10

"Oh, but look here, that's bad! That's bad! I can see I shall have to
take you in hand, and commence my work of reform. Oh, I'm a great
reformer, a Zwingli and Savonarola* in one. I couldn't count the
number of people I've led into the right way. It takes some finding,
you know. Strait is the gate*—Damned strait sometimes. A damned 15
tight squeeze . . ." Argyle was somewhat intoxicated. He spoke with
a slight slur, and laughed, really tickled at his own jokes. The man
Levison smiled acquiescent. But Lilly was not listening. His brow
was heavy and he seemed abstracted. He hardly noticed Aaron's
arrival. 20

"Did you see the row yesterday?" asked Levison.

"No," said Aaron. "What was it?"

"It was the socialists. They were making a demonstration against
the imprisonment of one of the railway-strikers. I was there. They
went on all right, with a good bit of howling and gibing: a lot of young 25
louts, you know. And the shopkeepers shut up shop, and nobody
showed the Italian flag, of course. Well, when they came to the Via
Benedetto Croce, there were a few mounted carabinieri. So they
stopped the procession, and the sergeant said that the crowd could
continue, could go on where they liked, but would they not go down 30
the Via Verrocchio, because it was being repaired, the roadway was
all up, and there were piles of cobble stones. These might prove a
temptation and lead to trouble. So would the demonstrators not take
that road—they might take any other they liked.—Well, the very
moment he had finished, there was a revolver shot, he made a noise, 35
and fell forward over his horse's nose. One of the anarchists had shot
him. Then there was hell let loose, the carabinieri fired back, and
people were bolting and fighting like devils. I cleared out, myself.
But my God—what do you think of it?"

"Seems pretty mean," said Aaron. 40

"Mean!—He had just spoken them fair—they could go where they liked, only would they not go down the one road, because of the heap of stones. And they let him finish. And then shot him dead."

"Was he dead?" said Aaron.

5   "Yes—killed outright, the *Nazione*＊ says."

There was a silence. The drinkers in the café all continued to talk vehemently, casting uneasy glances.

"Well," said Argyle, "if you let loose the dogs of war,＊ you mustn't expect them to come to heel again in five minutes."

10   "But there's no fair play about it, not a bit," said Levison.

"Ah, my dear fellow, are you still so young and callow that you cherish the illusion of fair play?" said Argyle.

"Yes, I am," said Levison.

"Live longer and grow wiser," said Argyle, rather contempt-

15 uously.

"Are you a socialist?" asked Levison.

"Am I my aunt Tabitha's dachshund bitch called Bella," said Argyle, in his musical, indifferent voice. "Yes, Bella's her name. And if you can tell me a damneder name for a dog, I shall listen, I assure

20 you, attentively."

"But you haven't got an aunt called Tabitha," said Aaron.

"Haven't I? Oh, haven't I? I've got *two* aunts called Tabitha: if not more."

"They aren't of any vital importance to you, are they?" said

25 Levison.

"Not the very least in the world—if it hadn't been that my elder Aunt Tabitha had christened her dachshund bitch Bella. I cut myself off from the family after that. Oh, I turned over a new leaf, with not a family name on it. Couldn't stand Bella amongst the rest."

30   "You must have strained most of the gnats out of your drink, Argyle," said Lilly, laughing.

"Assiduously! Assiduously! I can't stand these little vermin. Oh, I am quite indifferent about swallowing a camel or two—or even a whole string of dromedaries. How charmingly Eastern that

35 sounds! But gnats! Not for anything in the world would I swallow one."

"*You're* a bit of a socialist though, aren't you?" persisted Levison, now turning to Lilly.

"No," said Lilly. "I was."

40   "And am no more," said Argyle sarcastically. "My dear fellow, the

only hope of salvation for the world lies in the re-institution of slavery."

"What kind of slavery?" asked Levison.

"Slavery! *Slavery*! When I say *slavery* I don't mean any of your damned modern reform cant. I mean solid sound slavery on which the Greek and the Roman world rested. *Far* finer worlds than ours, my dear chap! Oh *far* finer! And can't be done without slavery. Simply can't be done.—Oh, they'll all come to realise it, when they've had a bit more of this democratic washer-women business."

Levison was laughing, with a slight sneer down his nose.

"Anyhow, there's no immediate danger—or hope, if you prefer it—of the re-instituting of classic slavery," he said.

"Unfortunately no. We are all such fools," said Argyle.

"Besides," said Levison, "who would you make slaves of?"

"Everybody, my dear chap: beginning with the idealists and the theorising Jews, and after them your nicely-bred gentlemen, and then perhaps your profiteers and Rothschilds,* and *all* politicians, and ending up with the proletariat," said Argyle.

"Then who would be the masters?—the professional classes, doctors and lawyers and so on?"

"What? Masters? They would be the sewerage slaves, as being those who had made most stinks."

There was a moment's silence.

"The only fault I have to find with your system," said Levison, rather acidly, "is that there would be only one master, and everybody else slaves."

"Do you call that a fault? What do you want with more than one master? Are you asking for several?—Well, perhaps there's cunning in *that*.—Cunning devils, cunning devils, these theorising slaves—" and Argyle pushed his face with a devilish leer into Aaron's face. "Cunning devils!" he reiterated, with a slight tipsy slur. "That be-pissed Epictetus* wasn't the last of 'em—nor the first. Oh, not by any means, not by any means."

Here Lilly could not avoid a slight spasm of amusement.

"But returning to serious conversation," said Levison, turning his rather sallow face to Lilly. "I think you'll agree with me that socialism is the inevitable next step—"

Lilly waited for some time without answering. Then he said, with unwilling attention to the question:

"I suppose it's the logically inevitable next step."

"Use logic as lavatory paper," cried Argyle harshly.

"Yes—logically inevitable—and humanly inevitable at the same time. Some form of socialism is bound to come, no matter how you postpone it or try variations," said Levison.

5 "All right, let it come," said Lilly. "It's not my affair, neither to help it nor to keep it back, or even to try varying it."

"There I don't follow you," said Levison. "Suppose you were in Russia now—"

"I watch it I'm not."

10 "But you're in Italy, which isn't far off. Supposing a socialist revolution takes place all round you. Won't that force the problem on you?—It is every man's problem," persisted Levison.

"Not mine," said Lilly.

"How shall you escape it?" said Levison.

15 "Because to me it is no problem. To Bolsh or not to Bolsh, as far as my mind goes, presents no problem. Not any more than to be or not to be. To be or not to be is simply no problem—"

"No, I quite agree, that since you are already existing, and since death is ultimately inevitable, to be or not to be is no sound
20 problem," said Levison. "But the parallel isn't true of socialism. That is not a problem of existence, but of a certain mode of existence which centuries of thought and action on the part of Europe have now made logically inevitable for Europe. And therefore there is a problem. There is more than a problem, there is a dilemma. Either
25 we must go to the logical conclusion—or—"

"Somewhere else," said Lilly.

"Yes—yes. Precisely! But *where* else? That's the one half of the problem: supposing you do not agree to a logical progression in human social activity. Because after all, human society through the
30 course of ages only enacts, spasmodically but still inevitably, the logical development of a given idea."

"Well, then, I tell you.—The idea and the ideal has for me gone dead—dead as carrion—"

"Which idea, which ideal precisely?"

35 "The ideal of love, the ideal that it is better to give than to receive,* the ideal of liberty, the ideal of the brotherhood of man, the ideal of the sanctity of human life, the ideal of what we call goodness, charity, benevolence, public spiritedness, the ideal of sacrifice for a cause, the ideal of unity and unanimity—all the lot—all the whole beehive
40 of ideals—has all got the modern bee-disease, and gone putrid,

stinking—And when the ideal is dead and putrid, the logical sequence is only stink.—Which, for me, is the truth concerning the ideal of good, peaceful, loving humanity and its logical sequence in socialism and equality, equal opportunity or whatever you like.—By this time he stinketh—and I'm sorry for any Christus who brings him to life again, to stink livingly for another thirty years: the beastly Lazarus of our idealism."*

"That may be true for you—"

"But it's true for nobody else," said Lilly. "All the worse for them. Let them die of the bee-disease."

"Not only that," persisted Levison, "but what is your alternative? Is it merely nihilism?"

"My alternative," said Lilly, "is an alternative for no one but myself, so I'll keep my mouth shut about it."

"That isn't fair."

"I tell you, the ideal of fairness stinks with the rest.—I have no obligation to say what I think."

"Yes, if you enter into conversation, you have—"

"Bah, then I didn't enter into conversation.—The only thing is, I agree in the rough with Argyle. You've got to have a sort of slavery again. People are not *men*: they are insects and instruments, and their destiny is slavery. They are too many for me, and so what I think is ineffectual. But ultimately they will be brought to agree—after sufficient extermination—and then they will elect for themselves a proper and healthy and energetic slavery."

"I should like to know what you mean by slavery. Because to me it is impossible that slavery should be healthy and energetic. You seem to have some other idea in your mind, and you merely use the word slavery out of exasperation—"

"I mean it none the less. I mean a real committal of the life-issue of inferior beings to the responsibility of a superior being."

"It'll take a bit of knowing, who are the inferior and which is the superior," said Levison sarcastically.

"Not a bit. It is written between a man's brows, which he is."

"I'm afraid we shall all read differently."

"So long as we're liars."

"And putting that question aside: I presume that you mean that this committal of the life-issue of inferior beings to someone higher shall be made voluntarily—a sort of voluntary self-gift to the inferiors—"

"Yes—more or less—and a voluntary acceptance. For it's no pretty gift, after all.—But once made it must be held fast by genuine power. Oh yes—no playing and fooling about with it. Permanent and very efficacious power."

5   "You mean military power?"

"I do, of course."

Here Levison smiled a long, slow, subtle smile of ridicule. It all seemed to him the preposterous pretentiousness of a megalomaniac —one whom, after a while, humanity would probably have the
10   satisfaction of putting into prison, or into a lunatic asylum. And Levison felt strong, overwhelmingly strong, in the huge social power with which he, insignificant as he was, was armed against such criminal-imbecile pretensions as those above set forth. Prison or the lunatic asylum. The face of the fellow gloated in these two inevitable
15   engines of his disapproval.

"It will take you some time before you'll get your doctrines accepted," he said.

"Accepted! I'd be sorry. I don't want a lot of swine snouting and sniffing at me with their acceptance.—Bah, Levison—one can easily
20   make a fool of you. Do you take this as my gospel?"

"I take it you are speaking seriously."

Here Lilly broke into that peculiar, gay, whimsical smile.

"But I should say the blank opposite with just as much fervour," he declared.

25   "Do you mean to say you don't *mean* what you've been saying?" said Levison, now really looking angry.

"Why, I'll tell you the real truth," said Lilly. "I think every man is a sacred and holy individual, *never* to be violated. I think there is only one thing I hate to the verge of madness, and that is *bullying.** To see
30   any living creature *bullied*, in *any* way, almost makes a murderer of me. That is true. Do you believe it—?"

"Yes," said Levison unwillingly. "That may be true as well. You have no doubt, like most of us, got a complex nature which—"

C R A S H !

35   There intervened one awful minute of pure shock, when the soul was in darkness.

Out of this shock Aaron felt himself issuing amid a mass of terrible sensations: the fearful blow of the explosion, the noise of glass, the hoarse howl of people, the rushing of men, the sudden gulf, the
40   awful gulfing whirlpool of horror in the social life.

He stood in agony and semi-blindness amid a chaos. Then as he began to recover his consciousness, he found himself standing by a pillar some distance from where he had been sitting: he saw a place where tables and chairs were all upside down, legs in the air, amid débris of glass and breakage: he saw the café almost empty, nearly everybody gone: he saw the owner, or the manager, advancing aghast to the place of débris: he saw Lilly standing not far off, white as a sheet, and as if unconscious. And still he had no idea of what had happened. He thought perhaps something had broken down. He could not understand.

Lilly began to look round. He caught Aaron's eye. And then Aaron began to approach his friend.

"What is it?" he asked.

"A bomb," said Lilly.

The manager, and one old waiter, and three or four youths had now advanced to the place of débris. And now Aaron saw that a man was lying there—and horror, blood was running across the floor of the café. Men began now hastily to return to the place. Some seized their hats and departed again at once. But many began to crowd in—a black eager crowd of men pressing to where the bomb had burst—where the man was lying. It was rather dark, some of the lamps were broken—but enough still shone. Men surged in with that eager, excited zest of people, when there has been an accident. Grey carabinieri, and carabinieri in the cocked hat and fine Sunday uniform pressed forward officiously.

"Let us go," said Lilly.

And he went to the far corner, where his hat hung. But Aaron looked in vain for his own hat. The bomb had fallen near the stand where he had hung it and his overcoat.

"My hat and coat?" he said to Lilly.

Lilly, not very tall, stood on tip-toe. Then he climbed on a chair and looked round. Then he squeezed past the crowd.

Aaron followed. On the other side of the crowd excited angry men were wrestling over overcoats that were mixed up with a broken marble table-top. Aaron spied his own black hat under the sofa near the wall. He waited his turn and then in the confusion pressed forward to where the coats were. Someone had dragged out his, and it lay on the floor under many feet. He managed, with a struggle, to get it from under the feet of the crowd. He felt at once for his flute. But his trampled, torn coat had no flute in its pocket. He pushed and struggled, caught sight of a section, and picked it up. But it was split right down, two silver stops were torn out, and a long thin spelch* of wood was curiously torn off. He looked at it, and his heart stood still. No need to look for the rest.

5 He felt utterly, utterly overcome—as if he didn't care what became of him any further. He didn't care whether he were hit by a bomb, or whether he himself threw the next bomb, and hit somebody. He just didn't care any more about anything in life or death. It was as if the reins of his life slipped from his hands, and he would let 10 everything run where it would, so long as it did run.

Then he became aware of Lilly's eyes on him—and automatically he joined the little man.

"Let us go," said Lilly.

And they pushed their way through the door. The police were just 15 marching across the square. Aaron and Lilly walked in the opposite direction. Groups of people were watching. Suddenly Lilly swerved—in the middle of the road was a large black glisten of blood, trickling horribly. A wounded man had run from the blow and fallen here.

20 Aaron did not know where he was going. But in the Via Tornabuoni Lilly turned towards the Arno, and soon they were on the Ponte Santa Trinita.

"Who threw the bomb?" said Aaron.

"I suppose an anarchist."

25 "It's all the same," said Aaron.

The two men, as if unable to walk any further, leaned on the broad parapet of the bridge and looked at the water in the darkness of the still, deserted night. Aaron still had his flute section in his hand, his overcoat over his arm.

30 "Is that your flute?" asked Lilly.

"Bit of it. Smashed."

"Let me look."

He looked, and gave it back.

"No good," he said.

35 "Oh no," said Aaron.

"Throw it in the river, Aaron," said Lilly.

Aaron turned and looked at him.

"Throw it in the river," repeated Lilly. "It's an end."

Aaron nervelessly dropped the flute into the stream. The two men 40 stood leaning on the bridge-parapet, as if unable to move.

"We shall have to go home," said Lilly, "Tanny may hear of it and be anxious."

Aaron was quite dumbfounded by the night's event: the loss of his flute. Here was a blow he had not expected. And the loss was for him symbolistic. It chimed with something in his soul: the bomb, the smashed flute, the end.

"There goes Aaron's Rod, then," he said to Lilly.

"It'll grow again. It's a reed, a water-plant—you can't kill it," said Lilly, unheeding.

"And me?"

"You'll have to live without a rod, meanwhile."

To which pleasant remark Aaron made no reply.

Chapter XXI.

Words

He went home to bed: and dreamed a strange dream. He dreamed that he was in a country with which he was not acquainted. Night was coming on, and he had nowhere to sleep. So he passed the mouth of a sort of cave or house, in which a woman, an old woman, sat. Therefore he entered, and though he could not understand the language, still his second self understood. The cave was a house: and men came home from work. His second self assumed that they were tin-miners.

He wandered uneasily to and fro, no one taking any particular notice of him. And he realised that there was a whole vast country spreading, a sort of underworld country, spreading away beyond him. He wandered from vast apartment to apartment, down narrow corridors like the roads in a mine. In one of the great square rooms, the men were going to eat. And it seemed to him that what they were going to eat was a man, a naked man. But his second self knew that what appeared to his eyes as a man was really a man's skin stuffed tight with prepared meat, as the skin of a Bologna sausage. This did not prevent his seeing the naked man who was to be eaten walk slowly and stiffly across the gangway and down the corridor. He saw him from behind. It was a big and handsome man in the prime of life, quite naked and perhaps stupid. But of course he was only a skin stuffed with meat, whom the grey tin-miners were going to eat.

Aaron, the dream-Aaron, turned another way, and strayed among the vast square rooms, cavern apartments. He came into one room where there were many children, all in white gowns. And they were all busily putting themselves to bed, in the many beds scattered about the room at haphazard. And each child went to bed with a wreath of flowers on its head, white flowers and pink, so it seemed. So there they all lay, in their flower-crowns in the vast space of the rooms. And Aaron went away.

He could not remember the following part. Only he seemed to have passed through many grey domestic apartments, where were all women, all greyish in their clothes and appearance, being wives of

286

the underground tin-miners. The men were away and the dream-Aaron remembered with fear the food they were to eat.

The next thing he could recall was, that he was in a boat. And now he was most definitely two people. His invisible, *conscious* self, what we have called his second self, hovered as it were before the prow of the boat, seeing and knowing, but unseen. His other self, the palpable Aaron, sat as a passenger in the boat, which was being rowed by the unknown people of this underworld. They stood up as they thrust the boat along. Other passengers were in the boat too, women as well, but all of them unknown people, and not noticeable.

The boat was upon a great lake in the underworld country, a lake of dark-blue water, but crystal clear and very beautiful in colour. The second or invisible Aaron sat in the prow and watched the fishes swimming suspended in the clear, beautiful dark-blue water. Some were pale fish, some frightening-looking, like centipedes swimming, and some were dark fish, of definite form, and delightful to watch.

The palpable or visible Aaron sat at the side of the boat, on the end of the middle seat, with his naked right elbow leaning out over the side. And now the boat entered upon shallows. The impalpable Aaron in the bows saw the whitish clay of the bottom swirl up in clouds at each thrust of the oars, whitish-clayey clouds which would envelope the strange fishes in a sudden mist. And on the right hand of the course stakes stood up in the water, at intervals, to mark the course.

The boat must pass very near these stakes, almost touching. And Aaron's naked elbow was leaning right over the side. As they approached the first stake, the boatmen all uttered a strange cry of warning, in a foreign language. The flesh-and-blood Aaron seemed not even to hear. The invisible Aaron heard, but did not comprehend the words of the cry. So the naked elbow struck smartly against the stake as the boat passed.

The rowers rowed on. And still the flesh-and-blood Aaron sat with his arm over the side. Another stake was nearing. "Will he heed, will he heed?" thought the anxious second self. The rowers gave the strange warning cry. He did not heed, and again the elbow struck against the stake as the boat passed.

And yet the flesh-and-blood Aaron sat on and made no sign. There were stakes all along this shallow part of the lake. Beyond was deep water again. The invisible Aaron was becoming anxious. "Will he never hear? Will he never heed? Will he never understand?" he thought. And he watched in pain for the next stake. But still the flesh-and-blood Aaron sat on, and though the rowers cried so acutely that the invisible Aaron almost understood their very language, still the Aaron seated at the side heard nothing, and his elbow 5 struck against the third stake.

This was almost too much. But after a few moments, as the boat rowed on, the palpable Aaron changed his position as he sat, and drew in his arm: though even now he was not aware of any need to do so. The invisible Aaron breathed with relief in the bows, the boat 10 swung steadily on, into the deep, unfathomable water again.

They were drawing near a city. A lake-city, like Mexico.* They must have reached a city, because when Aaron woke up and tried to piece together the dream of which these are mere fragments, he could remember having just seen an idol. An Astarte* he knew it as, 15 seated by the road, and in her open lap were some eggs: smallish hen's eggs, and one or two bigger eggs, like swan's, and one single little roll of bread. These lay in the lap of the roadside Astarte ... And then he could remember no more.

He woke, and for a minute tried to remember what he had been 20 dreaming, and what it all meant. But he quickly relinquished the effort. So he looked at his watch: it was only half-past three. He had one of those American watches with luminous, phosphorescent figures and fingers. And tonight he felt afraid of its eerily shining face.

25 He was awake a long time in the dark—for two hours, thinking and not thinking, in that barren state which is not sleep, nor yet full wakefulness, and which is a painful strain. At length he went to sleep again, and did not wake till past eight o'clock. He did not ring for his coffee till nine.

30 Outside was a bright day—but he hardly heeded it. He lay profitlessly thinking. With the breaking of the flute, that which was slowly breaking had finally shattered at last. And there was nothing ahead: no plan, no prospect. He knew quite well that people would help him: Francis Dekker or Angus Guest or the Marchese or Lilly. 35 They would get him a new flute, and find him engagements. But what was the good? His flute was broken, and broken finally. The bomb had settled it. The bomb had settled it and everything. It was an end, no matter how he tried to patch things up. The only thing he felt was a thread of destiny attaching him to Lilly. The rest had all 40 gone as bare and bald as the dead orb of the moon. So he made up

his mind, if he could, to make some plan that would bring his life together with that of his evanescent friend.

Lilly was a peculiar bird. Clever and attractive as he undoubtedly was, he was perhaps the most objectionable person to know. It was stamped on his peculiar face. Aaron thought of Lilly's dark, ugly face, which had something that lurked in it as a creature under leaves. Then he thought of the wide-apart eyes, with their curious candour and surety. The peculiar, half-veiled surety, as if nothing, nothing could overcome him. It made people angry, this look of silent, indifferent assurance. "Nothing can touch him on the quick, nothing can really *get* at him," they felt at last. And they felt it with resentment, almost with hate. They wanted to be able to get at him. For he was so open-seeming, so very outspoken. He gave himself away so much. And he had no money to fall back on. Yet he gave himself away so easily, paid such attention, almost deference to any chance friend. So they all thought: Here is a wise person who finds me the wonder which I really am.—And lo and behold, after he had given them the trial, and found their inevitable limitations, he departed and ceased to heed their wonderful existence. Which, to say the least of it, was fraudulent and damnable. It was then, after his departure, that they realised his basic indifference to them, and his silent arrogance. A silent arrogance that knew all their wisdom, and left them to it.

Aaron had been through it all. He had started by thinking Lilly a peculiar little freak: gone on to think him a wonderful chap, and a bit pathetic: progressed, and found him generous, but overbearing: then cruel and intolerant, allowing no man to have a soul of his own: then terribly arrogant, throwing a fellow aside like an old glove which is in holes at the finger-ends. And all the time, which was most beastly, seeing through one. All the time, freak and outsider as he was, Lilly *knew*. He knew, and his soul was against the whole world.

Driven to bay, and forced to choose. Forced to choose, not between life and death, but between the world and the uncertain, assertive Lilly. Forced to choose, and yet, in the world, having nothing left to choose. For in the world there was nothing left to choose, unless he would give in and try for success. Aaron knew well enough that if he liked to do a bit of buttering, people would gladly make a success of him, and give him money and success. He could become quite a favourite.

But no! If he had to give in to something: if he really had to give in,

and it seemed he had: then he would rather give in to the little Lilly
than to the beastly people of the world. If he had to give in, then it
should be to no woman, and to no social ideal, and to no social
institution. No!—if he had to yield his wilful independence, and give
5   himself, then he would rather give himself to the little, individual
man than to any of the rest. For to tell the truth, in the man was
something incomprehensible, which had dominion over him, if he
chose to allow it.

As he lay pondering this over, escaping from the *cul de sac* in which
10 he had been running for so long, by yielding to one of his pursuers:
yielding to the peculiar mastery of one man's nature rather than to
the quicksands of woman or the stinking bog of society: yielding,
since yield he must, in some direction or other: yielding in a new
direction now, to one strange and incalculable little individual;
15 as Aaron lay so relaxing, finding a peculiar delight in giving his soul
to his mind's hero, the self-same hero tapped and entered.

"I wondered," he said, "if you'd like to walk into the country with
me: it is such a nice day. I thought you might have gone out already.
But here you are in bed like a woman who's had a baby.—You're all
20 right, are you?"

"Yes," said Aaron. "I'm all right."

"Miserable about your flute?—Ah well, there are more flutes. Get
up then." And Lilly went to the window, and stood looking out at the
river.

25 "We're going away on Thursday," he said.

"Where to?" said Aaron.

"Naples. We've got a little house there for the winter—in the
country, not far from Sorrento—I must get a bit of work done, now
the winter is coming. And forget all about everything and just live
30 with life.—What's the good of running after life, when we've got it in
us, if nobody prevents us and obstructs us?"

Aaron felt very queer.

"But for how long will you settle down—?" he asked.

"Oh, only the winter.—I am a vagrant really: or a migrant. I must
35 migrate. Do you think a cuckoo in Africa and a cuckoo in Essex is
one *and* the same bird?—Anyhow, I know I must oscillate between
north and south, so oscillate I do. It's just my nature. All people don't
have the same needs."

"Perhaps not," said Aaron, who had risen and was sitting on the
40 side of the bed.

"I would very much like to try life in another continent, among another race. I feel Europe becoming like a cage to me. Europe may be all right in herself. But I find myself chafing. Another year I shall get out. I shall leave Europe. I begin to feel caged."

"I guess there are others that feel caged, as well as you," said Aaron.

"I guess there are."

"And maybe they haven't a chance to get out."

Lilly was silent a moment. Then he said:

"Well, I didn't make life and society. I can only go my own way."

Aaron too was silent. A deep disappointment was settling over his spirit.

"Will you be alone all winter?"

"Just myself and Tanny," he answered. "But people always turn up."

"And then next year, what will you do?"

"Who knows? I may sail far off. I should like to. I should like to try quite a new life-mode. This is finished in me—and yet perhaps it is absurd to go further. I'm rather sick of seekers. I hate a seeker."

"What," said Aaron rather sarcastically—"those who are looking for a new religion?"

"Religion—and love—and all that. It's a disease now."

"Oh, I don't know," said Aaron. "Perhaps the lack of love and religion is the disease."

"Ah—bah! The grinding the old millstones of love and God is what ails us, when there's no more grist between the stones.* We've ground love very small. Time to forget it. Forget the very words religion, and God, and love—then have a shot at a new mode. But the very words rivet us down and don't let us move. Rivets, and we can't get them out."

"And where should we be if we could?" said Aaron.

"We might begin to be ourselves, anyhow."

"And what does that mean?" said Aaron. "Being yourself—what does it mean?"

"To me, everything."

"And to most folks, nothing. They've got to have a goal."

"There is no goal. I loathe goals more than any other impertinence. Gaols, they are. Bah—jails and jailors: gaols and gaolers—"

"Wherever you go, you'll find people with their noses tied to some goal," said Aaron.

"Their wagon hitched to a star*—which goes round and round like an ass in a gin," laughed Lilly. "Be damned to it."

Aaron got himself dressed, and the two men went out, took a tram and went into the country. Aaron could not help it—Lilly put his back up. They came to a little inn near a bridge, where a broad stream rustled bright and shallow. It was a sunny warm day, and Aaron and Lilly had a table outside under the thin trees at the top of the bank above the river. The yellow leaves were falling—the Tuscan sky was turquoise blue. In the stream below three naked boys still adventurously bathed, and lay flat on the shingle in the sun. A wagon with two pale, loving, velvety oxen drew slowly down the hill, looking at each step as if they were going to come to rest, to move no more. But still they stepped forward. Till they came to the inn, and there they stood at rest. Two old women were picking the last acorns under three scrubby oak-trees, whilst a girl with bare feet drove her two goats and a sheep up from the water-side towards the women. The girl wore a dress that had been blue, perhaps indigo, but which had faded to the beautiful lavender-purple colour which is so common, and which always reminded Lilly of purple anemones in the south.

The two friends sat in the sun and drank red wine. It was midday. From the thin, square belfry on the opposite hill the bells had rung. The old women and the girl squatted under the trees eating their bread and figs. The boys were dressing, fluttering into their shirts on the stream's shingle. A big girl went past, with somebody's dinner tied in a red kerchief and perched on her head. It was one of the most precious hours: the hour of pause, noon, and the sun, and the quiet acceptance of the world. At such a time everything seems to fall into a true relationship, after the strain of work and of urge.

Aaron looked at Lilly, and saw the same odd, distant look on his face as on the face of some animal when it lies awake and alert, yet perfectly at one with its surroundings. It was something quite different from happiness: an alert enjoyment of rest, an intense and satisfying sense of centrality. As a dog when it basks in the sun with one eye open and winking: or a rabbit quite still and wide-eyed, with a faintly-twitching nose. Not passivity, but alert enjoyment of being central, life-central in one's own little circumambient world.

They sat thus still—or lay under the trees—for an hour and a half. Then Lilly paid the bill, and went on.

"What am I going to do this winter, do you think?" Aaron asked.

"What do you want to do?"

"Nay, that's what I want to know."

"Do you want anything? I mean, does something drive you from inside?"

"I can't just rest," said Aaron.

"Can't you settle down to something?—to a job, for instance?"

"I've not found the job I could settle down to, yet," said Aaron.

"Why not?"

"It's just my nature."

"Are you a seeker? Have you got a divine urge, or need?"

"How do I know?" laughed Aaron. "Perhaps I've got a *damned* urge, at the bottom of me. I'm sure it's nothing divine."

"Very well then. Now, in life, there are only two great dynamic urges—do you believe me—?"

"How do I know?" laughed Aaron. "Do you want to be believed?"

"No, I don't care a straw.—Only for your own sake, you'd better believe me."

"All right then—what about it?"

"Well then, there are only two great dynamic urges in *life*: love and power."*

"Love and power?" said Aaron. "I don't see power as so very important."

"You don't see because you don't look. But that's not the point.— What sort of urge is your urge? Is it the love urge?"

"I don't know," said Aaron.

"Yes you do. You know that you have got an urge, don't you?"

"Yes—" rather unwillingly Aaron admitted it.

"Well then, what is it? Is it that you want to love, or to be obeyed?"

"A bit of both."

"All right—a bit of both. And what are you looking for in love?— A woman whom you can love, and who will love you, out and out and all in all and happy ever after sort of thing?"

"That's what I started out for, perhaps," laughed Aaron.

"And now you know it's all my eye!" Aaron looked at Lilly, unwilling to admit it. Lilly began to laugh.

"You know it well enough," he said. "It's one of your lost illusions, my boy. Well then, what next? Is it a God you're after? Do you want a God you can strive to and attain, through love, and live happy ever after, countless millions of eternities, immortality and all that? Is this your little dodge?"

Again Aaron looked at Lilly with that odd double look of mockery and unwillingness to give himself away.

"All right then. You've got a love-urge that urges you to God, have you? Then go and join the Buddhists in Burmah, or the newest
5 fangled Christians in Europe. Go and stick your head in a bush of Nirvana or spiritual perfection. Trot off."

"I won't," said Aaron.

"You must. If you've got a love-urge, then give it its fulfilment."

"I haven't got a love-urge."

10 "You have. You want to get excited in love. You want to be carried away in love. You want to whoosh off in a nice little love-whoosh and lose yourself. Don't deny it. I know you do. You want passion to sweep you off on wings of fire till you surpass yourself, and like the swooping eagle swoop right into the sun. I know you, my love-
15 boy."

"Not any more—Not any more. I've been had too often," laughed Aaron.

"Bah, it's a lesson men never learn. No matter how sick they make themselves with love, they always rush for more, like a dog to his
20 vomit."

"Well, what am I to do then, if I'm not to love?" cried Aaron.

"You want to go on, from passion to passion, from ecstasy to ecstasy, from triumph to triumph, till you can whoosh away into glory, beyond yourself, all bonds loosened and happy ever after.
25 Either that or Nirvana, opposite side of the medal."

"There's probably more hate than love in me," said Aaron.

"That's the recoil of the same urge. The anarchist, the criminal, the murderer, he is only the extreme lover acting on the recoil. But it is love: only in recoil. It flies back, the love-urge, and becomes a
30 horror."

"All right then. I'm a criminal and a murderer," said Aaron.

"No you're not. But you're a love-urger. And perhaps on the recoil just now. But listen to me. It's no good thinking the love-urge is the one and only. *Niente!** You can whoosh if you like, and get
35 excited and carried away loving a woman, or humanity, or God. Swoop away in the love direction till you lose yourself.—But that's where you're had. You can't lose yourself. You can try. But you might just as well try to swallow yourself. You'll only bite your fingers off in the attempt. You can't lose yourself, neither in woman nor
40 humanity nor in God. You've always got yourself on your hands in

the end: and a very raw and jaded and humiliated and nervous-neurasthenic self it is, too, in the end. A very nasty thing to wake up to is one's own raw self after an excessive love-whoosh. Look even at President Wilson: he love-whooshed for humanity, and found in the end he'd only got a very sorry self on his hands.

"So leave off, leave off, my boy. Leave off love-whooshing. You can't lose yourself, so stop trying. The responsibility is on your own shoulders all the time, and no God which man has ever struck can take it off. You *are* yourself and so *be* yourself. Stick to it and abide by it. Passion or no passion, ecstasy or no ecstasy, urge or no urge, there's no goal outside you, where you can consummate like an eagle flying into the sun, or a moth into a candle. There's no goal outside you—and there's no God outside you. No God, whom you can get to and rest in. None. It's a case of

> Trot, trot to market, to buy a penny bun,
> And trot trot back again, as fast as you can run.*

But there's no God outside you, whom you can rise to or sink to or swoop away to. You can't even gum yourself to a divine Nirvana moon. Because all the time you've got to eat your dinner and go to the W.C. There is no goal outside you. None.

"There is only one thing, your own very self. So you'd better stick to it. You can't be any bigger than just yourself, so you needn't drag God in. You've got one job, and no more. There inside you lies your own very self, like a germinating egg, your precious Easter egg of your own soul. There it is, developing bit by bit, from one single egg-cell which you were at your conception in your mother's womb, on and on to the strange and peculiar complication in unity which never stops till you die—if then. You've got an innermost, integral unique self, and since it's the only thing you have got or ever will have, don't go trying to lose it. You've got to develop it, from the egg into the chicken, and from the chicken into the one-and-only phoenix, of which there can only be one at a time in the universe. There can only be one of you at a time in the universe—and one of me. So don't forget it. Your own single oneness is your destiny. Your destiny comes from within, from your own self-form. And you can't know it beforehand, neither your destiny nor your self-form. You can only develop it. You can only stick to your own very self, and *never* betray it. And by so sticking, you develop the one and only phoenix of your own self, and you unfold your own destiny, as a dandelion unfolds itself into a dandelion, and not into a stick of celery.

"Remember this, my boy: you've never got to deny the Holy Ghost which is inside you, your own soul's self. Never. Or you'll catch it.*
5 And you've never got to think you'll dodge the responsibility of your own soul's self, by loving or sacrificing or Nirvanaing—or even anarchising and throwing bombs. You never will ..."

Aaron was silenced for a moment by this flood of words. Then he said, smiling:

10 "So I'd better sit tight on my soul, till it hatches, had I?"

"Oh yes. If your soul's urge urges you to love, then love. But always know that what you are doing is the fulfilling of your own soul's impulse. It's no good trying to act by prescription: not a bit. And it's no use getting into frenzies. If you've got to go in for love and
15 passion, go in for them. But they aren't the goal. They're a mere means: a life-means, if you will. The only goal is the fulfilling of your own soul's active desire and suggestion. Be passionate as much as ever it is your nature to be passionate, and deeply sensual as far as you can be. Small souls have a small sensuality, deep souls a deep
20 one. But remember, all the time, the responsibility is upon your own head, it all rests with your own lonely soul, the responsibility for your own action."

"I never said it didn't," said Aaron.

"You never said it did. You never accepted. You thought there was
25 something outside, to justify you: God, or a creed, or a prescription. But remember, your soul inside you is your only Godhead. It develops your actions within you as a tree develops its own new cells. And the cells push on into buds and boughs and flowers. And these are your passion and your acts and your thoughts and your expressions,
30 your developing consciousness. You don't know beforehand, and you can't. You can only stick to your own soul through thick and thin.

"You are your own Tree of Life,* roots and limbs and trunk. Somewhere within the wholeness of the tree lies the very self, the
35 quick: its own innate Holy Ghost. And this Holy Ghost puts forth new buds, and pushes past old limits, and shakes off a whole body of dying leaves. And the old limits hate being empassed, and the old leaves hate to fall. But they must, if the tree-soul says so ..."

They had sat down again during this harangue, under a white wall.
40 Aaron listened more to the voice than the words. It was more the

sound value which entered his soul, the tone, the strange speech-music which sank into him. The sense he hardly heeded. And yet he understood, he knew. He understood oh, so much more deeply than if he had listened with his head. And he answered an objection from the bottom of his soul.

"But you talk," he said, "as if we were like trees, alone by ourselves in the world. We aren't. If we love, it needs another person than ourselves. And if we hate, and even if we talk."

"Quite," said Lilly. "And that's just the point. We've got to love and hate moreover—and even talk. But we haven't got to fix on any one of these modes, and say that's the only mode. It is such imbecility to say that love and love alone must rule. It is so obviously not the case. Yet we try and make it so."

"I feel that," said Aaron. "It's all a lie."

"It's worse. It's a half lie. But listen. I told you there were two urges—two great life-urges, didn't I.—There may be more. But it comes on me so strongly, now, that there are two: love, and power. And we've been trying to work ourselves, at least as individuals, from the love-urge exclusively, hating the power-urge, and repressing it. And now I find we've got to accept the very thing we've hated.

"We've exhausted our love-urge, for the moment. And yet we try to force it to continue working. So we get inevitably anarchy and murder.—It's no good. We've got to accept the power motive, accept it in deep responsibility, do you understand me? It is a great life motive. It was that great dark power-urge which kept Egypt so intensely living for so many centuries. It is a vast dark source of life and strength in us now, waiting either to issue into true action, or to burst into cataclysm. Power—the power-urge. The will-to-power —but not in Nietzsche's sense.* Not intellectual power. Not mental power. Not conscious will-power. Not even wisdom. But dark, living, fructifying power. Do you know, what I mean?"

"I don't know," said Aaron.

"Take what you call love, for example. In the real way of love, the positive aim is to make the other person—or persons—happy. It devotes itself to the other or to others.—But change the mode. Let the urge be the urge of power. Then the great desire is not happiness, neither of the beloved nor of oneself. Happiness is only one of many states, and it is horrible to think of fixing us down to one state. The urge of power does not seek for happiness any more than for any other state. It urges from within, darkly, for the displacing of

the old leaves, the inception of the new. It is powerful and
self-central, not seeking its centre outside, in some God or some
beloved, but acting indomitably from within itself.

"And of course there must be one who urges, and one who is
5 impelled. Just as in love there is a beloved and a lover: The man is
supposed to be the lover, the woman the beloved. Now, in the urge
of power, it is the reverse. The woman must submit, but deeply,
deeply submit. Not to any foolish fixed authority, not to any foolish
and arbitrary will. But to something deep, deeper. To the soul in its
10 dark motion of power and pride. We must reverse the poles. The
woman must now submit—but deeply, deeply, and richly! No sub-
servience. None of that. No slavery. A deep, unfathomable free
submission."

"You'll never get it," said Aaron.

15 "You will, if you abandon the love idea and the love motive, and if
you stand apart, and never bully, never force from the conscious will.
That's where Nietzsche was wrong. His was the conscious and
benevolent will, in fact, the love-will. But the deep power-urge is not
conscious of its aims: and it is certainly not consciously benevolent or
20 love-directed.—Whatever else happens, somewhere, sometime, the
deep power-urge in man will have to issue forth again, and woman
will submit, livingly, not subjectedly."

"She never will," persisted Aaron. "Anything else will happen,
but not that."

25 "She will," said Lilly, "once man disengages himself from the
love-mode, and stands clear. Once he stands clear, and the other
great urge begins to flow in him, then the woman won't be able to
resist. Her own soul will wish to yield itself."

"Woman yield—?" Aaron re-echoed.

30 "Woman—and man too. Yield to the deep power-soul in the
individual man, and obey implicitly. I don't go back on what I said
before. I do believe that every man must fulfil his own soul, every
woman must be herself, herself only, not some man's instrument, or
some embodied theory.—But the mode of our being is such that we
35 can only live and have our being whilst we are implicit in one of the
great dynamic modes. We *must* either love, or rule. And once the
love-mode changes, as change it must, for we are worn out and
becoming evil in its persistence, then the other mode will take place
in us. And there will be profound, profound obedience in place of
40 this love-crying, obedience to the incalculable power-urge. And men

must submit to the greater soul in a man, for their guidance: and women must submit to the positive power-soul in man, for their being."

"You'll never get it," said Aaron.

"You will, when all men want it. All men say, they want a leader. Then let them in their souls *submit* to some greater soul than theirs. At present, when they say they want a leader, they mean they want an instrument, like Lloyd George. A mere instrument for their use.—But it's more than that. It's the reverse. It's the deep, fathomless submission to the heroic soul in a greater man. You, Aaron, you too have the need to submit. You, too, have the need livingly to yield to a more heroic soul, to give yourself. You know you have. And you know it isn't love. It is life-submission. And you know it. But you kick against the pricks. And perhaps you'd rather die than yield. And so, die you must. It is your affair."

There was a long pause. Then Aaron looked up into Lilly's face. It was dark and remote-seeming. It was like a Byzantine eikon at the moment.

"And whom shall I submit to?" he said.

"Your soul will tell you," replied the other.

APPENDIX I

Cancelled extracts – *Aaron's Rod* typescript

Note on the texts

The two short extracts printed here (182:36–186:34 and 237:7–274:5) are cancelled passages from TS (pp. 292–9, 445–8) of *Aaron's Rod*. There is no Textual apparatus, but one editorial emendation has been made in square brackets in the second extract.

I

As he lay thinking of nothing and feeling nothing except a certain weariness, or dreariness, or God-knows-what, he heard a noise of many people and many voices in the street below. Rising, he went on to his little balcony. Came up from below the most frightening of all noises: the hoarse chaffered resonance of a mob in uneasy cry. It was men—all men—mostly youths—rather shabby but not particularly poor, wearing the inevitable black hat of the working people. They were all talking, and haranguing with one another, and making fierce demonstrative gestures at one another, and moving forward in that curious ebbing, revolving, reluctant, motion of an Italian crowd. Dark, they filled the street below with their ebbing, rotatory flood: and the upturned faces seemed pale, and the hands in gesticulation seemed to fly like sparks. They had no flag or badge: were evidently workmen of some sort: and the mob consisted of little gangs or clotted groups, which clotted groups, pressed more together, formed a serious crowd. But still it had no fixed purpose, but seemed to drift desultorily forward, talking and haranguing. Aaron saw a shopman in a white coat hastily fixing up his last shutter, a little ahead: then dart indoors like a white rabbit. And the crash of his down-sliding iron door-front, as he pulled it safe to earth, resounded above the curious swelling, tearing noise of the crowd.

Suddenly, however, some one caught sight of the Italian tricolor hanging directly opposite Aaron's hotel, and a shout was lifted. Many voices shouting many things, suddenly swelled in a wave of sound, like a great puff of smoky flame, up past Aaron's face, from the street below. Many faces were lifted pale from the darkness of the mob; many upturned faces, and mouths opening strangely in shouts, away below there. And still there seemed no one uniting emotion in it all. Still there seemed only a jolting, massive discord of voices, as group-voice smote against group-voice. They seemed to be exhorting one another—and exhorting themselves. They seemed to be urging a sort of growling, strangled passion into heat and flame. And the passion seemed to bubble and spurt irregularly.

The whole crowd had come to a stop immediately below the hotel, and all were now looking up at the green and white and red tricolor which stirred damply in the early evening light, from under the broad eaves of the house opposite. Aaron looked at the long flag, which drooped almost unmoved from the eaves-shadow, under the sky of light. Then he looked down at the packed black shoulders of the mob below, and at the curious clustering pattern of a sea of black hats. He could hardly see anything but hats and shoulders, uneasily moving like boiling pitch away beneath him. But the shouts came up hotter and hotter. The passion was beginning to fuse. It was a terrible noise, unspeakably depressing to the soul, the sound of this mass of men trying to work up a deep, slow, strangled anger to a pitch where it would take fire, and release itself into action. The shouts rose in pitch, and became more unanimous. The curious hot sound of the rising blood, and that most peculiar prolonged roaring resonance of a really angry mob now began to fill the street. Loud thuds and crashes as men beat and smashed at the great green door of the house. Stones rattled against the green shutters of the closed windows, and clanged against the iron wrought fencing of the little balconies. But the house heeded nothing, and the Italian flag hung heavily drooping. The pale stone house with its green shutters, and its balconies beneath each window—balconies with fine wrought-iron work on the first floor, with simpler iron-work on the second floor, and only a sort of grille for the top floor: this rather handsome, oldish stone house stood utterly unmoved, whilst the black sea at its foot urged and lashed itself towards a frenzy which still would not properly enkindle.

Suddenly there was a lull—then shouts, half-encouraging, half derisive. And Aaron saw a smallish-black figure of a youth, clinging like a monkey to the front of the house, and by the help of the heavy stone-work ornamentation climbing up the massive iron grille of the ground-floor windows, up like a black cat on to the projecting upper entablature above this window, clinging like a fly to the stone ornamentation and working himself up, gripping the balcony of the first-floor windows with his hands and swinging himself again like a black monkey upwards. He was on the balcony of the first floor windows. But he did not stay a moment—not a second. On he went, upwards, clambering up the wrought-iron scrolls, and flowers of the fencing, up on to the rail of the balcony, then again, in the same way catching hold of the shutters and inserting his fingers in the lattice and simply working himself upwards, cleaving to the housefront like a black fly, and never for one single instant hesitating or relaxing, but all the time, with strange, non-human quickness wriggling his way upwards to the windows of the second floor. How he did it no one knew, though they watched him with their own eyes.

At first the crowd had shouted, half-derisive, half-cheering. Then they had begun to get excited, as the lad wriggled himself so strangely, up the flat height. Then, as he reached the second floor, the feeling became intense. Voices, distinct, individual voices called to him, apparently giving directions. Sudden strange flashes of passionate exclamation broke out—

Bravo! Bravo!—and then what was probably the name: *Gino! O-Gi! Gi'i! Gino!* All the time, from below, these sudden flashes of passionate sound, above the deep murmur of the crowd, the deep, slow murmur that was like the swarming of bees, deep, pleased excitement. The shouts grew fewer after the climber had left the second storey and was working his way, a perilous small black figure cleaving like a black lizard or wall-newt to the house-front, working his way slowly and with great difficulty over the stone copings above the window, towards the balcony of the third floor. If he fell now he would be smashed to pieces. The crowd in the street had stood back from the walls of the house, so as to watch the progress upwards, and so, also, as to be out of the way if he *did* fall. There he was, working his way as it seemed cleaving against the almost overhanging housefront, high up, working, never still for a second, never for a hairs' breadth of a second relaxing his grip and his tension of progress. He seemed as if mesmerised—in some trance cleaving his way across the high and beetling house-front.

Till he grasped the topmost balcony. Then a ragged shout of pent-up anxiety and delight burst from the crowd. A wild and ragged shout of mixed feelings. But Aaron could understand no word, except *Bravo! Bravo!* and the reiterated *Gino!* The climber climbed on unheeding, as if he really were some black lizard, oblivious of human sounds. He scrambled on to the balcony and up the rail and up the shutters, till he grasped the flag-pole itself, which was fitted into a socket under the broad eaves. There he busily undid the ropes. And then, instead of hauling down the flag, he swarmed along the flag-pole, caught hold of the eaving of the roof, and swung himself up on to the roof's edge. There he knelt for a moment, drawing in the flag-rope from underneath, and the flag with it. And then he stood up, with the tricolor bunched up in one hand, and waved it raggedly at the crowd below.

Then a roar of delighted excitement went up, a roar, and strange wild whistlings, ear-piercing whistlings and shrillings and great, wide-throated howlings of excitement. It was excitement rather than enthusiasm. Meanwhile Gino suddenly threw down the flag. He threw it well clear, so that it dropped uneasily through the middle air, not far from Aaron's face. He never forgot the red-white-and-green dropping in mid-space before his eyes. And then the uplifting of innumerable pale, metal-gold hands, snatching, cruel: the clutched intensity of the black central knot of men, as the flag dropped plunging: the hands, the wrists, like a myriad-headed snake suddenly striking: and the gaudy red-white-and-green flashing for one moment among the hands and wrists, above the black hats, and then coming asunder, like sparks, and then disappearing altogether in the blackness. The crowd surged and swayed as black water when some great weight has fallen into it: and the roar was of strange anger: strange, strange, unaccountable cold rage.

And now the black figure on the roof-edge crouched and began the terrible descent, clinging and swarming down the now bare flag-pole, slithering down with a little smack on to the first balcony. The crowd below heaved, surged, roared, shouted *Bravo!*, worked with many passions. Some heeded, some did not heed the descent of the black climber, as he clutched his most perilous way downwards. Madness was in the street, madness in the air: the madness of an unresolved passion, an unresolved desire. What was it, what was it the crowd wanted? Why, why had the youth scaled the housefront? Neither he nor anyone else really knew. It was a kind of frenzy of baffled passion. But what passion? What passion? Neither he nor anyone knew. He scrambled his way anxiously over the topmost balcony-rail, as if he wanted now to be down.

And suddenly went a new shout through the mob: a new cry: a sharp new cry, part anger, part warning, part fear. There was a sudden veering movement away from the house. And just as suddenly, as if it had happened by magic, Aaron saw a posse of carabineers in the grey-green Italian uniform in the street, quite near. A yell went up, defiant, rage, fear. A great yell, and the air seemed dark. And at the same moment, sudden shots, as the carabineers rushed. And as if shot, the climber fell from the house-front. Aaron saw him fall. And yet, when he looked down, there was nothing to be seen in the street but the last vanishing specks of the black crowd. And the street was empty—empty, save for the posse of nervously-advancing carabineers in grey-green uniform. The black mob gone—melted like a dream. Gone—carrying the fallen climber with them. And the carabineers, far from rushing in pursuit, looking round cautiously and holding revolvers ready.

Gone!—the street empty! And the sergeant of the carabineers mustering his men, with their revolvers, to march them away. They marched away tentatively—and the street was quite empty—quite empty. It had gone like a dream. All had passed like a dream. Even the prosaic grey-green carabineers.

II

He forgot, perhaps, that this was how he had treated her. His famous desire for her, what had it been but this same impertinent appropriation of her female physical being to his own uses and ends. Or perhaps he did not quite forget. But to act in a certain mode, and to be the object of another's action in this self-same mode, those are two quite different things. Aaron was almost staggered at the way she used him, appropriated him, physically. Not in the passion-moments, but afterwards. As now, when she used him to curl herself up against, and to touch, and again to nestle deeper into! He didn't want it, not at all. She just appropriated him. Perhaps earlier he had appropriated her in a different, but equally, preposterous fashion.

However it may be, a certain deep dislike of her now began to creep into him. Nothing is more offensive to any wholesome individual, man or woman, than to feel that he or she is appropriated and made to serve the other person's gratification, or convenience. No wholesome person can bear to [be] made use of. And if it be a case of: "I'll let you make use of me, if you'll let me make use of you," this, indeed, is a bargain, but it is a bargain one always regrets, whilst one remains oneself, and whole. A bargain one not only regrets, but resents and deeply begrudges.

So with our friend Aaron. He dimly realised that it was a bargain, and that now he was paying his share of it, when this woman nestled to him and felt him. And he knew he was resenting his share. But he paid up, as he must, holding her close and still, as she wished. But he knew it was the last time. He disliked her for the bargain he had made with her. He had begun it. Yet none the less, he disliked her for the bargain he had made with her. Though she had in no way cheated him. Perhaps she had been more generous than he. But this was the last time. This time he was decided. At the bottom of his soul he disliked her. Or if not her, then her whole motive. Her whole life-mode. Perhaps his own too.

APPENDIX II

Maps of Eastwood and Florence (*c.* 1918)

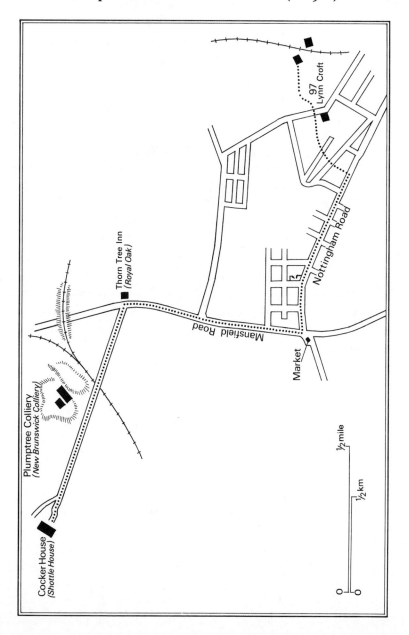

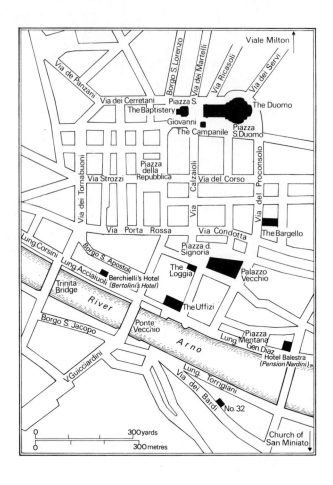

EXPLANATORY NOTES

EXPLANATORY NOTES

5:2   **The Blue Ball** All chap. titles in TS were added in ink in DHL's hand. On several occasions, however, more than one title occurred to him – see notes on 39:2, 56:2, 65:4, etc.

5:8   **It was Christmas ... evening.** The opening scenes of the novel are probably drawn from DHL's visit to the Midlands during Christmas 1918 when there was the threat of a general strike. 1919 brought nationwide strikes in the police force and railways but the miners did not strike until 1920 and 1921.

5:9   **Aaron Sisson**   The character is partly drawn from the miners' check-weighman (see note on 36:17), Thomas Cooper, who was a flautist and lived next door to the Lawrences when they moved in 1902 to 97 Lynn Croft Road in East-wood. (An actual 'Aaron Sisson', killed in action on 30 July 1915, is buried in Eastwood cemetery).

In the Old Testament Moses's brother was Aaron whose rod 'budded, and brought forth buds, and bloomed blossoms, and yielded almonds' (Numbers xvii. 8). As Moses's brother, Aaron was his chief helper in leading the Israelites out of Egypt, and in sustaining them during their forty years wandering in the desert, prior to entering the promised land. The flowering rod signifies that as head of the Levites, the priestly caste, he is favoured by God and confirmed as a spiritual leader. DHL may have seen the Biblical story as a parallel to the state of England in his time; that is, a nation wandering in the wilderness, seeking for spiritual leadership. The novel suggests that it is in artists, like Aaron and Lilly, that spiritual power is found. As a keen botanist DHL would also have been aware that the yellow mullein (*Verbascum thapsus*), commonly called 'Aaron's Rod', was reputed to have strong healing properties and to ward off evil. Possibly DHL recalled that Hermes gave mullein to Ulysses to keep off the magic of Circe, significant given the encounter between Aaron and the Marchesa in the novel. (See *Letters*, iv. 175). The title may also have a phallic significance.

5:12   **Miners Union** In 1914 every coalfield had its own District Union, part of the Miners Federation of Great Britain. After the war, however, disputes arose between those who believed power should remain with the district association and those who favoured a strong central Federation to negotiate with the Conservative Government for wage rises and reduction in working hours. See notes on 7:36 and 56:27.

7:36   **throw-in ... butties** 'Butty' is a coal-mining term denoting a stall man or contractor who has a few men under him in the mine. DHL's father was a butty: 'All the earnings of each stall were put down to the chief butty, as contractor, and he divided the wages again, either in the public-house or in his own home', *Sons and Lovers* (1913), chap. IV (see also chap. VIII). In 1919 the increasingly powerful left-wing of the Nottingham Miners Association proposed to abolish the inequalities of the 'butty' system. Understandably this plan was opposed by the more prosperous butties (hence 'the butties won't have it') but won popular support from the miners as a whole, and the 'all-throw-in' system was established, i.e. all adults engaged on a coal-face (or stall) shared equally in the contract earnings.

11:28 **"While ... watched—"** 'While shepherds watched their flocks by night', traditional Christmas carol.

12:3 **American oil-cloth** Canvas backing enamelled with oil to make it waterproof, used as a tablecloth in poor and working-class households.

17:2 **Royal Oak** There was a 'Royal Oak' public house in Watnall, near Eastwood, but the location specified here makes it certain that DHL is recreating the 'Thorn Tree' (no longer in existence) in Nether Green. See note on 19:17.

18:37 **Sherardy, the Hindu.** DHL knew two Indian doctors – Dr Russell (a Parsee Eastwood doctor) and Dr Dhuryabhai Mullan-Feroze (1874–1959), with whom he went to a party during the Christmas holidays of 1918. Dr Feroze also attended DHL in February 1919 when he was seriously ill with flu. See *Letters*, iii. 312–13.

19:17 **Mrs. Houseley.** Possibly based on the beer retailer of the 'Thorn Tree', Ellen Wharton. See references to 'a pint at Ellen's' and 'Ellen's' in *Sons and Lovers* (1913), chaps. I and II. 'Housley' is a local name, common in Newthorpe (s. of Eastwood); there were several Housleys associated with public houses and the beer trade at this time.

19:40 **Me an' a',"** 'Me and all', i.e. 'me too' (dialect).

21:36 **stunts** Stumps, tails (dialect).

23:33 **India ... national rule,** The British government had committed itself in principle to a gradual advancement to self-government in India as early as 1917, though it was not until 1935 that growing nationalist pressure forced a large measure of representative government.

25:39 **Shottle Lane ... Colliery.** DHL's recreation of Cockerhouse Road ... The colliery is probably Plumptree colliery, about 500 yards along on the right, walking towards Cocker House. The colliery itself was disused by 1916 but the pit-bank (26:22) could still have been smouldering in 1918.

26:2 **The Lighted Tree** Perhaps suggested by an incident in 1917 (recorded in Asquith 341–2) when a practical joke was played on a house-party.

26:15 **Shottle House, where the Bricknells lived;** Cocker House, the home of the Brentnalls at the end of Cockerhouse Road, no longer exists. Alfred W. Brentnall (1834–1924) was Estate Agent and Cashier to Barber Walker & Co., the leading mining company in Eastwood.

26:30 **Jim,** Based on Capt. J. R. White (1879–1946), a member of the Gordon Highlanders, who fought in the Boer War and was active in Irish political life, having helped to organise a strike in Dublin in 1913. Like White, 'Jim' was for a time not permitted to live in Ireland (see 76:12). White met DHL in London in

1917 and visited the Lawrences at Chapel Farm Cottage, Hermitage, Berkshire, early in 1918.

26:31 **Julia…Robert Cunningham,** 'Julia' is drawn from Hilda Doolittle (1886–1961), American poet and writer, at this time married to Richard Aldington (1892–1962), poet, novelist and biographer who had met DHL in 1914 and became a close friend. Hilda lent the Lawrences her room at 44 Mecklenburgh Square, London, following their expulsion from Cornwall in October 1917. That same autumn Aldington started his liaison with Dorothy Yorke (see note on 'Josephine Ford' below), whom he later married. H. D. began an affair with Cecil Gray ('Cyril Scott', see note below). See *Bid Me to Live* by 'H. D.' (New York, 1960), where H. D. also calls herself 'Julia'.

27:2 **pieces of futurism, Omega cushions** Futurism in art (which rejected the past and glorified youth and the future) was a movement that preceded cubism, dadaism and surrealism. See *Letters*, ii. 180–4. The 'Omega workshops', founded by Roger Fry in 1913 and active in London until 1919, were concerned with interior decoration and design. They aimed to popularise the new sensibility of modern art by making decorative articles for everyday use. Duncan Grant (1885–1978), the painter, who had met DHL during the war, was closely associated with the workshops.

27:24 **Josephine Ford,** Dorothy ('Arabella') Yorke (b. 1892), an American friend who knew the Lawrences during the war, in Mecklenburgh Square (see *Letters*, iii. 173 n. 3). Originally parts of TS read 'Hay' for 'Ford' but these were revised by DHL with this exception and the one at 45:3.

28:2 **Cyril Scott,** Modelled on Cecil Gray (1895–1951), composer and music critic, a neighbour of the Lawrences in Cornwall in 1917 (see *Letters*, iii. 128 n. 1). DHL also knew of (and possibly had met) an actual Cyril Scott, musician and composer, through Lady Cynthia Asquith (1887–1960); see Asquith 354–7.

30:23 *poupée* Doll, puppet (French).

32:37 *pas seul* A dance (or figure) for one performer (French).

33:35 **floor,** In TS (p. 44) 'floor' has been crossed out in pencil on three occasions and 'ground' substituted. Both A1 and E1 print 'ground' here, since the character is out of doors when he falls, but DHL often used 'floor' in this context. There are similar usages on 34:19 and 87:14 (TS pp. 45, 121) below and in other novels.

36:8 **Beldover?"** DHL's version of his home town Eastwood, near Nottingham. Cf. *The Rainbow* (1915), chap. xiv; *Women in Love* (1920), chaps. i and ix.

36:15 *de haut en bas.* Scornfully, superciliously (French).

36:17 **checkweighman,"** 'The representative of the men, who checks the weight of coals at the surface, on behalf of the workers at a colliery', Joseph Wright, *The English Dialect Dictionary*, 6 vols. (1896–1905).

39:2 **The Pillar of Salt** Lot's wife was turned to a pillar of salt when she looked back in the flight from Sodom and Gomorrah, the cities doomed to destruction by God (Genesis xix. 26). Earlier titles for this chapter, crossed out by DHL, were:

'The House-Breaker' and 'The Home Touch'. Cf. *Fantasia of the Unconscious* (1922), chap. XV: 'You've got to know that you're a man, and being a man means you go on alone, ahead of the woman, to break a way through the old world into the new ... And if you don't know which direction to take, look round for the man your heart will point out to you. And follow—and never look back. Because if Lot's wife, looking back, was turned to a pillar of salt, these miserable men, for ever looking back to their women for guidance, they are miserable pillars of half-rotten tears.' See also *Letters*, i. 98.

43:17 **takes his hook.** Is off on his own business. Cf. 98:11 and note.

45:3 **a box at the opera** Lady Cynthia, a close friend of the Lawrences, had been given a box at the opera for the 1917 season. The Lawrences went several times as her guests. See Asquith 335 and Brigit Patmore, 'Conversations with D. H. Lawrence', *London Magazine*, iv (June 1957), 35–6.

45:10 **Lilly and Struthers ... painter.** Rawdon Lilly is drawn from DHL himself (his wife, Tanny, from Frieda); Struthers is modelled on the painter Augustus John (1878–1961) whose studio DHL visited on 1 November 1917 with Lady Cynthia (see Asquith 361).

46:2 **Verdi—*Aida*.** DHL and Augustus John attended a performance of Verdi's tragic opera *Aida* (1871) on 13 November 1917 as guests of Lady Cynthia. See Asquith 361, 369; Cynthia Asquith, *Remember and Be Glad* (1952), p. 142; Augustus John, *Chiaroscuro* (1952), p. 85.

46:37 ***Merde!*** Shit! (French).

48:18 **scalp** TS (p. 67) reads 'scrap' and this was followed by A1. Since E1 printed 'scalp', which makes better sense in the context, it is probable that DHL corrected what is almost certainly a typist's error in the typescript which was setting-copy for E1.

52:32 ***À la bonne heure!***" 'Well and good!' (French).

56:2 **Talk** An earlier, deleted title for this chapter was 'After the Theatre' (TS p. 78).

56:15 **the bowler hat?** In wearing this hat, normally worn during the day, particularly in business hours, Aaron has committed a social solecism. He should have worn a top-hat.

56:26 **Adelphi ... *fons et origo*** A fashionable area in central London originally planned by Robert Adam (see note on 56:31) in 1768. DHL went to a party there on the evening of the Armistice and held forth long and bitterly about the war and its aftermath; see Harry T. Moore, *The Priest of Love*, rev. ed. (New York, 1974), p. 295; Asquith 376; Nehls, i. 479... The Latin phrase means the spring and source of.

56:27 **Labour and Robert Smillie, and Bolshevism.** Jim is referring to the complicated negotiations carried out between the Government and the Miners Federation of Great Britain under the leadership of Robert Smillie (1857–1940) – President of the Federation from 1912 to 1921 and an outspoken left-wing trade unionist – which included a formal demand by the Federation in January 1919 for a

30% wage rise a six-hour working day, the payment of demobilised miners at full union rates and the nationalisation of the coal industry. Other issues included demands for the withdrawal of British troops from Ireland and Russia. See A. R. Griffin, *The Miners of Nottinghamshire: 1914–1944* (1962), pp. 38–65; see also *Letters*, iii. 284–5.

56:31 **Adams rooms ... Heal's** Robert Adam (1728–92), eminent Scottish architect, town planner and interior designer, particularly famous for his planning of elegant town houses, which he often supervised down to the last detail of furnishing ... a fashionable furniture store in London specialising in modern crafts and design.

57:20 **Mrs. Browning** Modelled on Brigit Patmore (1882–1965), the writer, who met DHL through Ford Madox (Hueffer) Ford before 1914 and was part of the Lawrence–Aldington circle in 1917.

58:1 **fools make, rushing in,"** *An Essay on Criticism* (1711) by Alexander Pope (1688–1744), l. 625 ['For *Fools* rush in where *Angels* fear to tread'].

58:21 **sing Tosti's 'Farewell'** Francesco Paolo Tosti (1846–1916), Italian composer and singing master to the royal family, settled in London and wrote popular drawing-room songs of which 'Good-bye' was the best known.

59:25 **Bloomsbury.** Residential and academic district of London with a reputation as an artistic and intellectual centre.

60:24 **What price** What do you think of (slang).

61:15 **Amersham."** A town in Buckinghamshire, 26 miles on a main rail line from London.

62:16 **Mock Turtle—"** See chaps. IX and X of *Alice's Adventures in Wonderland* (1865) by Lewis Carroll (1832–98).

65:4 **The Dark Square Garden ... Soho,** Bloomsbury Square, near the British Museum, one of the first squares to be laid out in London in 1665. An earlier, deleted title for this chapter read 'Love Episode' (TS p. 91) ... a district in central London, well known for its bohemian life, restaurants and continental food shops.

73:2 **A Punch in the Wind** Events in this chapter closely follow White's visit to the Lawrences early in 1918. See Moore, *The Priest of Love*, pp. 285–6 and Richard Aldington, *Portrait of a Genius, But...* (1950), p. 224.

73:3 **cottage in Hampshire** The Lawrences lived in Chapel Farm Cottage, Hermitage (near Newbury), Berkshire 18 December 1917–2 May 1918, 22 October–19? November 1918, and occasionally during 1919 until Frieda's departure for Italy in October and DHL's in November of that year.

73:5 **a fine blonde.** In TS (p. 101) 'a fine blonde' has been crossed out and the phrase 'strong and fair' substituted in pencil in a hand that is not DHL's but may be Frieda's. A1 incorporated the pencilled substitution; E1 retained the original phrase.

75:23 **Russo-Japanese war,** February 1904–August 1905 from which Japan emerged victorious.

76:1   **a Japanese lover** Cf. the episode in *Mr Noon*, ed. Lindeth Vasey (Cambridge, 1984), pp. 119–20, where Johanna (who is modelled on Frieda Lawrence) encounters a Japanese man.

77:39   *manqué.*" Imperfect (French).

81:18   **locomotor ataxia:** A disorder of the nervous system (caused by syphilis) which results in difficulty in co-ordinating voluntary movements such as walking.

86:2   **Low-water Mark** Aaron's illness and the massage Lilly gives him may be based on events in the second half of February 1915 when John Middleton Murry (1889–1957), then a friend of DHL's, collapsed with a severe case of flu and was nursed by DHL at Greatham, Sussex. See Murry's *Between Two Worlds* (1935), p. 331. An earlier, crossed-out title for this chapter was 'Covent Garden' (TS p. 120).

86:14   **coster's barrow.** Originally a coster was an apple-seller and fruiterer who usually sold his fruit on the street. Now, in London, a man who sells fruit, vegetables, fish etc. from a barrow.

87:12   **setts** Squared stones, generally granite, used for paving.

90:23   **Bovril?**" Brand name for concentrated beef essence which, mixed with hot water, makes a nourishing drink.

94:7   **a calomel pill.** Mercurous chloride, a purgative.

96:38   **Lloyd George and Northcliffe** David Lloyd George (1863–1945), Prime Minister December 1916–October 1922. Viscount Northcliffe (1865–1922), the leading newspaper journalist and proprietor, at first supported Lloyd George's Coalition Government but later denounced him. For DHL's hostility to Lloyd George see *Letters*, iii. 48 and 118.

96:40   **pro bono publico ... bonum publicum** For the good of the public ... the public good (Latin).

97:9   **kick against the pricks.** To protest against the inevitable. See Acts ix. 5 and xxvi. 14.

97:16   **A lot of little Stavrogins ... ear.**" Stavrogin, the enigmatic protagonist in Dostoevsky's novel *The Possessed* (1871), unaccountably and outrageously bites the ear of a local dignitary at a party. For DHL's view of the novel and the incident, see *Letters*, ii. 537 and 542–3.

98:8   **break my bread** To share food; a common allusion in the Scriptures (Acts ii. 42, 46) and specifically to the Last Supper.

98:11   **to take their hook into death.** To die, i.e. take one's hook or staff and depart this life.

104:33   **fridge** Chafe, rub (dialect).

107:22   **What by that?**" 'What of it?' or 'So what?' (dialect).

108:2   **Pelléas.** *Pelléas and Mélisande*, opera (first produced in 1902) by Claude Debussy (1862–1918).

110:8　**the fantasies of a certain Leo Frobenius**, DHL read *The Voice of Africa* (1913; English trans. 1918) by the German explorer and anthropologist Leo Frobenius (1873–1938), in April 1918. Frobenius attributed a common origin to the cultures of Oceania and West Africa, an idea which appealed to DHL. Cf. 'Foreword' to *Fantasia of the Unconscious* and *Letters*, iii. 233.

110:32　**Kabyles.** Berbers of Algeria or Tunisia.

110:37　**jealous God**. Exodus xx. 5.

112:20　**the Guards**, An elite army division, whose officers are socially superior, attached to the person of the Sovereign.

112:24　*Rosemary*," A popular comedy (1896) by L. N. Parker (1852–1914) and M. Carson.

113:5　**one day** On several occasions in TS DHL corrected or deleted words which E1 printed as they stood in Secker's copy of the typescript. Here (p. 162) he corrected 'the other' (which E1 printed) to 'one day'. Similarly in 106:10 above 'Poor' has been deleted in TS (p. 150) but appears in E1, and in 113:2 'hell' (p. 162) appears as the uncorrected 'hill' in E1 (see Textual apparatus).

113:15　**Battenbergs ... Guelphs ... Battenberg** The Battenberg family rose to international prominence in the nineteenth and twentieth centuries (the Royal House of Great Britain combines the Houses of Guelph, Wettin and Windsor) and in Britain changed its name to Mountbatten in 1917. Herbertson is specifically referring to Prince Louis Alexander Battenberg (1854–1921), created Marquess of Milford Haven in 1917. See also Asquith 52.

121:27　**to obey ... he did.** There is a discrepancy between A1 and E1 here. TS (p. 177) originally ended with the typed line 'Aaron did not find his friend at home when he called', to which is added, in DHL's hand, the text as it appears here and in A1. But E1 reads slightly differently and also adds two sentences between 'to obey' and 'If in', and another sentence between 'quits' and 'He was'. Presumably when he was correcting the E1 typescript at the same point DHL made slightly different alterations. See entries in Textual apparatus for 121:24, 25, 27.

123:19　**familiar old** Both A1 and E1 incorrectly printed 'odd' here because the TS typist (p. 180) superimposed 'l' on 'd' to correct 'odd' to 'old'.

129:2　**Novara** A town and commune in northwest Italy, w. of Milan. DHL substituted 'Novara' for 'Turin' when revising TS (pp. 192ff.) where he stayed for two nights on his journey through Italy in November 1919. See note on 130:39.

129:7　**Lady Artemis Hooper ... taxi-cab.** DHL's recreation of Lady Diana Cooper (1892–1986), a friend of Lady Cynthia, and of a similar accident that happened to her. See Asquith 52.

130:39　**Sir William Franks'**. DHL's recreation of Sir Walter Becker (1855–1927) at whose villa near Turin DHL stayed 15–17 November 1919 on his way to Florence. See *Letters*, iii. 417; cf. Nehls, ii. 12–13 where Norman Douglas quotes a letter from Sir Walter recalling his impression of DHL's visit. See also note on 138:37.

131:29 **Torinese.** Turinese, the dialect of Turin in northern Italy. DHL seems to have forgotten that he has changed the setting to Novara.

131:37 **park wall** In TS (p. 194) 'pink' has been crossed out and 'park' substituted in a hand that is not DHL's but presumably that of its original typist, or of Seltzer, or of his American typist.

134:17 *The Graphic ... Country Life,* A weekly illustrated newspaper founded in 1869 ... an illustrated periodical founded in 1897; both directed at the country gentry and read by those a little lower in the social scale who aspire to the latter.

134:33 **Greuze** Jean-Baptiste Greuze (1725–1805), French painter of rustic genre scenes and portraits.

134:39 **the Somme** Perhaps the most bitterly fought battle of World War I in France, July–November 1916, in which the Allies lost 600,000 men (two-thirds of them British) and the German army 615,000.

135:1 *Connu!* *Connu!* Known! Known! (French). Cf. *Sea and Sardinia* (1921), chap. VI.

136:17 **Beecham's operas ...** *Ivan.* Sir Thomas Beecham (1879–1961), conductor, composer and operatic impresario, conducted several operas (including *Ivan the Terrible* and *Boris Godounov*, see note on 136:32) during the 1917 season when DHL went as Lady Cynthia's guest. See note on 45:3 ... *Ivan the Terrible*, opera by the Russian composer Rimsky-Korsakov (1844–1908), first produced in St Petersburg in 1873 and in London in 1913.

136:27 **where the wretched Austrians are.** Austria was treated as a defeated enemy at the close of World War I; she was forced to give independence to or to cede large tracts of her pre-war territories to other nations and to pay heavy reparation to the Allies.

136:32 **Moussorgsky ...** *Boris* ... *Kovantchina,"* Mussorgsky (1839–1881), Russian composer of the operas *Boris Godounov* (1869) and *Khovantshchina* (1886). The former enjoyed great popularity in London and was performed each year 1916–19; the latter was produced at Covent Garden in November 1919.

137:2 *cachet* Capsule (French).

138:37 **There were three orders ... State of Ruritania,** Sir Walter Becker, a wealthy ship-owner, founded and maintained a hospital in Turin for the British Expeditionary Force in Italy and was knighted in 1918. His decorations included the KBE (Knight Commander of the Order of the British Empire) and that of Knight Commander of the Crown of Siam (where he had been Consul-General). 'The State of Ruritania' refers to the imaginary kingdom created by Anthony Hope (1863–1933) in *The Prisoner of Zenda* (1894).

142:16 **casting his ... the waters.** Cf. Ecclesiastes xi. 1.

148:28 **"Gli Alpi—si signore."** 'The Alps—yes sir.' (Italian).

148:31 **end of September,** DHL's chronology is confused; cf. 210:28 only a few days later, when it is November.

150:2   **Wie es Ihnen Gefällt** As you like (German).

151:28   *The Queen.* Illustrated British weekly periodical founded in 1861, directed at the middle and upper classes.

152:35   **the cock-feathers of the Bersaglieri.** A crack corps in the Italian army who wear a cock's long green tail-feathers in their hats.

156:24   **'Signora! Signora ... Vengono qui!'** 'Madam! Madam! Get up! Immediately! Madam! They are coming!'— and I said, 'Who? Who are they, who are coming? Who?'—'The Novaresi! The Novaresi are coming. Coming here!' (Italian).

160:17   **veil ... earth** At the moment of Christ's death the heavens darkened, the earth quaked and the curtain of the Temple of Jerusalem was rent: 'And behold, the veil of the temple was rent in twain from the top to the bottom', Matthew xxvii. 51. Thus, a veil which hides religious mysteries.

161:22   **iron tablet** With irresistible authority (cf. God's giving Moses the Ten Commandments engraved on tablets of stone, Exodus xxiv. 12, xxxi. 18).

163:32   **Wells'** *Invisible Man.* Novel (1897) by H. G. Wells (1866–1946).

163:39   **Mrs. Mackenzie's Dead.** A typical family fire-side game, popular from *c.*1890 in which each player must repeat what has been said and done by the first player, thus: the player at one end says 'Mrs Mackenzie's Dead'; the next in line asks 'How did she die?'; the head of the line replies, 'With one finger up, just like I' and performs the action. Question and answer move around the semi-circle till all have one finger up. The questions start again, but the second answer (e.g. 'with one eye shut') must be added to the previous action, so that each player in turn shuts an eye while still holding up a finger, and so on.

166:22   **The lily toils and spins hard enough,** 'Consider the lilies of the field, how they grow; they toil not, neither do they spin', Matthew vi. 28.

166:40   **Whitman's "Dalliance of Eagles."** 'The Dalliance of Eagles' (1880) by Walt Whitman about whom DHL was writing between June 1918 and 1922. See chap. XII in *Studies in Classic American Literature* (1923) and an early version of this essay in *The Symbolic Meaning*, ed. Armin Arnold (Arundel, 1961).

167:22   **risky ... risky?** TS (p. 256) originally read 'immoral'; the first occurrence was crossed out by DHL to read 'dangerous' and then all three entries were altered again to 'risky'.

169:39   **bonne bouche ... Fortuna gentilissima!** A nice mouthful, a tid-bit (French) ... Fortune most kind! (Italian).

170:30   **ruddier than the cherry.** From Polyphemus' aria in *Acis and Galatea* (1721) by Handel (1685–1759), perhaps suggested by the Major's 'crucified cyclop' single eye (170:14).

170:34   **taking no thought for the morrow.** Matthew vi. 34 ['Take therefore no thought for the morrow; for the morrow shall take thought for the things of itself. Sufficient unto the day is the evil thereof', AV].

171:20　**The child was always father to the man,** Cf. 'The Child is father of the Man' in Wordsworth's 'My heart leaps up' (1807).

172:37　**united-we-stand.** 'By uniting we stand, by dividing we fall', 'Liberty Song' (1768) by John Dickinson (1732–1808). 'United we stand, divided we fall' became a watchword of the American Revolution.

173:38　*coeur à coeur.* Heart to heart (French).

175:1　**Queen Victoria … Victorian Majesty,** Sir Max Beerbohm (1872–1956), caricaturist and belletrist, whose drawings first appeared in the *Strand Magazine* for 1892. See *The Poet's Corner* (1904) for the drawing DHL mentions.

175:9　**His eye … watches me.** A popular hymn by C. H. Gabriel ['… And I know He watches me'].

175:33　**as if at a Café Chantant,** A cafe provided with a stage for singing and other entertainment (French).

175:36　*vivace Schumann* Lively, vivaciously (Italian). Robert Schumann (1810–56) was a prolific composer for the piano and for voice.

176:33　**"Ye Banks and Braes," and *Caro mio ben,*** The famous song (1792) by Robert Burns (1759–96), and a popular song by the Italian composer Giuseppe Giordani (*c.*1753–98).

178:2　**XX Settembre** A date significant in the unification of Italy. On 20 September 1870 'Victor Emmanuel's Bersaglieri entered Rome … And so Italy was made—modern Italy', *Movements* 291.

180:28　**the white cross of Savoy** The arms of the House of Savoy which united Italy under the banner of Vittorio Emanuele, King of Piedmont and subsequently King of Italy (1860). See *Movements* chap. XXVIII on the unification of Italy.

181:7　**the *Corriere,*** The Milan newspaper *Corriere della sera* or 'The Evening Chronicle' was admired by DHL. 'I recall much praise of the Italian newspaper at the expense of the English ones. How much better than *The Times* was the *Corriere della Sera!*' (Carswell 152). See also *Letters,* ii. 135 and *Sea and Sardinia,* chap. VIII.

182:34　**reckitt's blue** Deep blue, from the old-fashioned laundry product manufactured by Reckitt's Co. in block form (used to make laundry appear whiter).

185:23　**carabinieri** Italian army corps which is also a police force.

186:23　**a prisoner between them.** There is a slight inconsistency in sense here stemming from the very extensive revision in TS of the pages describing the riot. In the unrevised version the young man falls from the second floor – hence Angus' subsequent comment 'Did you see him fall!' (187:12) – whereas in the revised version he climbs down unhurt and is marched off by the carabinieri. For the unrevised version of this scene see Appendix I.

186:34　**The scene was ended.** DHL witnessed more than one such scene in Florence. See Carswell 153; *Movements* 316.

186:36　**two young men:** Possibly suggested by Jan Juta (b. 1897), the South African painter who illustrated *Sea and Sardinia* in 1921, and his friend the Welsh painter Alan Insole. Cf. the description of the two young men in *Sea and Sardinia*, chap. VIII, and *Letters*, iv. 158. Juta and Insole were guests of the Lawrences at Taormina late in January 1921.

187:39 **Siena** The typist typed this correctly but DHL later altered the entries adding an extra 'n', thus giving the French spelling 'Sienna' (TS pp. 266ff). The spelling in both English and Italian has only one 'n' and is used here.

189:14 **Scriabin.** Alexander Scriabin (1872–1915), Russian musician and composer who was in London in 1914 giving piano recitals.

189:17 **Lacrimae Cristi,** Literally 'tears of Christ'; a Neapolitan and Sicilian wine.

190:9 *Strega* A sweet liqueur, made at Benevento in Italy. 'Strega' means 'witch'.

190:17 *Frutta ... Natura Morta* The fruit ... Still life (Italian).

197:22 *le style, c'est l'homme.* 'Le style est l'homme même' ('The style is the man himself)', from Buffon (1707–88), *Discours Académiques*.

197:23 **Merthyr.** An industrial town (Merthyr Tydfil) and district in south Wales, once important for its production of coal, iron and steel.

198:22 *bella figura.* A fine figure (Italian).

200:35 **the mysterious revolution would be effected.** DHL is referring to the illusory and brief period of post-war prosperity which was rapidly followed by inflation and the virtual economic collapse of Italy, before the rise of Fascism in the 1920s.

202:9 *New Statesman* British weekly periodical founded in 1913. Some of DHL's early work was published there.

202:12 **Mais—cette place était *réservée*—**" 'But—this place was reserved—' (French).

202:31 **"Già! Già.** [202:26] ... **"C'è posto là,"** 'Right! Right!' ... 'They must travel in the first class—*first class!*' ... 'There is room there,' (Italian).

203:15 **Firenzuola** 'Little Florence', a town *c.* 25 km. n. of Florence through which the railway passes.

205:10 **"Buon' appetito,"** 'Good appetite', customarily said at meal times (Italian).

205:20 **Bertolini's hotel, on the Lungarno** [205:14] ... **Ponte Vecchio** DHL's recreation of Berchielli's Hotel on the banks of the Arno river in Florence ... 'The Old Bridge', lined with shops.

205:40 **Perhaps it was ... stairs ..."** From 'An Expostulation' by Isaac Bickerstaff (?1735–1812?) ['... right to dissemble your love, / But—why ... downstairs?'].

206:30 **the Uffizi ... San Miniato.** The chief public gallery of Italian paintings in Florence and one of the finest in Italy ... the church of San Miniato, completed in 1062 (façade in the 12th century), stands on a hill overlooking Florence and is typically Florentine with its decoration of many-coloured marble panels.

206:31 **group of statuary in the Piazza Mentana** A crude and melodramatic war memorial to Italian unification, commemorating the battle of Mentana in 1867 when Giuseppe Garibaldi (1807–82) was defeated by the French. See *Movements* 290–1.

206:34 **"Pension Nardini."** DHL's recreation of the Hotel Balestra, 5 Piazza Mentana, where Norman Douglas and Maurice Magnus also stayed. DHL had stayed there 19 November–9 December 1919 and again in April 1921. 'Nardini' was possibly suggested by the Hotel Nardini where Douglas later had rooms. See 'Introduction' to *Memoirs of the Foreign Legion* (1924), pp. 12–13, where DHL calls it the Cavelotti. See also *Letters*, iii. 423–4.

210:3 **Pergolesi ... Scarlatti ... Corelli.** Giovanni Pergolesi (1710–36) ... Domenico Scarlatti (1685–1757) ... Arcangelo Corelli (1653–1713), eminent Italian composers. Although Corelli's favoured instruments for his music were the violin and viol, Aaron could readily have found his music transposed for the flute.

211:18 **Palazzo Vecchio ... Piazza della Signoria.** 'The Old Palace', begun between 1298 and 1334. With the Piazza it formed the political centre of Florence (Savonarola, see note on 277:13, was executed here).

211:25 **Bandinelli.** Bartolomeo Bandinelli (1488–1559), Florentine sculptor; his marble colossi in the Piazza della Signoria were ridiculed by Benvenuto Cellini (1500–71) whose *Autobiography* (trans. J. A. Symonds, 1888) DHL had read in 1907. Cf. DHL's letter to Earl Brewster, 9 June 1927.

211:34 **the great naked David [211:23] ... Michelangelo** The marble statue of David (*c.*1504) has become a symbol of Florence and her art. DHL made it the central symbol in his essay 'David' (possibly written while he was working on *Aaron's Rod*), seeing it as 'the presiding genius of Florence' and an emblem of 'The pride of the fulfilled self' (*Phoenix* 61 and 64). The original statue was moved to the Galleria dell' Accademia in 1873 so DHL (and Aaron) would have seen the copy in the Piazza della Signoria.

212:9 **the distant equestrian statue;** A large bronze of Cosimo Medici by Giambologna (1529–1608), erected in 1594.

212:19 **the bronze Perseus ... Benvenuto Cellini's dark hero ... the Loggia!** Cellini, Florentine goldsmith, metal-worker and sculptor whose bronze Perseus (1545–54) is reckoned his masterpiece ... the roofed gallery of the Loggia dei Lanzi or della Signoria was constructed in the second half of the 14th century. It houses sculptures by Giambologna, Pio Fedi and various originals and copies of antique sculpture.

215:1 **James Argyle ... Algy Constable ... Louis Mee ... Walter Rosen.** By all accounts recreations of Norman Douglas's (1868–1952) circle in Florence in the autumn of 1919 and the spring of 1921 (see Introduction, p. xxii and n. 15). Douglas was clearly aware of DHL's penchant for describing his acquaintance in fiction: 'I am going to try to prevent his meeting certain other people, because he is a damned observant fellow and might be so amused at certain aspects of Florentine life as to use it for "copy" in some book: which would be annoying' (Weintraub 193). For Douglas's reaction to himself as Argyle, see Nehls, ii. 10–15 ... 'As Constable, Reggie [Turner, d.1938] is drawn to near-photographic realism' (Weintraub 195; see also 196–7)... Mee is drawn from Maurice Magnus (1876–1920), whose acquaintance with DHL is chronicled in 'Introduction' to *Memoirs of the Foreign Legion* ... Walter Rosen is drawn from Leo Stein (1872–1947), Gertrude Stein's brother: 'I have never met Gertrude Stein, but if you remember the deaf fellow in *Aaron's Rod*, that is her brother' (Letter to Koteliansky, 10 April 1926); see also Weintraub 285, n. 14.

215:29 **wise virgins ... bridegroom cometh—!** See the parable of the wise and foolish virgins, Matthew xxv. 1–13.

217:24 *mots.* Epigrammatic, witty sayings (French). See also Weintraub 189.

217:28 **Rich as Croesus,** Croesus, the last king of Lydia (*c.* 560–546 BC) whose rich and peaceful court attracted the wisest men of Greece; his name became proverbial for wealth.

218:37 **Avanti!"** Forward! (Italian).

219:9 **Siamo nel paradiso.** We are in paradise (Italian).

219:17 **Algy had ... flat was kept.** Reggie Turner's flat on the Viale Milton which DHL would have visited on one of his trips to Florence. See Weintraub 197.

219:30 **the Marchesa Del Torre,** The character of the Marchesa may have been suggested by the American wife of the Marchese Carlo Torrigiani, whose Sunday at-homes and dinners were famous in Florence. 'Ever since the First World War, Reggie had dined with the Marchesa and her guests every Sunday night he was in Florence' (Weintraub 230). Like the Marchesa in the novel, she 'had lived most of her life in Europe' and was 'one of Algy's [Reggie's] lionesses' (219:31–4).

220:1 **the Marchese ... cavalry,** Cf. 'a very well-known horsey Marchese in an Italian cavalry regiment,' *The Lost Girl*, ed. John Worthen (Cambridge, 1981), note on 132:22.

222:29 *comble* Height, summit (French).

224:33 **salotta.** Either 'salotto', a drawing-room or reception room, or 'saletta', the diminutive of 'sala' (as seems likely from the context here; see 226:34), a small lounge (Italian).

227:24 **To read ... nonsense.** Cf. 'The Nightingale' which DHL wrote a few years later in June 1926 (*Phoenix* 40–4).

229:8 **Bargello,** Dating from 1255, the building is now the National Museum and principally houses sculpture.

229:9 **He had been robbed.** In the autumn of 1919 DHL was indeed robbed of his wallet in Florence. See Catharine Carswell's account of his reaction to this (and to another robbery) in Carswell 118–19. Also cf. *Sea and Sardinia*, chap. VIII.

232:2 High Up over the Cathedral Square E1 prints an alternative title, 'Nel Paradiso' (see Introduction, p. xxxv).

232:6 Baptistery. Though possibly originating as early as the 5th century (there is disagreement over its precise date), the Baptistery was probably constructed in the 8th century and is built of alternating layers of white and dark blue marble in the traditional Romanesque style of Tuscany.

232:21 Giotto's tower, The Campanile, or bell-tower, which stands beside the façade of the Cathedral, was designed by the painter Giotto (*c.*1267–1337) in 1334. Like the Cathedral, which also dates from the beginning of the 14th century (although the façade which DHL admired is late 19th century neogothic), it is built of horizontal layers of pink, green and white marble. Cf. 'Giotto's tower, The lily of Florence blossoming in stone' from 'Giotto's Tower' by Henry Wadsworth Longfellow (1807–82) whose poetry DHL knew.

232:24 Firenze—Fiorenze ... The Fiorentini, The Italian word for flower is 'fiore'; Fiorente, 'the city of flowers', was the old Latin name for Florence. The arms of Florence are three red lilies on a white background; see also 258:7.

234:7 The devil looking over Lincoln," Said of a vitriolic critic or backbiter. The devil is supposed to have looked over Lincoln Cathedral, maligning men's devotion. Cf. *The Rainbow*, ed. Mark Kinkead-Weekes (Cambridge, 1989), 103:36n.

235:12 The Blessed Damosel looked down The opening line of Dante Gabriel Rossetti's (1828–82) poem of that title. Cf. *The White Peacock*, ed. Andrew Robertson (Cambridge, 1983), p. 85; *Letters*, i. 51.

235:38 Höflichkeiten ... bin ich. 'Formalities ... No formalities. I'm a plain man' (German).

236:10 Town of Peabodys and piss-en-lits—" From the context it appears that Argyle is punning rather heavily, i.e. 'pee-body'; *pissenlits* (in TS incorrectly typed 'pris-en-lits') is French for dandelion but also means 'wet the bed'. See also Carswell 152 on DHL's painting 'Dandelions'.

236:26 mistkäfer Dung-beetle (German).

237:39 panettone, A cake typical of Torino, usually associated with Christmas and Easter.

238:10 *éprise*. In love with, smitten with (French).

238:13 "And run ... like Alcibiades?" A brilliant Athenian general and statesman and a pupil of Socrates, Alcibiades (*c.* 450–404 BC) was so vain that he refused to play the flute lest he spoil the shape of his mouth.

239:20 a time to love ... loving." 'A time to love, and a time to hate', Ecclesiastes iii. 8.

243:40 maquereaux Pimps, procurers (French).

244:4 a Madame Bovary, The eponymous heroine of Gustave Flaubert's (1821–80) realist novel (1856) who after two unhappy love affairs poisons herself. See *Letters*, ii. 101.

245:37   *pis-aller.* Last resource, worst course (French).

246:27   **Like Saint . . . pillar.** Simeon Stylites, an ascetic, said to have spent thirty years on a pillar near Antioch until his death in 459.

249:11   **Aubrey Beardsley** (1872–98), artist and illustrator and a leading figure of the *fin-de-siècle*, whose decadent drawings at once fascinated and repelled DHL. 'Think of the malice, the sheer malice of a Beardsley drawing, the wit and the venom of the mockery', article sent to Willard Johnson, 12? October 1922 (*The Collected Letters of D. H. Lawrence*, ed. Harry T. Moore, New York, 1962, ii. 725). See also *Letters*, ii. 118 and *The White Peacock*, ed. Robertson, p. 159.

249:23   *ébloui.* Dazzled (French).

250:26   **Botticelli's Venus on the shell."** 'The Birth of Venus', now in the Uffizi Gallery, by Sandro Botticelli (1445–1510).

251:39   **"Age cannot wither . . . stale—"** *Antony and Cleopatra* II. ii. 241.

254:1   **the fire-music putting Brunnhild to sleep.** In Act III of Richard Wagner's opera *The Valkyrie* (produced in 1870, the second in the cycle of four operas *The Ring of the Nibelung*), Brünnhilde – one of the Valkyries – has disobeyed her father, Wotan, king of the gods. Her punishment is to lose her divinity and to become a mortal woman. Wotan causes her to fall into a trance and surrounds her with fire. The opera ends with the fire-music. Brünnhilde is awakened by Siegfried in the last act of the third opera in the cycle, *Siegfried*. Cf. *The Trespasser*, ed. Elizabeth Mansfield (Cambridge, 1982), p. 106.

255:4   **like Trilby . . . Yvette Guilbert . . . me in tune."** Trilby is the eponymous heroine of George du Maurier's (1834–96) novel (1894). Originally an artist's model, she becomes a famous singer under the hypnotic influence of Svengali, a Hungarian musician who plays a flageolet to awaken her talent. When Svengali dies, Trilby loses her ability to sing, languishes and dies soon after. 'Malbrouk s'en va-t-en guerre' is an 18th century French song that Trilby sings: the tune is that of 'For he's a jolly good fellow' . . . Yvette Guilbert (1867–1944) was a French singer of great popularity in London and the USA.

255:20   **"Derriere [255:7] . . . assis dessous."** A traditional French country song, possibly dating from the early 18th century.

> Behind my father's house
> *Fly fly my heart, fly!*
> Behind my father's house
> There is a sweet apple tree.
> *Very sweet, yes very sweet*
> *Very sweet, yes very sweet*
> *There is a sweet apple tree.*
>
> There beautiful princesses
> *Fly fly my heart, fly!*
> Three beautiful princesses
> Are sitting beneath it.
> *Very sweet, yes very sweet*
> *Very sweet, yes very sweet*
> *Are sitting beneath it.*

259:3   the book of *chansons*?" Recalling her meeting with DHL in the winter of 1918, Catherine Carswell mentions 'a little manual of French songs which he carried about everywhere like a Bible' (Carswell 105).

259:14   *Trois ... En passant ... ma blonde ...* 'Three young drummers' (a French soldiers' song, probably from the Napoleonic wars) ... 'Passing through Lorraine' (a traditional French song, with many variations, dating from the 17th century, about a girl with wooden clogs who meets three captains) ... 'Beside my blonde girl' (a very old drinking or marching song, still sung today as a round for children).

265:2   Cleopatra, but not Anthony An earlier, deleted title for this chapter is simply 'Anthony' (TS p. 433).

265:15   Settignano, Hamlet a few km. e. of Florence. DHL knew it well (see *Letters*, iii. 592 and n. 3).

265:34   the cypresses, in Tuscany. Cf. 'Cypresses', written in September 1920, *The Complete Poems of D. H. Lawrence*, ed. Vivian de Sola Pinto and Warren Roberts (1964), i. 296–8. Also see Nehls, ii. 49–50.

269:27   Corinna Wade, Probably based on Vernon Lee (pseudonymn for Violet Paget, 1856–1935), novelist, essayist and feminist living in the English Florentine colony. See Weintraub 180 and 284 n. 12.

269:30   influence of woman ... Periclean day. Possibly a reference to Aspasia, a courtesan who became attached to Pericles (*c*. 495–429 BC), the Athenian statesman, and for whom he divorced his wife. The political enemies of Pericles attacked her but Aspasia's brilliance and intellectual ability transcended scandal and she lived on in Athens after Pericles' death.

270:22   Veneziano ... tutto matto—'" A traditional Italian rhyme: The Venetian is a great gentleman/The Paduan a good doctor./The Vicenzean eats cats/The Veronese is quite crazy.

270:34   Byzantines ... far other ages. A reference to the Eastern empire of Constantine the Great (*c*. 274–337) and its influence which survived, though much diminished, until the middle of the 15th century. See *Movements*, chap. II ('Constantinople'), particularly 16–19. Constantinople is now Istanbul.

270:36   Anna Comnena ... Tancred! Daughter of the Byzantine Emperor Alexius Comnenus, Anna Comnena (1083–1148) wrote a history of his reign ... Tancred (d.1112), a Norman lord of s. Italy and one of the leaders of the First Crusade, warred against both Turks and Byzantines. DHL's characterisation of Anna in *Movements* is amusing:

> Anna Comnena, daughter of the Emperor, a young, clever princess, wrote her memoirs in which we may still read her account of the visit of these Crusaders to her father's capital. She did not like the counts and nobles of the north. She thought them the merest barbarians, insolent, overbearing, vulgar, gaping greedily at the treasures of the palace. Their rude manners disgusted the delicate little lady, their very names, so uncouth, offended her Greek tongue. Some, she allows, were handsome, but all were uncivilised. (*Movements* 114–5. See also 118, 134–55).

271:9 **Galluzzo,** Village 5 km. s. of Florence.

273:28 **But himself … Moses's sister Miriam.** An obscure reference since Miriam, who with Aaron rebelled against Moses, was cursed with leprosy by God, though cured at Moses' intercession. Nevertheless she was exiled from the camp of the faithful for seven days (Numbers xii. 15).

275:35 **the Piazza Vittorio Emanuele … the café** The old name for the present Piazza della Repubblica … the 'Paskowski', where DHL often went and invited friends to meet him (see Weintraub 194).

277:13 **reformer, a Zwingli and Savonarola** Ulric Zwingli, Swiss reformer and theologian (1484–1531) may be said to have begun the Swiss Protestant Reformation around 1522. Girolamo Savonarola (1454–98), Italian reformer and martyr, who preached against corruption in the Church and government and whose authority in Florence was paramount from 1490 until the year of his execution; see *Movements* 181–6.

277:15 **Strait is the gate** Matthew vii. 13–14 (AV).

278:5 **the *Nazione*** The *Nation*, the leading Florence newspaper.

278:8 **let loose the dogs of war,** *Julius Caesar* III. i. 273 ['let slip the …'].

279:17 **Rothschilds,** The most famous of all European banking dynasties, founded in 1744.

279:32 **Epictetus** Greek philosopher (*c.* 55–*c.*135) associated with the Stoics. Epictetus taught that there is only one thing that belongs entirely to an individual – his God-given will, or purpose, which cannot be thwarted or compelled by anything external.

280:35 **better to give than to receive,** Acts xx. 35 ['It is more blessed to give …'].

281:7 **By this time … our idealism."** Jesus raised Lazarus, the brother of Martha and Mary, from the dead (John xi. 1–44). Martha sought to dissuade him, saying: 'Lord, by this time he stinketh: for he hath been *dead* four days' (John xi. 39). DHL echoes Nietzsche here in denouncing the idealism of love. See Introduction, pp. xxvi–xxvii.

282:29 **the real truth … *bullying*.** Lilly's statement of 'the real truth' of his beliefs is strikingly similar to DHL's often expressed detestation of 'bullying'. Cf. *Movements*, 'Epilogue' 312–21.

284:2 **spelch** A 'spelk' is a splinter or small strip of wood.

288:11 **A lake-city, like Mexico.** Mexico City is built on a dry lake-bed. See *The Plumed Serpent* (1926) where the pagan religious revival is centred on Lake Chapala, w. of Mexico City.

288:14 **An Astarte** The mother goddess of Phoenicia; the deity of sexual activity, fertility, maternity and war, sometimes erroneously identified as a moon goddess. For DHL she symbolised not only the life-giving power of woman but also her suffocating possessiveness. Cf. *Women in Love*, chap. XIX 'Moony' (ed. David Farmer, Lindeth Vasey and John Worthen, Cambridge, 1987, pp. 244–65).

291:26 millstones ... stones. An echo of Friedrich von Logau (1604–55), *Sinngedichte* (trans. by Henry Wadsworth Longfellow): 'Though the mills of God grind slowly, yet they grind exceeding small'.

292:1 Their wagon hitched to a star 'Hitch your wagon to a star', from 'Civilisation' by Ralph Waldo Emerson (1803–82).

293:20 dynamic urges in *life*: love and power." Cf. 'Epilogue' (written in September 1924) to *Movements*; see Introduction, pp. xxvi–xxvii.

294:34 *Niente*! Nothing! (Italian).

295:16 Trot, trot ... can run. A variant of the nursery rhyme:

> Trit trot to market to buy a penny doll;
> Trit trot back again, the market's sold them all.

Iona and Peter Opie, *Oxford Nursery Rhyme Book* (1955).

296:4 deny the Holy Ghost ... catch it. Cf. 'The blasphemy against the Holy Ghost shall not be forgiven ...', Matthew xii. 31.

296:33 Tree of Life, The tree growing in the middle of the Garden of Eden (Genesis ii. 9) the eating of whose fruit would give immortality; also, in Revelation xxii. 2, a tree in the heavenly Jerusalem whose leaves are for healing the nations. Cf. 'Foreword' to *Fantasia of the Unconscious*, and 'The tree of life. The tree of knowledge' in chap. IV.

297:29 The will-to-power—but not in Nietzsche's sense. 'Only where there is life, there is will, but not unto life, but ... will unto power', Friedrich Nietzsche (1844–1900), *Thus Spake Zarathustra* (trans. Tille, 1899), p. 164. DHL was also familiar with *The Will to Power* (1887), but he was re-reading *Zarathustra* in 1916. Cf. also Count Dionys in 'The Ladybird' on power, submission, obedience, and *The Plumed Serpent*, ed. L. D. Clark (Cambridge, 1988), pp. 72–80.

TEXTUAL APPARATUS

TEXTUAL APPARATUS

The following symbols are used to distinguish states of the text:

TS = Corrected typescript
A1 = American first edition
E1 = English first edition
E1a = Second printing, English first edition

All subsequent impressions in DHL's lifetime reproduced *E1* in England and *A1* in USA.

Whenever the *TS* reading is adopted, it appears within the square bracket with no symbol. When an editorial emendation has been chosen, it appears with its appropriate source-symbol within the square bracket. Rejected readings follow the square bracket, in chronological sequence (*A1* precedes *E1*), with their first source denoted. In the absence of information to the contrary the reader should assume a variant recurs in all subsequent states.

The following symbols are used editorially:

Ed. = Editor
Om. = Omitted
/ = Line or page break resulting in a punctuation, hyphenation or spelling error
~ = Repeated word in recording an accidental variant
P = Paragraph

In order to reduce the difficulty of tracing variants in *A1* for one lengthy passage omitted from *E1*, these variants are given in individual entries and are indicated by the note '*see also following entries to* ...'

5:12	Miners] ~' *E1*	6:37	Father] father *E1*
5:21	tree—? *Ed.*] Tree—? *TS, E1*	7:1	indoors,] ~; *E1*
	Tree? *A1*	7:20	tonight *A1*] to-night *TS, E1*
5:25	Wheer] Where *E1*	7:22	his dinner] the table *E1*
5:32	Father] father *E1*	7:31	today *A1*] to-day *TS, E1*
6:4	top-most] topmost *A1*	7:40	packets,] ~ *E1*
6:4	in *A1*] on *TS, E1*	8:5	Freer? *A1*] ~?. *TS* ~?— *E1*
6:5	coat-less *TS, E1*] coatless *A1*	8:21	Union *A1*] union *TS, E1*
6:12	path,] ~; *E1*	8:29	colour *TS, E1*] color *A1*
6:13	clear,] ~; *E1*	9:6	Millicent—.] ~. *A1* ~— *E1*
6:21	bough,] ~; *E1*	9:11	"Don't] "~, *A1*
6:30	swinging] ~, *E1*	9:14	drop *TS, E1*] top *A1*

9:21　will—.] ~.— *A1* ~. *E1*

9:31　aw Mother] ~, mother *E1*

9:35　love!] ~? *E1*

9:38　Look Mother] ~, ~ *A1*
　　　~ mother *E1*

9:39　Yes, it's lovely] Lovely *E1*

10:1　Look Father] ~, ~ *A1* ~ father
　　　E1

10:17　dark-blue colour] dark blue
　　　color *A1* dark blue colour *E1*

10:19　it] ~, *A1*

10:32　daresay *TS, E1*] dare say *A1*

10:36　drop. It *TS, E1*] ~, it *A1*

10:38　Oh-h-h] Oh—h—h *E1*

11:9　pretty] ~, *E1*

11:11　No *TS, E1*] ~, *A1*

11:28　Shep-ep-ep-ep-herds]
　　　Shep—ep—ep—ep—herds *E1*

11:38　Sisson *TS, E1*] ~, *A1*

12:20　Ay] ~, *E1*

12:34　air,] ~ *E1*

13:5　good-humoured *E1*]
　　　good-humored *TS*

13:15　Father] father *E1*

13:29　*you TS, E1*] you *A1*

13:33　Father] father *E1*

13:37　Shall] shall *E1*

13:37　Father] father *E1*

14:9　practicing *Ed.*] practising *TS*

14:12　o'clock: *TS, E1*] ~; *A1*

14:19　you Father] ~, ~ *A1* ~, father
　　　E1

14:38　holders] ~, *E1*

15:14　Goodnight—Goodnight ...
　　　Goodnight *Ed.*] Good-night—
　　　Good-night ... Good-night *TS*
　　　Good-night—Good-night, ...
　　　Good-night, *A1*

16:2　Sixpence *E1*] Six-pence *TS*

16:6　twopence *TS, E1*] two-pence
　　　A1

16:12　they? *A1*] ~?. *TS*

17:4　market-place *Ed.*] market place
　　　TS

17:7　public houses *Ed.*]
　　　public-houses *TS*

17:11　low] ~, *E1*

17:20　you, *A1*] ~. *TS* ~! *E1*

17:30　high-coloured *A1*]
　　　high-colored *TS*

18:2　indeed.] ~? *A1* ~! *E1*

18:6　Well] ~, *E1*

18:12　thick] ~, *E1*

18:28　please!] ~? *A1*

18:39　Why] ~, *E1*

19:19　*always TS, E1*] always *A1*

19:19　patronising *TS, E1*] patronizing
　　　A1

19:40　a',] a'—, *E1*

20:5　here] ~, *E1*

20:6　Kirk. *TS, E1*] ~, *A1*

20:18　world—] ~. *E1*

21:14　money,] ~: *E1*

21:14　of— —] ~— *A1*

21:35　t'other *TS, E1*] t' other *A1*

22:3　you] *you E1*

22:19　nay,] ~ *E1*

22:28　in the middle of] deep estab-
　　　lished in *E1*

22:28　invisible] obstinate *E1*

22:29　waited, never to be] was never
　　　E1

22:30　For] ~, *E1*

22:30　course] ~, *E1*

22:30　go,] ~; *E1*

22:38　benevolence] philanthropy *E1*

23:7　innermost] *Om. E1*

23:9　made] left *E1*

23:9　saw her ... all women] had
　　　come to her once too often. To
　　　her and to every woman *E1*

23:11　help in] help *E1*

23:11　game!] ~. *E1*

23:12　whiskey] the whiskey *E1*

23:15　feel] have felt *E1*

23:16　melting and swimming] swim-
　　　ming and flowing *E1*

23:16　oneness with the dark] dark-
　　　ness *E1*

23:17　white] cold white *E1*

23:17　wide-eyed *E1*] wide eyed *TS*

23:19　more] a more *E1*

23:22　his] the *E1*

23:27　answered, "it *TS, E1*] ~. "It
　　　A1

24:37　of people] *Om. E1*

24:37 and for a race much] for a race which is even *E1*
24:38 children] little children *E1*
24:39 other *TS, E1*] other's *A1*
25:1 that] which *E1*
25:4 speech] ~, *E1*
25:5 secret] secret lustful *E1*
25:5 a *TS, E1*] the *A1*
25:7 on the pit-bank ... all-righteous newspaper; *Ed.*] on ... pit bank ... newspaper; *TS* at the miners' meeting—or the all-benevolent newspaper— *E1*
25:8 revulsion,] ~ *A1*
25:9 love and good-will] good-will and love *E1*
25:10 good-will! *A1*] good will! *TS* good-will. *E1*
25:10 Self-righteous] All righteous *E1*
25:11 poison gas] poison-gas *E1*
25:13 said] ~, *E1*
25:36 "Royal Oak." *A1*] ~~. *TS, E1*
25:39 high-road *TS, E1*] highroad *A1*
26:2 The Lighted Tree] "THE LIGHTED TREE" *A1* THE LIGHTED TREE *E1*
26:6 *en masse A1*] en masse *TS*
26:12 dark, *TS, E1*] ~ *A1*
26:16 Colliery] colliery *E1*
26:17 accent,] ~ *E1*
26:23 refuse fire] refuse-fire *E1*
26:24 pleasant] ~, *E1*
26:25 dead end] dead-end *E1*
26:35 silvery grey] silvery-grey *E1*
27:12 Michelangelo *Ed.*] Michael-Angelo *TS*
27:14 glass] ~, *E1*
27:24 Ford *A1*] Hay *TS, E1* see notes
27:28 chin too] ~, ~, *E1*
27:37 She too] ~, ~, *E1*
27:40 man] ~, *E1*
28:5 husband, Robert Cunningham, a *A1*] husband, Robert Cunningham, was a *TS* husband. Robert Cunningham was a *E1*
28:9 rear—] ~, *E1*

28:12 eyelid *Ed.*] eye-lid *TS*
28:23 well-bred *Ed.*] well bred *TS*
28:28 blunt, *TS, E1*] ~ *A1*
28:40 Oh *TS, E1*] ~, *A1*
28:40 right! *TS, E1*] ~? *A1*
29:4 No] no *A1* No, *E1*
29:9 nervous, *TS, E1*] ~ *A1*
29:29 Oh] ~, *A1*
29:35 furtively] ~, *E1*
30:2 cigarettes, *TS, E1*] ~ *A1*
30:5 Ah] ~, *A1*
30:7 Eh] eh *E1*
30:22 Goodnight] Good night, *A1* Good-night, *E1*
30:26 grey-silk] grey silk *E1*
31:2 twenty-two *A1*] twenty two *TS, E1*
31:5 shining] moist *E1*
31:7 naïve] naive *A1*
31:22 Yes] ~, *A1*
31:26 Jim] ~, *E1*
31:33 Christmas tree *Ed.*] Christmas-tree *TS*
31:34 Oh *TS, E1*] ~, *A1*
31:36 What—!] ~! *E1*
31:39 Oh *TS, E1*] ~, *A1*
32:1 *No TS, E1*] ~, *A1*
32:1 *No!*] No! *A1* no! *E1*
32:3 let's.] ~! *E1*
32:5 lawn. *TS, E1*] ~? *A1*
32:13 Oh *TS, E1*] ~, *A1*
32:13 say—!] ~! *E1*
32:35 Why] ~, *E1*
33:1 Oh *TS, E1*] ~, *A1*
33:4 Indian] ~, *E1*
33:6 bicycle lamp *Ed.*] bicycle-lamp *TS*
33:18 Why—y—y *TS, E1*] Why-y-y *A1*
33:24 intruder: *TS, E1*] ~; *A1*
33:29 him,] ~ *E1*
33:33 loud] ~, *E1*
33:35 floor,] ground *A1* ground, *E1* see notes
33:39 himself, *TS, E1*] ~ *A1*
34:4 doubled-up *TS, E1*] doubled up *A1*
34:9 articulate.] ~: *E1*

34:19 floor] ground *A1* grass *E1*
34:26 embarrassed *A1*] embarassed *TS*
34:28 he] the stranger *E1*
35:6 remarked *TS, E1*] replied *A1*
35:6 chap—] ~. *E1*
35:11 unmoving] unchanged *E1*
35:15 right] ~, *A1*
35:21 new-comer *A1*] newcomer *TS*
35:28 handsome] ~, *E1*
36:6 road—.] ~—*A1* ~. *E1*
36:8 enquired *Ed.*] inquired *TS*
36:15 *haut Ed.*] *haute TS*
36:32 will—] ~. *E1*
36:36 Oh] ~, *A1*
37:7 now—] ~. *E1*
37:11 pale] ~, *E1*
37:23 quiet, *TS, E1*] ~ *A1*
37:26 Oh] ~, *A1*
37:34 Robert] ~, *E1*
37:36 Jim *TS, E1*] ~, *A1*
38:17 house mate] house-mate *E1*
39:2 The Pillar of Salt] "THE PILLAR OF SALT" *A1* THE PILLAR OF SALT *E1*
39:17 downhill *Ed.*] down-hill *TS*
39:32 into *TS, E1*] in to *A1*
39:32 grate] grating *E1*
40:1 —'ning...—'ning *TS, E1*] -'ning...-'ning *A1*
40:8 this time] *Om. E1*
40:9 bare-headed *A1*] bareheaded *TS, E1*
40:10 coat-less *Ed.*] coatless *TS*
40:10 slippered] ~, *E1*
40:20 Mrs. Sisson] his wife *E1*
40:27 goodnight] good night *A1* good-night *E1*
40:27 Goodnight] Good night *A1* Good-night, *E1*
41:10 shortish] ~, *E1*
41:11 the blind] the bind *E1*
41:19 Now] ~, *E1*
41:34 weak] ~, *E1*
41:39 No] ~, *A1*
42:3 it,] ~. *E1*
42:12 No...No *TS, E1*] ~,...~,*A1*
42:23 with *TS, E1*] *Om. A1*

42:26 emotional] ~, *E1*
42:37 letter—"] ~" *E1*
43:8 said] ~, *E1*
43:10 Well-well, well-well] ~—~, ~—~ *E1*
43:14 Well-well, well-well] ~—~, ~—~, *E1*
43:32 fair-haired *TS, E1*] fairhaired *A1*
43:37 thought *TS, E1*] ~, *A1*
44:5 *you*] you *E1*
44:8 oriental *Ed.*] Oriental *TS*
44:8 tread] ~, *E1*
44:10 portrait, *TS, E1*] ~ *A1*
44:17 by] my *E1*
44:18 girl—.] ~——*A1* ~. *E1*
44:20 *pince-nez E1*] pince nez *TS*
44:40 again, *TS, E1*] ~ *A1*
45:3 Ford *A1*] Hay *TS see note on* 27:24
45:4 evening: *TS, E1*] ~; *A1*
45:6 front *TS, E1*] the front *A1*
45:11 front *TS, E1*] the front *A1*
45:12 front *TS, E1*] the front *A1*
45:13 full-swing] noisy *E1*
45:19 Bohemians *TS, E1*] bohemians *A1*
45:28 tight] ~, *A1*
45:31 far-off *Ed.*] far off *TS*
46:2 *Aida*] *Aïda E1*
46:4 social] fashionable *E1*
46:10 *Aida*] *Aïda E1*
46:25 large *TS, E1*] ~, *A1*
46:29 fat *TS, E1*] ~, *A1*
47:7 blonde *TS, E1*] blond *A1*
47:9 Oh *TS, E1*] ~, *A1*
47:25 *too wonderful TS, E1*] too wonderful *A1*
48:1 go *TS, E1*] to go *A1*
48:1 alone? *TS, E1*] ~! *A1*
48:15 Oh yes,] ~, ~, *A1* ~~. *E1*
48:18 scalp *E1*] scrap *TS see notes*
48:24 scene *TS, E1*] ~, *A1*
48:30 offered. *P* When] ~. When *E1*
48:40 Oh *TS, E1*] ~, *A1*
48:40 Why *TS, E1*] ~, *A1*
49:2 *Scott.*] ~! *E1*
49:21 answer] ~, *E1*

49:27 Oh *TS, E1*] ~, *A1*
49:32 re-appear *TS, E1*] reappear *A1*
50:2 Who—? I—?] ~? ~? *E1*
50:15 wife Tanny] ~, ~, *A1*
50:23 course *TS, E1*] ~, *A1*
50:25 experiment— *TS, E1*] ~—. *A1*
50:29 But] ~, *E1*
50:32 Oh] ~, *E1*
50:33 him] ~, *E1*
50:37 see] ~, *E1*
51:3 off, *TS, E1*] ~. *A1*
51:10 might—!] ~!— *E1*
51:18 Josephine] ~, *E1*
51:18 Oh yes] ~, ~, *A1* ~, ~ *E1*
51:23 Julia.] ~, *E1*
51:24 Rob-ert] *Rob*-ert *E1*
51:28 well-nourished] well nourished *E1*
51:30 Rob-ert] *Rob*-ert *E1*
51:30 young!] ~. *E1*
51:33 old *TS, E1*] Old *A1*
51:36 Julia. Josephine] ~. *P* ~ *E1*
52:1 they] ~, *A1*
52:32 *À Ed.*] *A TS*
53:15 What] what *E1*
53:18 he?] ~! *E1*
53:29 man] ~, *E1*
54:10 Oh *TS, E1*] ~, *A1*
54:16 than's good for us] than we bargain for *E1*
54:24 said. *A1*] ~, *TS*
54:34 Oh *TS, E1*] ~, *A1*
54:35 *we've TS, E1*] we *A1*
55:5 half-smiling *TS, E1*] half smiling *A1*
55:6 an' *TS, E1*] and *A1*
56:5 downstairs *Ed.*] down-stairs *TS*
56:15 hat?] ~. *E1*
56:22 Adelphi] the Adelphi *E1*
56:25 working-man] working man *E1*
56:28 Labour *TS, E1*] labour *A1*
56:31 Heal's *E1*] Heale's *TS*
56:33 chesterfield *TS, E1*] Chester-field *A1*
57:5 Bohemia *E1*] bohemia *TS*
57:6 *Aida A1*] Aida *TS*
57:10 bohemian] Bohemian *E1*
57:13 bohemian] Bohemian *E1*

57:20 concentrated] ~, *E1*
57:28 Alas *TS, E1*] ~, *A1*
57:29 upper lip *Ed.*] upper-lip *TS*
57:31 meet." She *A1*] ~." she *TS* ~," she *E1*
57:39 you] ~, *E1*
58:16 though, *TS, E1*] ~? *A1*
58:18 am *TS, E1*] ~, *A1*
58:21 'Farewell' *E1*] ~ *TS*
58:29 free] down *E1*
58:30 pathos!] ~. *E1*
58:35 Oh *TS, E1*] ~, *A1*
58:39 Yes] ~, *A1*
59:6 hearth-rug] hearthrug *E1*
59:40 Why] ~, *A1*
60:1 an *TS, E1*] and *A1*
60:1 vile] rotten *E1*
60:13 twitching,] ~: *E1*
60:17 Why] ~, *A1*
60:20 it!] ~? *E1*
60:21 Oh *TS, E1*] ~, *A1*
60:25 machine guns *Ed.*] machine-guns *TS*
60:31 But *TS, E1*] ~, *A1*
60:31 Robert,] ~; *E1*
60:34 Ah] ~, *A1*
61:13 Oh *TS, E1*] ~, *A1*
61:17 Oh] ~, *A1*
61:19 side-board *Ed.*] sideboard *TS*
61:36 Oh *TS, E1*] ~, *A1*
61:36 drawled *TS, E1*] ~, *A1*
62:6 Jim.—] ~,— *A1* ~. *E1*
62:9 LOVE IS ... RESPIRATION *TS, E1*] Love is the soul's respiration *A1*
62:21 WHEN YOU ... BREATHES IN] When you love, your soul breathes in *A1* WHEN YOU LOVE, YOUR SOUL BREATHES IN. *E1*
62:22 And then on the next line.] *Om. A1* And then ... line:— *E1*
62:23 WHEN YOUR ... BLOODY REVOLUTION *TS, E1*] When your soul breathes out, it's a bloody revolution *A1*
62:25 say] ~, *E1*

62:30 I'M DYING ... I AM] I'M
DYING, AND I KNOW I AM *A1*
I'm dying, and I know I am *E1*

62:34 am, *TS, E1*] am. *A1*

63:5 Tanny, *TS, E1*] ~ *A1*

63:7 Clariss. "She's *A1*] ~. "she's
TS ~, "she's *E1*

63:8 working people *TS, E1*]
Working People *A1*

63:11 Oh] ~, *A1*

63:15 right—] ~.— *A1* ~. *E1*

63:15 it *TS, E1*] Om. *A1*

63:24 wife Tanny] wife *A1* wife,
Tanny, *E1*

63:26 stairs—] ~, *E1*

64:9 soldiers *A1*] Soldiers *TS*

64:18 jaded, *TS, E1*] ~ *A1*

65:5 burgundy *TS, E1*] Burgundy
A1

65:10 schoolteacher] school teacher
E1

65:10 years] ~' *E1*

65:16 midland] Midland *E1*

65:27 No, *TS, E1*] ~ *A1*

65:30 blond, *A1*] ~ *TS*

66:9 some] a bit of *E1*

66:10 myself—] ~. *E1*

66:15 will be hurt] are going to suffer
so *E1*

66:17 Ah *TS, E1*] ~, *A1*

66:17 to feel—] to love. *E1*

66:25 Oh *TS, E1*] ~, *A1*

66:26 be a lover ... or to] go on being
a lover, to her or *E1*

66:34 amiable-looking *A1*]
aimiable-looking *TS*

66:35 amiable *A1*] aimiable *TS*

67:16 know.] ~! *E1*

67:23 it *TS, E1*] It *A1*

67:36 on.—] ~—*A1* ~. *E1*

67:38 her, *TS, E1*] ~ *A1*

68:4 miserably] piqued *E1*

68:10 be *TS, E1*] Om. *A1*

68:17 Oh] ~, *A1*

68:36 But] Yes! But *E1*

68:37 Oh *TS, E1*] ~, *A1*

69:5 forward, *TS, E1*] ~ *A1*

69:7 suggestion, *TS, E1*] ~ *A1*

69:26 wild] ~, *E1*

69:28 Square *TS, E1*] square *A1*

70:11 realised ... realised *TS, E1*]
realized ... realized *A1*

70:22 nothing,] nothing if you like, *E1*

70:23 Why *TS, E1*] ~, *A1*

70:33 Square] square *E1*

70:38 Yes] ~, *E1*

71:18 Nay!] ~, *E1*

73:4 a fine blonde *TS, E1*] was
strong and fair *A1 see notes*

73:6 acquaintances,—] ~— *E1*

73:7 telegram, *A1*] ~ *TS*

73:8 4.30 *TS, E1*] 4:30 *A1*

73:22 stooped] stooped, *A1* stopped
E1

73:28 A.1. *Ed.*] A.I. *TS* A1, *E1*

73:29 Oh] ~, *A1*

74:4 one.] one: there before them all
in the pretty cottage
living-room. *E1*

74:7 Well] ~, *E1*

74:7 nice,] ~! *E1*

74:24 No] ~, *A1*

74:29 tea *TS, E1*] ~, *A1*

74:30 postoffice *Ed.*] post-office *TS*
post office *E1*

74:36 Saving] saving *E1*

75:10 But] but *E1*

75:25 fire, *TS, E1*] ~ *A1*

75:29 cracked] mad *E1*

75:29 awful,—] ~— *E1*

75:32 man—It] ~.—~ *A1* ~—it *E1*

76:31 busy—] ~.— *A1* ~. *E1*

76:33 Sir] sir *E1*

77:3 always *TS, E1*] *always A1*

77:11 *ad infinitum A1*] ad infinitum *TS*

77:21 oneself] one's self *E1*

77:33 abstraction.] ~? *E1*

77:34 Lilly—"a] ~. "A *E1*

77:39 *manqúe A1*] manqúe *TS, E1*

78:7 self-conscious *A1*] self
conscious *TS*

78:17 Christianity—At] ~.—~ *A1*
~—at *E1*

78:23 Lilly however] ~, ~, *E1*

78:27 agree? *P* Suddenly] ~? Suddenly *A1*

78:35 say] ~: *E1*
79:7 I] ~, *A1*
79:11 slimy creepy] ~, ~, *E1*
79:12 intimacy.—] ~:— *E1*
79:14 *people*——] ~—— *E1*
79:25 journey] ~— *E1*
79:31 Lois, *TS, E1*] ~ *A1*
79:33 Marlow *E1*] Marlowe *TS*
79:34 postoffice] post office *E1*
79:36 postoffice *A1*] post-office *TS* post office *E1*
80:4 junction-town] junction town *A1*
80:5 message] ~— *E1*
80:5 3.40 *TS, E1*] 3:40 *A1*
80:13 said, "it's *A1*] ~. "It's *TS*
80:16 burgundy *TS, E1*] Burgundy *A1*
80:30 any where *TS, E1*] anywhere *A1*
80:33 Yes] ~, *A1*
80:34 Oh *TS, E1*] ~, *A1*
80:40 Technically ... oh yes!] Technically ... oh, yes! *A1 Om. E1*
81:6 *be*] be *E1*
81:7 Quiet *A1*] quiet *TS, E1*
81:18 ataxia] ataxy *E1*
81:26 arm-chairs *Ed.*] arm-/chairs *TS, E1* armchairs *A1*
81:30 God!] ~, *E1*
81:36 time] ~, *E1*
82:1 it?] ~, *E1*
82:8 rickety] ricky *E1*
82:14 disgusting—] ~. *E1*
82:19 will— —] ~ —— *A1* ~— *E1*
82:26 winded, *TS, E1*] ~ *A1*
83:19 Yes] ~, *A1*
83:26 was] seemed *E1*
83:30 kind: *TS, E1*] ~, *A1*
83:33 Jim. "Never] ~; "never *E1*
83:36 Oh *TS, E1*] ~, *A1*
84:8 feel—] ~. *E1*
84:9 feel—] ~. *E1*
84:16 But *TS, E1*] ~, *A1*
84:26 station] ~, *E1*
84:37 others] *Om. E1*
85:10 play at little Jesus,] try to make a little Jesus of yourself, *E1*

86:11 cockney *Ed.*] Cockney *TS*
87:5 bonnet.] ~! *E1*
87:6 cabbage-leaves. *TS, E1*] ~? *A1*
87:14 floor *TS, E1*] ground *A1 see note on* 33:35
87:25 cockney] Cockney *E1*
87:25 it *A1*] ~. *TS* ~: *E1*
87:25 Drank.] ~! *E1*
87:27 d'you *TS, E1*] d' you *A1*
87:30 some,—Come] ~,—come *A1* ~. Come *E1*
87:36 you! *TS, E1*] ~? *A1*
87:37 you. *TS, E1*] ~? *A1*
87:38 Market. *TS, E1*] ~? *A1*
88:5 bare-headed] ~, *E1*
88:8 cockney] Cockney *E1*
88:12 Aaron: *A1*] ~. *TS* ~: —*E1*
88:16 turned, *TS, E1*] ~ *A1*
88:30 papers. Books] ~, books *E1*
88:40 half a crown] half-a-crown *E1*
89:11 Sir] sir *E1*
89:25 boil,] ~: *E1*
90:13 water bottle] water-bottle *E1*
90:37 And] and *A1*
90:39 Ay!— *TS, E1*] ~! *A1*
91:9 now—Though] ~—though *A1* ~. Though *E1*
91:16 though—? *TS, E1*] ~? *A1*
91:19 naïve *Ed.*] naive *TS*
92:7 half-opened *A1*] half opened *TS, E1*
92:10 street-door *Ed.*] street door *TS*
92:23 Oh *TS, E1*] ~, *A1*
93:7 in] on *E1*
93:13 flu, *A1*] ~ *TS*
95:28 round— —] ~— *A1*
95:31 freesias *Ed.*] freezias *TS*
95:35 cold] ~, *A1*
96:31 himself.] ~: *A1* ~, *E1*
96:32 him ...] ~.... *A1* ~. *E1*
96:35 say,] ~ *E1*
96:40 *bonum publicum E1*] bonum publicum *TS*
97:1 power. *TS, E1*] ~? *A1*
97:2 authority. *TS, E1*] ~? *A1*
97:11 alone. *TS, E1*] ~? *A1*
97:21 Europeans] wastrels *E1*
97:24 orientals] Orientals *E1*

97:27 They] they *A1*
97:27 Asiatic—Even] ~—even *A1*
~. Even *E1*
97:28 wallowers.—The] ~—the *A1*
~. The *E1*
98:2 right *TS, E1*] ~, *A1*
98:10 Others] others *E1*
98:23 inobtrusive] unobtrusive *E1*
98:38 into *TS, E1*] from *A1*
99:23 *Egoïsme Ed.*] *Egoisme TS*
99:25 *Egoïsme Ed.*] *Egoisme TS*
99:34 It's *TS, E1*] it's *A1*
99:36 Ay—! *TS, E1*] ~! *A1*
100:1 myself,] ~ *E1*
100:2 are:] ~; *E1*
100:5 sorry to, *TS, E1*] ~, too *A1*
100:8 the] their *E1*
100:15 know— *TS, E1*] ~, *A1*
100:15 bed, *A1*] ~. *TS*
100:20 Ah women!— *TS, E1*] ~, ~—
A1
100:22 crime.] ~! *E1*
100:25 to bring them up] for a woman
E1
100:25 first. They'd *A1*] ~,—They'd
TS ~,—they'd *E1*
100:26 that] that's *E1*
101:4 curling, *TS, E1*] ~; *A1*
101:15 self-conceit—] ~. *E1*
102:9 Oh] ~, *A1*
102:10 that:] ~ *E1*
102:12 despatched *TS, E1*] dispatched
A1
102:18 Oh *TS, E1*] ~, *A1*
102:25 Maud Allen Wing *TS, E1*]
Maud Allen Wing A1
102:32 can you *TS, E1*] can't you *A1*
103:15 Why *TS, E1*] ~, *A1*
103:22 else?] ~. *E1*
103:28 But there *TS, E1*] There *A1*
103:28 mes] me's *E1*
104:12 got?] ~. *E1*
104:16 colourless *E1*] colorless *TS, A1*
104:31 soul,] ~ *E1*
105:1 Ah *TS, E1*] ~, *A1*
105:3 do *TS, E1*] ~, *A1*
105:19 believe *TS, E1*] ~, *A1*
105:36 tall *TS, E1*] ~, *A1*

106:10 Lilly] Poor Lilly *E1*
107:33 right] ~, *A1*
107:35 else: *TS, E1*] ~; *A1*
107:36 Malta *TS, E1*] ~, *A1*
107:37 Oh *TS, E1*] ~, *A1*
108:2 *Pelléas A1*] Pelléas *TS*
108:20 think, *TS, E1*] ~ *A1*
108:25 you *TS, E1*] ~, *A1*
109:9 myself: *TS, E1*] ~; *A1*
109:31 patches *TS, E1*] ~, *A1*
109:32 advantages. *TS, E1*] ~? *A1*
110:13 No] ~, *A1*
110:24 it— *A1*] ~.— *TS*
110:29 *Pelléas A1*] Pelléas *TS*
110:39 re-appeared *E1*] reappeared
TS
111:3 that *TS, E1*] ~, *A1*
111:22 way—.] ~—*A1* ~. *E1*
111:31 postoffice *Ed.*] post office *TS*
112:24 *Rosemary E1*] 'Rosemary' *TS*
112:27 Oh *TS, E1*] ~, *A1*
112:28 soda. *TS, E1*] ~? *A1*
112:29 soda. *TS, E1*] ~? *A1*
112:36 be—] ~. *E1*
113:2 hell] hill *E1*
113:5 one] the other *E1 see notes*
113:8 boy] ~, *A1*
113:8 poured] poured out *E1*
113:10 But I like ... it. Why ...
[113:16] Guards, too—"] But
... it? Why ... too—" *A1 Om.*
E1
113:21 imitator— *A1*] ~.— *TS*
113:23 Oh *TS, E1*] ~, *A1*
113:35 invited—] ~. *E1*
113:38 only:] ~, *A1* ~; *E1*
114:32 perfect—It] ~. ~ *E1*
114:34 Now] ~, *E1*
114:39 No] ~, *E1*
115:5 thing, *TS, E1*] ~ *A1*
115:6 1916— *TS, E1*] 1916, *A1*
115:9 Well] ~, *A1*
115:13 Innes—] ~. *E1*
115:18 know—Yes—] ~.~, *E1*
115:27 quiet] ~, *E1*
115:35 real] rear *E1*
115:38 Guards *E1*] guards *TS*
115:39 charge—] ~. *E1*

116:2 animated] ~, *E1*
116:7 *vice versa E1*] vice versa *TS*
116:18 Well] ~, *A1*
116:32 thing—] ~. *E1*
117:1 look.—] ~— *E1*
117:6 Well] ~, *A1*
117:25 them—] ~. *E1*
117:39 regular: Think] ~. ~ *A1*
117:39 it.] ~! *E1*
117:39 course] ~, *A1*
118:11 belly-ache *Ed.*] bellyache *TS*
118:22 Yes] ~, *E1*
118:26 No] ~, *A1*
119:14 oh *TS, E1*] Oh, *A1*
119:15 That] ~, *E1*
120:4 asked, *TS, E1*] ~ *A1*
120:23 sight] ~, *E1*
120:25 we] you *E1*
120:27 There was no] No *E1*
120:28 only] always *E1*
120:30 anyhow,] ~? *A1*
120:32 life-spirit *Ed.*] life spirit *TS*
120:33 None] '~ *A1*
120:34 smoke.] ~.' *A1*
120:35 killed, *TS, E1*] ~ *A1*
120:36 death-choice—] ~. *E1*
120:36 will not] *will not E1*
120:38 never] *never E1*
121:1 bed:] ~. *A1*
121:3 anyhow. *TS, E1*] ~? *A1*
121:13 Oh *TS, E1*] ~, *A1*
121:17 Oh *TS, E1*] ~, *A1*
121:21 took it rather as] felt it was *E1*
121:22 quite] perfectly *E1*
121:23 on] upon *E1*
121:23 Aaron's] ~, *E1*
121:24 at all] *Om. E1*
121:24 obey.] obey. Rather he curled his fine nose, worldly-wise. People who make calls on other people's souls are bound to find the door shut. *E1 see note on* 124:27
121:24 chose] chooses *E1*
121:25 street-door] worldly house-door *E1*
121:25 world-friend—] world-caller, *E1*

121:25 let it be quits.] it is nearly quits. Aaron accepted the *quid pro quo. E1*
121:27 thought] felt *E1*
122:6 bohemian] Bohemian *E1*
122:8 already] always *E1*
122:27 fascinated] fascinated him *E1*
122:29 dishevelled *TS, E1*] disshevelled *A1*
123:19 old] odd *A1 see notes*
123:39 frame, *TS, E1*] ~ *A1*
124:6 irony: *TS, E1*] ~. *A1*
124:27 And again ... boiled.] *Om. E1*
125:30 months, *TS, E1*] ~? *A1*
125:31 doing. *TS, E1*] ~? *A1*
125:33 months. *TS, E1*] ~? *A1*
126:1 pretence *TS, E1*] pretense *A1*
126:16 them. *TS, E1*] ~? *A1*
127:11 strange, *TS, E1*] ~ *A1*
128:1 she too *TS, E1*] ~, ~, *A1*
128:4 wrist, *A1*] ~. *TS* ~ *E1*
128:6 she too *TS, E1*] ~, ~, *A1*
128:14 He too *TS, E1*] ~, ~, *A1*
129:10 her, *TS, E1*] ~ *A1*
129:20 Yes—] ~, *A1*
130:8 bit *TS, E1*] ~, *A1*
130:10 flute] ~, *E1*
130:11 of Miss] or Miss *E1*
130:24 *tête-à-tête Ed.*] tête-à-tête *TS* tete-à-tete *A1* tête-a-tête *E1*
130:25 beauties:] ~; *E1*
130:39 Franks'] Franks's *E1*
131:2 wet *TS, E1*] ~, *A1*
131:16 yes—or-right] Yes—orright *A1* yes—orright *E1*
131:17 Franks.] ~? *A1* ~.— *E1*
131:22 cabman *A1*] cab-man *TS, E1*
131:32 Or-right] Orright *A1*
131:32 or-right] orright *A1*
131:36 rainy *TS, E1*] ~, *A1*
131:39 there—" in *TS, E1*] ~." In *A1*
132:18 doorway *A1*] door-way *TS*
132:31 tall *TS, E1*] ~, *A1*
132:33 No signore *TS, E1*] ~, Signore *A1*
133:4 dark *TS, E1*] ~, *A1*
133:15 length *TS, E1*] ~, *A1*

133:17 manservant *A1*] man-/ servant *TS* man-servant *E1*

133:20 manservant] man-servant *E1*

133:22 turkish] Turkish *A1*

133:29 re-appeared *TS, E1*] reappeared *A1*

133:31 thin *TS, E1*] ~, *A1*

133:32 dinner-jacket *Ed.*] dinner jacket *TS*

134:2 oh … oh *TS, E1*] ~, … ~, *A1*

134:2 Well *TS, E1*] well, *A1*

134:7 well *TS, E1*] ~, *A1*

134:12 nuisance— *TS, E1*] ~. *A1*

134:17 *The Graphic A1*] The Graphic *TS*

134:17 *Country Life A1*] Country Life *TS*

134:31 turkish] Turkish *A1*

135:1 *Connu! Connu! A1*] Connu! Connu! *TS Connu! Connu! E1*

135:8 young *TS, E1*] ~, *A1*

135:12 khaki:] ~— *E1*

135:14 hostess'] hostess's *E1*

135:23 new-comer *Ed.*] newcomer *TS*

135:25 vol-au-vents *TS, E1*] vol au-vents *A1*

136:2 beautiful *TS, E1*] ~, *A1*

136:6 due] dues *E1*

136:18 *Ivan A1*] Ivan *TS*

136:22 right *TS, E1*] ~, *A1*

136:26 necessary *TS, E1*] ~, *A1*

136:28 hostess'] hostess's *E1*

136:31 *Boris … Boris A1*] Boris … Boris *TS*

136:32 *Kovantchina A1*] Kovantchina *TS, E1*

136:33 *Kovantchina A1*] Kovantchina *TS*

136:36 really. *TS, E1*] ~? *A1*

136:36 oh no—But] ~, ~—but *A1* ~ ~. But *E1*

137:8 marsala *TS, E1*] Marsala *A1*

137:16 you: *TS, E1*] ~! *A1*

137:16 glad indeed *TS, E1*] ~, ~ *A1*

137:20 marsala] Marsala *A1*

137:21 Sir] sir *E1*

137:22 Sir] sir *E1*

137:28 Now] ~, *A1*

137:30 it: *TS, E1*] ~; *A1*

137:30 marsala] Marsala *A1*

138:4 practice] practise *E1*

138:5 practice] practise *E1*

138:6 practice] practise *E1*

138:6 Ah *TS, E1*] ~, *A1*

138:9 practice … practice *A1*] practise … practise *TS, E1*

138:11 Sir] sir *E1*

138:14 fire: *TS, E1*] ~, *A1*

138:17 couch; *TS, E1*] ~: *A1*

138:18 wife: *TS, E1*] ~, *A1*

138:22 *crème TS, E1*] crème *A1*

138:29 capacity *TS, E1*] ~, *A1*

138:30 bought but not] but not to *E1*

139:13 wonderful— *TS, E1*] ~, *A1*

139:25 goes." And] ~"—and *E1*

139:28 Oh] ~, *A1*

139:29 tall *TS, E1*] ~, *A1*

139:32 Sir] sir *E1*

139:32 tall *TS, E1*] ~, *A1*

139:33 forwards. "But] ~, "but *E1*

139:35 honour *A1*] honor *TS*

139:37 Italian—] ~. *E1*

140:20 yourself] ~, *A1*

140:24 Ah *TS, E1*] ~, *A1*

140:28 Splendid *TS, E1*] splendid *A1*

140:29 naïvely *Ed.*] naively *TS*

140:34 Sir] sir *E1*

140:36 man!] ~? *E1*

140:37 Why *TS, E1*] ~, *A1*

140:39 honoured *A1*] honored *TS*

140:40 little *TS, E1*] ~, *A1*

141:7 frail *TS, E1*] ~, *A1*

141:8 honours *A1*] honors *TS*

141:9 hard-money-woman *TS, E1*] hard-money woman *A1*

141:18 Pinned on] Pinned-on *A1*

141:21 *crème TS, E1*] crème *A1*

141:30 were] ~, *A1*

141:33 Italy! *TS, E1*] ~? *A1*

141:36 Oh *TS, E1*] ~, *A1*

142:5 Oh *TS, E1*] ~, *A1*

142:8 received] reserved *E1*

142:25 ability *TS, E1*] ~, *A1*

143:6 Now *TS, E1*] ~, *A1*

143:10 kindhearted *Ed.*] kind-hearted *TS*

143:19 illness] ~, *A1*
144:6 flute *TS, E1*] ~, *A1*
144:9 point. I cannot see his point.
  TS, E1] point. I cannot see his
  point. I cannot see his point. *A1*
144:16 him: *TS, E1*] ~; *A1*
144:20 honours *A1*] honors *TS*
144:27 It *TS, E1*] Is *A1*
144:31 worse. *TS, E1*] ~? *A1*
144:34 No *TS, E1*] ~, *A1*
145:16 Sisson?] ~. *E1*
145:16 catechism *A1*] catachism *TS*
145:28 death *TS, E1*] ~, *A1*
145:30 young man, *TS, E1*] ~ ~ *A1*
146:1 Oh *TS, E1*] ~, *A1*
146:18 Lilly *TS, E1*] ~, *A1*
146:21 word] ~, *A1*
146:23 Oh *TS, E1*] ~, *A1*
146:25 careful *TS, E1*] ~, *A1*
146:36 Why *TS, E1*] ~, *A1*
147:7 Oh *TS, E1*] ~, *A1*
147:18 half repentant *TS, E1*] half-
  repentant *A1*
147:18 half depressed *TS, E1*] half-
  depressed *A1*
147:24 that *TS, E1*] ~, *A1*
147:36 Half-past *Ed.*] Half past *TS*
147:38 half-past *Ed.*] half past *TS*
147:40 hostess'] hostess's *E1*
148:3 soft *TS, E1*] ~, *A1*
148:4 deep *TS, E1*] ~, *A1*
148:6 deep *TS, E1*] ~, *A1*
148:7 soft *TS, E1*] ~, *A1*
148:17 half-amused *A1*] half amused
  TS, E1
148:23 Yes] ~, *A1*
148:28 si *TS, E1*] ~, *A1*
148:28 signore. *A1*] ~, *TS*
148:31 clear *A1*] dear *TS*
148:33 hovering] lowering *E1*
148:34 skypanthers] sky-panthers *A1*
148:36 house] ~, *E1*
149:2 fine *TS, E1*] ~, *A1*
149:13 long *TS, E1*] ~, *A1*
149:17 drawing-room *A1*] drawing
  room *TS*
149:18 menservants] manservants *A1*
  men-servants *E1*

150:2 Gefällt] GEFAELLT *A1*
  GEFÄLLT *E1*
151:6 old *TS, E1*] ~, *A1*
151:14 and new] a new *A1*
151:17 oh *TS, E1*] ~, *A1*
151:22 no one *A1*] no-one *TS*
151:24 *The Graphic E1*] the Graphic
  TS the *Graphic A1*
151:26 Aaron *TS, E1*] ~, *A1*
151:28 *The Queen A1*] The Queen *TS*
151:38 big *TS, E1*] ~, *A1*
151:39 little *TS, E1*] ~, *A1*
152:3 bright *TS, E1*] ~, *A1*
152:4 Novaresi] Novarese *A1*
152:21 Lire] lire *A1*
152:30 9.00 *Ed.*] 9. 0 *TS, E1* 9:00 *A1*
152:34 time *TS, E1*] ~, *A1*
153:1 Aaron however] ~, ~, *A1*
153:4 new *TS, E1*] ~, *A1*
153:15 Pekinese] Pekingese *E1*
153:17 Pekinese] Pekingese *E1*
153:25 Goodness] goodness *A1*
153:28 Oh] ~, *A1*
153:37 Aaron] ~, *A1*
154:1 Ah] ~, *A1*
154:5 fire-place *Ed.*] fireplace *TS*
154:25 homage too *TS, E1*] ~, ~, *A1*
154:27 it *TS, E1*] ~, *A1*
154:30 money. *TS, E1*] ~? *A1*
155:8 there?] ~! *A1* ~. *E1*
155:12 Ah *TS, E1*] ~, *A1*
155:23 hostess'] hostess's *E1*
155:24 good-humour *TS, E1*] good
  humour *A1*
155:31 philanthropies] philanthropics
  E1
156:21 room *TS, E1*] ~, *A1*
156:28 said 'Get *TS, E1*] ~, "get *A1*
157:10 shirt sleeves *Ed.*] shirtsleeves
  TS
157:24 alien, as *TS, E1*] ~; ~ *A1*
158:24 headstrong] head-strong *E1*
159:27 him, *TS, E1*] ~ *A1*
159:28 all-beneficent] all beneficent
  E1
159:38 deep *TS, E1*] ~, *A1*
160:1 ah *TS, E1*] ~, *A1*
160:6 oh *TS, E1*] ~, *A1*

160:10 oh *TS, E1*] ~, *A1*
160:11 time,] ~ *E1*
160:14 tremendous *TS, E1*] ~, *A1*
161:7 mad. *TS, E1*] ~! *A1*
161:10 mad too *TS, E1*] ~, ~ *A1*
161:18 flat *TS, E1*] ~, *A1*
161:38 Oh *TS, E1*] ~, *A1*
162:7 cold *TS, E1*] ~, *A1*
162:8 relax:] ~; *E1*
162:13 or] nor *E1*
163:13 half consciousness] half-consciousness *E1*
163:15 gulf] golf *E1*
163:19 etc;] etc.; *A1*
163:22 normal: *TS, E1*] ~; *A1*
163:29 abnormal? *TS, E1*] ~. *A1*
163:32 Wells' *A1*] Well's *TS* Wells's *E1*
164:5 manoeuvred *TS, E1*] manoeuvered *A1*
165:25 present—;] ~; *A1*
165:28 receiver.] ~? *E1*
165:32 give *TS, E1*] gives *A1*
165:35 man. And] ~. *P* And *E1*
166:40 "Dalliance of Eagles." *Ed.*] ~ ~ ~. *TS*
167:16 practice *E1*] practise *TS*
167:22 Risky] Immoral *E1 see notes*
167:29 entrée *TS, E1*] *entrée A1*
167:33 so.] ~! *A1* ~? *E1*
167:33 old-fashioned— *A1*] ~.— *TS*
168:3 me *TS, E1*] ~, *A1*
168:10 Why] ~, *E1*
168:37 unfortunate!] ~. *E1*
169:7 Why] ~, *A1*
169:18 Why] ~, *A1*
169:22 And of course] ~, ~ ~, *E1*
169:26 honour *A1*] honor *TS*
169:28 Now] ~, *A1*
169:30 port: *TS, E1*] ~, *A1*
169:30 days! *A1*] ~.! *TS* ~. *E1*
169:34 No Sir—No Sir] ~, sir; ~, sir *A1* ~ sir—no sir *E1*
169:35 fortune] Fortune *E1*
169:35 who, *TS, E1*] ~ *A1*
169:37 *bouche TS, E1*] *bouchée A1*
169:38 Ah yes] ~, ~, *A1*
169:39 fortune] Fortune *E1*

169:39 *Fortuna gentilissima A1*] Fortuna gentilissima *TS, E1*
170:17 Oh] ~, *A1*
170:22 oh] ~, *A1*
170:23 Sir] sir *E1*
170:30 portglass] port glass *A1*
170:34 Well *TS, E1*] ~, *A1*
171:5 sea—] ~,— *E1*
171:6 Now] ~, *E1*
171:10 destination— *TS, E1*] ~. *A1*
171:19 Sir] sir *A1*
171:25 Aaron *TS, E1*] ~, *A1*
171:30 A.1.] A.I. *A1* A1 *E1*
172:17 a] *Om. E1*
172:22 damned! *TS, E1*] ~. *A1*
172:27 so *TS, E1*] ~, *A1*
173:8 trouser-buttons *Ed.*] trouser buttons *TS*
173:16 oh *TS, E1*] ~, *A1*
173:17 roly-poly cake-walk *TS, E1*] roly-poly-cake-walk *A1*
173:27 coffee: *TS, E1*] ~. *A1*
173:28 waiting *TS, E1*] ~, *A1*
173:35 alone] ~, *A1*
173:40 Venice of course] ~, ~ ~, *A1*
174:6 Aaron,] ~ *A1*
174:9 *crème de menthe. TS, E1*] *crème de menthe! A1*
174:15 drawing-room *E1*] drawing room *TS*
174:27 *crème TS, E1*] *crème A1*
175:22 aude *TS, E1*] *aude A1*
175:25 rapt *Ed.*] wrapt *TS*
175:33 Bravo!,] ~! *A1*
175:33 Chantant,] ~— *E1*
175:34 around *TS, E1*] round *A1*
176:9 *vivace A1*] *Vivace TS*
176:16 Well] ~, *A1*
176:25 away:] ~, *E1*
176:26 quiet *TS, E1*] quite *A1*
176:32 sang— *TS, E1*] ~ *A1*
176:32 "Ye Banks and Braes," *Ed.*] ~ ~ ~ ~, *TS, E1* Ye Banks and Braes, *A1*
178:4 Franks' *A1*] Frank's *TS*
178:6 act *A1*] art *TS*
178:14 another: *TS, E1*] ~; *A1*
178:21 him: *TS, E1*] ~; *A1*

178:22 direction: *TS, E1*] ~, *A1*
179:40 third class *Ed.*] third-class *TS*
180:28 tricolor *TS, E1*] tricolour *A1*
180:33 housefront] house front *E1*
180:37 passed:] ~, *E1*
181:7 *Corriere E1*] Corriere *TS* Cor-
rière *A1*
181:10 waiter too] ~, ~, *A1*
181:29 endless restless] ~, ~, *E1*
181:40 side altar] side-altar *E1*
182:6 shallow] ~, *E1*
182:16 was *TS, E1*] *Om. A1*
182:27 vermouth] Vermouth *E1*
182:40 procession,] ~ *E1*
183:1 fist] hand *E1*
183:2 powerful: *TS, E1*] ~, *A1*
183:3 into *TS, E1*] to *A1*
183:6 tricolor,] tricolour, *A1*
tri-color— *E1*
183:6 closed, but the] closed: *E1*
183:7 railway-men's *TS, E1*] railway
men's *A1*
183:8 felt] *Om. E1*
183:14 set purpose,] fixed purpose and
sharp will, *E1*
183:15 jarring of steel] scraping of
steel and copper *E1*
183:16 men—] ~; *E1*
183:16 male,] ~ *E1*
183:17 swirling like a little pool]
clustering thick before the shop
E1
183:20 frowsty looking] frowsty-
looking *A1*
183:22 mockery—] ~: *E1*
183:23 acrid derision—the] derision,
acrid. The *E1*
183:24 on. Almost] ~. *P* Almost *E1*
183:25 disappeared] began to disappear *E1*
183:28 way. Only] ~. *P* Only *A1*
183:28 flying—] ~: *E1*
183:28 tricolor] tricolour *A1* tri-color
E1
183:33 tricolor] tricolour *A1* tri-color
E1
184:2 ringing of ... the shop-door.]
banging of the shop door and a

ringing of the bell of the guilty
house-door. *E1*
184:5 street *TS, E1*] ~, *A1*
184:8 flag—] ~: *E1*
184:8 again turned] now turned
again *E1*
184:9 knock with their knuckles] beat
with their fists *E1*
184:10 They looked ... the flag.] *Om.*
E1
184:11 rose] arose *E1*
184:12 something again.] again, with
rapid gestures. *E1*
184:13 floors] apartments *E1*
184:13 entrance was] entrances were
E1
184:14 caretaker.] caretaker to be
found. *E1*
184:15 that] *Om. E1*
184:20 flag] gaudy flag *E1*
184:20 procession] mob *E1*
184:21 below. *A1*] ~: *TS*
184:23 half derisive] half-derisive *A1*
184:24 smallish-black] smallish black
E1
184:27 stone-work] stonework *E1*
184:28 under] beneath the *E1*
184:29 He did not stop there,] There
he did not stop, *E1*
184:30 away] his way *E1*
184:31 below,] ~ *E1*
184:31 sheer] a frenzy of *E1*
184:38 magically] ~, *E1*
184:39 passed] had passed *E1*
185:6 house] house-front *E1*
185:7 third floor] third-floor *E1*
185:8 it—] ~: *E1*
185:9 his] one *E1*
185:11 down.] down, it was in his
hand. *E1*
185:11 prolonged] long *E1*
185:12 flame,] ~ *E1*
185:13 hand] fist *E1*
185:17 unheard] unheeded *E1*
185:23 carabinieri] Carabinieri *E1*
185:26 greeny-grey ... them wildly]
sturdy, greeny-grey Carabinieri, like a posse of foot-

soldiers, rushing thick and wild and indiscriminate on the crowd, with a frenzied excitement which must have been based on fear: a sudden, new, excited crowd in uniform attacking the civilian crowd and laying about blindly, furiously, *E1*

185:31 in a terror of frenzy.] into a terror of frenzy. *A1* into it in a frenzy of panic. *E1*

185:35 carabinieri] Carabinieri *E1*

185:36 fled—] ~, *E1*

185:39 window-ledges] window ledges *E1*

185:40 again] ~, *A1*

185:40 ran—] ~: *E1*

186:4 time,] ~ *E1*

186:5 carabinieri] Carabinieri *E1*

186:8 the] *Om. E1*

186:11 dispersed] disappeared *E1*

186:12 carabinieri] Carabinieri *E1*

186:13 foolishly let themselves] let themselves foolishly *E1*

186:14 taken: perhaps] ~; ~ *A1* ~. Perhaps *E1*

186:14 half a dozen men,] half-a-dozen ~: *E1*

186:14 half a dozen prisoners;] half-a-dozen ~: *E1*

186:15 more. The] ~. *P* The *E1*

186:19 towards] to *E1*

186:19 began, in humiliation,] began in cautious dejection *E1*

186:21 surrounded] seized *E1*

186:22 they marched ... a prisoner] marched authority, triumphant and thankful to have got off so lightly. The dejected youth was marched away *E1*

186:24 protest,] ~ *E1*

186:24 a few shouts of anger and derision] *Om. E1*

186:25 carabinieri] Carabinieri *E1*

186:27 shout.] shout or threat. *E1*

186:28 pretending] ready to pretend *E1*

186:30 Nevertheless *TS, E1*] ~, *A1*

186:30 watched,] ~ *E1*

186:30 the] *Om. E1*

187:5 ruddy *TS, E1*] ~, *A1*

187:14 Yes! *TS, E1*] ~. *A1*

187:16 window *TS, E1*] *Om. A1*

187:25 good *E1*] gold *TS*

187:39 Siena *E1*] Sienna *TS see notes*

188:3 Why *TS, E1*] ~, *A1*

188:8 Siena *E1*] Sienna *TS*

188:10 "very lovely," *A1*] '~ ~', *TS* '~ ~,' *E1*

188:13 Well *TS, E1*] ~, *A1*

188:23 know,] ~ *E1*

188:25 Therefore *TS, E1*] ~, *A1*

189:4 Half-litre *Ed.*] Half litre *TS*

189:11 Oh] ~, *A1*

189:13 Oh] ~, *A1*

189:14 Scriabin—] ~.— *A1* ~. *E1*

189:26 No] ~, *A1*

189:28 Oh] ~, *A1*

189:36 Well] ~, *A1*

189:39 should *TS, E1*] ~, *A1*

190:1 Oh] ~, *A1*

190:2 decent—] ~. *E1*

190:9 *Stega*] Strega *A1*

190:15 *Frutta:*] *Frutte, A1 frutta:* *E1*

190:17 *Natura Morta*] *natura morta E1*

190:24 naïve] naive *E1*

190:31 near, *TS, E1*] ~ *A1*

190:32 dark-blue *TS, E1*] dark blue *A1*

190:34 Yes. *TS, E1*] ~, *A1*

191:9 Oh *TS, E1*] ~, *A1*

191:9 incredible!—] ~? *E1*

191:13 course? *TS, E1*] ~. *A1*

191:17 recitals *TS, E1*] ~, *A1*

191:20 but *TS, E1*] *Om. A1*

191:25 half rising] half-rising *A1*

191:36 glad:] ~; *A1* ~ *E1*

192:8 He too *TS, E1*] ~, ~, *A1*

192:11 *nice*] nice *A1*

192:15 Oh] ~, *A1*

192:19 friend] ~, *E1*

192:40 Slade—] ~. *E1*

193:37 nasty] ~, *E1*

194:4 war hero *Ed.*] war-hero *TS*

194:14 listened too *TS, E1*] ~, ~, *A1*

194:21 Well *TS, E1*] ~, *A1*

194:32 psychoanalysed]
    psycho-analysed *E1*
195:3 right *TS, E1*] ~, *A1*
196:12 first class *Ed.*] first-class *TS*
196:12 third class *Ed.*] third-class *TS*
196:20 right *TS, E1*] ~, *A1*
196:24 first class] first-class *E1*
196:26 third class *Ed.*] third-class *TS*
196:27 Well *TS, E1*] ~, *A1*
196:33 Well *TS, E1*] ~, *A1*
197:17 Well *TS, E1*] ~, *A1*
197:31 awful *TS, E1*] ~, *A1*
197:39 Oh] ~, *A1*
198:11 See] see *E1*
198:14 Oh dear *TS, E1*] ~, ~, *A1*
198:23 first class] first-class *E1*
198:26 He too *TS, E1*] ~, ~, *A1*
198:26 fascinating] as fascinating *A1*
    so fascinating *E1*
198:40 Sometimes, oh *TS, E1*] ~. Oh,
    A1
199:1 of ten *TS, E1*] or ten *A1*
199:15 life: *TS, E1*] ~, *A1*
199:17 high *TS, E1*] ~, *A1*
199:19 a *TS, E1*] *Om. A1*
199:21 them *TS, E1*] ~, *A1*
199:24 third class *Ed.*] third-class *TS*
199:27 holding] who is holding *E1*
199:33 third class] third-class *E1*
200:6 genuine.] ~? *A1*
200:8 Lunch time *Ed.*] Lunch-time
    TS
200:14 impressed: oh *TS, E1*] ~. Oh
    A1
200:29 wait.] ~? *E1*
200:29 suppose.] ~? *E1*
200:32 third class] third-class *E1*
200:36 second class] second-class *E1*
200:36 first class] first-class *E1*
200:37 third class] third-class *E1*
200:38 Oh *TS, E1*] ~, *A1*
201:16 third class] third-class *E1*
201:31 Aaron:] ~, *A1*
201:36 it *TS, E1*] ~, *A1*
202:7 Oh] ~, *E1*
202:24 first class] first-class *E1*
202:27 [in] prima classe *Ed.*] prima
    classa *TS*

202:27 *classe Ed.*] *classa TS*
202:29 at *TS, E1*] to *A1*
202:29 first class] first-class *E1*
202:35 first class] first-class *E1*
203:3 third class *Ed.*] third-class *TS*
203:8 first class *Ed.*] first-class *TS*
203:9 third class *Ed.*] third-class *TS*
203:12 Apennines] Appenines *E1*
203:12 sulphureous *TS, E1*] sulphu-
    rous *A1*
203:29 creep *TS, E1*] creak *A1*
203:31 fellow-passenger *Ed.*] fellow
    passenger *TS*
203:31 them,] ~ *E1*
204:23 fellow-passenger] fellow pas-
    senger *E1*
204:24 good.] ~? *E1*
204:31 fellow-passenger] fellow pas-
    senger *A1*
204:32 fellow-passenger] fellow pas-
    senger *E1*
205:3 gipsy *TS, E1*] gypsy *A1*
205:5 clothes] ~, *A1*
205:10 Buon' appetito *E1*] Buon
    'appetito *TS*
205:26 Liras] lire *A1* liras *E1*
205:27 Liras] lire *A1* liras *E1*
205:27 six-shillings-and-sixpence *TS,
    E1*] six-shillings-and-six pence
    A1
205:34 Well *TS, E1*] ~, *A1*
205:39 your love to dissemble] to dis-
    semble your love *E1*
205:40 the stairs ... *TS, E1*] stairs? ...
    A1
206:1 Then morning] The morning
    then *E1*
206:11 Trinita *Ed.*] Trinità *TS*
206:11 left,] ~ *E1*
206:12 river *A1*] River *TS*
206:15 cobble stones *Ed.*]
    cobble-stones *TS*
206:18 district:] ~ *E1*
206:21 Oh *TS, E1*] ~, *A1*
206:21 *Oh TS, E1*] ~, *A1*
206:33 notice-plate *Ed.*] notice plate
    TS
207:1 maidservant] maid-servant *A1*

207:8 eyes—] ~, *E1*
207:12 Oh Good-morning] ~, good-morning *A1*
207:19 How] how *E1*
207:29 red tiled] red-tiled *E1*
207:34 half-past *TS, E1*] half past *A1*
208:2 Oh *TS, E1*] ~, *A1*
209:17 Oh] ~, *A1*
210:11 dining-room *E1*] dining room *TS*
210:15 halfway] half-way *E1*
210:15 preoccupied *TS, E1*] pre-occupied *A1*
210:18 maidservant] maid-servant *A1*
210:22 half a dozen] half-a-dozen *E1*
210:39 Oh *TS, E1*] ~, *A1*
211:19 flat, *TS, E1*] ~ *A1*
211:29 trickling *A1*] trinkling *TS*
211:34 Palace] palace *A1*
212:22 strong, *TS, E1*] ~ *A1*
212:23 palace! *TS, E1*] ~. *A1*
213:21 Oh] ~, *A1*
213:23 *miles TS, E1*] miles *A1*
213:24 *rushed TS, E1*] rushed *A1*
213:24 people,] ~ *A1*
213:27 oh *TS, E1*] Oh *A1*
213:28 *odd*!!] ~! *A1* ~!! *E1*
213:28 So *more*] so more *E1*
213:28 Oh *TS, E1*] ~, *A1*
214:6 favour *A1*] favor *TS*
214:18 oh] ~, *A1*
214:31 soliloquy] in soliloquy *E1*
215:5 But *TS, E1*] ~, *A1*
215:16 Oh *TS, E1*] ~, *A1*
215:17 your *TS, E1*] a *A1*
215:28 eyebrows *Ed.*] eye-brows *TS*
215:28 lamp-oil!—] ~— *A1* ~! *E1*
215:37 done,] ~ *A1*
215:38 egg.—I ... [216:5] boys. *P* "Then ... [216:9] were so.] egg." *P* "Then ... so. *A1* egg. *E1*
216:9 But *TS, E1*] ~, *A1*
216:14 They can't ... not doing it.] *Om. A1*
216:15 Ha-ha! Saving ... their urine ... ha!—ha!—ha!] Ha-ha! Saving ... the waste matter of

their bodies ... Ha! ha!—ha! *A1 Om. E1*
216:27 Well *TS, E1*] ~, *A1*
216:34 somebody—"] ~'''— *E1*
216:36 far-off *Ed.*] far off *TS*
217:7 shaky: *TS, E1*] ~, *A1*
217:9 Goodnight *Ed.*] Good-night *TS*
217:15 he too *TS, E1*] ~, ~, *A1*
217:23 drawing-rooms *TS, E1*] drawing rooms *A1*
217:25 eleven-and-threepence *TS, E1*] eleven-and-three-pence *A1*
217:27 but of course] ~, ~ ~, *E1*
217:29 nineteen-and-twopence *TS, E1*] nineteen-and-two-pence *A1*
217:37 him,] ~ *A1*
218:21 tea-parties *E1*] teaparties *TS*
218:25 had of course] ~, ~ ~, *E1*
218:34 Look *TS, E1*] look *A1*
218:37 Avanti *TS, E1*] *Avanti A1*
218:39 cathedral square *E1*] Cathedral square *TS* Cathedral Square *A1*
219:3 twelve—] ~.—*A1* ~. *E1*
219:3 —tomorrow] —Tomorrow *A1* —to-morrow *E1*
219:5 come *TS, E1*] *Om. A1*
219:8 forget—Just] ~.—~ *A1* ~—just *E1*
219:9 Siamo nel paradiso *TS, E1*] *Siamo nel paradiso A1*
219:21 Which] ~, *E1*
219:37 well-dressed *Ed.*] well dressed *TS*
220:1 Colonel's *TS, E1*] colonel's *A1*
220:16 white—] ~.—*A1* ~. *E1*
220:35 Ah *TS, E1*] ~, *A1*
220:39 anyhow—] ~. *E1*
221:3 Why *TS, E1*] ~, *A1*
221:7 Paris] Rome *E1*
221:7 Paris,] Paris often, *E1*
222:6 smiled] ~, *E1*
222:31 collapsed—] ~.—*A1* ~. *E1*
222:36 tea-party *E1*] teaparty *TS*
223:21 Oh *TS, E1*] ~, *A1*

223:29 Ambassador to Paris] ambassador to Paris *A1* a famous figure
in Europe *E1*

223:40 Half-past *E1*] Half past *TS*

224:2 manservant] man-servant *A1*

224:28 shut-upedness *A1*] shut-/
upedness *TS* shutupedness *E1*

225:2 Ah *TS, E1*] ~, *A1*

225:15 No] ~, *A1*

225:19 don't—But] ~—but *A1*

225:35 Saturdays] Sundays *E1*

226:1 to me] ~ ~, *A1*

226:8 know. *TS, E1*] ~? *A1*

226:17 me—But] ~—but *A1* ~. But
E1

226:18 you.] ~? *A1*

226:20 do *TS, E1*] ~, *A1*

226:33 Listen] ~, *A1*

226:39 Enough light will] There will
be enough light *E1*

227:18 melody: *TS, E1*] ~, *A1*

227:18 animation: *TS, E1*] ~, *A1*

228:4 castle-keys. *Ed.*] castle keys.
TS

228:15 Saturdays] Sundays *E1*

228:33 these] this *E1*

228:35 Emanuele *Ed.*] Emmanuele *TS*

229:15 him *TS, E1*] ~, *A1*

230:3 effects— *TS, E1*] ~. *A1*

230:10 reserve: *TS, E1*] ~, *A1*

230:14 always. With] ~, with *E1*

230:18 "It] ~ *A1*

230:37 you…"] ~. … . *A1*

230:38 active *TS, E1*] ~, *A1*

231:2 forever *Ed.*] for ever *TS*

231:9 sleep: *TS, E1*] ~, *A1*

232:2 High Up … Square] HIGH
UP OVER THE CATHEDRAL
SQUARE *A1* NEL PARADISO *E1*
see notes

232:4 small hotel] house *E1*

232:5 no one *A1*] no-one *TS, E1*

232:15 tram-cars,] ~ *E1*

232:19 façade *A1*] facade *TS*

232:28 gothic *TS, E1*] Gothic *A1*

232:29 love it,] ~ ~; *E1*

232:31 rose: *TS, E1*] ~; *A1*

232:32 heavy *TS, E1*] ~, *A1*

233:11 In November] So late in the
year *E1*

233:14 south *TS, E1*] South *A1*

233:21 oh *TS, E1*] ~, *A1*

233:22 Liras] lire *A1* liras *E1*

233:36 And *TS, E1*] An *A1*

233:38 nowadays—] ~. *E1*

234:5 siamo nel Paradiso *TS, E1*]
siamo nel paradiso A1

234:10 respectable—] ~. *E1*

234:11 But respectability … sick.
What?] *Om. E1*

234:20 Seems I've … region.] *Om. E1*

234:31 Well *TS, E1*] ~, *A1*

234:36 whiskey.] ~? *A1*

235:4 façade *A1*] facade *TS*

235:4 red tiled *Ed.*] red-tiled *TS*

235:11 Oh *TS, E1*] ~, *A1*

235:11 fun! *TS, E1*] ~.— *A1*

235:11 The Blessed … balcony. I'd …
down. Ha-ha-ha … a — —.]
Om. A1 The Blessed …
balcony. Ha-ha-ha … a— *E1*

235:16 charming.—Zinnias]
~—zinnias *E1*

235:17 oh *TS, E1*] ~, *A1*

235:20 red tiled *Ed.*] red-tiled *TS*

235:27 Why didn't … at my crucial
moment with … days. I am …
[235:36] my boy."] Why … at
any crucial moment.—I am …
boy." *A1 Om. E1*

235:38 Kerl] ~, *E1*

236:1 tomorrow—] ~. *A1*
to-morrow— *E1*

236:2 Delighted—.] ~— *E1*

236:3 "Not yet … sell. I … [236:10]
piss-en-lits—" *Ed.*] "Not …
pris-en-lits—" *TS Om. E1*
"Not … sell." *A1*

236:17 can, *A1*] ~ *TS*

236:18 so *TS, E1*] ~, *A1*

236:26 mistkäfer *E1*] mistkafer *TS*

236:40 loggia—] ~.— *A1* ~. *E1*

237:1 very glad *TS, E1*] ~ ~, *A1*

237:17 ingénu *Ed.*] ingenu *TS, E1*
ingénue *A1*

237:21 Chickens *A1*] Chicken *TS, E1*

237:23 cheap] cheep *E1*
237:26 Squeaked] squeaked *A1*
237:27 luggage stool *Ed.*] luggage-stool *TS*
237:32 featherless—Then] ~— then *A1* ~. Then *E1*
237:33 do.—] ~— *E1*
237:39 panettone *Ed.*] panetone *TS*
237:41 panettone *Ed.*] panetone *TS*
238:9 it *TS, E1*] ,*A1*
238:10 much *TS, E1*] ~,*A1*
238:10 I too *TS, E1*] ~, ~,*A1*
238:18 you] ~,*A1*
238:25 Ah *TS, E1*] ~,*A1*
238:33 Ah *TS, E1*] ~,*A1*
239:3 "And never ... [241:31] *any means.*"] *Om. E1 see also following entries to* 241:26
239:12 But] ~,*A1*
239:15 Oh] ~,*A1*
239:23 Ah] ~,*A1*
239:24 Indeed ... Indeed] ~, ... ~, *A1*
239:39 hate] ~,*A1*
240:4 Ah] ~,*A1*
240:16 right] ~,*A1*
240:23 what] ~,*A1*
240:38 Argyle. *A1*] ~, *TS*
241:1 things— *Ed.*] ~.— *TS*
241:7 people] ~,*A1*
241:19 alone—] ~.*A1*
241:20 Thank] thank *A1*
241:20 —nothing] (~ *A1*
241:21 alone—] ~),*A1*
241:26 Oh] ~,*A1*
241:37 Ah *TS, E1*] ~,*A1*
242:19 childish—But] ~—but *A1* ~. But *E1*
242:23 be separate—] separate— *A1* be separate. *E1*
242:24 true— *TS, E1*] ~.*A1*
242:40 my *TS, E1*] my *A1*
243:3 it, a *TS, E1*] ~ ~ *A1*
243:5 unbelieving—] ~.— *A1* ~. *E1*
243:10 same, *TS, E1*] ~ *A1*
243:39 Oh *TS, E1*] ~,*A1*
243:39 shopkeepers *A1*] shop keepers *TS*

243:40 maquereaux *Ed.*] maquéreaux *TS*
244:1 husband-maguereaux *Ed.*] husband-maquereaux *TS, E1* husband-maquéreau *A1*
244:7 maquereau *TS, E1*] maquéreau *A1*
244:9 going— *TS, E1*] ~.— *A1*
244:17 Women. Oh *TS, E1*] ~ oh *A1*
244:35 love—] ~. *E1*
244:35 Oh *TS, E1*] ~,*A1*
245:9 obeyed: *TS, E1*] ~,*A1*
245:31 *doesn't TS, E1*] doesn't *A1*
246:2 this too *TS, E1*] ~, ~,*A1*
246:9 "And then ... [246:14] cried Argyle.] *Om. E1*
246:15 wife *TS, E1*] ~,*A1*
247:3 ipso facto] *ipso facto E1*
247:32 Aaron] ~,*A1*
249:7 gauzy *A1*] gauzey *TS*
249:30 Oh *TS, E1*] ~,*A1*
250:9 Well *TS, E1*] well *A1*
250:26 shell *TS, E1*] Shell *A1*
250:27 "Yes!—] "~! *A1*
250:41 Manfredi *TS, E1*] ~,*A1*
251:9 sham wistfulness *TS, E1*] sham-wistfulness *A1*
251:10 charm *TS, E1*] charms *A1*
251:15 morning-feeling *TS, E1*] morning-feelings *A1*
251:33 also, *TS, E1*] ~ *A1*
251:38 her *TS, E1*] *Om. A1*
253:11 palm-trees *Ed.*] palm trees *TS*
254:1 Brunnhild *TS, E1*] Brunnhilde *A1*
254:3 morning-awakening *TS, E1*] morning awakening *A1*
254:22 the *TS, E1*] *Om. A1*
254:24 practice *Ed.*] practise *TS*
254:27 Oh ... Oh *TS, E1*] ~, ... ~,*A1*
255:2 Guilbert] Gilbert *E1*
255:4 Malbrouk *TS, E1*] Malbrouck *A1*
255:33 play—] ~, *E1*
256:28 Bravo] ~,*A1*
257:7 so] ~,*A1*
258:21 above] *Om. E1*
258:24 hill] across *E1*

258:28 practice *Ed.*] practise *TS*
258:28 manservant] man-servant *E1*
258:31 manservant] man-servant *E1*
258:32 shoulders] ~, *A1*
258:37 odd] ~, *E1*
259:40 or *TS, E1*] nor *A1*
260:21 him—] ~, *E1*
261:25 yet, *TS, E1*] ~ *A1*
261:25 at ... of passion,] *Om. A1*
261:27 Even as ... felt it.] *Om. A1*
261:30 And again ... liberation,] *Om. A1*
261:31 he] He *A1*
261:33 But afterwards ... [262:11] part, really.] *Om. A1*
262:12 When he] When, after a long sleep, he awoke and *A1*
262:12 awakedness *TS, E1*] awakeness *A1*
262:14 up, *TS, E1*] ~ *A1*
262:14 even before ... shirt he] *Om. A1*
262:35 bedlinen] bed linen *A1*
262:38 faint feeling *TS, E1*] faint-feeling *A1*
262:39 knew] know *E1*
263:4 jeweller's] jewellers' *E1*
263:8 marsala *E1*] Marsala *TS*
263:9 marsala *E1*] Marsala *TS*
263:10 more. He *TS, E1*] ~, he *A1*
263:26 postoffice *Ed.*] post office *TS*
264:9 débris *A1*] debris *TS, E1*
265:18 trees *A1*] tree *TS*
266:2 Nay] nay *E1*
266:32 teatime] tea-time *E1*
266:34 blue] ~, *E1*
266:35 corn-flowers *E1*] corn-/flowers *TS* cornflowers *A1*
266:37 a *TS, E1*] the *A1*
267:12 No,—] ~—*A1*
267:31 Why *TS, E1*] ~, *A1*
267:31 Goodness yes!] ~, ~! *A1 Om. E1*
267:34 A.I.] A-I. *A1* A I. *E1*
267:40 practicing *Ed.*] practising *TS*
268:16 marsala *E1*] Marsala *TS*
268:37 that] ~, *E1*
269:2 rod] ~, *A1*

269:17 well connected *TS, E1*] well-connected *A1*
269:33 littérateur *TS, E1*] litterateur *A1*
269:34 not-very-important social] social not-very-important *E1*
269:36 well-dressed *Ed.*] well dressed *TS*
270:6 Much *A1*] Must *TS*
270:6 nerve-wracking *Ed.*] nerve-racking *TS*
270:7 life—] ~. *A1*
270:9 Ah *TS, E1*] ~, *A1*
270:11 Oh *TS, E1*] ~, *A1*
270:20 dottore *TS, E1*] dotore *A1*
270:23 *Veneziano TS, E1*] *Veneziana A1*
270:23 signore *TS, E1*] Signore *A1*
270:27 kings *TS, E1*] king *A1*
270:33 Interesting] interesting *A1*
271:1 so *TS, E1*] *Om. A1*
271:1 free lance] free-lance *E1*
271:9 Galluzzo *Ed.*] Galuzzo *TS*
271:28 conversationalist *TS, E1*] ~, *A1*
271:38 him.] ~? *E1*
272:7 night,] ~ *A1*
272:7 in his extreme,] *Om. A1*
272:9 long] ~, *E1*
272:9 of electric ... [272:17] And this night] of electric fire, a ... gratifying sensation. *P* This night *A1* of electric fire. *P* This night *E1* excruciating, but also an intensely gratifying sensation. *P* This night *E1a*
272:18 morning, *TS, E1*] ~ *A1*
272:19 And then ... again.] *Om. A1*
272:24 hair.] ~? *E1*
272:27 round *TS, E1*] around *A1*
272:27 and his slow ... lifting her, *TS, E1*] *Om. A1*
272:33 Did he ... immortality!—But ... same time] *Om. A1* But did he ... immortality. But ... time *E1*
272:35 it *TS, E1*] It *A1*
272:36 And she touched ... and quivered,] *Om. A1*
272:37 and clung] And she clung *A1*

272:38 Of his actual ... of a fetish. *TS*,
     E1] Afraid of him as of a fetish!
     A1
273:1 the phallic fear:] *Om. A1*
273:3 some way *TS, E1*] ~ ~, *A1*
273:6 treated] ignored *E1*
273:10 all] always something, all *E1*
273:13 terrible] own terrible *E1*
273:14 victim!] ~. *E1*
273:15 welter of] *Om. E1*
273:16 himself] ~, *E1*
273:17 different—] ~: *E1*
273:17 victim—] ~; *E1*
273:19 There, as in ... deeper into!]
     Om. A1
273:20 didn't want it,] did not want
     it— *E1*
273:22 love-contact,] ~. *A1* love
     contact. *E1*
273:22 and his soul ... his breast.] *Om.*
     A1
273:24 apart] was apart *A1*
273:25 She lay ... him. And] *Om. A1*
273:26 he] He *A1*
273:27 her,] ~—*A1*
273:27 magic] ~. *A1*
273:27 male ... nipples.] *Om. A1*
273:28 far-off *Ed.*] far off *TS*
273:28 Moses's *Ed.*] Moses' *TS*
273:28 There lay the ... and then] *Om.*
     A1
273:30 she] She *A1*
273:35 There was ... then carrion.]
     Om. A1
273:39 apart] ~, *A1*
274:6 greater] more *E1*
274:7 lay] lay there *E1*
274:7 so,] ~ *E1*
275:6 thought] ~, *E1*
275:20 Mediaeval] Mediæval *E1*
275:35 Vittorio Emanuele *Ed.*] Vittoria
     Emmanuele *TS*
276:2 vermouth *A1*] Vermouth *TS*
276:20 others however] ~, ~, *E1*
276:22 coffee-pot *Ed.*] coffee pot *TS*
276:38 no one *A1*] no-one *TS*
277:10 Or the ... That's bad!] *Om.*
     E1

277:15 Damned] damned *A1*
277:26 shopkeepers *Ed.*] shop-keepers
     TS
277:30 liked *A1*] like *TS, E1*
278:5 *Nazione Ed.*] Nazione *TS*
278:19 damneder] demneder *E1*
278:37 You're *A1*] You're *TS, E1*
279:12 it—of *E1*] ~.—~ *TS* ~.—Of
     A1
279:17 perhaps *TS, E1*] ~, *A1*
279:21 Masters? *TS, E1*] ~. *A1*
279:22 stinks *TS, E1*] smells *A1*
279:30 and *TS, E1*] And *A1*
279:31 That be-pissed] That
     be-fouled *A1 Om. E1*
280:1 "Use logic ... harshly.] *Om.*
     E1
280:20 socialism *A1*] Socialism *TS*
281:1 stinking—] ~.—*A1* ~. *E1*
281:4 By *TS, E1*] But *A1*
282:34 C R A S H] CRASH *E1*
283:16 débris *A1*] debris *TS*
283:18 café *A1*] cafe *TS*
283:31 tip-toe *Ed.*] tiptoe *TS*
284:1 section,] ~ *E1*
284:20 Tornabuoni *TS, E1*] Tourna-
     buoni *A1*
284:22 Trinita *E1*] Trinità *TS*
284:35 Oh *TS, E1*] ~, *A1*
285:8 water-plant—you] ~. You *E1*
286:12 realised *TS, E1*] realized *A1*
286:17 a naked *TS, E1*] naked *A1*
286:22 and *TS, E1*] *Om. A1*
286:23 But of course] ~, ~ ~, *E1*
287:10 them *A1*] the *TS, E1*
287:12 dark-blue *Ed.*] dark blue *TS*
287:21 whitish-clayey] whitish clayey
     E1
288:15 lap *TS, E1*] ~, *A1*
289:7 he] the *E1*
290:1 little] devilish little *E1*
290:12 bog *TS, E1*] bogs *A1*
290:14 individual;] individual: *A1*
290:22 Ah *TS, E1*] ~, *A1*
291:38 jailors:] ~, *A1* ~! *E1*
292:8 falling—*A1*] ~.— *TS*
292:37 circumambient *A1*] circum-
     nambient *TS*

293:14 me—?] ~? *E1*
293:19 Well *TS, E1*] ~, *A1*
293:26 Yes] ~, *A1*
293:37 Well *TS, E1*] ~, *A1*
294:8 must. *A1*] ~, *TS*
294:11 love-whoosh *TS, E1*] love whoosh *A1*
294:16 —Not] —not *A1*
294:32 No] ~, *A1*
294:32 you're a love-urger *E1*] you've a love-urger *TS* you've a love-urge *A1*
295:6 off, leave *Ed.*] ~, Leave *TS* ~. Leave *A1*
295:15 Trot ... run *TS, E1*] '~ ... ~' *A1*
295:16 trot trot *TS, E1*] ~, ~ *A1*
295:19 Because ... and go to the W.C.] Because ... and digest it. *A1 Om. E1*
296:6 Nirvanaing *TS, E1*] Nirvaning *A1*
296:9 said, *TS, E1*] ~ *A1*
296:11 Oh *TS, E1*] ~, *A1*
297:3 understood] ~, *A1*
297:3 oh, *TS, E1*] ~ *A1*
297:16 I.—] ~? *A1*
297:19 love-urge *A1*] love urge *TS, E1*
298:4 And of course] ~, ~ ~, *E1*
298:5 The] the *E1*
298:40 power-urge *A1*] power urge *TS*

Of the compound words which are hyphenated at the end of a line in this edition, only the following hyphenated forms should be retained in quotation:

6:13 non-luminous
12:2 white-scrubbed
12:15 blue-and-white
13:5 good-humoured
18:17 reddish-brown
38:14 drawing-room
43:32 fair-haired
44:12 woe-begone
45:33 high-pitched
56:24 arm-muscles
87:6 cabbage-leaves
94:17 self-repulsion
99:25 self-conscious
105:1 word-splitting
106:8 self-sufficient
118:28 dream-logged
134:24 creamy-coloured
135:12 good-looking
139:38 pinning-on
149:18 clean-shaven
152:19 money-changing
152:34 cock-feathers
155:24 good-humour
155:33 storing-up
159:3 life-source
174:15 drawing-room
174:34 vacant-seeming
181:38 rose-hearted
182:7 big-patterned

182:25 half-elegant
182:28 heart-eating
183:12 southern-shaped
184:24 fair-haired
185:38 ground-floor
186:37 well-coloured
188:30 old-fashioned
198:37 mid-summer
199:30 tight-bound
203:16 summit-station
204:18 cross-legged
205:27 six-shillings-and-sixpence
212:22 hawk-head
212:40 amber-coloured
215:28 lamp-oil
219:24 Mid-Victorian
228:4 castle-keys
230:1 pocket-book
232:32 earth-substance
239:40 tram-driver
240:11 love-apostle
247:6 self-knowledge
252:22 decay-sweetness
269:20 old-fashioned
276:4 torch-bearer
287:1 dream-Aaron
294:14 love-boy
295:1 nervous-neurasthenic
297:1 speech-music